THE STORY OF
CHE GUEVARA

THE STORY OF
CHE GUEVARA

Lucía Álvarez de Toledo

HarperCollins Publishers Ltd

The Story of Che Guevara
Copyright © 2010 Lucía Álvarez de Toledo. All rights reserved.

Published by HarperCollins Publishers Ltd
First published in Great Britain in 2010 by Quercus

First Canadian edition

Lines from *La Canción Desesperada* © Fundación Pablo Neruda

HarperCollins books may be purchased for educational, business, or sales promotional use through our Special Markets Department.

HarperCollins Publishers Ltd
2 Bloor Street East, 20th Floor
Toronto, Ontario, Canada
M4W 1A8

www.harpercollins.ca

Library and Archives Canada Cataloguing in Publication information is available upon request

ISBN 978-1-44340-566-9

Text designed and typeset by Helen Ewing
Picture research: Bronagh Woods
Maps: Bill Donohoe
Index: Alison Worthington

Printed and bound in the United States
RRD 9 8 7 6 5 4 3 2 1

In Memoriam

Guglielmo Biraghi
Rodolfo Kuhn
José González Aguilar
Andrea Morales Vidal
Juan Carlos Frugone

'Quítate de la acera
mira que te tumbo
que aquí viene el Che Guevara
acabando con el mundo.'

'Stop hanging around on the sidelines
And be careful not to fall
Because here comes Che Guevara
On his way to change the world.'

Contents

Introduction

His name, as it appeared in his first passport, was Ernesto Guevara de la Serna. He was known at different times as Teté, Fúser, Tatu, Fernando or Ramón. He received an official Cuban passport when a decree declared him 'a Cuban citizen by birth' in 1959 – an unusual tribute to his role in the Cuban Revolution – though he renounced it when he went off to fight in the Congo. From then on, he possessed several false passports with assumed names such as Adolfo Mena-González: a businessman from Uruguay, whose identity he used to enter Bolivia for what was to be his final campaign.

The world knows him as Che. The nickname was given to him by his comrades-in-arms in Mexico, when they were training for the invasion of Cuba in 1955 – and he loved it. 'For me,' he said, 'Che represents the most essential, the most loved aspect of my own life. How could I not like it? The first and second names of a person are small things, personal, insignificant. In contrast, I like it very much when people call me Che.'

At the time, 'Che' was widely used in Latin America to refer to Argentines. It is an allusion to an interjection with which we pepper our conversation. It has now been definitively hijacked by Guevara, but it reminds us of one crucial and often ignored aspect of his life: he was an Argentine.

I, too, am an Argentine, born in 1938 (which makes me ten years younger than Ernesto) into a family from the same social milieu, with Spanish ancestry traceable to similarly unsavoury servants of the crown and empire. We were marked by the same background and political events: Perón and Eva; de facto pro-Nazi military presidents; an economy directed by the UK; an intellectual life heavily influenced by French thinkers, ever since our

1

founding fathers looked to the encyclopaedists and Jean-Jacques Rousseau in drafting our constitution and laws; the all-pervading right-wing Roman Catholic church; the Spanish republican exiles; the crude onslaught on our culture by the dominating economic power of the USA.

So perhaps it is natural that I have always been fascinated by the story of Che Guevara. Like most Argentines, I followed his meteoric career throughout his extraordinary short life. I remember vividly the stir it caused in Buenos Aires, in 1957–8, when the newspapers started mentioning the Argentine doctor who had become a comandante in the Cuban Revolution. A young man with hardly any training was leading his troops in one victory after another across the island of Cuba, not many years after he had been declared unfit for military service by the Argentine army.

It was around the same time that those of us who had fluent English or French used to make our way to the dressing rooms of the artists performing at the Gran Rex or Cine Opera on Corrientes Avenue and introduce ourselves, offering to show them the city, take them out and entertain them. On one occasion we found ourselves escorting Ella Fitzgerald to a small, dark, smoky basement bar in downtown Buenos Aires where we knew the pianist was good and she would not be mobbed by autograph hunters. The visiting performers often felt sufficiently at home to grab a microphone and delight us with a private recital. Phrases like *con swing* (with swing) or *una total falta de swing* (a total lack of swing) became part of our local jargon. To swing like Ella meant you were in; anyone 'incapable of swing' had something seriously wrong with them.

It wasn't all about musical ability. Though he was tone deaf, Che Guevara was the epitome of swing. He had allure, charisma and nonchalance, and he could lead a guerrilla army with such panache that he made it look effortless. We were all head over heels in love with him. The same applied to his comrade-in-arms, Camilo Cienfuegos, with his wide-brimmed hat, skinny body and flowing beard. I distinctly recall the arrival of a friend who generally took himself rather seriously at our apartment block in Buenos Aires, on New Year's Eve 1959. He danced a kind of gauche samba down the corridor, singing '*los barbudos bajaron de la Sierra*' (the bearded ones came down from the mountains), as news bulletins informed us that Cienfuegos had marched on Havana and was at Camp Columbia Barracks. He was soon followed by Che and his men, who were in Santa Clara, poised to descend on the Cuban capital and take the fortress of La Cabaña.

Though I was unaware of it then, a number of people within my social circle were to play significant roles within Guevara's life and afterlife. I remember an evening in 1961, for example, when a group of us were going out to dinner at La Cabaña, one of Buenos Aires' famous beef restaurants. Horacio Rodríguez-Larreta, a friend who worked as an adviser to the Ministry of Foreign Affairs, was due to come along. As we were leaving the apartment where we had gathered for drinks, Horacio rang to say he had been summoned by the president to his residence on the outskirts of Buenos Aires and would join us later. When he eventually turned up at the smart restaurant, I noticed that his shoes were covered in mud. Horacio was a dapper dresser, one of the most elegant men in the city. I laughed and asked if he had been to see the president in those shoes. He said the president had invited him to chat outdoors, walking in the vast gardens where the sprinklers had just been turned off, perhaps because he thought that his residence was bugged by the military intelligence service.

Many years later, when I interviewed Horacio for a documentary about Che I was planning with Pepe González-Aguilar, I discovered that the president had summoned him because he wanted to know, in detail, what had been discussed by Guevara and Richard Goodwin, Kennedy's envoy to the Punta del Este Conference in August 1961. Horacio, who was a linguist, had been their interpreter.

Another link came through former members of the French Resistance, who had taken up residence in Buenos Aires after Paris came under German occupation. Musicians inspired by Django Reinhardt also made their way to our city, formed groups and played with great success. There were tea rooms in the centre of town where you could listen to jazz in the afternoon and evening. Tatave Moulin, who had been in the Resistance, had a small restaurant just behind Harrods (a store identical to the one in London) where people gathered to hear him sing, play the accordion and enjoy his wonderful home-made French food. He and his friend, the actor Maurice Jouvé, hogged all the roles requiring a foreign accent in Argentine films and television and were always charming, friendly and a joy to be with. They made you think they did not have a care in the world. We did not know that their extracurricular activities in the 1960s included assisting such local left-wing organisations as Che Guevara's failed guerrilla movement in Salta, northern Argentina, led by Jorge Ricardo Masetti.

By 1961, when we were in our early twenties, I was in charge of continuity on several short films directed by Rodolfo Kuhn, a close friend who had returned from film school in the USA and had managed to put together a small budget to produce his first feature. To save money on locations, he was shooting some scenes in the apartment I shared with my sisters.

One evening the assistant director, Pepe González-Aguilar, was late. When he turned up we all upbraided him. We did not want the neighbours to complain about the people and equipment entering and leaving the building after midnight. Pepe explained that he had dropped in on the Guevaras, who lived a few blocks away. They had received a phone call from Ernestito (as Che was known to his family) in Havana, so everyone had queued up to speak to him. By now he was probably the most famous man on the continent. It was highly unusual for someone we knew to be in the international news almost daily, behaving in such an iconoclastic manner and being so irreverent towards the USA.

A couple of years later, in 1963, I was a rookie journalist with Radio Municipal of Buenos Aires, part of the state-owned National Broadcasting System of Argentina. Because I had had an English education, I was in charge of writing, producing and presenting a weekly programme called 'La Vida y la Música en Gran Bretaña y las Naciones de la Comunidad Británica', about life and music in Britain and the Commonwealth. There was an atmosphere of excitement and expectation in the corridors of the radio station (then housed in the basement of the Teatro Colón, the huge opera house in Buenos Aires). We were at the centre of literary and political debate, and the most prominent writers and artists were constantly arriving to be interviewed. Jorge Luis Borges, who had a five-minute programme straight after mine, stood listening from the technician's booth until my signature tune came on air.

It was there that I often ran into Albino Gómez, a career diplomat who was also a journalist. During one of the short periods of democracy in the 1960s he had been one of President Frondizi's close aides – and the man responsible for dealing with Che Guevara's secret visit to Argentina in 1961.

4

Another political journalist who was often at the radio station was Tomás Eloy Martínez. He was writing for *Primera Plana*, a weekly magazine that carried the story of Guevara from his arrival on the scene in Cuba to his death in Bolivia. Tomás went on to become a much-lauded novelist who wrote extensively about the phenomenon of Peronism in Argentina. He also became the champion of Ciro Bustos, the man unjustly blamed for betraying Che Guevara in Bolivia who suffered years of ostracism and rejection for a crime he did not commit. Though I moved to London in 1968, these two writers remained firm friends.

Che Guevara kept touching my life in unexpected ways. In December 1987, I went to Havana to attend a film festival. Rodolfo Kuhn had died suddenly in Mexico and was being honoured for his documentary about the relatives of the 'disappeared' of Argentina, the Mothers of Plaza de Mayo. (These were a large group of women, some of the mothers of the many women and men who 'disappeared' during the Dirty War of 1976–83, who used to gather every Thursday in the Plaza de Mayo in front of Government House, wearing white scarves, to protest to whoever was in power. Their action took some guts.)

When the London contingent turned into the driveway of the legendary Hotel Nacional, we were confronted by a huge hoarding which covered the whole façade. This depicted Kuhn as well as various notable guests. I was deeply moved. Che Guevara looked down on us from the hoarding too. It was twenty years since his death and yet he was still everywhere. The man had turned into an island in the Caribbean. He had become the spirit of Cuba.

At five thirty in the morning, I was woken by men drilling holes in the road outside the hotel, repairing pipes. When I complained about the noise, the concierge simply said the men had to start early as they were doing voluntary work before going to their regular jobs. They were members of the Che Guevara Voluntary Brigades.

One day, out shopping in downtown Havana, I got drenched by a sudden shower. A battered old Dodge taxi stopped and asked me where I was going. I knew he was not allowed to pick up foreigners, for whom there are special taxis, but when he heard my accent the driver said, 'If Che could risk his life for us, I can risk a fine for you. Jump in.'

It was a strange feeling for an Argentine to see another Argentine so deeply embedded in Cuba's psyche. At first I thought it was only in Havana – the festival included many documentaries about him – but as I left the city, I realised it was a national celebration. One evening I travelled to Matanzas with the Brazilian delegation to the festival. During the two-hour journey I started feeling dizzy. When we arrived, I decided to stay in the bus and relax since I had already seen the film, but the driver was concerned for me and insisted I should visit the outpatient department of a hospital which was just across the road. The doctor on duty was a young woman. As soon as I opened my mouth she grinned and said, 'And what is the Argentine *compañera*'s problem?' She had recognised my accent. I told her. She put aside the book she was reading and wrote me a prescription. Then she pointed to her book and said, 'He had that accent as well.' It was Che Guevara's *Reminiscences of the Cuban Revolutionary War*.

During the same trip a documentarist asked me to help him research Santería, a local religion which is an amalgam of Catholicism and the Yoruba faith African slaves brought with them. We were talking to an Afro-Cuban who was showing us the altar in his home. To my amazement, there, amidst the figures of Yemanyá, Oshún and Oxalá, was Che Guevara. There was no dissuading this old black peasant: Guevara, according to him, was black and Cuban, and had joined the pantheon of Santería's gods because of his sacrifices for his fellow men. Although he could not stand adulation, this was the sort of accolade I suspect Che would have relished, since it transcended the race, social class, background and nationality into which he was born. I had never come across a whole nation (albeit a tiny one) so totally in love with their hero, but that is how it felt. It was infectious and moving.

I returned home to Buenos Aires in late 1989, after twenty-five years abroad. I was to travel to northern Argentina to work on an Argentine-British co-production. Before leaving, I dropped in on Juan Martín Guevara, Che's youngest brother, at Nuestra América, the huge bookshop, depot and agency for Latin American books, Havana cigars and Cuban rum that he ran. A democratic government had been installed and Juan Martín had just been released from jail, where he had served eight years of a twelve-year sentence for revolutionary activities and had contracted chronic viral hepatitis. I told him I intended to go to Bolivia and follow the route of Che's guerrillas in 1967. Juan Martín lent me a book, *De Ñacahuasú a La Higuera*, by Adys Cupull and Froilán González, a couple of historians who had done exactly that when posted to the Cuban embassy in Bolivia. I was going to visit the places where Che and his men had seen action and interview the Bolivian generals who had been instrumental in his downfall, as well as the inhabitants of the villages who witnessed the events at the time. Long before Bolivia had discovered Che's potential as a tourist attraction, I would be following his route from Ñacahuasú to Vallegrande.

Towards the end of my journey, I went to La Higuera, the village where the guerrillas were taken as prisoners in 1967. I stood in the middle of the dirt track that passes for a road outside the telegraphist's house, which Guevara mentions in his diary. A woman came out of the house and walked towards me. She turned out to be the telegraphist's daughter. When I mentioned I had come to see the place where Guevara died, she said she had been there, aged nineteen at the time. Then she cast a look around her and said, 'Look at us. Nothing has changed since then. El Comandante came too soon. We were ignorant and did not understand him. We abandoned him and he died because of us, when he had come to save us so that we could have a better life, and here we are, just as we were before he came or maybe even worse.' I was struck by her words.

When I returned to Buenos Aires several weeks later my sister Celia handed me a large cardboard box which had seen better days. She had collected articles about Che and hidden the box. 'Since you are so interested,' she said. She had also hung a photograph of Che in my room.

'Where did that appear from?' I asked.

'We all had his picture,' she said.

'I never knew you were a leftie,' I said, bemused.

'You don't understand,' she replied. 'His death touched us all. He transcended ideology. Che', my sister explained, 'stood up for his continent against immense odds. He was one of us. We could identify with him. He had rejected privilege and power. And when he went to his death, he possessed nothing. Like Gandhi. Like Christ.

'You don't know what went on here all these years,' she said. 'On the surface, we all pretended everything was okay because we were terrified. People got killed because they appeared in the address book of someone the police suspected of left-wing activities. Life under Isabel Perón and her witch doctor minister López-Rega was so awful that we all cheered when the military ousted them. [López-Rega had created a paramilitary force called *Alianza Anticomunista Argentina* (AAA or Triple A) which persecuted and terrorised everybody who dared to disagree with them.] We did not know that what came afterwards would be just as terrible. Thirty thousand people were "disappeared".

This is an account of Guevara's life written by a Latin American, a native of Buenos Aires and a woman. I hope to give a sense of why it is that, more than forty years on, his angry and determined image on a black and red banner is still seen at the head of demos everywhere from Buenos Aires to Berlin to Kathmandu. I want to put him back in his Latin American context and convey what that means to readers in Europe, North America and the rest of the world. I will explain why he is admired by those who knew him intimately – and also far more widely, right across the political spectrum in Latin America – for his integrity, his courage and charisma, his commitment to the poor and hostility to the United States. This feeling is shared by many people who are totally out of sympathy with revolutionary violence, his economic doctrines and other political beliefs.

I have looked at the published material on Che in four languages and have tried to assemble, examine and assess the conflicting evidence as carefully as possible, but this is also a personal, insider's book. It draws on a background which allows me to see things other biographers have missed or failed to understand. The country I describe in the early chapters is the one I knew as a child and adolescent, when I was growing up in the Barrio Norte of downtown Buenos Aires, only a few blocks from Che's family home. We went to the same places (I often watched the rugby team he played for in San Isidro – in fact it was on these playing fields that he earned the nickname Fúser, which is a contraction of Furibundo Guevara de la Serna – Furious Guevara de la Serna – as players would say 'here comes Fúser' when they saw him approaching at breakneck speed and throwing himself into the melee with gusto. His tackles were notably fierce) and knew many of the same people. Perhaps even more crucially, we spoke the same language.

Argentine Spanish is full of colloquialisms brought by the different nationalities invited to immigrate before and after the Second World War. By incorporating all these into its lyrics, the tango helped forge a language, *lunfardo*, that is only spoken and understood by those who grew up in Argentina and Uruguay. Many wonder why those of us who are tone deaf, like Guevara and myself, know such lyrics by heart, failing to realise that they are part of our collective psyche as the language of our capital city. Buenos Aires is a port on the widest river in the world, open to newcomers of all races and persuasions, and this language can often express far better how we *porteños* feel than the expressions in traditional Spanish that came with the conquistadores.

A nice example of his *porteño* irony appears in Che's diary of his Bolivian campaign. Like several of his other published works, this consists of notes he was writing to himself as an aide-memoire to form the basis of a book. He never had the opportunity to revise it, since he was dead twenty-four hours after it was taken from him. The tone is notably confidential and informal, revealing the person rather than the public persona. At one point, though they had only a couple of mules and horses, Che describes how he 'spurred on the cavalry'.

Since few of those who have written about him have been natives of Buenos Aires, they have often been unaware of our linguistic nuances and distinctive tone. When he is visiting the Inca ruins in Cuzco on which the conquistadores built their churches, he says, in *Back on the Road*, that he has a *matete* in his head, an Argentine colloquialism for a muddle. Yet someone translated it as 'motet', a mistake that successive biographers have adopted unthinkingly. One Italian text even has him consuming vast amounts of marihuana (*hierba* in Spanish), when he was actually drinking maté (*yerba mate* in Spanish), an infusion which is Argentina's staple drink, made from the leaves of *Ilex paraguariensis*; it is similar to green tea.

The black beret which Che chose to wear in the Sierra as part of his uniform and persona has now become a generic symbol of rebellion, modishly worn by pop stars and even, in cartoons, by Princess Diana. Yet within the Argentine context it has a far more specific meaning, since it arrived with the Basque immigrants from Spain and is the trademark of the peons or lowly hired hands in the rural establishments of his childhood.

When his earlier biographers wanted to explore Che's origins they had to start by interviewing his family, friends and those who knew him well. Half the population of Argentina had something to say about him, and dozens of would-be experts crept out of the woodwork. Guevara, it seemed, grew up simultaneously in different towns, dated girls who weren't even born when he left the country for good and performed many other equally impossible feats.

Many of those close to him felt they had been misrepresented by writers unsympathetic to Che's politics and refused to grant any more interviews. When I embarked on this project, I had the advantage of already knowing some of the people he grew up with. Speaking Spanish with a marked Buenos Aires accent perhaps made people who didn't know me accept that I was not a total outsider. I was researching Che because he is part of my heritage, the history of my whole continent.

My background and experience have also allowed me to address some of the more persistent myths that have grown up around Che in the decades after his death: claims that he was a member of the aristocracy or a serial womaniser; that he killed women and children and held mock executions when he was the comandante of the fortress of La Cabaña; that he had limited guerrilla skills; that there was a rivalry between him and Castro which forced him to leave Cuba; that Castro effectively killed him by abandoning him in Bolivia; that he went to Bolivia because he was a desperate man who had run out of options.

Finally, because I am a woman, I feel no need to compete with Che in the macho stakes or to cut him down to size. Many of the men who have written about him seem compelled to attack him, as if the mere fact that he once existed casts a doubt on their masculinity. How can they not notice that he was made of sterner stuff than them, as they see how he dragged his asthma uncomplainingly across various theatres of war, was a prolific writer, never stopped learning, was revered by his comrades, had boundless energy and faith in the future of his ideas? In Cuba to this day there are men who will tell you how hurt they still feel that he did not pick them to go with him to Bolivia, even knowing now that it would have meant almost certain death.

The exact nature and value of Guevara's legacy remain disputed, whether we locate it in the Cuban Revolution, a vision for the continent now emerging with the ascent to power of socialists in Bolivia, Uruguay, Ecuador, Venezuela and Brazil, or even his dream of a United States of Latin America. Yet he is undoubtedly one of the most remarkable figures of the twentieth century and a continuing inspiration for many in the twenty-first.

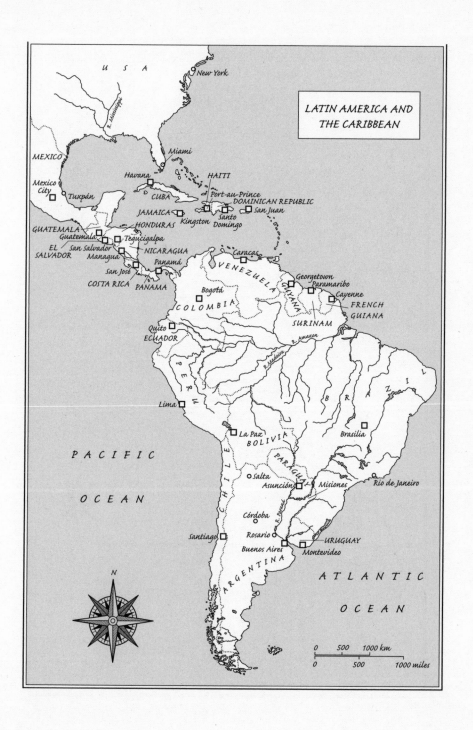

LATIN AMERICA AND
THE CARIBBEAN

U S A

New York

R. Mississippi

MEXICO

Miami

Mexico
City   Tuxpán

Havana

HAITI

CUBA   Port-au-Prince
                    DOMINICAN REPUBLIC
JAMAICA   San Juan
          Kingston   Santo
GUATEMALA HONDURAS   Domingo
Guatemala Tegucigalpa
EL   San Salvador   NICARAGUA   Caracas
SALVADOR Managua   VENEZUELA
        San José   Panamá   Georgetown
COSTA RICA PANAMA   Paramaribo
                                              Cayenne
                Bogotá   GUYANA   FRENCH
                COLOMBIA   GUIANA
                                    SURINAM
Quito
ECUADOR

                            R. Amazon

                      R. Madeira

PERU   B R A Z I L

Lima

            La Paz   Brasília
            BOLIVIA

PACIFIC   PARAGUAY

                Salta   Rio de Janeiro
                Asunción   Misiones
OCEAN

                Córdoba
        CHILE   R. Paraná
Santiago   Rosario   URUGUAY
        Buenos Aires   Montevideo

                            ATLANTIC

        ARGENTINA   OCEAN

N

            0   500   1000 km

            0   500   1000 miles

ONE

(1928–1930)

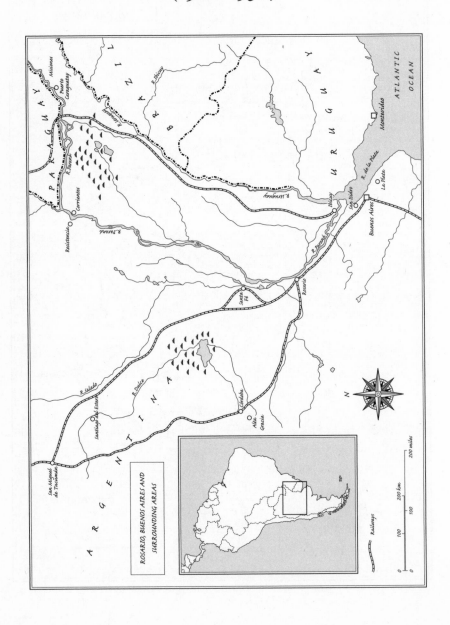

ROSARIO, BUENOS AIRES AND SURROUNDING AREAS

Che was born Ernesto Guevara de la Serna in the port city of Rosario, in the province of Santa Fé in Argentina. His date of birth was probably 14th June 1928. Some of his biographers mention a different date even though the photograph of his birth certificate has appeared in various publications. One went so far as to state that the birth certificate was falsified to conceal the fact that the Guevaras had only been married for seven months when their first child was born. Anyone who knew them would also know that sort of detail did not concern them. The Guevaras were never interested in conventional behaviour or in any of the taboos of the social class into which they had been born. In fact, according to Roberto Guevara de la Serna, one of Ernesto's siblings, the date change was merely an act of vindictiveness on the part of a journalist who was excluded from Mrs Guevara's intimate circle during her final days in a Buenos Aires clinic in 1965, when she was dying from breast cancer. Unfortunately, the journalist's date, 14th May 1928, has now been perpetuated in most of the ensuing biographies.

So, will we ever know Ernesto's actual date of birth? I am inclined to believe that the date on the birth certificate is the correct one. Does it really matter? Only if you believe in horoscopes and astral charts. In any case, Ernesto was somebody who set his own agenda right from the start; he was in a hurry to be born and so Rosario it was, whatever the date.

The city of Rosario, the second largest port in the country, had a population of around 300,000 at the time of Ernesto's birth. Because Argentina then exported grain, leather and beef and imported manufactured goods, Rosario was a busy hub. The various products did not travel in containers or by plane, but were shipped in the holds of cargo vessels to and from Europe, the United States and the Far East.

Rosario has belatedly decided to claim Ernesto Che Guevara as its son and to honour him with a huge statue made of bronze keys, donated by thousands of *guevaristas* to the sculptor Andrés Zerneri. It was inaugurated on 14th June 2008, the day he would have turned eighty. Ernesto Che Guevara has come a long way in the country of his birth, from having his works banned for decades by successive military governments to being honoured with a four-metre-high statue, as well as a postage stamp. However, Ernesto's birth in Rosario was totally accidental. The family did not have any link to the city at

Statue of Che made with bronze keys donated to the sculptor, inaugurated on June 14, 2008

the time. Even now, the only connection is the fact that Ernesto's youngest brother, Juan Martín, was captured there when he was a guerrilla member of the Ejército Revolucionario del Pueblo (People's Revolutionary Army), fighting against the self-appointed military government of General Jorge Rafael Videla: this was the man responsible for the Dirty War, which lasted from 1976 to 1983 and which 'disappeared' 30,000 Argentines suspected of having left-wing leanings.

Ernesto Guevara-Lynch and his wife Celia de la Serna both came originally from Buenos Aires, the capital city of Argentina, where their families still lived. In 1928, the Guevaras were living at their *yerba mate* plantation in Puerto Caraguatay in the territory of Misiones. They were travelling to Buenos Aires down the Paraná river for the birth of their first child when Celia went into labour prematurely and they were forced to make a halt. Rosario is halfway between Misiones and Buenos Aires and, in those days, it used to take up to a week to get to the capital.

Members of both their families came to celebrate the birth of Ernestito, as he would be called well into adulthood in order to avoid confusion with his father, who was also called Ernesto. More than thirty years later, when Ernesto's parents arrived in Havana after the triumph of the Cuban Revolution, Camilo Cienfuegos, Ernesto's fellow guerrilla comandante and closest friend, could not control himself and collapsed in fits of laughter on hearing Ernesto's parents address him as Ernestito. The legendary Comandante Guevara, the scourge of the Sierra Maestra, the strategist of the defining victory of Santa Clara which sent the dreaded dictator Fulgencio Batista packing, was addressed by his parents using the diminutive form of his name, as if he were a mere child.

Ernestito spent the first two years of his life in Puerto Caraguatay, on his parents' plantation on the banks of the Paraná river. The jungles of Paraguay were visible across the water, as the river is the frontier between the two countries. Guevara Senior, who was a master builder and had studied architecture for a couple of years, built his family a house which they referred to as *la calesita*, or the merry-go-round; although the house itself was square, the poles supporting its overhanging roof did make it look rather like a merry-go-round. The house had pillars, wall panels and a roof all made of timber, but no joinery or ordinary nails: it was held together by galvanised iron beams. The secret of the design was that the stresses were evenly distributed. Nevertheless, Guevara Senior was amazed when the house was able to withstand a hurricane, which lasted several hours and uprooted many ancient trees in the surrounding forest.

Guevara de la Serna family home in Puerto Caraguatay, Misiones, 1928

The population of Argentina when Ernestito was growing up was approximately 12 million (the 1914 census gave it as 8,612,000; the following census, in 1947, as 15,894,000). Most of those with Spanish surnames had been there since before Argentina became a republic. It was the parents of the great-grandparents of Ernesto's generation who brought about independence from the Spanish, so that our recent history – and all

Argentine history is recent – had been made by men and women whose surnames were still current in Argentina. Children studying at school felt a real sense of belonging when the exploits of their forefathers were described in class.

Many of the founding families of Argentina originally came from the Basque region of Spain, and Guevara is a Basque surname. They grew rich because they owned fertile land and reared livestock, and they were known as the *oligarquía vacuna*, or cattle oligarchy. At best, Argentina became a country of highly educated people – there are five Argentine Nobel laureates – as well as of immense rural establishments, which grew wheat and reared livestock.

Biographers have often said that the Guevaras were members of the aristocracy. Those who make this assertion fail to understand the social structure of Argentina. For criollos (those born on American soil of Spanish stock), the citizens of a nation that is scarcely two hundred years old, the connotation of the word aristocracy is entirely different from its meaning for Europeans. It is almost pejorative, because our forefathers had chosen not to have an aristocracy: in 1813, in the preamble to the new constitution drawn up after we obtained independence from the Spanish crown, the Asamblea General Constituyente declared all men were born equal. As well as this, the ousted representatives of the Spanish crown were often both titled and corrupt and this had left the criollos with a bitter aftertaste.

The Guevaras were landed gentry of Spanish and Irish stock and the de la Sernas were landed gentry of Spanish ancestry. If Guevara Senior boasted that Viceroy Peralta of Peru was one of Ernesto's ancestors it was to emphasise the fact that his son came from a privileged background – he was white, had been given an education and always had enough to eat – and therefore had not become a revolutionary out of self-interest.

Ernesto's parents belonged to the enlightened Argentine bourgeoisie. They would have been appalled at being described as aristocrats. As their families grew larger, their original fortunes were shared out with an ever-growing number of siblings in each generation. Ernesto Guevara Senior had always needed to earn a living, something he tried to do with varying degrees of success. He and his wife had the values of an educated class, and their four eldest children all went to university and graduated. Ernesto was a doctor, Celia is an architect, Roberto a lawyer, and Ana María, now deceased, was an architect as well.

The more enlightened criollos, such as the Guevaras, did not perceive themselves as Europeans and regarded the aboriginal tribes that populated the continent before the arrival of the Spanish as *paisanos*, their fellow Americans. One such man in Argentina's past was José de San Martín, the country's foremost general who liberated his own people from the Spanish in the 1810s. After obtaining permission from the Pehuenche tribe to ride through their territory, he then crossed the Andes on horseback at the head of three armies – that of his fellow Argentines, one formed by Chilean and one by Peruvian patriots – to liberate both Chile and Peru as well. Meanwhile, Simón Bolívar, another criollo, was advancing southward from the top of the continent, liberating the regions that were to become the countries of Venezuela, Colombia and Ecuador.

In a General Order to his army on 27th July 1819, San Martín referred to the Indians as *paisanos*, or our countrymen. His rousing words were: '*Compañeros* of the Army of the Andes, we will have to wage war as best we can; even if we do not have money, there will be meat and some tobacco. When we run out of clothes, we will dress in the cloth that our women weave for us; otherwise we will go around naked like our countrymen the Indians. Let us be free and the rest does not matter at all ... *Compañeros*, let us swear that we will not lay down our arms until we see our country totally liberated or die like men of courage.' San Martín, who had been educated in Spain, was an officer and a gentleman. Going in to battle naked would not have been the natural thing for him to do; however, his words are proof of the importance those born on American soil, whether aborigines or criollos, attached to being free from European dominance.

But most members of the *oligarquía vacuna* were no more humane than their colonial masters had been when it came to the treatment of the aboriginal population. The new Argentine ruling class had divided the land taken from the Spanish among themselves. They left the majority of the inhabitants – not only the Indians but those of mixed blood such as the gauchos (who made up the majority of the rural population and worked as hired hands on horseback for the landowners), as well as members of the lower echelons of society such as artisans, soldiers, labourers, farmers and peons – merely to survive in utter poverty. This is doubly immoral when one considers the wealth of the land to which they had helped themselves. Successive governments, always formed by members of the new white oligarchy, considered it their right to continue to dispossess their fellow Argentines by means of laws that enshrined their privileges and benefited them and their clansmen only.

Argentina's population is mainly white. It seems that the Spanish who conquered the region, which was known as the Provincias Unidas del Sur (United Southern Provinces) during their rule, were particularly brutal. They were also the carriers of such European diseases as smallpox, cholera and tuberculosis. These plagues were new to the Americas and the native population had no antibodies to them. There are still pockets of Indian tribes throughout Argentina, but in the rest of Latin America the local aboriginal tribes seem to have fared slightly better, as young Guevara was to discover during his travels. Unlike Argentina, most of Hispanic South and Central America has populations mainly of indigenous origin. I say they fared 'slightly better' in that they were still alive; but theirs was a miserable, deprived existence, no better than that of slaves, although officially the status was not applied to them – as it was to the Brazilian population of African origin, who had been transported there expressly as slaves by the Portuguese who ruled that part of the Americas.

It must be said, however, that recent research seems to indicate that Argentines are not as ethnically white as many would like to think. Argentine historian Ricardo Herren, in his *La Conquista Erótica de las Indias* (The Erotic Conquest of the Indies), informs us that, when the Spanish conquistadores arrived in Latin America without their women, they indulged in carnal knowledge of the local Indian female population, thus producing the first '*mestizos*' or people born in America of mixed Spanish and aboriginal parentage. In recent years, the DNA centre in Buenos Aires has been put in charge of matching the children of the 'disappeared' with their relatives, some of whom are still alive and hoping to be reunited with them. The findings of the centre show that as many as 56 per cent of the samples analysed have some indigenous blood.

Ernestito's father once said rather grandly that the blood of his Irish ancestors, who had been rebels and patriots, ran through his son's veins. Both the Guevaras and the Lynches were established Argentine families who had taken the road of self-imposed exile in the early nineteenth century, during the violent and tyrannical dictatorship of Juan Manuel de Rosas (1829–32; 1835–52). He ran a reign of terror until he was finally deposed and exiled to Britain. Anyone who refused to join his militias was his enemy. Francisco Lynch refused and left with his family for Uruguay. From there he travelled north until he reached California and settled in San Francisco.

Juan Antonio Guevara also left Argentina because of his political ideas. As he was from the province of Mendoza, which lies at the foot of the Andes, he crossed the cordillera and lived in Chile for a while. Later he joined forces with his brothers and a group of friends from Argentina to travel to California, where the discovery of large gold fields in 1849 attracted men from all over the world.

Francisco Lynch and Juan Antonio Guevara were Ernesto Guevara-Lynch's grandparents. Their offspring, Ana Lynch and Roberto Guevara, who had been born in the United States, returned to Argentina and eventually got married. They had twelve children, one of whom was Ernesto Guevara-Lynch, father of Ernesto Che Guevara de la Serna who could so easily have been a citizen of the United States of America.

Ernestito's mother was no less notable in her ancestry. Celia de la Serna y de la Llosa was the youngest child of Edelmira de la Llosa and Juan Martín de la Serna, descendants of two of the most patrician Argentine families of Spanish origin. Juan Martín de la Serna had inherited a vast fortune in the shape of several country establishments or ranches, known in Argentina as estancias, which he managed using modern farming methods. He was an intelligent man who had become a lawyer at twenty-two and was a professor in the Faculty of Law of the University of Buenos Aires. He died when Celia was not yet two years old, and his wife died when Celia was seven. Celia's eldest sister, Carmen, took over the running of the household when their mother died.

Celia had been educated by the nuns of the Sacred Heart and grew up as a devout Roman Catholic; it was thought she might even become a nun herself. Initially in favour of self-flagellation and mortification of the flesh, she soon realised she did not have a vocation and that the nuns' real interest in receiving her into the church was that she would come with a substantial dowry.

Her sister Carmen, who would marry the communist poet Cayetano Córdoba-Iturburu, became a surrogate mother to Celia after the death of their parents. The Córdoba-Iturburus were undoubtedly an important influence during Celia's youth. Ernesto Guevara Senior was already a convinced socialist when Celia married him, and she would become one with the passage of time. She picked up some of her political knowledge from her husband originally but, as her son's meteoric career developed, she became an avid student of socialism, political reform and the means to create a more egalitarian society.

Celia met Guevara Senior through the Echagües, a family to whom he was very close, and for a time they were just friends. When Celia wanted to get married and collect her inheritance she was not allowed to do so because she was underage: in Argentina at the time, the age of majority was twenty-two. To force a decision, she ran away from home and went to stay with her other sister, Edelmira, who was married to Ernesto Moore. Edelmira arranged for Guevara Senior and Celia to be married in a private ceremony, to which the sisters' brother Jorge was the only member of the de la Serna clan invited. Afterwards, off the couple went to their maté plantation at Puerto Caraguatay in Misiones.

Misiones was not a province when the Guevaras lived there, but one of several 'territories' which would eventually be elevated to provinces by the national government in Buenos Aires. It was a wild, unknown area. Guevara Senior tells us, in his memoir *The Young Che*, that he bought the land with an inheritance he received from his father. I see no reason to disbelieve him, although some biographers claim he used his wife's money for it.

It was not uncommon in Argentina for people to pool their resources when they got married. Couples needed more than one source of income to support themselves, since income from the land was largely dependent on external factors such as climate, plagues, locusts, insects and, in the case of livestock, diseases such as foot-and-mouth, which Argentine cattle farmers are struggling to eradicate to this day. However, Celia was a minor and an orphan when she and Guevara Senior married, although she did later inherit arable land and livestock as well as an income in bonds.

Misiones was an idyllic place. According to Guevara Senior, the naturalists Friedrich von Humboldt and Aimé Bonpland, who arrived in the area in the 1850s, to carry out explorations, were so captivated by their surroundings that they were unable to leave, and stayed on for years, as if bewitched. Others who wrote eloquently about their fascination with the region included Félix de Azara, who had been sent there by the Spanish crown to settle a border dispute between the colonies either side of the river; Martin de Moussy, a French scientist who was employed by the Argentine authorities to carry out geographical studies and who explored the Uruguay and Paraná rivers; and Moisés Bertoni, a Swiss scientist who lived in Misiones and Paraguay, carrying out studies in agriculture, botany, zoology and meteorology. Their works were read all over Europe.

Everything in Misiones is larger than life. The jungle is impenetrable, and the trees so enormous that sunlight cannot get through, making the forests dark, humid and mysterious. There are animals that are found only in this region, such as the *yaguareté*, a jaguar capable of splitting open a bull; the *onza*, a cross between a cat and a panther; and the *yacaré*, which is a giant alligator. The vegetation indigenous to the region includes the *lapachos*, huge trees whose timber is used in the construction industry, and the *tacuaras* and *tacuarembós*, species of very strong reeds found on the banks of the rivers of northern Argentina which are used to make furniture. The native Indians used the *tacuaras* to make their spears when fighting the advancing colonising armies. In turn, those armies would themselves learn to use the *tacuaras* as spears.

When Ernesto Moore and his wife Edelmira de la Serna de Moore came to Puerto Caraguatay with their two sons on a visit, they too were seduced by the place and stayed for months. Ernestito and his cousins, who were approximately the same age, thoroughly enjoyed themselves playing outdoors and were often taken for rides through the forest by the new addition to the family, Carmen Arias – a Galician woman who had come to help with the housework and to look after Ernestito. She stayed with the family until she got married eight years later but remained close to them always. Guevara Senior tells us how, when he was out inspecting his maté plantation, he could hear the children shrieking with laughter as they drove past at full speed in their buggy pulled by a couple of mules, with Carmen singing to them at the top of her voice.

They were happy years, although it was not an easy life. According to Guevara Senior, the insects found in the area can be lethal to humans, who must learn to identify them and treat their skin when it has come into contact with them. The *mbarigui*, gnats and *uras* are tiny insects that are barely visible and yet can cause enormous damage: they can pass through a mosquito net and arrive by the hundreds. The *pique* is almost too small to be seen and lives between the floorboards of houses until it can crawl under the toenails of someone walking barefoot. If it has been fertilised, it will explode into thousands of new *piques* that make galleries under the skin, causing enormous pain as well as infections.

The foreman in Guevara Senior's plantation was an expert at removing *piques* from the toenails of small children when they were asleep and did so by applying heat to them with his cigarette. Once the insects had surfaced, he removed them with a gold pin. Ernestito was frequently subjected to this cure and so successfully that he never woke up while the operation was taking place. And then, of course, there were the malaria-carrying mosquitoes as well . . .

Misiones may have been a wonderful place for a child to grow up, surrounded by nature and enjoying the freedom of the outdoors, but it was also quite unusual for a privileged family, which had been accustomed to the comforts of city life, to choose to live there. In fact, Celia and Ernesto Guevara were a rather eccentric couple and others may have considered them a bit mad, but they were also very lovable and warm-hearted. When they were first married, the Guevaras were described by their friends and acquaintances as chaotic, restless and incredibly generous. Those who worked for them were always treated like family.

Many years later, after Ernestito's nanny, Carmen, had left their employment to get married, she learnt that the Guevaras were in financial distress, something that Celia had mentioned en passant in a letter to her. Just before Christmas, the Guevara children received a huge hamper full of chocolates and various kinds of sweets, fruit and jam from Carmen and her husband. In a letter to their parents, she said they had wanted to offer the little ones she loved so much some of the things children should have for Christmas.

TWO

(1930–1934)

The Guevaras had been in Misiones for a couple of years when Celia became pregnant again, so they returned to Buenos Aires in 1930 for the birth of their second child, a daughter whom they called Celia. They rented a house in the grounds of Martín Martínez-Castro's palatial residence in San Isidro. This arrangement had advantages for everyone. Martínez-Castro was married to Ernesto Guevara Senior's sister, María Luisa, so the children would be living next to their cousins, and they could all play together in the vast gardens of the mansion without much parental supervision. The Martínez-Castro children were slightly older than Ernestito and Celita and were happy to be given the responsibility of looking after their younger cousins, as is often the case with children.

San Isidro is an elegant residential area on the outskirts of Buenos Aires and Guevara Senior went to work not far from his new home at the Astillero Río de la Plata, a shipyard owned by his second cousin, Germán Frers-Lynch, in which he had invested some capital. Unfortunately, the shipyard burnt down and was not insured at the time. The oversight cost Guevara Senior his capital. The fire may have been caused by a jealous competitor who saw his business losing out to Frers' more successful designs. Guevara Senior was left with nothing but a sailing boat that went by the name of *Kid*, which he kept on the Paraná river near his home in Puerto Caraguatay. It was his local means of transport to and from his maté plantation. Frers also gave him the *Ala*, which was a proper yacht, apparently as some sort of compensation. This he kept on the Río de la Plata delta near Buenos Aires for use at weekends and holidays.

This stay in Buenos Aires was supposed to be temporary, but Ernestito began to suffer from the asthma which was to affect him throughout his

26

life. The doctors advised that the boy would not be able to breathe properly in the extremely humid climate of Puerto Caraguatay and the family was unable to return home.

Much has been written about Ernestito's asthma, including that it was the result of a too-close relationship with his mother. Time and medical research have proved this theory erroneous, but it would have been false in any event, since all the Guevara children suffered from asthma, though the other four had only very mild episodes of the condition and were able to go through their childhood and into adulthood without incident. There is no doubt that Ernestito was his mother's favourite and they enjoyed a particularly close relationship. This may have been because he was her firstborn or because he was unable to attend school regularly and she had to take over his education when he was bedridden. But it is also true that she refused to bring him up like an invalid and she must have been an inspiring example for him when he was growing up.

Rather than being someone who flouted conventions, Celia was a woman totally unconcerned by them. She had other priorities. She was extremely courageous, intelligent and generous. She was also highly educated and well read. She spoke French fluently and loved French literature, in particular poetry. She was always in high spirits and, during those early years before her son became a public figure, did not take anything too seriously. Although she was not a classic beauty, she was considered to be an extremely attractive woman. She had a strong personality and, in the Argentina of the period, and particularly in her social class, she was often among the first to adopt a new idea. She was one of the first women in Argentina to wear trousers in public, she drove her own car, had a personal bank account and wore her hair cut very short *à la garçon*.

Celia Guevara and Ernestito as a toddler

Calica Ferrer, a childhood friend of Ernestito, tells an anecdote about Celia's unconventional personality. Once, when they were all living in the province of Córdoba, the priest of the local church thought Celia had attended mass without wearing stockings (which was not allowed at the time) and proceeded to reprimand her as she was leaving the church. She laughed in his face, stuck her hands into the deep pockets of her skirt and pulled up her nylons, thus proving that she was wearing stockings. Transparent nylon stockings were a novelty at the time.

On 6th September 1930, General José Félix Uriburu toppled the democratically elected popular government of Hipólito Irigoyen, a lawyer who led the Unión Cívica Radical, a party of the centre. It marked the beginning of what became known as the Infamous Decade although it actually lasted to 1943. The de facto government of General Uriburu (1930–32) made substantial concessions to British capital, most of little benefit to the nation. This led to constant instability as well as a series of coups and counter-coups and frequent changes of government, some fraudulent, some democratic, some dictatorial.

The net result of the Infamous Decade was that the armed forces were never far from the seat of power in Argentina, a situation which was to last, on and off, for many years to come. (It can be argued that they were eventually forced to stay out of politics only when defeat at the hands of the British in the Malvinas/Falklands war of 1982 brought shame and discredit to the military.) Naturally, the military's constant interference in democratic institutions had an effect on the views and outlook of those who were growing up at the time. It is exhausting to be continually denied civil liberties by men in uniform.

Ernestito continued to have severe bouts of asthma and his doctors now advised that the family leave San Isidro. The climate of their chalet near the river was not conducive to his recovery, as it was too humid. The family moved to an apartment on the fifth floor of a block in central Buenos Aires, not far from Palermo, the vast park which is the lungs of the city. Roberto, the Guevaras' third child, was born there on 18th May 1932. Ernestito made frequent visits to the park. He enjoyed the fresh air and his father taught him how to ride his tricycle, but his health did not improve. The doctors recommended that they move to the hills in the province of Córdoba, an area famous for its benign climate. In fact, the entire province of Córdoba, in central Argentina, has long been considered a sort of vast sanatorium for those suffering from lung infections.

The Guevaras travelled to Córdoba on the night train. Guevara Senior had intended to send his wife and children with their nanny ahead of him, as he had to finish some business in Buenos Aires. He took his family to the station but, just as they were about to leave, Ernestito began to show the symptoms of an asthma attack. His father did not have the heart to leave him and got on the train without any luggage. Thus, their arrival in Córdoba was quite inauspicious. Guevara Senior tells us that he was wearing new shoes which were too tight, he had his whole family in tow, his eldest son was ill and he was generally not a happy man.

The family took an apartment at the Plaza Hotel in Córdoba, with windows which opened onto San Martín Square. They could feel the dry mountain air. It was sunny, the square was shaded by beautiful old trees and, not far from it, they could see the old cathedral the Jesuits had built in the previous century. Guevara Senior noticed that his boy's asthma had eased. The child had not been able to sleep all night on the train because of the severity of the attack and now he was breathing normally. He thought his son would soon be cured and they would all go happily back to Buenos Aires, where their families and friends lived and where he had his business and his home.

The local paediatrician, Dr Soria, was put in charge of Ernestito's health. He warned them not to be too optimistic, as it would take some time for the child to show permanent improvement. So, in order to settle his family, Guevara Senior rented a house in the neighbourhood of Argüello where, inexplicably, Ernestito's asthma got worse. They had planned to stay in the hills for four months, but this period was soon over and Ernestito's health continued to have its ups and downs. It could not be said that the new arrangements had benefited him in any way.

An old friend, Dr Fernando Peña, suggested they try Alta Gracia, a small town near Córdoba, at the foot of the Sierras Chicas. He had lived there himself for many years and could vouch for its excellent climate. In desperation, the Guevaras decided to follow Dr Peña's advice. They took rooms at the Hotel de la Gruta in Alta Gracia and, almost immediately, their eldest child began to breathe more easily. Encouraged by this development,

Guevara Senior rented a house in the area of Villa Carlos Pellegrini, at the foot of the slopes.

The town of Alta Gracia was divided into two neighbourhoods, which the locals referred to as El Alto and El Bajo. The lower section, or El Bajo, was the old quarter, which had grown up around the church and other colonial structures of the seventeenth century built by the Jesuits. There was some tourist trade, and ponchos, rugs, leather goods, souvenirs and handicrafts of dubious taste were displayed for sale. The poorer inhabitants of the town lived in this area. The Guevara home was in El Alto, which was the residential section, where the houses were more spacious and grand, although most had fallen into disrepair. People who came for their holidays rented houses in this area. The social life of the locals and the summer tourists took place at the Sierras Hotel where they went to play cards, have drinks and be seen. In winter, however, El Alto was inhabited only by those who had come to recover from their pulmonary ailments.

The Guevaras arrived in the province of Córdoba in 1933, when Ernestito was five years old, and stayed until 1944, when he turned sixteen. Their new home was surrounded by woods and soon the children were running around, making friends and generally having a good time. Ernestito even had asthma-free periods and was able to enjoy playing outdoors with all the other children. However, he was not completely cured. He still suffered from sporadic attacks, which could be violent and confine him to bed for long periods, and was regularly using an inhaler. His parents were determined that he should lead as normal a life as possible. They encouraged him to practise sports, to swim and enjoy the outdoors, and he determined early on he would not let it bring him down or interfere with anything he wanted to do. (When he played rugby as a teenager, he would arrange for a friend to carry the inhaler and run up and

Ernestito aged five, in Alta Gracia

down the sidelines throughout the game, so as to be near him when an attack happened.)

It can be said that his asthma defined him. As a long-time bedridden child myself, I know that children who suffer chronic illnesses develop mechanisms to cope. Being immobile would have given Ernestito time to think, and think beyond his years because his life had been altered for ever. He was forced to decide whether he would be a victim or a survivor. His strength of character made the choice easy: Ernestito did not choose victimhood. Once he had made his choice there was no going back.

Looking death in the face when he was choking and could not breathe gave him a different perspective on life. At an age when children are normally fantasising about becoming intrepid explorers or infamous pirates, Ernestito was acquainting himself with his own mortality. The proximity of death changes the thoughts of a young child. It is no longer something that happens to adults. The child makes contingency plans to be able to handle it if it comes. His own fragility makes him value all he has: a loving family, a home, friends, enough to eat, holidays, books . . . He becomes aware of his own resourcefulness. He makes better use of his time because he cannot take it for granted that he has any. He lives in the moment.

In Ernestito's case this gave him a kind of determination and sense of invulnerability, which was the opposite of what you'd expect of someone with his condition. I do not believe Ernesto Guevara set out to prove anything to others but, years later in conversation with Uruguayan writer and friend Eduardo Galeano, his mother said, 'My son spent all his life trying to prove to himself that he could do all the things that he should not have been able to do.'

In his teens Ernesto discovered the German poet Rainer Maria Rilke, who claimed death was just the dark side of life and one should embrace the ambiguity. It is not surprising that he fell in love with this idea. The fact that he did not fear death and considered it an inevitability conditioned his behaviour and perhaps gave him an advantage over his enemies. In Cuba many years later, Fidel Castro compared his two best men: he said Camilo Cienfuegos was the most courageous man there was but Che was totally fearless and flung himself into danger oblivious of the possibility of death. Castro was surprised Guevara had made it alive to the end of the revolutionary struggle.

On 28th January 1934, Ana María, the Guevaras' fourth child, was born. The family was living in a house which had been uninhabited for a long time. It was the last one on the old road leading to the hills and there was a popular superstition that spirits resided in it. The locals referred to it as 'the house of ghosts' although its real name was Villa Chichita. In his memoirs, Guevara Senior tells us he was convinced that the ghosts were a tall story but the local people's belief in them meant he was able to rent the house cheaply. It was ideal for his family.

One night, as he was reading in bed, he heard a noise coming from the kitchen in the basement. The noise was stopping and starting of its own accord. He knew nobody would be in the kitchen at that time of night and wondered if Dr Peña was playing a practical joke. He went to the kitchen, having picked up his revolver on the way, and switched on the light. There was no more noise. He went back to bed. The noise started again, so he went back to the kitchen. Again the noise stopped. When the noise started a third time, he went to the kitchen and closed the door behind him. The noise started again. He switched on the light. It came from two hinged wooden lids to the coal storage: these shook when the wind blew in through the broken panes in the kitchen windows. If the kitchen door was open, the pressure subsided, the lids did not rattle and the noise stopped. The lids were silent during the day because the wind from the north blew only at night. The house lost its mysterious appeal for the children once the ghosts proved to be nonexistent, but their parents were able to sleep at night.

The family eventually moved out of Villa Chichita, because it was too cold in winter, to Villa Nydia, a large house surrounded by land. This is now the Che Guevara museum, but at the time Villa Nydia was also rather run down. Celia's country estate was enduring a lengthy period of drought and the price of maté from their plantation in Misiones had plummeted, so the family's income was greatly reduced. They continued, however, to live their carefree bohemian existence. There was so much activity in the house, as the children were growing up and brought their friends home with them, that it was given the nickname 'Vive como quieras' (Do as you please), which was the Spanish title of Frank Capra's film You Can't Take It with You. Villa Nydia seemed more like a youth club than a family home.

THREE

(1934–1941)

It was during the Guevaras' prolonged stay in Alta Gracia that Ernestito and Calica Ferrer became friends. Calica's father, Dr Carlos Ferrer-Moratel, was now the Guevara family doctor. Since he was a specialist in pulmonary infections, Alta Gracia was an obvious place for him to practise. Carlos Figueroa, another close friend of Calica and Ernestito from that period in Alta Gracia, used to say they had all been thrown together by the Koch bacillus, the cause of tuberculosis. It was thought the dry mountain air, abundant and wholesome food and lots of rest were beneficial to the health of those suffering from this, as well as asthma and other lung diseases. At the time, there was a stigma attached to tuberculosis, so those who were afflicted by it and could afford to would buy a house in the locality and endure their fate as best they could.

The Guevara and Ferrer parents were good friends and shared political leanings, as they both sympathised with the socialist party of Alfredo Palacios. This was unusual for members of their social class and in sharp contrast to the rest of the population of the province, which was extremely right wing and staunchly Roman Catholic. In those days, the established church in Argentina exerted its influence over both politicians and ruling-class families. The more conservative elements of society did not reject the Ferrer or Guevara families, since Ferrer, Guevara-Lynch and de la Serna were established patrician surnames and members of these families would always be tolerated by other patrician families. In fact, something that always surprises me during my visits to Argentina is how readily the members of the oligarchy, against whose privileges Ernesto Che Guevara fought all his adult life, are prepared to pretend his political stance was not that radical. At worst, they consider him a little mad or eccentric, but will never go as far as calling him a traitor to his class.

Celia was patrician down to her fingernails, Calica tells us in his recollections of his childhood. She could be seen wearing her pearls and playing bridge at the Sierras Hotel, where the elite congregated. She smoked cigarettes made of dark tobacco, something which only men did at the time. She was tall and slim and full of life, looking and moving like someone of great distinction, and she usually carried a book with her. She was cultured, elegant and refined; she voiced her opinions and did not shy away from any subject. She could be sarcastic and ironic but she also accepted it gracefully when she was made the butt of a joke. She had a huge sense of humour and cared enormously for her children. This care she extended to all her children's friends, regardless of where they came from.

Ernestito, fifth from right; Calica, sixth from right; Ana María Guevara, seated; Alta Gracia, 1938

When Ernestito began mixing with the children of their extremely poor neighbours or the boys who worked as caddies at the golf club, she greeted them like the rest of his friends and opened her house to them, not only so they could all play together but also to ensure they got their afternoon tea, in case that was their only meal before bed. Afternoon tea was known as *la leche* since children would drink a glass of milk or a cup of milky coffee, tea or maté, with bread and butter and jam or honey. Bread and butter with sugar was also very popular. A soup plate with caster sugar was placed at the centre of the tea table and children could press their slice of buttered bread against it so the sugar stuck to the butter. Another popular delicacy was, and still is, *factura*, which can best be described as a distant cousin of Danish pastry in various shapes and sizes, sometimes filled with jam or custard. In Argentina, wheat flour is not dyed to make it look white, and we Argentines are convinced that our flour tastes better than anyone else's.

Guevara Senior was an impressive man: tall, good-looking and a sportsman. He wore thick glasses for his astigmatism and affected a distant and haughty air, but it was just a façade. In actual fact he was an extremely sensitive and kind man. During their eleven-year stay in the province of Córdoba, he became frustrated because provincial life provided few career opportunities, and the irregularity of their income from the maté plantation in Puerto Caraguatay (which they held on to until 1947) or Celia's country establishment forced him and his family to have a rather nomadic existence, moving house more often than they would have liked.

His creditors nicknamed him 'Urquiza, the terror of Caseros' after Brigadier-General Justo José de Urquiza, a patriot who had won a decisive battle at Monte Caseros in 1852, against the tyrant Rosas. He was the scourge of his enemies and terrified the population of his province with his stern justice. Guevara Senior found this nickname as amusing as everybody else. Although he was often a late payer he always honoured his debts, and when he was not able to pay those in his employment punctually – the women who helped with the children, the cooking and the domestic chores – he always paid them with interest to compensate.

When they lived in Puerto Caraguatay, he was nicknamed 'the communist' because he made a point of paying his labourers in cash though it was the custom to

Ernestito with his parents, Celia and Ernesto

35

pay them with vouchers. The workers were mostly Guaraní Indians, who had been subdued by the Jesuits when they colonised the region. After the Jesuits were forced to leave by order of the Spanish crown in 1767, the new plantation owners behaved as if they owned the Indians as well as the land. The labourers worked under armed guard and were constantly in debt to their masters, who owned the general stores and sold them overpriced supplies, food and clothing of very poor quality. Because the vouchers they were paid with were only redeemable at these stores, they were unable to obtain even basic goods elsewhere. Being perpetually in debt meant they had to renew their contracts and were never able to escape their miserable existence. If they attempted to run away through the forests, they were tracked down like wild beasts by armed thugs on the payroll of the landowners and either killed or brought back in chains to continue their bondage.

Guevara Senior had employed several men from the region to work in his maté plantation. One day, his foreman sent one of them to the house with a payment order for 95 pesos. Guevara Senior took the order and was about to give the man the exact amount of money owed to him when the man asked if he could be paid with a 100 peso note. Surprised, Guevara Senior asked, 'Why do you want a hundred peso note?' The man replied, 'I have never seen one, Master.'

Guevara Senior handed it to the man, who gave him the change he had brought wrapped up in his handkerchief. The man stared at the note and turned it in his hand. He looked at it as if he were hypnotised. 'You know, Master, we can never earn this sum,' he said. Guevara Senior invited him to sit down and share a few matés and that was how he found out what the life of the Indians was really like in Misiones.

The Guevaras were atheists, in spite of Celia's upbringing by the nuns. If they attended Sunday mass every now and then, it was more as a social occasion than a religious one. The children were exempted from catechism lessons at school, usually something only the few Jewish parents requested. However, the morals and ethics the Guevaras taught their children could have been mistaken for a Christian education. It was just that Celia and Ernesto detested the clergy and their hypocrisy: they saw them as allies of the rich and those who exploited the poor.

The Sierras Hotel, where many of the social activities of Alta Gracia took place because of its Olympic-size swimming pool, golf course and tennis courts, had been built by the British when they were laying railway lines the length and breadth of Argentina. It was identical to one they built in Calcutta in the heyday of the Raj and it possessed many salons, terraces, galleries and dining rooms. Guests met for drinks before dinner at the glamorous bar and there was an orchestra to which people danced in the evening. Whether in Argentina or India, the British provided themselves with a luxurious, pseudo-European venue in which to reproduce their lifestyle.

Celia, in the meantime, drove the children around in her 1926 Maxwell convertible, which had a front seat for two and an open space at the back, meant for the luggage, in which her own children and their friends travelled, piled up and giggling uncontrollably. Occasionally someone would fall out and have to be picked up from the side of the road. Celia drove the children to school, but she also took them on excursions to the hills where they might have a picnic and go for a swim.

Calica, whose real name is Carlos, and his brothers, Jorge (nicknamed Gordo or Fatso) and Horacio (nicknamed Chacho), were members of this group, as were the González-Aguilar children, newly arrived from Spain. Alongside these Ernestito had other friends, the children of the working-class people who lived in a kind of improvised shanty town near the Guevara home. Tiki and Ariel Bildoza belonged to this group. Many years later, in 1953, Tiki (who became a gendarme) saw Ernestito again in La Quiaca, where he was guarding the border between Argentina and Bolivia, when Ernestito and Calica were on their way north to Venezuela.

Tea parties, birthday parties, get-togethers to play the guitar or dance, ping-pong championships, canasta or *truco* tournaments (*truco* is a traditional Argentine card game), barbecues, excursions to the hills, swimming in the streams, riding – these were the summer pastimes of *el elenco estable* (the permanent cast) of Alta Gracia and the children of the families who came for the summer.

Many of these activities took place at the homes of the girls in the group, which was how the parents managed to keep them under their watchful eyes. One way the boys had of seducing girls was the *guitarreada* (a get-together to play the guitar and sing). The *guitarra criolla* is the direct descendant of the guitars which came with the Spanish colonisers. Most of the teenagers who holidayed or lived in Córdoba were amateur guitarists and could play and sing provincial folk songs, and sometimes even tangos. Ernestito and Calica absolutely loathed the *guitarreadas* because they were both tone deaf and so unable to participate actively. The boys who could play and sing were the centre of attention and got all the adulation from the girls.

Ernestito was incapable of recognising even the national anthem, which he must have heard many times at school, and was hopeless at dancing. As he was growing up and started wearing long trousers, his uncles gave him their old clothes, which he wore without bothering to have them altered. He enjoyed being casually dressed and sometimes even looking rather ridiculous. In spite of this, he managed to attract girls with his good looks and the way he talked to them. He always asked the less attractive ones to dance because he felt for them if they were left as wallflowers. According to Calica, the girls they went to parties with felt sorry for Ernestito because he could not dance. They would invite him to spend an afternoon with them so they could teach him, and he would end up having tea at their homes, eating all that he could stuff himself with, then have a totally fruitless dance lesson but a wonderful time.

Ernestito and Calica could only compete in the popularity stakes when they were outdoors, showing off their horsemanship – both were good riders and able to make their horses rear up, which earned them some kudos. And if they went out riding in the hills, they might find a secluded place for a moment of intimacy with their chosen conquest and steal a kiss from her. The grown-ups, meanwhile, were enjoying their own sports, such as golf or tennis, and the occasional fox hunt in true English style.

The Guevaras usually spent part of the long summer holidays by the sea at a resort called Mar del Plata, some four hundred kilometres from Buenos Aires. Surprisingly, Ernestito's asthma was not exacerbated by the extremely humid climate. They also went to stay on the estates or farms of relatives and friends. One of these was an estancia in Galarza, in the province of Entre Ríos, which belonged to Ernesto Moore, who was married to Celia's sister Edelmira. It was a perfect example of a gaucho ranch. The large house was surrounded by a vast area of pastureland and the Moore family raised livestock.

Ernesto Moore had an English father and an Irish mother. He even looked Irish himself: tall, slim and bony, with deep blue eyes and covered in freckles. He had grown up on his country estate when it belonged to his parents and was a perfect gaucho, dressing like one and taking part in all the work alongside his hired hands. This included rounding up the animals and taking them to the small farms within the estancia where the gauchos lived and worked. There the livestock were branded, treated and castrated as necessary. The gauchos would also break in wild horses, which they often achieved without once being thrown off. Some could remain mounted without grabbing on to the saddle and controlled the horse using only a whip. These activities would end in an *asado*, a feast in which a whole animal was barbecued and served accompanied by red wine. Ernestito took part in all this, and was always hanging around with the gaucho children.

Guevara Senior's mother, Ana Lynch, was someone else the family often stayed with. She was born in San Francisco and came to Argentina at the age of twelve, when her parents came home from exile to reclaim their lands. She had taken over the management of her country estate in Portela, in the province of Buenos Aires, and built a large house there when she married Roberto Guevara. Since hospitality was paramount, it had eleven bedrooms, a huge dining room and several bathrooms. Her farm was part of a much larger estancia called San Patricio, which had belonged to her father, Francisco Lynch. She grew corn, alfalfa, wheat and flax and bred cattle and sheep, which were sent to the local abattoir when they had been fattened up. She also reared horses and, when she had a full house, as many as fifteen or twenty riders could be seen galloping across her fields.

Ernesto and Celia Guevara spent many a summer at Portela with their children who, as they grew older, would also bring their friends. Ernestito had a particularly close relationship with his grandmother, who doted on him. Perhaps it was from her that he inherited his love of the outdoors and his interest in nature. Her treat was to take him out in the evening in her four-wheeled American carriage and drive through the stables to inspect the animals or down the rows of fruit trees, picking the ripe apples off the branches on their way.

At the end of the summer, those who had gone to Alta Gracia for their holidays made their way back to Buenos Aires, as the school year was about to start. In Argentina, it is divided into two terms: the first one runs from early March to July and the second, after a fortnight of winter holidays, from late July to early December. Thus the summer holidays last for three months, from early December to the beginning of March, since it is then extremely hot in many parts of Argentina.

Celia and Ernesto Guevara with their four children in the seaside resort
of Mar del Plata

When the summer visitors left, Alta Gracia calmed down and returned to its normal existence: fewer people, less traffic, fewer parties, less fun. And the local children went back to school as well. That is, the children of the bourgeoisie, because the children of the poor, of those who were either badly paid or unemployed, did not attend school, although it was compulsory and free – and it was possible to get a decent education at the state schools at the time. Instead they helped their parents, either by staying at home to look after their younger siblings or by doing menial chores, such as running errands or working in the kitchen at the Sierras Hotel, acting as caddies at the golf course, or going out into the streets carrying a basketful of home-made pasties or cakes to sell. These children often sold their goods at the railway station to the passengers on board the frequent trains that stopped briefly on their way to and from the capital.

Ernestito was unable to attend school regularly himself, albeit for a different reason, and he befriended many of these children. He went to their homes and saw for himself that a whole family often slept all in one room on a couple of mattresses on the floor, using newspapers for blankets. On several occasions, Celia was unable to find the *guardapolvos* Ernestito was supposed to wear to school because he had given them away to less fortunate children. (A *guardapolvo* is a white coat children wear over their clothes to protect them from wear and tear. It is the equivalent of the uniform worn by children who attend private schools.)

Argentines were enduring the Infamous Decade of the 1930s at home, but the nation's international reputation did not suffer. The Argentine foreign minister, Carlos Saavedra-Lamas, was awarded the Nobel Peace Prize in 1935 for his mediation in the 1932–5 Chaco War between Bolivia and Paraguay. Buenos Aires sponsored an international peace conference and Argentina rejoined the League of Nations in 1936, after a thirteen-year absence.

In the same year, part of the Spanish army, under General Franco, took up arms against the Republic. The Spanish Civil War had begun. In view of its colonial past, cultural identity, language and ancestry, Argentina could not fail to take a serious interest, and the civil war would colour Argentine lives for years to come.

Argentine diplomats posted throughout Europe worked hard to secure the safe evacuation of Spaniards who sought asylum in their embassies and consulates. Argentina condemned hostage-taking, the bombing of open cities and attacks on non-combatants and, because it did not take sides, was able to be of assistance to Spaniards affected by the conflict, whatever their political persuasion. Opinion and public sympathy were sharply divided, with the military, the established church, and the upper classes on the whole pro-Franco whilst the rest of the population were overwhelmingly pro-Republican.

Cayetano Córdoba-Iturburu, the communist poet and journalist married to Carmen de la Serna, left for Spain as war correspondent for the evening broadsheet *Crítica* when the conflict broke out. Carmen and her children arrived from Buenos Aires and moved in with the Guevaras. Her husband's stay in Spain would last a year. In order to prevent his articles falling into the hands of Franco's supporters, the enemies of the Spanish Republic, Córdoba-Iturburu sent them to his wife with his personal letters to her. Once everyone had read them in Alta Gracia, Carmen forwarded the articles to the newspaper. The Guevara household thus had first-hand knowledge of events at the front in Spain.

While the Spanish Republic was still fighting for its survival, the Guevaras and their close friends worked very hard for it. Towards the end of 1938, a Spanish republican family arrived in Alta Gracia. The father, Dr Juan González-Aguilar, had stayed behind in Barcelona where he was the Head of Army Sanitation, in charge of the evacuation of refugees to France through the western Pyrenees. He had managed to smuggle the poet Antonio Machado and his mother across the frontier in an ambulance, as if they were wounded combatants. González-Aguilar's wife and their four children were immediately welcomed by the Guevaras, who helped them to settle down. The children of the two families were of similar ages and they all became fast friends.

Pepe González-Aguilar, who was to become Ernestito's friend later on in life when the difference in years no longer mattered, following him to Cuba once the revolution had triumphed, used to tell me many stories about his family's friendship with the Guevaras. Years later, when he and I were working together, he told me that Celia Guevara had taken it upon herself to nurse him back to health when the family arrived in Alta Gracia. He was a nervous and frightened four-year-old who was having a tough time adapting to his new circumstances; he missed his father and had been bewildered by their change of residence, as they had lived in Buenos Aires for a while when they first arrived from Spain. He would not eat and was growing more emaciated by the day.

One lunchtime, Celia prepared a plate of gnocchi especially for him. When she told him the dish was an Italian delicacy, Pepe refused to allow the fork to pass his lips. The Italian fascists were the enemy, he blurted out to her. Celia quietly disappeared into the kitchen and returned with the same plate of gnocchi, which she had smothered beyond recognition in tomato sauce. She announced that this red dish was called Russian potatoes. This time round, Pepe relished the treat and ate it all up. She told him the story years later when he was a grown man and they laughed together at her cunning and inventiveness.

The Spanish refugee composer, Manuel de Falla, also came to live in Alta Gracia. The Argentine writer, Daniel Moyano, wrote a short story which tells how he and Ernestito used to climb up the peach trees in de Falla's garden to steal the fruit. The composer would appear at a first-floor balcony and shout at them to help themselves to the fruit but not to damage the tree. Daniel Moyano came from an extremely poor family, his mother took in washing and ironing from the well-to-do families of Alta Gracia. When Ernestito came down from the tree with his shirt full of ripe peaches he gave them all to Daniel: he could not take them home as his mother would punish him severely for stealing. Daniel ended the story by saying that both de Falla and Guevara were eventually immortalised in their country's currency. De Falla's image appeared on the Spanish 100 peseta bill, while Guevara's face can still be seen on the 3 peso note in Cuba.

Córdoba-Iturburu sometimes included newspaper articles and magazines published by the Republic with his letters and so, when Spanish intellectuals began to arrive in Argentina as refugees after the Republic lost the war, the Guevaras were already familiar with the works of people like the poet Rafael Alberti, who spent many years in exile in Alta Gracia. After Franco's death in 1975, he returned triumphantly to Spain to take up a seat in parliament. Argentina's cultural life was greatly enhanced and enriched by such figures.

Another well-known Spanish republican to arrive in Alta Gracia was General Enrique Jurado, the hero of the Battle of Guadalajara, in which the republican army under his command defeated Franco's nationalist forces and prevented them from entering Madrid. It was a decisive republican victory at the time and greatly boosted morale. General Jurado was a modest man, unlike the Argentine generals, who modelled themselves on their German counterparts. He never spoke of his own exploits but always praised his men and the officers under his command.

Ernestito was riveted by his stories. During the war, he had followed the development of the conflict on a huge map hung on his bedroom wall, on which he and his brother Roberto pinned little flags marking the positions of both armies, their advances and retreats. In fact, both Ernestito and Roberto knew the names of all the republican generals by heart and would recite them at the slightest provocation, much as other children rattled off the names of their preferred football team.

In 1939 France and Britain recognised Franco's government in Spain. Hitler advanced on Prague in March that year and, while the summer was coming to an end in Alta Gracia, a world war loomed on the horizon. A Conservative government was in power in Argentina when the Second World War broke out in 1939 and it was torn between its pro-German instincts and its traditional economic dependence on Great Britain, but Argentina was to remain neutral.

Argentina's dependence on Britain had increased during the Infamous Decade. In London, on 1st May 1933, Julio A. Roca Junior, representing the Argentine government, and Sir Walter Runciman, representing Britain, had signed the Roca-Runciman Treaty for the export of a fixed quota of Argentine meat to the UK. The terms were extremely unfavourable for Argentina. Under the treaty, the UK would continue to buy Argentine beef provided its price was lower than that of other suppliers. In exchange for this 'favour', Argentina lifted most taxes on British products and undertook to prevent the creation of Argentine companies that might rival the British-owned ones in the refrigerated meat-packing industry. The Central Bank of the Argentine Republic was created, with several British officials on its board. A British corporation was granted the concession for the transport system for the capital city. Transport by road would not compete with the railway system built and owned by the British.

Without seeming to realise the enormity of what he was saying, Julio A. Roca Junior stated that Argentina would now be part of the British Empire. The unfortunate phrase was echoed by another member of his delegation who said, 'Argentina is one of the most precious jewels of His Gracious Majesty's crown.' Senator Lisandro de la Torre of the Progressive Democratic Party stated that it could not be said that Argentina had attained the status of a British colony because Britain did not impose on its dependent territories the humiliation it imposed on Argentina. British colonies were all allowed to manage their own quotas of meat exports.

There was a long history behind this state of affairs. Britain had coveted the region which became Argentina since before 1810, when it attained independence from Spain. Britain went to war with Spain in 1804. In June 1806, the British invaded Buenos Aires, intending to annex the Viceroyalty of the River Plate to the British Empire. They managed to take the city and help themselves to the country's treasury, which they sent to England, before they were ousted on 12th August by the population's volunteer militia. They invaded a second time in June 1807, but this time the locals were better prepared to defend their city. When the British marched through the narrow streets of Buenos Aires they were greeted by boiling oil poured from the balconies and roofs of buildings. It was said that every male member of the population, including the black slaves and Indians, took part in the defence. The British retreated, and the Union Jack would never again fly over mainland Argentina.

Nevertheless, it didn't stop Britain becoming the main trading partner in an unequal relation with Argentina for many decades to come, up to and beyond the 1930s. The cattle oligarchy had always been pro-British, and spoke English as well as Spanish. They thought of themselves as superior to the less well-educated masses whom they had dispossessed and condemned to a miserable existence in a country which is rich beyond belief. They were devout Roman Catholics and their church condoned their attitude.

The United States of America were also penetrating the area with their ideology, as part of a trend that had been going on for almost a century: they had developed the notion that Latin America was their 'back yard'. In 1848 the United States had signed the Treaty of Guadalupe Hidalgo with Mexico. This ended hostilities between the two countries and established the Rio Grande as their boundary, which meant that the USA acquired territories from Mexico that were to become the states of California, Nevada, Utah, part of Arizona, New Mexico and Wyoming. The Republic of Texas, whose independence Mexico had never recognised, had already been annexed in 1845. The USA had also acquired vast tracts from France in 1803, through the Louisiana Purchase, and had bought Florida from Spain in 1819. It was seventy years since independence and the USA had hugely enlarged its territory. The country George Washington had founded on the principles of liberty and equality was no longer recognisable.

Just as the USA was expanding, Argentina was shrinking since territories that had been part of the Viceroyalty of the River Plate – Paraguay, Bolivia and Uruguay – had seceded. It was natural for the USA to look towards South America next. The concept of Manifest Destiny, a phrase coined in 1839 to justify the US's push westward, was used in 1845 by John O'Sullivan – the editor of an influential New York newspaper – to endorse the proposed annexation of Texas and was from then on picked up by the media. O'Sullivan was only articulating the long-held belief that white Americans had a divine right to occupy the entire American continent. It was their God-given duty to spread their values to the less fortunate Native Americans and Hispanics. Their real motive was greed and power. In 1823 the USA had introduced the Monroe Doctrine, warning Europeans against committing further acts of colonisation in the Western hemisphere at a time when many Latin American countries had or were about to become independent from Spain. Eventually the USA would use the doctrine to justify its own expansionist intentions, its right to unilateral intervention and hegemony.

Meanwhile, towards the end of 1939, a German pocket battleship, the *Graf Spee*, had been causing great damage to the British merchant navy and, after fighting what became known as the Battle of the River Plate against three much smaller British ships, it was scuttled by its skipper outside the Bay of Montevideo in Uruguay. The German sailors who had survived the sinking of their vessel were interned in the province of Córdoba, where there was already a large community of German origin in Calamuchita, not far from Alta Gracia.

Guevara Senior was a founder member of a group called Acción Argentina, which supported the Allied cause and had branches all over the country. Its members came from different political parties but all shared anti-fascist ideas. In its declaration of intent, the organisation denounced attempts by foreign powers to invade Argentina, and invited citizens to organise themselves in groups to monitor and counter such attempts.

Nazi cells had already been introduced into Argentina by Hitler's government. These operated clandestinely and could have surfaced at any time had the war reached our continent. Hitler himself had said that, once the Nazis won the war in Europe, they would conquer the underdeveloped regions of South America. The Central Organisation of Germans Abroad and the Information Office of the German Railways were really created as fronts to cover up the activities of the Nazis in South America. Members of the German embassy in Buenos Aires, who were also part of these Nazi networks, were eventually declared personae non gratae and forced to leave the country for taking advantage of their diplomatic immunity to conduct improper activities. The government probably wanted to avoid a public scandal which might uncover even more irregularities.

Guevara Senior's group discovered a Nazi spy network operating out of La Falda in the province of Córdoba, a mere eighty kilometres from Alta Gracia: a hotel with a powerful radio transmitter was in touch with Berlin every night. When the group of members of Acción Argentina travelled there to inspect the premises, Ernestito, who was twelve at the time, went with them. The group prepared two lengthy and detailed reports full of relevant data and presented them to the Office of the President of the Republic, together with reports drafted by members from other regions the length and breadth of the country. They were binned without a thought by pro-German President Castillo.

FOUR

(1941–1950)

As the Nazis advanced through Europe, the Guevara children and their friends repeated the place names they heard the grown-ups talk about until they were part of their daily vocabulary. At times, they were more concerned with these faraway places than with what they were being taught at school. The Spanish refugees had brought the European conflict into their lives and they had made it their own. The boys no longer played cowboys and Indians; now they used the ditches that had been dug in the streets to repair the sewage system as the trenches in which their rival armies fought their own wars.

In 1941, at the age of thirteen, Ernestito finished his primary education at the Escuela Pública San Martín, a state-run school which the three older Guevara children attended. He did not go to school regularly until he was nine years old, and he only went then because the authorities forced his parents to send him: education was compulsory, and a visit by an inspector had revealed his poor attendance record. He had been perfectly happy at home being educated by his mother and following the school curriculum with the help of his younger siblings, who were responsible for bringing home the day's lessons.

Once at school, he was an indifferent student and occasionally had behaviour problems, according to his teachers. He was hyperactive and restless and would obviously have preferred to be somewhere else. He obtained good marks in history and made sustained improvements in natural sciences, reading, writing, geography and geometry, but showed a lack of interest in drawing, gymnastics and music. His teachers remembered him as an intelligent boy who led his fellow students in games during the breaks from class, but who did not seem very interested in the school syllabus.

There was no secondary school in Alta Gracia, so in 1942 he travelled daily to Córdoba city to study for his *Bachillerato* (Baccalaureate) at the Colegio Nacional Deán Funes. His sister, Celia, had also completed her primary studies and enrolled in a school in the provincial capital. In the summer of 1943, when he was fifteen, the family decided they should move to the city. This would spare their two eldest children the daily bus ride of about forty kilometres each way, and Guevara Senior had now embarked on a construction project based in Córdoba city. It was the start of a slightly more prosperous period in the family fortunes, with Guevara Senior at last in a permanent job. His business partner was a local architect and their firm received commissions to build several houses. As a Master Builder, Guevara Senior supervised their construction.

The Guevaras moved to a house in Calle Chile, in the residential area called Nueva Córdoba. The González-Aguilar family also moved to Córdoba and rented a house not far from the Guevaras, so the children continued to see each other every day and stayed close friends. Unfortunately, the neighbourhood had been built on ground which was prone to landslides and, since the Guevaras were the first family to occupy their house, they were also the first to suffer from the subsidence, which opened large cracks in the walls. Guevara Senior, in spite of or perhaps because of his building knowledge, did not seem too concerned that a crack in the ceiling over his bed allowed him to see the stars at night. The only precaution he took was to move the children's beds away from the walls, as cracks had also appeared in their rooms. Beside the more or less luxurious houses of the middle classes, the poor of the city had built their homes of discarded cardboard, zinc sheeting and tin, and the Guevaras' house was next to a *villa miseria*, as shanty towns are known in Argentina.

On 18th May 1943, the Guevaras' fifth and last child, Juan Martín, was born in this house. Pepe González-Aguilar tells us that, in spite of their atheism, the Guevaras had their child christened and his parents were Juan Martín's godparents. When the older children heard their atheist, left-wing, free-thinking parents replying in Latin to the priest who was conducting the ceremony, they got the giggles and had to leave the church.

On 4th June 1943, President Castillo was ousted by a military coup and replaced by Arturo Rawson. He, in turn, was replaced by General Pedro Ramírez, who was then forced to resign and was himself replaced by his vice-president, General Edelmiro J. Farrell, in 1944. A certain Colonel Perón, whom nobody really knew, was behind the coup that initiated this chain of events. Both pro-Germans and pro-Allies rejoiced, as it was not clear what the ideology of the new rulers was.

The fascist leanings of the military soon began to show: they sacked university professors who demanded that the country be returned to democracy, and all political parties were banned. The United States ordered an economic blockade against Argentina, demanding that the Argentine government break relations with the Axis powers. The government chose to obey. Everyone rejoiced except Ernestito, who was furious. Nobody could understand the teenager's reaction. He had always been a staunch anti-Nazi. It even took his parents a long time to understand that what he objected to was the country caving in to US pressure. It was the beginning of his lifelong hatred of US imperialism – a feeling that would colour his political development from then on.

Ernestito was still attending the Colegio Nacional Deán Funes in Córdoba, where he had met Tomás Granado. They were the same age and in the same grade, and they had become close friends. Tomás had an older brother, Alberto, aged twenty-one, who was studying biochemistry and pharmacology at the University of Córdoba. He was putting together a rugby team called Estudiantes. Ernestito wanted to play and asked to be given a chance to join them; Alberto gave him a try. They practised two evenings a week and Ernestito proved himself a tough player in spite of his physique – he was not very robust and had skinny arms. But his friendship with Alberto went well beyond sport, as they were both avid readers.

Ernestito always carried a book with him and had already read Baudelaire, Mallarmé, Verlaine, Dumas and Zola in the original French. He also enjoyed reading American writers, such as Faulkner and Steinbeck, in translation. Though as keen on literature as Ernestito, Alberto was also actively interested in biochemistry and medicine. He had a social conscience and was researching the Hansen bacillus, which causes leprosy. He came from a humble background and had experienced the injustices of the political system first-hand. They would eventually travel together across Latin America, and Alberto would follow his friend to Cuba to help cement the revolution once it had triumphed.

The weakness of General Franco's Spain after the civil war meant it would be a very long time before it – the original imperial power – exerted any influence on most Latin Americans. And the same was true of defeated Italy, the country from which a large portion of the population of Argentina had emigrated. And of course Nazi Germany was anathema to the young men of the Argentine bourgeoisie with left-wing leanings. There was a strong socialist movement in Argentina, led by Alfredo Palacios, a man of great personal prestige and charisma and an impressive orator, while the Unión Cívica Radical was a party of the centre, supported by the middle classes at the time. The Americans, with their paranoia, were busy controlling the mainstream media so that little information came out of the Soviet Union and few were converted to the communist cause.

Colonel Perón had concealed his fascist leanings while in an obscure job at the Department of Labour, but he had gradually begun to acquire a certain popularity with the lower echelons of society. He managed to turn his department into the Secretariat for Labour and Social Welfare and implemented a series of measures which were to benefit the working classes. He was appointed Minister of Defence as well, and this enabled him to put his cronies in the army in key positions. Then in June 1944 he became vice-president of the republic, under President Farrell.

When Argentina was forced by the USA to declare war on the Axis early in 1945, it was no secret that Perón was an admirer of Mussolini, while other members of the government had openly fascist leanings. However, political prisoners, with the exception of communists, were set free, university professors who had been sacked were rehabilitated, and a law was passed allowing some activity by political parties. There was talk of elections in the near future. The USA made the mistake of sending a new ambassador to Argentina, Spruille Braden of the Braden Copper Company, who openly became the champion of the opposition when, as a diplomat, he should not have been so blatantly partisan. It gave Perón the opportunity to coin the catchphrase 'Braden or Perón', as if they were the only two possible options: either you were with the USA or you were with the proletariat.

The Communist Party of Argentina took sides with Braden, something they have never been allowed to forget.

With the end of the war in the Pacific in 1945, many took the opportunity to march against Perón and soon there were clashes in the streets of Buenos Aires and other major cities, between the middle classes and the police who defended the government. Pro-Perón groups, known as the Alianza Libertadora Nacionalista (they would soon feel betrayed by Perón and change sides), appeared in the streets using violent paramilitary tactics. The Federation of University Students and the Communist Youth Movement armed themselves and there were serious clashes, with dead and wounded on both sides.

Alberto Granado was one of the student leaders taken into custody in Córdoba during these clashes. Ernesto (he had managed to drop the diminutive and only his family still called him Ernestito) and Alberto's brother, Tomás, went to visit him and take him food. Alberto tried to persuade the two, who were both still studying for the Baccalaureate at secondary school, to mobilise their fellow students and march against the government. Ernesto flatly refused, saying that he would only join a demonstration if someone gave him a gun. The police in Argentina carried Colt 45s as standard equipment and he was not prepared to face them unarmed.

There was an attempt by the opposition to organise an uprising against Farrell and Perón. General Rawson, the man who had been president for forty-eight hours in 1943, led the uprising, but it failed, and the government announced a state of siege and imposed a curfew. A faction of the army demanded that Perón be withdrawn from office and replaced by a civilian vice-president until elections could be held.

On 13th October 1945, Perón was detained and sent to the island of Martín García, off the Argentine coast, where there is a military prison. The news spread like wildfire. The opposition celebrated, while the trade unions, pro-Perón since they were impressed by his populist streak and saw him as their champion, called a general strike for the 18th. But the military and the opposition parties did not reach an agreement, as the army was divided and some of its members were pro-Perón. On 17th October the workers marched to the city centres instead of going to their place of work. In Buenos Aires, Córdoba, Tucumán, Rosario and throughout the country, a loud roar was heard: 'Perón! Perón! Perón!' The middle classes felt threatened. Everyone rushed home, and shops closed their doors in a hurry. Celia Guevara, who had gone out elegantly attired, came across a group of demonstrators in the street. She was ordered to shout 'Viva Perón'. She shouted 'Death to Perón' instead. The police quickly intervened and rescued her from the furious mob.

There was a power vacuum: the politicians could do nothing, and neither could the military. The police force did not want to attack the people. The country had never seen anything like it. By nightfall, Perón had been brought back from the island and spoke to the masses from the balcony of the Casa Rosada, the palace of government. His speech was transmitted to the whole country by the state broadcasting system. On 24th February 1946, general elections took place. Perón won by a huge margin, to the astonishment of many. But in the province of Córdoba, which was and would always remain anti-Perón, the Unión Democrática, a coalition of parties opposed to Perón, won.

The government of President Perón was not easy to define. There was a drive for industrialisation, which made many rich quickly. The need for labour in the new factories meant that many abandoned their rural homes and settled in the outskirts of the capital. This totally changed Buenos Aires. The proletariat invaded the centre of the city and took over the streets, cinemas, restaurants and dance halls. The horrified bourgeoisie referred to these new arrivals as *cabecitas negras* (little black heads, after a South American bird of that name, the *Carduelis magallanica*) because most of them were small, dark and stocky. Perón referred to his followers as the *descamisados* or shirtless. He used both terms affectionately, whereas for the opposition they were pejorative. There was a shortage of housing for the newcomers so shanty towns sprang up in many neighbourhoods. But more schools than ever were built and education reached the furthermost corners of the country.

Perón served his six-year term in office and was re-elected in 1952 for a further six years, only to be ousted by a military junta in 1955. He had committed a fundamental economic mistake: he did not invest the financial reserves accumulated during the Second World War when Argentina had remained neutral and sold beef and wheat to Britain. Instead of developing the oil, iron and coal industries, building power stations and roads, modernising transport and mechanising agriculture, he simply distributed the wealth.

Just as there cannot be a successful economic policy that does not attend to social justice, there cannot be social justice without a solid economic base. The failure of his policies led to confrontation between the different social strata. The situation could only end in violence. Perón's party, now renamed the Partido Justicialista, had started out as a national movement in spite of all the errors committed in the political, economic and social spheres, but by Perón's second mandate it had become a faction. Paradoxically, once in power his party had turned into an extremist movement, isolated from the people as a whole as it in turn isolated the working classes, trying to turn them into the party's only political support. And then he attacked the Roman Catholic church and consequently fell out with the devout who were forced to make a choice; so the military intervened and toppled him.

Right from the start of his presidency, Perón had turned the country into a haven for Nazi war criminals such as Josef Mengele, Adolf Eichmann, Klaus Barbie and Erich Priebke, as well as for many Croatian fascists including their leader Ante Pavelic, wanted in Europe for acts of genocide. Once Perón's guests were in the country they were able to lead normal lives without having to pay for their crimes: they were given new identities and assistance so they could integrate into the local society, learn the language and behave as any other immigrant in a land of opportunity, as Argentina was at the time.

At the end of the summer of 1946, the Guevara family returned to Buenos Aires for good. To begin with, they stayed with Guevara Senior's mother in her home at Calle Arenales 2208. Ernesto remained in Córdoba to finish his studies. He and Tomás Granado had managed to obtain jobs in the materials analysis department of the Provincial Roads Directorate. He had a salary of 200 pesos and free lodgings, so his only expenses were for food and books, he told his father in a letter. He enjoyed the job because he got on very well with the engineers who were in charge of the works and he felt they trusted him. His predecessor had not done a good job and he had to work overtime to carry out overdue tests relating to ten kilometres of roads. He would soon be promoted to foreman and even contemplated studying engineering with Tomás Granado, who had just enrolled at the University of Córdoba. But at the beginning of 1947 Ernesto completed his Baccalaureate, quit his job and returned to Buenos Aires.

His paternal grandmother, Ana Lynch de Guevara, was seriously ill. They had always enjoyed a special relationship and he looked after her without leaving her bedside for seventeen days. When she died, he was inconsolable. Shortly afterwards, he decided to enrol in the Faculty of Medicine at the University of Buenos Aires, and it has often been said that this decision was motivated by seeing his grandmother die and by his mother's recent serious operation for breast cancer.

The Guevaras bought an old house on the corner of Calles Aráoz and Mansilla, where they occupied the first floor as there were tenants on the ground floor. Through a close friend, his father found Ernesto a job in the Buenos Aires City Council's Supplies Division. From then on he combined his studies with work and supported himself. He spent more time than was necessary at work simply because there he had peace and quiet to read and write. He was writing what he referred to as a philosophical dictionary, which helped him to clarify his ideas and classify what he read. He kept this habit for many years, improving and updating his entries as he learnt more about the subjects he covered. His essays about Marx and Engels were eventually published by his estate in 2007 under the title *A Biographical Synthesis of Marx and Engels.*

It was not long before he gave up this job and decided to go into business with his old friend from Córdoba, Carlos Figueroa, who was now living in Buenos Aires too, reading law. They started manufacturing an insecticide in the garage of the Guevara home, based on a product called Gamexane, which the Ministry of Agriculture was using with great success to combat plagues of locusts in the countryside. After carrying out some tests, they bought a large amount of it and of talcum powder and some little round boxes which could contain 100 grams of a mixture made up of 80 per cent talcum powder and 20 per cent Gamexane. They marketed the product under the name Vendaval, which means windstorm. Housewives bought it and, according to Carlos Figueroa, pronounced it excellent. But just when they thought they had a profitable business, they were forced to stop producing the mixture because everything in the Guevara household above the garage tasted and smelled of it. And it was toxic as well, so soon both Ernesto and an assistant he had employed were suffering from mild poisoning.

Luckily, Ernesto was now given a job by Dr Salvador Pisani, a prestigious scientist who specialised in allergies. He ran his own Instituto de Investigaciones Alérgicas and was well known throughout the country. Ernesto had been to see him as a patient and had experienced a marked improvement as a result of the treatment the doctor had prescribed. Dr Pisani noticed Ernesto's potential as a scientific researcher and offered him a part-time job in his laboratory. Dr Pisani's theory was that people who suffered from certain allergies could be desensitised, using injections he prepared in his own laboratory. These consisted of a mixture containing semi-digested foodstuffs. There was great empathy between the men and Ernesto learnt a lot at Pisani's side.

Dr Pisani had bought some modern electrical equipment from Sweden, to be used to grind human entrails for their tests. When it arrived, Ernesto decided to try out the apparatus, so he took some entrails from the Faculty of Medicine, where he was studying. They came from people who had died of infectious diseases. When preparing the mixture to put into the apparatus, he did not realise he should use a rubber seal to prevent the infected particles coming into contact with his hands. A couple of days later, he developed a very high temperature and confined himself to bed. His father came home, saw his condition, called an emergency medical service and asked for a heart stimulant, as well as telephoning Dr Pisani. Guevara Senior, helpless and in utter desperation, watched his son grow progressively worse. Soon, both the nurse with the stimulant and Dr Pisani arrived. The doctor stayed for several hours, watching over his patient and administering medicines. The family anxiously waited up all night until, at about six in the morning, Ernesto began to recover.

Ernesto got out of bed and began to get dressed. His father waited until he went for his jacket before asking him where he thought he was going. Ernesto said he had to sit an exam in a couple of hours. There was no point in arguing with him: he had made up his mind. What could have been described as stubbornness when he was a child was now proving to be a tenacious willpower which would overcome any of his handicaps and limitations and take him wherever he wanted to go.

In 1947 Ernesto became eligible for National Military Service, which was compulsory and by conscription. He received his summons and, according to his family, when the date for his medical examination came up he took a very cold shower before turning up at the barracks, knowing that the cold would give him an almighty asthma attack. He was consequently exempted as physically unfit. He had no intention of wasting a year of his life when he wanted to carry on with his studies. 'For once,' he said, 'my shitty lungs have done something useful for me.'

His first asthma attack had occurred in similar circumstances, after Celia took him swimming at the San Isidro Club near their home. When Guevara Senior arrived to take them to lunch he noticed that the child was shivering and not breathing properly, but the problem was only diagnosed as asthma much later.

The Faculty of Medicine of the National University, where Ernesto attended lectures and practical classes from 1947 until his graduation in 1953, is an old, grey, pseudo-Gothic building in downtown Buenos Aires. There he met Tita Infante, a young woman from Córdoba who was also studying to become a doctor. They studied together, carried out lab tests together, went to class together and shared a passion for literature as well.

Though Ernesto was shy, a bad dancer and a poor singer, girls always enjoyed his company

Tita, who was slightly older than Ernesto, was a committed communist, but she did not participate in the political activities of the students' union of which she was a member. Ernesto recoiled from the shallow interests of Argentine party politics and had still to define his own political position – he only had a militantly humanitarian concern for his fellow men. Tita and Ernesto often spent time together before and after lessons, and would meet at one of the cafés near the Faculty to discuss classes, and sometimes also at the Guevara home. On Wednesdays, they attended a class on the nervous system at the Museum of Natural Sciences, where they dissected fish and insects. They wrote to each other frequently after Ernesto left Argentina for good and their friendship lasted until Ernesto's death. They were able to confide in each other but, although they treated each other with great affection, they were never sentimentally involved.

Ernesto (far left) with friends in Córdoba

Félix Fernández-Madrid knew Ernesto from the San Isidro Club, where they had both played rugby for a time, and they met again at the Faculty of Medicine. Their younger brothers, Talo and Roberto, both law students, were also friends and fellow rugby players. Fernández-Madrid went on to practise medicine in the USA. He wrote a book called *Che Guevara and the Incurable Disease,* the title referring not to Ernesto's asthma but to the fear and paranoia felt by a society that will not confront the misery and economic oppression of large sections of the population.

In his book he tells us that, at the time they were students, tuition at the National University was free, and there was only a minimal registration fee. This meant that thousands of students would enrol, as the entrance examination was easy as well. The huge numbers attending classes put a strain on the resources, professors, classrooms and materials, but the practical and theoretical exams were rigorous, which meant that the drop-out rate was high. After seven years, only about 10 per cent of the original number of students would graduate.

Alberto Granado (third from right) and Ernesto (first from right), Córdoba

The classes in the foundation year were anatomy, histology and embryology. The first big hurdle was anatomy. Students arriving punctually for their lectures were unable to enter the auditorium, as it would already be filled to capacity. This was not really a big problem because the textbooks were excellent. The students' bible was the Spanish translation of the French classic by Testut. The practical exams were considered exacting and nobody dared miss a session at the morgue, where the demonstration of anatomical dissections took place. The classes were packed and it was impossible to see anything. The answer to this was to obtain a corpse and carry out the dissections on one's own, consulting books and diagrams.

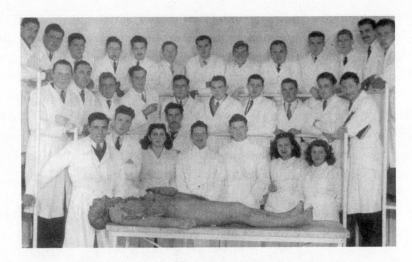

The Faculty of Medicine in the morgue, Buenos Aires. Ernesto is sixth
from right, last row

The students would avail themselves of cadavers from the lunatic
asylum, where it was easier to find corpses because many inmates had been
abandoned by their families or were foreigners who had no relatives to
claim them. The morgue attendants would prepare the corpses
by injecting formalin to preserve them. The students were able to buy a
whole body and work on it for several weeks in the morgue. Once, Ernesto
took a leg from the morgue so that he could study it with one of his
friends, Adalberto Larumbe, at his home. He wrapped the leg up in
newspapers and took the Underground. As the papers began to unwrap,
the toes appeared. The passengers on the train did not know what to make
of it and gave him strange looks. Ernesto enjoyed the shock he caused and
arrived at his friend's home in fits of laughter.

Fernández-Madrid and Ernesto sometimes shared a cadaver and studied
together, meeting at each other's homes, as well as in cafés and at the Faculty.
By 1950, they had finished the basic curriculum. Physiology, physics and
biological chemistry required few practical sessions and were on the whole
theoretical. Only pathology had microscopy and autopsy requirements.

FIVE
(1950–1951)

Throughout the six years in which Ernesto studied medicine off and on, he never sought to distinguish himself or to obtain high marks. He just wanted to pass the tests and graduate as quickly as possible, in spite of the many interruptions caused by the trips he embarked on during that period.

On 1st January 1950, taking advantage of the summer holidays, Ernesto set out for northern Argentina on a bicycle trip. He had equipped his bicycle with a small Micron motor but was careful to play down his intentions and did not give details of his planned itinerary, as members of his family were already saying he would not get any further than Pergamino, some two hundred and thirty kilometres from Buenos Aires, let alone the northern provinces.

He took some reading material with him as well as several notebooks in which to record his impressions, and this became his habit for the rest of his life. During the trip he wrote many letters home telling his parents his whereabouts and giving vivid descriptions of what he saw. But it is the notebooks, written in pencil and on the hoof, that give us an insight into his thoughts and state of mind. He wrote wherever he could: on the side of the road when he was forced to halt, and during his overnight stops at hospitals, police stations or wherever he could scrounge some hospitality.

His father found some of these notebooks in the basement of his elder sister Beatriz's apartment quite accidentally in 1972, long after Ernesto's death in 1967. There had been a freak storm in the city and the basements in downtown Buenos Aires were flooded. Beatriz, who was over eighty by then, was bedridden and suffering from paralysis, so she asked her brother to deal with the situation. Hercilia, their younger sister, had already been

61

down to see the concierge and told him to burn everything. When Guevara Senior arrived, the concierge was surrounded by tenants from other apartments in the block who were indicating which of their damaged possessions should be thrown into the fire. The boiler was on and the operation was proceeding apace.

The concierge showed Guevara Senior a couple of trunks that belonged to his family, in which he found all sorts of rubbish: old shoes, bits of clothing, newspaper cuttings and many more useless objects. There were also books, which he immediately recognised as belonging to his son Ernesto, and among them were the notebooks. It was evident to him that poor old Beatriz, who had been Ernestito's favourite aunt and had been appointed guardian of his possessions when he left home for the last time (although nobody knew then that he would never come back), had been overwhelmed by the number of papers and books he had entrusted to her. So she had put them away in a trunk and totally forgotten about them.

Ernesto had his picture taken before he left: he sits on his bicycle, in sunglasses, a cap and a leather jacket, carrying his spare tyre across his chest, the very picture of a sportsman. When he returned from the trip, he wrote to the importers of the motor asking them to repair it for him and mentioned the distance he had travelled – 4,700 kilometres. Both his letter and photograph were eventually used in an advertisement to promote the motor, in exchange for which it was repaired for free. The photograph also made it to the cover of the prestigious sports magazine *El Gráfico*.

Ernesto had set himself the target of reaching Pilar, some fifty kilometres from Buenos Aires, on the first leg. He started off using his motor but, after San Isidro, on the outskirts of the city, he decided to turn it off and continue pedalling. Another cyclist caught up with him and they went on together, passing Pilar and then San Antonio de Areco in the morning. There the two young men parted company after breakfast.

By the afternoon, Ernesto had reached Pergamino. This was as far as he expected to go on his second leg but, encouraged by his achievement, he chose to push himself further and continue on to Rosario in spite of being quite tired. He hung on to the back of a fuel lorry, which afforded him a rest from pedalling, and by eleven that night had reached his intended destination for the day. By now, he tells us in his diary, his body was screaming for a mattress but his will opposed it and he carried on. During a downpour at two in the morning, from which he protected himself with a canvas cape his mother had packed for him, he recited a poem by Ernesto Sábato at the top of his voice and laughed heartily at the weather.

Ernesto on his bicycle with two of the Granado brothers in Córdoba

It was six in the morning when he reached Leones and around ten when he went through Bel Ville and hooked on to the tail of another lorry that took him as far as Villa María, 600 kilometres from his starting point. Ten kilometres later, a car caught up with him and he asked the driver to tow him, but not to exceed 60 kilometres an hour. After some ten kilometres he realised he had punctured his rear wheel and fell off. He inspected the bicycle and noticed that the motor had been rubbing against the rear tyre, exposing the inner tube, which had been damaged. His spare inner tube was beyond repair and he was exhausted, so he slept by the side of the road. A couple of hours later, he flagged down an empty lorry and asked the driver to take him as far as Córdoba.

He arrived at the Granado household exactly 41 hours and 17 minutes from the time he started. When Tomás Granado arrived home some days later they left for Tanti on their bicycles with Grego, the third Granado brother. After a day or so there was relentless rain and it seemed pointless to sit in a tent, so the three friends decided to take it down and put it away. They were packing their belongings when they heard the rushing sound of a stream coming towards them; as it got nearer, the sound turned into a roar. People came out of the houses, shouting that the stream was approaching and they were in danger of being carried away by it. They collected their gear together and Ernesto, who was holding their machete, cut the tent's final guy rope and shouted, 'Charge, my brave ones', as if it were a scene in a film. At the last minute, the three pulled all their belongings to one side as the stream raced past them. To Ernesto's disappointment, it was only about one and a half metres deep and therefore not very dangerous.

The Granado brothers then went home and Ernesto continued on to San Francisco del Chañar where Alberto, the third and eldest of the Granado brothers, worked in the hospital. The next day, Ernesto fell and broke eight spokes of the bicycle and it took him four days to get them repaired. Ernesto and Alberto finally left for Ojo de Agua, Alberto on his motorcycle and Ernesto on his bicycle. Alberto tried to tow Ernesto but the rope kept breaking and the fifty-five kilometres took four hours. Alberto then returned to San Francisco del Chañar while Ernesto went on with his journey to the province of Santiago del Estero, north of Córdoba. There he saw cacti six metres high, which he thought looked like candelabra.

Arriving at Loreto in the middle of the night, he asked for hospitality from the local police officer, who advised him to move there and set up a practice, since the place had no doctor and he would earn a lot of money as well as doing the locals a favour. Ernesto declined and was back on the road early in the morning, heading for the city of Santiago, where he had relatives of friends to visit. It was in Santiago, his diary tells us gleefully, that he was interviewed 'for the first time in my life'. It was almost as if he knew there would be many more interviews in the future. He let the journalist pay for the meal they ate together without compunction.

Although Ernesto came from a privileged background, he had no money for his travels. Instead, he relied on his luck to see him through, accepting and asking for hospitality wherever he could find it. He could offer his medical knowledge in exchange for a bed at hospitals and police stations (which were often the only places open to the public at all hours in provincial Argentina in the 1950s), and it seemed that nobody could deny him anything. He had the common touch. Policemen liked him; hospital clerks and nurses liked him; lorry drivers liked him. And of course, his own family adored him.

The strangest of episodes took place the following day when Ernesto continued on his way, this time to Tucamáno. He was inflating a tyre, about a kilometre from a village, when a tramp appeared from a nearby culvert. They struck up a conversation and the man told him he had been working on the cotton harvest in Chaco in the north, and that he was now contemplating making his way to the province of San Juan to work on the grape harvest. When Ernesto told him he was touring several provinces just for the experience, the man could not believe his ears: how could anyone make such a huge effort if not for profit?

The man decided he and Ernesto would do some business. Ernesto's protestations went unheeded so he followed his mentor, as he put it, out of curiosity. The two arrived at the first shop in the town and the tramp launched into a speech, claiming that 'this young man' was on a quest. He was on a grand tour of fourteen Argentine provinces collecting funds for a worthy cause: he intended to travel to Boulogne-sur-Mer in France, where the Liberator of Argentina, Chile and Peru, General San Martín (whom the tramp referred to at various points as the Saint of the Sword and the Great Captain) was buried. The enterprising and patriotic young man would lay a bunch of flowers at the grave once he had completed his feat, since it was the centenary of the death of General San Martín.

After a tour of the various shops in the main street, 112 pesos had been collected. The tramp then made the mistake of spending the money in a nearby bar, where he bought drinks for himself and Ernesto and a couple of passers-by, bragging about his exploit and mocking those who had been taken in. Someone must have ratted on him because, not much later, a policeman arrived to make enquiries about the young cyclist and promptly arrested Ernesto. It took him four hours to establish his innocence and be released. He went back to the culvert from which his would-be promoter had originally emerged and invited him to go on the road with him, but the tramp declined, letting 'the young cyclist' have 10 pesos from the remains of his kitty.

A downpour soon forced Ernesto to take cover and he spent the night at the local barracks (more precisely in the arsenal), some fifteen kilometres beyond Tucumán, leaving early next morning. The road out of Tucumán, he claimed, was one of the most beautiful in northern Argentina, with its luxuriant vegetation resembling a tropical forest. In this idyllic landscape he realised how much he hated urban life, whose noise shut out the melodious music of nature. He saw cities as the antithesis of peace and serenity and man's incessant travails as pointless and detrimental to nature.

He reached a police checkpoint at about midday and stopped for a rest. A motorcyclist on a brand new Harley-Davidson appeared and offered to tow him at 80–90 kilometres per hour. Ernesto knew this would be impossible and declined. He drank some coffee with the policeman and left for the north, only to see the Harley-Davidson being hauled down from a lorry. He enquired after the rider and was told that he was dead. He wrote that a man who goes looking for danger and dies without witnesses when taking a bend on the road becomes in retrospect an unknown adventurer imbued with a suicidal fervour, and that might have made the study of his personality interesting.

The magnificence of the surroundings near Lobería made him crave the company of a woman, whoever she might be, to share the experience and protect from the elements. Ernesto turned up at the hospital in Salta and introduced himself as a medical student, a penniless and exhausted cyclist. He was allowed to sleep on the soft seats of a vehicle, which he found a bed worthy of a king.

The next day he arrived in the city of Jujuy, the capital of the province of the same name, and again looked for a hospital, since by now he had decided there was no better way to know a country than by visiting its hospitals and meeting the people in them. He was allowed to sleep in one of the wards but not before he put his medical skills to the test, removing the worms and larvae that had taken up residence in the scalp of a two-year-old Indian boy. The child groaned throughout the extraction, while Ernesto counted the number of his victims, which were legion. He could not fathom out how such a small child could be so infested. When the boy's mother expressed her gratitude, Ernesto lusted for her briefly but reminded himself of his pariah status. Sleep calmed his desire and he had pleasant dreams. In the morning, when he was ready to move on, the child's mother shook his hand and he noticed that hers had calluses that were like spikes to the touch.

He arrived back in Salta the following day and went to visit his friends at the hospital, who marvelled at his speedy return. How could he have done the whole trip in one day? Had he had time to see anything on the way? He could not explain to them that he was not interested in the sites for tourists. The museums containing army memorabilia, the statues of patriots on horseback which adorn the main squares of Argentine towns, the churches of the Roman Catholic faith with their miracle-performing saints and relics, all left him cold. He did however have a passion for archaeology, for the evidence of the continent's past before the arrival of the Europeans. For Ernesto, the soul of a people was reflected in the sick who were in hospital, those in custody at police stations or the passers-by with whom he struck up a conversation during his travels.

He did not explain because he felt nobody would understand. He left instead to have a look at Salta, of which he had not seen very much the first time round. When night fell, he went to a police station and asked if he could sleep there. He spent some time with the policemen, took a nap and then decided to leave at around four, on his way back to Tucumán. At seven in the morning, he had a pleasant surprise when he saw a long line of lorries stuck in the mud. The drivers had taken time off to sleep and were now gathering to discuss what to do next. And among the lorry drivers was one he had already encountered. He made a bet with them: he would leave immediately and, if they caught up with him before the asphalt road into Tucumán, he would lose; but if they were unable to catch him, he would wait for them and they would buy him a lavish meal. Ernesto set off, ignoring his faulty brakes, the steep slopes, the dangerous curves and his own thirst and exhaustion, spurred on by the vision of a hearty meal of roast chicken and potatoes.

We will never know if he won the bet because the rest of his notebooks were not found. However, we do know that he visited Mendoza, where his aunt Maruja, one of his father's sisters, was spending her holidays. She did not recognise him when he turned up on her doorstep because he had grown a beard and had long hair, as well as being covered in dust. She took him in, had his clothes washed, helped him get his bicycle repaired, gave him a succulent lunch and forced some peso notes into his pocket, in spite of his reluctance to accept them. He was, of course, down to his last cents by then. He left Mendoza for Buenos Aires, crossing the province of San Luis en route.

He had seen the beauty of his country, he had enjoyed being on his own as well as in the company of close friends and members of his family. He had tested his strength and used his ingenuity, endured hardship as he travelled 4,700 kilometres and had fun as well! But the real experience had been his exposure to a parallel existence: that of the native population of the country, whose deprivation and extreme poverty he had now witnessed first-hand. It had been an education.

In October 1950, the Guevara family travelled to Córdoba where Carmen, one of the González-Aguilar children, was getting married. There was a big party at which Ernesto met Chichina Ferreyra: they fell head over heels in love with each other, as young people do. The Ferreyras were extremely rich and successful. Far from ordinary people, they were cultured, had travelled widely, and stood out in a Córdoba which was rather parochial and flat. Chichina's father had been on a trip up the Amazon and faced all sorts of perils. He and his brothers had been racing-car drivers at a time when there were barely roads in the country, and had piloted their own aircraft. One of the brothers had died when the ship in which he was travelling to Europe was sunk by the Germans during the war. He had been on his way to join General de Gaulle and his Free French forces. The Ferreyra clan loved art and music and owned a stud farm of Arab horses. Their country estate, Malagueño, had polo grounds, tennis courts and a large swimming pool.

A few months later, in early 1951, Ernesto took a job as a male nurse on board an Argentine merchant ship, the *Anna C*, which left from the southern port of Comodoro Rivadavia on the Atlantic coast of Argentina and travelled to ports in Brazil, Trinidad and Tobago, Curaçao, British Guiana and Venezuela. He went on four trips, which lasted several weeks, but decided he did not really enjoy the life of a sailor because too much time was spent at sea and there was too little opportunity to visit the places where they docked, so he gave it up.

During one of these trips he wrote the short story he called '*Angustia (Eso Es Cierto)*' (Anguish – The Only Certainty), which was later retrieved and published by his father's estate after his death. In it he describes his experiences on a visit to Trinidad, interlacing the account with pertinent quotations from famous writers and politicians (Ibsen, Pascal, Sartre, Nehru) and with his own philosophical musings. It is a surrealistic piece and, as he muses on his beliefs and the way he wishes to live life, the early seeds of his highly moralistic, ethical way of perceiving things can be detected. The final paragraph of the story is an indication of the heavily rhetorical style he developed later in life.

As he now lived in Buenos Aires, Ernesto would travel to Córdoba to see Chichina and stay with the Granados. At first the Ferreyras had accepted Ernesto and were amused by his eccentricities and by the fact that he seemed to make a point of looking unkempt and scruffy. They found him charming and entirely lacking in self-importance. They were impressed by his knowledge of literature, history and philosophy and enjoyed the stories he told of his trips on his bicycle. But when Ernesto expressed his desire to go travelling with Chichina (and marry her first), they were not amused. Chichina was underage and Ernesto did not have a cent to his name. She did not go with him on his next trip.

By now the family was growing weary of his criticism of all the things they stood for. The Ferreyras were devout Roman Catholics. They were upright, law-abiding citizens. They were not fascists, but nor were they left wing, and they admired Winston Churchill and Dwight Eisenhower. Winston Churchill was one of Ernesto's pet hates. At a time when Churchill was revered by most people for his stance against the Nazis, Ernesto considered him a conservative and backward politician who had refused women the vote, among other misguided policies. Although not yet a communist, Ernesto never wasted an opportunity to denigrate the Allies and praise the Soviet Union. He was interested in world politics and decolonisation, and was a staunch admirer of Gandhi, with his belief in non-violence (he was reading about him in Nehru's *The Discovery of India*). But, although he was not in favour of the USA or of Perón or the communists, he was not terribly interested in the party politics of his own country or in the activities of most of its politicians, whom he found unattractive and insincere.

The political situation in Argentina was still tense. Perón continued to oppose US imperialism and claim that the country was now economically viable. But he also persecuted the communists, even though they were a minority of little political importance. The right-wing broadsheet *La Prensa* was considered the organ of the US embassy, so the government first closed it and then expropriated it. In the elections of November 1951, Perón was returned to government. His wife, Eva Duarte, was by now a prominent figure on the political landscape as the champion of the poor and the disenfranchised. She had been a radio soap opera actress and was alleged to have had various dubious liaisons to further her career before she met Perón. She was universally hated by upper- and middle-class women, in spite of the fact that it was thanks to her that they now had the vote. She herself voted from her bed as she was terminally ill with cancer.

She died only a few months later, on 26th July 1952. She was given a state funeral although she had never held office, her body lying in state at the Ministry for Labour in downtown Buenos Aires. The queues of working-class men and women waiting, six or seven abreast, to pay their respects were several blocks long for many days, and many of them had come from the provinces. The army cooked three meals a day in huge pots on log fires for people to eat on the spot or take away with them. Breakfast was a piece of bread and *mate cocido* (a maté infusion served with milk, like tea), lunch and dinner was *puchero*, a traditional Argentine stew of meat and vegetables in broth. It was free, of course.

Argentine President Juan Perón and his wife Evita

It can be argued that Eva Perón and Ernesto Che Guevara were the two most charismatic political figures of twentieth-century Latin America. They shared a concern for the poor and downtrodden and a belief that they could do something about it, a mixture of optimism and rebelliousness. Each in their own way was passionate and combative, the qualities of a true revolutionary. They came from totally different backgrounds but they both became outsiders, turning their backs on the social sphere into which they had been born.

Eva was the youngest of five illegitimate children of a lower-middle-class provincial businessman who led a double life, as he had a wife and other children by her – a not uncommon occurrence in that social milieu at the time. Ernesto was the eldest son of an established patrician family whose lineage could be traced back to the Spanish nobility. She had received only a basic education, and had known rejection, hunger and humiliation, both as a child in her provincial home town and as a young woman looking for work in Buenos Aires. Her inauspicious beginnings coloured her attitude towards the disinherited of her country, the poor who had been taken advantage of first by their colonial masters and then by the cattle oligarchy. Ernesto had a loving family, an above-average education and came from the ruling class. His social background meant that he had access to more than most. But he also fled from the circumstances of his birth. His attitude to the dispossessed came from a sense of justice, while hers originated from her resentment and her need to belong. He rejected the institutions and social structure of his country as elitist and unfair, while she sought to be accepted by them (something that never happened). She defied convention because she was not accepted. He defied convention because he did not accept it.

Both captured the imagination of their contemporaries, she in Argentina, he in Cuba, and both eventually acquired international recognition. Both died young and this helped to cement their myths. Both were courageous, unconventional iconoclasts with a profound sense of themselves and their destiny. To an outsider their confidence could come across as arrogance. Each in their own way represented something quintessentially Argentine: a kind of individualism, a non-conformist spirit. Once in power, she succumbed to the lure of French haute couture and abundant jewellery as part of her new persona, while he wore his faded olive-green fatigues and his unkempt look almost as a statement of his status as a warrior and a man with no time for diversions from his quest.

SIX

(1951–1952)

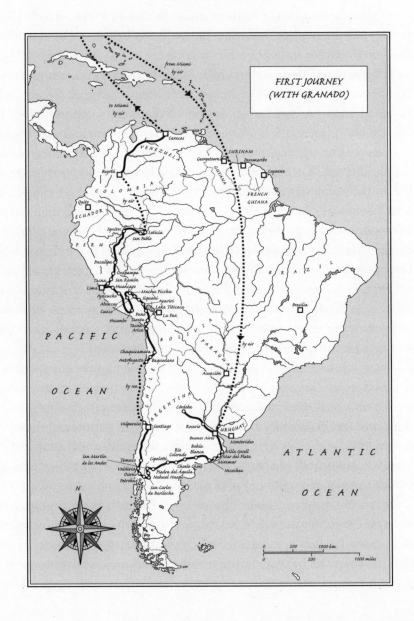

FIRST JOURNEY
(WITH GRANADO)

It was a year and a half after his bicycle tour that Ernesto and the eldest of the Granado brothers, Alberto, set off on a journey across Latin America on Alberto's motorcycle. Ernesto had dreamt of travelling with Chichina but, when this proved impossible, he seized Alberto's invitation to join him with both hands. Alberto was working at the hospital in San Francisco del Chañar as a leprologist, but he had always aimed to make the trip before his thirtieth birthday and he was now twenty-nine. They decided to leave at the end of December 1951, after Ernesto had sat his exams.

After much discussion, planning and organisation, Ernesto and Alberto set off on 29th December. They left Alberto's home in Córdoba on his old 1939 Norton 500cc motorcycle (nicknamed La Poderosa II, since the first Poderosa, or Powerful One, had been Alberto's bicycle), on which they dreamt of going all the way to the United States. In spite of this, they went south from Córdoba, instead of north. Their plan was to celebrate the New Year with the Guevara family in Buenos Aires and then drive to the coastal town of Miramar, still in the province of Buenos Aires, to say farewell to Chichina, who was spending the summer there. Then they would visit the southern Patagonian lakes before turning north to travel through Chile, Peru, Colombia and Venezuela.

The first stop was Ballesteros, where they camped under the eaves of a humble farmhouse and relished their first night as 'international trekkers', which is how they saw themselves. Then on to Rosario, where they visited Alberto's nieces who, of course, were very impressed by Ernesto. However, the girls did not impress them, as their main interests were radio soaps and women's magazines. In Buenos Aires they were subjected to all sorts of jokes and disparaging remarks about their means of transport, their disproportionate ambitions and lack of funds. Only Ernesto's mother had something positive to say. She took Alberto to one side and asked him to persuade Ernesto to come back at the end of the trip to finish his medical studies. 'A degree never hurts,' were her words.

On 4th January 1952, the pair left the Guevara household in Buenos Aires, the motorcycle loaded with so much gear that it looked like some kind of mechanical monster. They carried tents, a *parrilla* (a sort of mini-grill on which to barbecue meat), as well as utensils for cooking and preparing maté, camp beds, clothes, books, maps and the Smith & Wesson revolver which Guevara Senior had lent his son for the trip. As they drove through the parks of Palermo, where a multitude of vendors sold all sorts of souvenirs, trinkets and even pet animals, Ernesto bought, on impulse, a small puppy as a farewell present for Chichina. Its seller claimed it was a German shepherd but, of course, it was nothing of the sort: as it grew, or more precisely did not grow, it became apparent that it was a mongrel. Ernesto called the puppy Come Back, in English, but what Chichina was supposed to make of that we do not know.

They reached Villa Gesell on 6th January, and Alberto saw the sea for the first time in his life, at night by moonlight. It made a huge impression on him, as he recorded in his diary. Ernesto, on the other hand, considered the sea an old friend to whom he had often confided his innermost secrets. They stayed with an uncle of Ernesto's who fed them, gave them some tinned food to take with them on the next leg of the trip and saw the three of them off safely on their way to Miramar and Chichina. The poor little dog had a very tough time on the way to his destination, falling off the bike a couple of times, frequently being sick, and almost getting run over by a lorry.

The stay in Miramar lasted seven days, which was longer than they had originally planned, but Ernesto found it almost impossible to detach himself from Chichina. Much has been said about the romance of Ernesto and Chichina but Pepe González-Aguilar, who was dating one of her close friends at the time, told me their brief liaison has been exaggerated because of the man Ernesto became, as well as the fact that she is mentioned both in his and Granado's travel diaries. Whatever Ernesto's feelings were for her at the time, Chichina dumped him by letter while he was away.

Alberto found Chichina's entourage an eye-opener, as they were from a social class he had not come across before. He came from a working-class background and his parents were so poor that, when his younger brothers were born, he was sent to live with his grandmother, who brought him up. Alberto soon grew weary of the upper-class young men and women who thought they had some sort of divine right to do nothing with their lives but enjoy themselves, oblivious to what went on around them. Ernesto would discuss with them socialised medicine in the United Kingdom (something the Labour government of the time had just implemented), the precarious state of health and welfare in their own country and the role of the doctor in society. He invariably won the arguments with his greater knowledge and passion.

Now that Come Back had found a permanent home and a caring mistress, it was time to move on. At long last they left for Necochea, where Alberto had a colleague by the name of Tamargo, with whom he had shared a house when they were students. They had played sports together, clashed with the repressive police force and made the Students' Union of Córdoba more democratic. They had only been apart for four years but the distance between them was now palpable. Tamargo was very friendly and hospitable, but his wife could not conceal her horror at Ernesto's decision to go on a pan-American tour when he still had several subjects pending before graduation.

Ernesto thought her hostility towards them was due to a fear her husband might be lured into following their example, something that Ernesto thought impossible, declaring the man 'beyond redemption'. This had been obvious from the start, when Tamargo had been unable to disguise his shock at seeing Alberto turning up on a motorbike, covered in grease and dirt from head to foot. Alberto had been equally taken aback at seeing his old friend 'turned into a bourgeois small-time fossil who has forsaken his conscience to become a member of the exploiting classes, charging his patients more for lab tests than they are worth'.

Ernesto and the Granado brothers with La Poderosa at the
Granados' home in Córdoba

The pair left for Bahía Blanca. It was very hot, and they wandered around the city and the port while the bike was undergoing repairs, before setting off through the sand dunes of Médanos. Ernesto took the controls and, eager to make up for lost time, rode at full speed, thus managing to have what he described as the worst crash of the trip. He hurt his foot, which was scorched by a cylinder and took a long time to heal, while Alberto emerged miraculously unscathed. A heavy downpour forced them to look for shelter at a ranch, but not before falling off a couple more times. The ranch-dwellers were hospitable and helpful but the day would be remembered as the one on which they took nine tumbles.

The next morning they left for Choele Choel but fatigue got the better of them, and they decided to stop en route at Benjamín Zorrilla, where they slept happily in a room at the railway station. When they woke up, Ernesto knew he had caught the flu, for he was shaking uncontrollably. Alberto drove on to Choele Choel, with Ernesto half-asleep behind him, his head leaning on Alberto's shoulder. They were housed at the local hospital and a course of penicillin was prescribed for Ernesto. Their attempts to leave were frustrated by the doctor who emphatically declared, 'For flu: bed.' Several days went by, during which their every need was taken care of until, one fine morning, the doctor was finally satisfied with his patient's condition. Within an hour, they had upped and left in the direction of the lakes. After walking about twenty kilometres to Piedra del Águila to have the bike repaired (the handlebar had broken and needed welding to the frame) and spending the night at the mechanic's there, they rode on – with San Martín de los Andes as their intended destination.

The following day, they were having a breakfast of crackers and maté when a man walked up to them. In accordance with traditional Argentine hospitality, they invited him to join them for a round of maté. The man sat with them and commented on the high quality of their leather jackets and pouches. He asked them if they were not afraid to be travelling on their own in that desolate area, where they might be attacked by robbers who could leave them with no clothes, no money and no bike. Without saying a word, Ernesto took his father's revolver from the side of his boot and, aiming in the direction of the lake, shot from the hip. A duck which was swimming past gave a loud quack and fell on its side, dead. Their guest got up and left in a hurry, without finishing his maté or saying goodbye, while Ernesto shrieked with laughter.

On 13th February they crossed the border into Chile. The campaign for the elections to be held on 4th September was already under way. Both Ernesto and Alberto thought General Ibáñez del Campo would win. He had already been president from 1927 to 1931 and he was a populist as well as an authoritarian politician whose current programme had been influenced by that of General Perón in Argentina, whose support he enjoyed. Those who were able to do so had taken the route of self-imposed exile – among them the communist poet Pablo Neruda. Ernesto mentions in his diary that the candidate from the People's Front had the support of the communists. His name was Salvador Allende but it would be many years before their paths crossed in Cuba and even more before Allende reached the presidency, only to be ousted by a coup led by General Augusto Pinochet with the connivance of the then president of the United States, Richard Nixon.

Once on Chilean soil, Alberto and Ernesto set off for Temuco. It was drizzling and they had a puncture, but a van offered them a lift as they were attempting to repair it. They put La Poderosa – which was quickly turning into The Weakling – on the van and drove off with their benefactor at the wheel.

They left Temuco marvelling at the kindness and hospitality of the Chilean people, but had travelled less than a hundred metres when the bike threw them. Alberto was catapulted forward while Ernesto, who had fallen by the bike, had the presence of mind to get up and shut off the petrol. On closer inspection, they found that the aluminium chassis protecting the gearbox had hit the road and shattered into four pieces. But they did eventually arrive in Lautaro and had the bike fixed. It cost them the last of their capital and two days.

While waiting they decided to go to a dance in a not very respectable area of the town. There were lots of drunks, as well as some women who showed interest in the two foreigners. Alberto was dancing with an Indian woman who cared for the tango, while Ernesto had been singled out by a young woman who seemed to be willing to acquaint herself more intimately with him. Ernesto thought he had been given an invitation and tried to take her outside, but the woman spotted her husband and pretended that she was being dragged away against her will. Her husband came after Ernesto at full speed with a broken bottle. In the nick of time, Alberto managed to prevent the man hitting Ernesto over the head. The man fell, Ernesto turned round and, realising what had almost happened, fled. Alberto followed suit. It could have ended disastrously, but it was the most exciting thing that had happened to them in Lautaro: on the whole they were bored.

On the road again, they had yet another mishap: the bike's brakes went, just as they were trying to negotiate their way through a herd of oxen. They were going downhill, which meant the bike was picking up speed in spite of Ernesto using the gears to try to slow it down. As they approached the bank of a river, Ernesto managed to get it into first gear and Alberto jumped off. Ernesto drove on with his legs wide apart until the bike hit a hillock and he too jumped off. They ran over to the bike and switched off the petrol. It had been a close call and they were happy to be alive.

They attempted the ascent to Malleco, where there is a railway bridge purporting to be the highest in the Americas, but La Poderosa decided to call it quits. The two riders patiently waited most of the day for a lorry to give them a lift to the top. They slept in the town of Cullipulli but the next morning it was plain La Poderosa had given up the ghost. Alberto and Ernesto and the mortal remains of the bike were driven to the town of Los Ángeles by a passing lorry.

They were eventually allowed to stay at the fire station in Los Ángeles and, on their first night there, were woken up by the din of its alarm bell. They asked to be allowed to help and were given helmets and protective jackets. Within seconds, they had become two impromptu firemen on board the Chile-España fire engine, sweeping across town at top speed. In the distance, they saw the fire and smelt it, too, as the odour of burnt resin wafted in their direction. The building on fire was made of pine timbers and there was practically nothing left of it when they got there.

The firemen split into two groups. One group tackled the fire that had already reached the surrounding woods and the other attempted to extinguish the fire in the main building and the outhouse. The terrified meowing of a cat was heard. It was on the roof and could not find a way through the flames. Ernesto climbed up on the roof to look for it and came back clutching the kitten in his hand. There was a round of applause and the fire brigade decided to keep it as their mascot. This was not the first time Ernesto had shown he could disregard danger with nonchalance and aplomb.

To get to Santiago, they entered into a deal with a lorry driver. He would charge them 400 Chilean pesos for taking La Poderosa on board but would also hire them as porters at 50 pesos a day plus meals. Once in Santiago they realised that the cost of repairing La Poderosa was beyond their means and they made arrangements to leave the bike behind. It was the end of their stint as motorised gentlemen of the road and the beginning of their adventures as bums on foot.

Alberto was heartbroken at first, but Ernesto remarked that he did not really mind losing La Poderosa: being without transport put them on an equal footing with the poorest of the continent and they were able to see more, to meet more people and to experience first-hand how the least privileged of their fellow Americans endured their lot. While Alberto was able to revise and retouch his diary with a view to publication, this remark of Ernesto's was contemporaneous and some would say shows the beginning of his political identification with the poorest of the continent, whom he had now discovered were as destitute and downtrodden as those of his native Argentina.

Their next stop was Valparaíso, one of Chile's most beautiful cities, set in an impressive landscape. The mountains behind it are covered in trees and not far away there are glaciers where people go for winter sports all year round. To the west there is a bay with attractive beaches, and a few miles to the north is the jewel in the crown: Viña del Mar, the incredibly beautiful seaside resort favoured by the rich and famous of Chile and beyond.

When planning the trip they had hoped to visit Easter Island, but here their hopes were dashed. The next ship for Rapa Nui would not be leaving for almost a year. The president of the Society of Friends of Easter Island, a Mr Molina-Luco, promised them an invitation for the following year. Instead, they decided to avoid crossing the desert of northern Chile and travel to Antofagasta by sea.

One of Valparaíso's funicular railways

While in Valparaíso they made friends with the owner of a derelict fish shack which passed for a restaurant. He fed them for free twice a day, and asked Ernesto to visit an old woman who, like himself, had asthma. She was a pitiful sight, for she also had a heart condition. She lived in extreme poverty and was bedridden. Her room smelt of sweat and unwashed feet. Ernesto felt powerless, and it dawned on him that this was not only a medical problem but also a social issue. This was the lot of the proletariat all over the continent. Until recently, the woman had worked as a waitress, wheezing and panting but able to face life with dignity. Now, she was a burden on her relatives, who probably could not afford to look after her and consequently resented her. Ernesto gave the woman some tablets he carried with him and left, her words of gratitude echoing in his ears.

By now they had met the captain of a cargo ship at a shipping agency and persuaded him to let them stow away and then work their passage. They bid farewell to their friend, the proprietor of the *La Gioconda* fish shack restaurant, and waited until dark to board surreptitiously. As it turned out, they were only able to get on to the ship at nine in the morning when the crew arrived, and they spent a sleepless night dodging the officers on board, the stevedores who worked through the night and the police who guarded the port and the ship. Once on board, the plan was to hide in one of the toilets until the ship sailed. They had not counted on it being filthy, smelly and, in Alberto's words, 'brimming over with shit'.

At midday, a loud whistle announced that the engines were about to be switched on. They heard the screeching of the anchor as it was raised and knew they were on their way. Goodbye Valparaíso with its pelicans and seagulls, its pastel-coloured houses, its old funicular railways which take people up and down the city without effort or the risk of falling off its steep slopes, its beautiful landscape and its friendly inhabitants. On to Antofagasta and new adventures.

As soon as they were far enough from the port and there was no chance of being offloaded or sent back, they presented themselves on deck. On the way there, they scrounged a crust and some hot coffee from the kitchen attendant. When the captain saw them, he called them up to the bridge and gave them hell. He was play-acting, of course. He soon called the boatswain, informed him that the fait accompli would have to be accepted and told him to find them bunks and jobs. Ernesto got stuck with cleaning the toilets and Alberto was sent to the kitchen to peel onions. Later they had to clean the whole kitchen until it was spotless. They really had to work for their passage, but nobody was complaining.

When they had finished their tasks and the crew was asleep, they went on deck to admire the sea in the moonlight. Up on the bridge they found the captain playing canasta with another officer and the wireless operator. They were invited to join in and Ernesto won three hands paired with Alberto: they were unbeatable. In those days, canasta was the favourite card game in Argentina and we were all experts at it, until television took over as the main form of entertainment at home. The captain ordered that the cook be woken up to prepare a meal for them. After eating the food and drinking several glasses of wine, Ernesto and Alberto began to lose, which was just as well because otherwise they would have had to play through the night: the officers would not have accepted defeat. The next day, work seemed even harder because of the hangovers they were both nursing.

The ship docked at Antofagasta and they hitched a ride in a lorry which took them on the first leg of their journey to Chuquicamata, where they wanted to see the nitrate fields and the copper mines. The road wound between the hills of a reddish desert landscape. The only signs of human life were the telegraph posts and the asphalt strip of the road. Every couple of miles there was a water outlet which supplied the desert villages. The water came from the Bolivian side of the border, not far to the north.

They spent the night at Baquedano, where they met an impoverished couple on the road. He had been in jail for being a communist and was now finding it impossible to get work. The Communist party was banned in Chile and its members suffered both persecution and incarceration. He told them of the many injustices to which the miners were subjected by the owners of the mines and the local authorities. Many of his fellow workers had ended up at the bottom of the sea. The man had spent three months in prison, his children were in the care of a kind neighbour and he and his wife were on the road, on the verge of starvation, having lost everything. Alberto and Ernesto shared their maté, bread and cheese with them and then gave them one of their two blankets, huddling together under the remaining one. Ernesto later wrote, 'It was one of the coldest nights in my life, but also one which made me feel a little more brotherly toward this strange, for me anyway, human species.' He would not forget the plight of the Chilean miners easily.

The next morning, they left for Calama. From Calama they travelled on in a bus, crossing the desert at an altitude of more than 2,000 metres. When they reached Chuquicamata they were welcomed by the police superintendent, who gave them a tour round a section of a mine in his van. That evening, they were invited to lodge at the police station, where they were also fed. They were given a couple of camp beds and slept through the night in comfort, something they had not done for several days.

They went to see the American manager of the mine the next day. After making them wait for a long time, he gave them a lecture about the site not being a charitable institution or a tourist spot and then sent them round with a guide to show them the installations. Alberto, who was six years older and more politicised than Ernesto, tells us in his diary of the trip that no one could fail to realise that the place had enormous wealth and that the workers, the Araucanian people native to Chile, were being treated appallingly by the Americans who ran the plant.

Each worker, each machine operator, only knew what went on in his section. Men who had been at the mine for ten years might not know anything about the procedures in which they were not directly involved. This was calculated on the part of the company: the less the workforce knew, the less the trade union leaders would be able to discuss with them. The workers would sign any agreements that the company put before them without ever finding out if they were being cheated of their rights or duped in any way. In fact, the man acting as guide to Alberto and Ernesto had no compunction in informing them that, when the union called a meeting, he and other members of the management would invite several union officials to the local brothels so that the meeting never had the required quorum. On the one hand, he said the miners made excessive demands when they asked for a rise of 100 pesos (about one US dollar), but on the other he did not hesitate to mention that, if the mining complex was unproductive for just one day, the loss would be US$1 million.

The following day they visited a plant which was in the process of being built and Ernesto had to climb to the top of what was allegedly the tallest chimney in South America. At times his courage verged on craziness. They went to the town and saw for themselves the precarious conditions in which the workers lived, in prefabricated huts with no drains. The Americans, meanwhile, enjoyed proper housing, school buildings and even a golf course. They travelled on to the Empresa Salitrera de Toco, a nitrate plant, where they were greeted by a group of navvies who invited them to join them for a game of football. After the game, they all ate together and went to sleep at the road builders' camp, as if they had known each other all their lives.

After several days' travelling, during which they visited the Rica Aventura and Prosperidad nitrate plants and hitched a ride to Laguna, they were offered a lift by a lorry driver whom they had helped with a puncture. They were sitting on a pile of alfalfa in the back of the lorry when they reached the crest of a mountain and caught a glimpse of the sea below. It was the Bay of Iquique, renowned for its beauty. After a night in Iquique, another lorry took them to Arica by a road that crosses the Seven Pampas (desert plains separated by jagged hills). It turns into a corniche road which rises to about 2,000 metres and crosses the mountain range. In some places, the road is so high that the clouds and the condors can be seen below. The journey took twenty-four hours.

By now they were not far from the Tropic of Capricorn and the vegetation became luxuriant: they saw guavas and avocados, mangoes and papayas. They went to the local hospital and were invited by the director to stay the night. In the afternoon they went for a swim and then ate shellfish called *locos*, which can only be found on Chile's coast. They had been in Chile for thirty-eight days, enjoying Chilean hospitality and generosity at every stop.

They crossed over to Peru on 23rd March at the customs post at Chacalluta on the south bank of the River Lluta, Chile's northernmost point. They went through Tacna and on to Puno, on the banks of Lake Titicaca, and then to Cuzco via Sicuani. In Peru, there are lorries which operate as buses for the poor, who ride on top of the load, in the open. Ernesto observed in his diary that the drivers, who were of mixed race, treated them as if they were members of a superior race because they were white, and invited them to ride in the cab. He also noticed that the locals looked at them with indifference, and sometimes almost fearfully. He found it difficult to reconcile these people with the proud race that had frequently challenged the authority of the Incas and forced them to keep an army permanently guarding their frontiers. Those who did speak to them, however, sang the praises of Perón and Eva, who saw to it that the poor in Argentina had access to the same things as the rich and who did not exploit the poor Indians or treat them as harshly as they were treated in Peru.

They soon arrived at Cuzco, which had been the centre of the Inca world, or Tiawanakota Empire, and where the creed of Tiwantisuyo had been the norm: do not lie, do not kill, do not steal. Much later, in 1966, this knowledge would be crucial for Ernesto in Bolivia, in his dealings with the Aymara people, who had once been the serfs of the Inca. Cuzco has many Spanish colonial churches built on the Inca ruins: the Roman Catholic cathedral was built on the site of the Temple to Viracocha, the Jesuit church on the Temple of the Serpent, the convent on the House of the Sun Virgins and the Santo Domingo monastery on top of the temples of the Sun and the

Moon. The earthquake of 1950 had brought down the majority of the church towers, and it was rumoured that this was the vengeance of Viracocha, the mythical god of the Incas and the creator of man and all the divinities. General Franco had financed the reconstruction of the cathedral tower and on 7th April Ernesto and Alberto attended a ceremony to celebrate its inauguration. One of the largest bells in the world rang again, its peculiar sound caused by the gold contained in its alloy.

The event took place in the presence of the Spanish ambassador, and the military band played the Spanish national anthem in his honour, except that what they actually played was the Anthem of the Spanish Republic. The ambassador ran around like a thing possessed, demanding that the music be stopped. This, Ernesto decided, while roaring with laughter, was the vengeance of Tupac Amaru, the last Inca ruler who had been executed by the Spanish viceroy, Don Francisco de Toledo, in 1572.

During a visit to the museum, Alberto befriended a young Indian woman who worked in the ceramics section. Like most inhabitants of the region, she claimed to be descended from an ancient Quechua family. He saw her again in the evening and then went back to the museum the next morning. Her name was María Magdalena and although he flirted with her, she pretended not to be interested.

Finally they left for Machu Picchu, the lost city of the Incas that was discovered by Hiram Bingham in 1911. Machu Picchu is Quechua for Old Mountain and the site is located some 2,400 metres above sea level. It was built around the year 1460 but abandoned by the Inca rulers about a hundred years later. It is, however, still considered a sacred place. Remarkably, the Spanish conquistadores never found it, and it was therefore spared the usual plunder and destruction.

Ernesto and Alberto decided to spend several days in the area, to take in as much as they could. During an improvised game of soccer they had the good fortune to meet someone who offered them food and lodgings, after they were able to prove they were not the couple of vagabonds that their clothes seemed to suggest. That night in bed, Ernesto read Hiram Bingham while Alberto absent-mindedly perused a volume of letters by Simón Bolívar.

Suddenly, Alberto told Ernesto that he had the answer to the problems of the downtrodden Indians. He would marry María Magdalena, a direct descendant of Manco Capac II, and would turn into Manco Capac III; he would form an Indian political party, give people the vote, and thus start the new Tupac Amaru American Indian Revolution. 'Revolution without firing a shot? You're crazy,' was the reply with which Ernesto put an end to his reveries.

SEVEN
(1952)

Their next destination was the leprosarium at Huambo. At Abancay, they made a stop at the hospital, where they were lodged and fed and had a chance to wash their clothes. In return, they gave a talk for the nurses on clinical laboratory methods, something in which they were both quite experienced by now. They spent the day out visiting the area and in the evening, back at the hospital, gave a talk on leprosy and asthma. As if on cue, Ernesto had a huge asthma attack and needed two injections of adrenalin, one almost immediately after the other.

And then at Huancarama, further on the way to Huambo, he suffered another attack. At four in the morning he woke Alberto, desperate because his asthma had returned, intensified, and he could not breathe at all. Alberto had to make a bold decision, since they had run out of the adrenalin ampoules Ernesto used to calm his attacks when his inhaler was not sufficient. Alberto would inject him intravenously with a shot of calcium chloride in order to cause him stress, which would then stimulate his own adrenal medulla to secrete adrenalin. He needed water to sterilise the syringe and needle and got it from a little stream he had seen running past the farmhouse where they had camped for the night.

Ernesto calmed down after the injection, but quite soon Alberto was woken by Ernesto's moans. He looked like death and his body was arching off the ground, while his mouth contracted. Alberto was so stunned by this unusual development that he could not think what to do. He watched Ernesto for a while until the moaning subsided, his body resumed a normal position, he fell asleep and started snoring loudly. Normally, Alberto would have poked Ernesto in the ribs and told him to stop that infernal noise but now he found it comforting and gratifying. Ernesto was on the mend.

The following morning, they got up late and asked the town authorities for a couple of horses to ride to Huambo. The horses that were brought were skinny and tiny and it seemed ridiculous to expect them to take their weight. A young Indian led the way along the path, which is very rough. It skirts a series of hills covered in golden flowers, sometimes follows the edge of precipices and occasionally descends to river level. They passed villages where the locals were celebrating Easter, which entailed consuming large amounts of *chicha*, a liquor made from maize. Many had already collapsed in a drunken stupor on the side of the road. As the ground grew rougher, the horses they had disparaged proved their worth, climbing up and down the steep terrain without losing their footing. They had been riding for about three hours when they finally caught sight of Huambo.

All the time they had been on the road, they had been followed by an old woman and a boy. Ernesto and Alberto had not paid much attention to them: it was customary for Indians to trail people to whom they were trying to sell their produce and the woman was carrying a couple of baskets. It now transpired they were the owners of the horses which the authorities had requisitioned for the foreigners. The woman and boy had followed them to retrieve their animals and return home with them. They were a long way from where they lived. Ernesto and Alberto, appalled at the distress they had caused, dismounted, paid them and continued on foot.

After a brief stop to eat some fruit from a nearby tree, they set off along a path. The foliage was so dense that the sun could not penetrate it, and the path was soggy and muddy. Ankle-deep in mud, they finally emerged in front of the leprosarium at Huambo. It could not have been in a more remote and isolated place.

There were two separate sections: one for the healthy people and the other for the patients. The healthy area consisted of two rooms with mud walls and a thatched roof. One room was the dispensary, dining area and office and the other the pharmacy, consulting room and infirmary. They met the staff – three male nurses and one health-worker – who welcomed them warmly. The next morning they visited the patients' area, which was made up of four wings. These were mud huts without windows, each of which housed three or four patients. Hygiene and sanitation facilities were non-existent. Some patients were busy planting cassava, potatoes or maize. And that was it.

When they thought they had seen the worst, along came a band of children who were not infected but were almost certain to contract the disease: although they lived with their parents, who were infected, they had not been inoculated. Mr Montejo and his three assistants, Vivanco, Montoya and Valdivia, told them about the shortages they had to endure. Even the doctor did not turn up regularly. Mr Montejo told them the only scientist in the whole of Peru who cared about those affected by this scourge was Dr Hugo Pesce.

As time went by, Alberto and Ernesto saw that everything was not entirely bleak. To start with, the hospital did have drugs which were effective against leprosy, as well as medicines to combat anaemia. The food was quite good, and was supplemented by the vegetables the patients themselves grew. But the most positive factor was that Mr Montejo and his assistants treated the patients with respect, sympathy and even affection. They were also told a new sanatorium was being built nearby but, to their chagrin, they found it was just a larger version of the one they had already seen: a kind of warehouse to store the sick, Alberto remarked in despair. Ernesto's asthma attacks could come at any time, without warning, and he suffered another attack after the visit to the new leprosarium. It was severe enough to need an injection.

Mr Montejo had arranged for them to spend the night at a nearby farm. The owner greeted them very cordially and gave them a sumptuous dinner and a variety of exquisite Chilean wines. While they were at table, he quite casually explained to his guests how he turned vast swathes of land into arable soil (the land covered an area that went as far as the Vilcanota river, which was comparable to the distance back to Machu Picchu). He allowed the Indians the right to settle in virgin forests, which they cut down and turned into cultivable land. At that point he turned them out, forcing them to move to new ground where the process began all over again. At the end of this cycle, the Indians were relegated to the most arid areas and the land had been cleared at no expense.

Alberto and Ernesto were shocked at these revelations and said so, while poor Mr Montejo wondered whether it had been wise to introduce these people to each other when their views were so opposed. The following morning they left very early on horses provided by their host. Although he came to bid them farewell, his attitude was by now manifestly distant and gruff.

They arrived in Huancarama to find a carnival in progress. A great number of Indian men and women were dancing *carnavalitos* and playing the *quena*, an Andean flute. Most were very drunk and made obscene gestures as they passed by. Ernesto was having an asthma attack but, because of the celebrations, neither the local authorities nor the police were on duty. Alberto left him sitting helplessly in a corner, and went to find water to sterilise the needle and syringe. It suddenly began to rain, which solved Alberto's problem. He was able to boil the rainwater and inject his friend immediately. Ernesto promptly went to sleep.

The next two weeks brought more asthma attacks, more stays in hospitals and police stations, more carnival celebrations and religious processions, winding roads, stunning views, drunken Indians, starving children and sick women who asked them for help when they heard there were two doctors in the area. And they finally reached Lima, the capital of Peru and the city of the viceroys. More importantly, it was the place where Dr Hugo Pesce lived.

Dr Pesce was the famous leprologist to whom they had a letter of introduction. He had studied in Italy and returned home to practise, only to be deprived of his chair in Tropical Medicine at the University of Lima because he was a member of the Peruvian Communist Party. He was sent to a remote post in the Andes by the dictator Odría but took advantage of his time there to write a book, *Latitudes of Silence*, about the plight of the Indians and his experience among them. He had been a follower of José Carlos Mariátegui, a Peruvian Marxist thinker and founder of the Indigenist Party, who was among the first to blend nationalist and indigenous thought with international Marxism. Mariátegui's most famous work, *Seven Interpretative Essays on Peruvian Reality*, discussed the need for the downtrodden and disenfranchised of Latin America to embrace the path of socialism as a means of liberating themselves from the yoke of their white or foreign masters. In later years Ernesto Guevara would also be influenced by the works of Mariátegui but, during this period of his life, he hadn't chosen a political party with which to identify.

Dr Pesce arranged for Alberto and Ernesto to be lodged (for free, of course) at the Hospital de Guía, part of which was a leprosarium. His assistant Zoraida Boluarte took them under her wing and catered to their immediate needs, organising clean clothes and meals. She became really fond of them, and their friendship would continue as they corresponded over the years. Dr Pesce had Alberto and Ernesto round to dinner in his family home almost daily and they discussed a variety of subjects, which included not only leprosy and tropical diseases – he was an expert on malaria and had written several relevant papers on the subject, having discovered two new types of mosquito that carried the disease – but physiology, politics and philosophy as well. Alberto even credited him with introducing them to the works of César Vallejo, Peru's foremost poet of the people.

By now, Ernesto and Alberto had read Dr Pesce's *Latitudes of Silence* and found it uninspired and clichéd but they kept their opinions to themselves. Ernesto nicknamed Dr Pesce El Maestro, because he really admired him – for the breadth of his knowledge and the seriousness of the political convictions for which he had been ostracised, as well as for his decency and kindness to them.

After making arrangements for their onward trip (giving them letters of introduction, as well as the fares to the leprosarium at San Pablo, some clothes and money), Dr Pesce invited them for a farewell dinner on their last night in Lima. During the evening, Dr Pesce asked Ernesto what he thought of his book. Worried about what Ernesto might say, Alberto promptly stepped in and praised its merits: he had particularly cared for the descriptions of the psychology of the Indians. Dr Pesce addressed Ernesto again. Alberto butted in once more and said how much he had liked the description of the flooding Urubamba river. Mrs Pesce came to their rescue by expressing her own opinion and the subject was dropped.

But when they were making their farewells and Dr Pesce was shaking Ernesto's hand, he insisted that he wanted to know his opinion of the book. Ernesto told him flatly that it was not a good book, and that he could not believe that a Marxist scholar had described the psychology of the Indians in such negative terms. He thought it pessimistic and not worthy of a scientist and a communist. The doctor did not defend his work but rather acquiesced.

Alberto thought he would die of embarrassment. As far as he was concerned, Ernesto had ruined their farewell party simply because he was incapable of making a minor concession to the only weakness their benefactor had exhibited: his literary pretensions. As they walked towards their lodgings, some forty blocks away, Alberto exploded. He accused Ernesto of insensitivity. How could he have been so unkind to the man who had given them so much? Ernesto was pained. All he said was, 'Could you not see that I didn't want to say anything?' It was a manifestation of a habit he would never lose: his refusal to compromise, no matter what the consequences.

They took their leave of Zoraida Boluarte, whom they would always refer to as their guardian angel, and said goodbye to the patients at the leprosarium, who gave them an envelope containing some money they had collected, which moved them. They went off to find a man who had agreed to give them a lift in one of his lorries to Pucallpa, a town on the Ucayali river, across the central cordillera. There, on 25th May, Alberto and Ernesto boarded *La Cenepa*, a two-deck launch with a boat in tow carrying swine, timber and third-class passengers, which sailed down the Ucayali river for a week until it reached the Amazon. They were both happy on board in spite of the impossibility of getting a single night's decent sleep due to the swarms of mosquitoes which descended as the sun went down. After seven days' sailing they arrived in Iquitos. Within half an hour, a letter they brought with them from Maestro Pesce resulted in a room at the Centre for the Prevention of Yellow Fever, as well as meals at the local hospital.

They moved on to the San Pablo leprosarium, arriving on 8th June, and were greeted by Dr Bresciani, for whom they also had a letter from Dr Pesce. They stayed until 20th June and were able to assist in visits to patients and participate in laboratory tests, as well as play football with the inmates. The hospital was made up of several buildings on stilts, connected by wooden planks, so that people could move from one building to another without having to walk in the mud, as the rainfall was heavy and frequent. Leprosy was endemic on the banks of the Ucayali and Yaraví rivers. People had got used to seeing those afflicted around them and it was impossible to separate their children from them. On the positive side, the hospital was so welcoming that it had become a real home for the patients, who were able to live as normal a life as possible. Some grew tomatoes, yuccas and bananas, others ran shops which sold soft drinks. A few were so successful they had acquired their own motorboats. Doctors, nurses and patients all became their friends.

On 14th June, when Ernesto turned twenty-four, a birthday dinner party was organised in his honour in the canteen. There was dancing and food and drink, and at midnight the director made a congratulatory speech. Ernesto replied in a few moving words before they all danced the night away. He had had a few drinks and lost his characteristic incapacity to express his feelings. He thanked everyone for their kindness and generosity and then said, speaking on behalf of Alberto and himself, 'Although we are too insignificant to be spokesmen for such a noble cause, we believe, and this journey has only served to confirm this belief, that the division of America into unstable and illusory nations is a complete fiction. We are one single *mestizo* race with remarkable ethnographical similarities from Mexico down to the Magellan Straits. And so, in an attempt to break free from all narrow-minded provincialism, I propose a toast to Peru and to a United America.'

Whether he was consciously aware of it or not, Ernesto had made a choice: he had discarded his social class and his white European racial ancestry but not his nationality, because in his view to be an Argentine was to be part of that United America he was now discovering.

One of the nurses was the daughter of the chief of an Indian tribe who were hunting in the area, and the director had arranged for them to join in a monkey hunt the next day. They were taken a couple of kilometres upriver to a village where the chief was waiting for them, surrounded by many women and children. They all lived together in a shelter made of palm leaves. As the hunting group arrived at a clearing in the forest, they were instructed to paint their faces and hands with a mixture of monkey grease and *annatto* (a dye obtained from the seeds of the *Bixa orellana*, a small tropical tree), to neutralise human scent and keep the mosquitoes away. One of the hunters had a blowpipe in one hand and a dart dipped in curare in the other.

After a long wait, the monkeys' howls could be heard as they drew nearer. A couple of monkeys went by above the heads of the group, shrieking loudly. A horde of monkeys of all sizes followed them, their little ones clinging to them. Another troop went by and a few minutes later yet another. When the next group went by, the last monkey fell as the dart from the blowpipe hit it. The hunter explained that it was important to kill the last monkey, because otherwise the whole troop could alter its route and the hunting ground would become useless.

The rest of the hunters now returned to the group. The five monkeys taken were carried on poles back to the village where everybody was invited to share in the banquet. Ernesto and Alberto went for a short walk before supper and, as they returned, they could smell the roast. They were offered a drink of fermented cassava and then the meal was served on plantain leaves. The roasted baby monkey looked like an unborn child but Ernesto and Alberto glanced at each other, plucked up their courage and tucked in. However, they never did find out what monkey tastes like, because the roast had been smothered in very hot chillies.

As the time to leave the leprosarium approached, the patients built them a raft so they could sail down the Amazon to their next port of call: Leticia in Colombia. There were farewell speeches, songs and presents of butter, sausages, tinned meat, flour, eggs, lentils, bananas, papayas, chickpeas and poultry. They were also given a mosquito net, kerosene and a lantern. The patients would never forget the two young men who had not feared contagion and had moved freely among them. People normally wore gloves when they came into contact with them, but Ernesto and Alberto had categorically refused to.

Alberto went back to the leprosarium in 2003, as Walter Salles' consultant during the shooting of *The Motorcycle Diaries*, a film about their trip. Some of the patients, who had been between fourteen and twenty years old at the time, still remembered their two Argentine friends who had, in their own words, given them dignity and treated them with great affection and camaraderie.

The raft was named *Mambo-Tango* by the patients, who painted the name clearly on its side. They were on board for three days and nights and, with the current carrying them, went straight past Leticia, ending up in Brazil. After much discussion in Portuguese, a language neither of them spoke, they managed to persuade a local man to take them back as far as Leticia in his canoe, since it would have been impossible to sail their raft against the current.

Alberto and Ernesto on the raft called the *Mambo-Tango*, built for them by the
patients at the leprosarium of San Pablo

Like Peru and Chile, Colombia was governed by a dictator. He was
called Laureano Gómez and had won an election in 1950 because he was
the only candidate. In 1948, Jorge Eliécer Gaitán, the leader of the left wing
of the Liberal Party, had been assassinated. A popular uprising followed,
called El Bogotazo (after Bogotá, the capital of Colombia), but it was not
sufficiently well organised for the people to take power. The right had
finally imposed itself after weeks of street fighting. Guerrilla groups
emerged in various parts of the country and continued to emerge for years
to come. They are of many different political tendencies, even including
some who are right wing. Colombia has been an extremely violent country
ever since.

Leticia is a tiny frontier town over which much blood has been spilt,
since both Peruvians and Colombians claim it as theirs. When they reached
it, Alberto and Ernesto went to the customs police to explain their unusual
mode of arrival and ask that their passports be stamped. They were lodged
at the police headquarters and fed at the police station. When they went to
the port to exchange their Peruvian currency for Colombian pesos, they
struck up a conversation with some sailors who told them the first officer
of *El Cisne*, the motor launch on which they had sailed from Iquitos to San

Pablo, had talked about 'two scientists who were on a tour of all the leprosaria in the world'. They joked with each other about being preceded by their fame.

In the evening, one of the directors of the local football club came visiting. Perhaps influenced by the international reputation that Argentine football players enjoyed, he wanted them to stay and train the Independiente Sporting Football Club squad for a special match that was about to take place. They promised to visit the pitch the next day. Since they had managed to obtain half-price plane tickets to the capital city two weeks later, a little football might be the answer to the boredom of the small garrison town, where there seemed to be more men in uniform than civilians. They joined the football club and played alongside their trainees in the special match. Ernesto played goalkeeper and Alberto centre forward. Although they lost when the match went to penalties, they gave a good account of themselves and the club rewarded them with a higher fee than had originally been agreed.

The aircraft turned out to be a seaplane and it took them to Bogotá on 2nd July. They had been without any international news for several days and they now learnt about two encouraging developments. In Guatemala, President Jacobo Arbenz had passed an agrarian reform bill which would result in the expropriation of many hectares of land belonging to the United Fruit Company, a US concern that was hugely powerful in Central and South America. In Bolivia, where the Movimiento Nacionalista Revolucionario was now in power, the electoral system had been restructured to give the vote to a million people, mostly of indigenous origin.

Ernesto and Alberto hated the atmosphere of Bogotá. They were taken into police custody after Ernesto took out a penknife to draw a plan of the area on the pavement in order to find his bearings. Then they had an argument with the sergeant in charge, who told them to leave the country immediately. Ernesto said he would not leave without his knife. Another argument ensued and they were detained again. The Argentine consulate had to intervene and they were set free, but the police warned them to leave within forty-eight hours. As they had been denied permission to visit the leprosarium and had been unceremoniously thrown out of their lodgings, they did not want to stay in any case. Fortunately, they had made some friends on the university campus, where they had been going for their meals, and these kindly organised a collection to pay for their transport out of town.

They left on 14th July, via Cúcuta, and crossed the frontier with Venezuela at the bridge over the Táchira river, reminding themselves that it was Bastille Day for them, too, as they had managed to leave the restrictions of Colombia behind.

Venezuela had its own history of military dictators and juntas, some surprisingly enlightened. When Ernesto and Alberto crossed into Venezuela from Colombia, a civilian junta ruled the country, with Germán Suárez Flamenich at its head. Venezuela was a prosperous country because of its oil reserves, and people were flocking there to make their fortunes. The currency was strong and it was easy to save (although this went against Alberto and Ernesto, as their funds were in the much weaker Colombian peso). However, Venezuela made a good impression on them.

The journey from San Cristóbal to Barquisimeto was an eventful one, as they were travelling in a packed van which kept getting punctures and they wasted a lot of time trying to patch and repair the tyres. After Barquisimeto they reached Valencia, where they were surprised to encounter black people. They had not seen them anywhere else on their travels, as the populations of countries in the Andean region are mainly Indian and Spanish in origin. Caracas they found to be a modern and attractive city, the traffic as infernal as it is now. Ernesto had yet another asthma attack. An aunt of a friend was a real godsend since she helped them find decent lodgings at the Venezuelan Young Catholics boarding house, no less.

They had a letter of introduction from Dr Pesce to a Dr Convit and went to see him. After asking Alberto some pertinent questions in relation to his medical experience, he offered him a job there and then, with a salary of 500 bolívares plus lodgings at the hospital. Alberto said he would think about it, although he was bursting to accept. They went to visit the leprosarium at La Guaira. It was old and in serious need of a coat of paint, but it was just a few steps from the beautiful blue Caribbean Sea. After meeting Dr Convit again and making the acquaintance of Dr Bluemenfeld, who ran the laboratory, Alberto made up his mind. La Guaira it would be.

In the meantime, Ernesto had decided to go home. He was trying to get himself a transit visa for the USA, as the only way he could get home was by hitching a ride in a cargo plane. This travelled between Caracas and Buenos Aires, with a stopover in Miami, carrying thoroughbred horses which belonged to a business associate of his uncle, Marcelo Guevara-Lynch. After many comings and goings, Ernesto obtained his visa but, as luck would have it, the aircraft developed a mechanical fault and he had to stay in Miami for a month until it was repaired.

He had one dollar on him when he arrived in the USA on 26th July, and for several days he survived on a cup of milky coffee a day. He eventually made friends with a man who ran a coffee shop who offered him something to eat regularly. He lodged in a boarding house which was a long way from the public library where he spent his days, and he walked there and back, some fifteen kilometres. According to his father, Ernesto was allowed to board for free as he promised he would pay for his lodgings once he returned home, which he did. Jimmie Roca, a cousin of Chichina, was studying architecture near by and they spent time together as well. Jimmie was supported by his parents, so his personal situation was not as dire as Ernesto's, although he did not always reach the end of the month in funds.

Ernesto was eventually able to fly home in the cargo plane, now filled with boxes of fruit. His travelling companion was the groom who had accompanied the race horses on their way north. Of his American experience he would say, quoting José Martí, the hero of Cuban independence from the Spanish, 'I have seen the belly of the beast.' Some people were kind to him, he did not starve and he was able to indulge his passion for reading at the public library, but he was shocked by the racism he witnessed. Because of his Latin looks people often assumed he was from Puerto Rico. The territory had just become an Associated Free State as the result of a referendum. Many were unhappy with this, and Puerto Ricans were being closely watched by the police. When they asked him to identify himself, the police had difficulty accepting that he was a passenger in transit on a cargo aircraft under repair.

He found the Americans hostile and at their most aggressive when discussing the Korean War which was raging at the time. Senator Joseph McCarthy's anti-communist witch-hunt was in full swing and intellectuals and artists were either fleeing the country or in detention. The luxurious lifestyle of the tourists along the coast – the beaches, the huge swimming pools, the casinos and bars and the neon signs announcing cabaret stars – was in sharp contrast with life in the rest of the Americas.

The trip had lasted seven months and during that time Ernesto had managed to indulge his passion for archaeology, visit many sites and museums and read about them in public libraries on the way. He had put his medical knowledge to the test in the leprosaria he and Alberto had visited and he had seen the precarious conditions in which the poor of the continent lived. Now he was returning to Buenos Aires to finish his medical degree, as he had promised his mother. He had twelve subjects pending. In November 1952 he sat and passed three. In December he passed several more. By the end of the year he had only one subject outstanding and he had soon taken that too.

EIGHT

(1953)

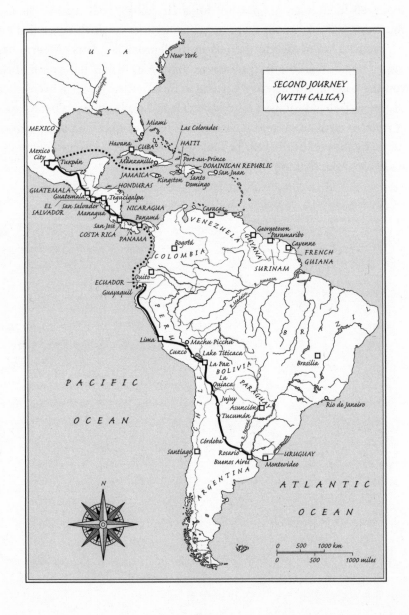

SECOND JOURNEY
(WITH CALICA)

Ernesto graduated to fulfil his promise to his mother, but he had no intention of setting up a practice or even of settling down. He still did not know what he wanted to do in life but he had seen enough of our *América morena* (America of colour) to feel he was Latin American rather than just Argentine and he certainly did not want to live within the constraints of the social class into which he had been born. He decided to go on the road once again.

According to Calica Ferrer, Ernesto's invitation to join him on his second trip around Latin America came as a challenge rather than a proposal. But then that was Ernesto's way of doing things. He had told Calica he would sit his remaining exams in twelve subjects, since that was what he had come home to do, and would then leave again. It was a crazy idea, but for Calica it was a privilege to be asked, to be chosen from among so many childhood friends, as the most suitable companion for this new adventure. When Ernesto was travelling with Granado, his letters home were read by all and sundry and the trip had become legendary. After all, it was quite unusual for an educated, upper-class young man to travel without well-laid plans or plenty of funds, to work in leper colonies, to sleep rough and not know where the next meal was coming from.

Ernesto was planning to travel all the way back to Caracas, where Alberto Granado was established and earning well as a scientist and researcher. He fantasised about Venezuela, with its strong currency and gorgeous women: how easy it would be for two well-brought-up young men to find suitable jobs for a while before travelling on to Paris, taking Granado with them as well. At the time, most educated Latin Americans dreamt of Paris as the Mecca of culture, knowledge, art, worldliness and chic. Ernesto spoke fluent French, taught to him by his mother, as a result of which he had become acquainted with the work of French writers and poets. His father was intellectually very cosmopolitan and his library included innovators such as Freud and Marx as well as novelists: Faulkner, Stevenson, Conrad, Jack London; and Latin American writers such as Pablo Neruda and José Martí. The range of books available to Ernesto was unusually broad and liberal. Upper-class Argentines read literature of the imagination but the opportunity to read Marx and Freud and the revolutionaries of European thought was quite unusual.

On 11th April 1953, Ernesto obtained his university degree. He called his mother from a public phone box and said, 'This is Doctor Guevara de la Serna speaking.' The stress was on the word doctor, and she was thrilled. Ernesto then went to see Calica and flung his university carnet in his face saying, 'Here you are, you fool. I was not going to graduate? Get ready, Calica. We are leaving soon.'

Ernesto's first passport photo

Their departure, on 7th July, was quite an event, Calica tells us. All their relatives were there, as well as friends, ex-girlfriends and current flames. As they did not have official fiancées and the current flames were more than one a head, they ran the risk of a scene at the station but, equally, they could not stop them coming to say goodbye. And since they were going away, what they left behind did not matter all that much any more.

Calica and Ernesto had deliberately chosen to travel second class because they had limited funds and the price of the second-class ticket was half that of a first-class one. They needed to stretch their money as far as possible if they were to reach their destination, Venezuela, right at the top of the continent. Ernesto later wrote in his diary that the ladies in expensive fur coats and high heels and the men in custom-made suits were in stark contrast with the rest of the passengers in their section of the train, who were humble people of indigenous origin. They had come down from the north to find some menial work in the capital and were now going home, wearing their traditional ponchos and carrying their babies on their backs. They travelled with their poultry and the occasional little green parrot, their maté and gourd and kettle. Some had cats or dogs.

Calica's suitcase was full of elegant outfits, since he was a smart dresser. Ernesto's, on the other hand, weighed a ton because it contained lots of books. When Calica complained about it, Ernesto simply said that those were the books he was reading at the time. Calica thought good clothes would help them get jobs, lodgings and girls. He was wearing his knee-high leather boots which his grandmother had given him and which had been made by López-Taibo, the city's most renowned bootmaker. He wore them throughout the trip. Ernesto was wearing navy fatigues and short lace-up boots to which he had helped himself: his brother Roberto was doing his military service in the navy and they were part of his uniform. Ernesto, who always wore his hair very short anyway, now looked like a conscript. But the clothes he wore were warm and hard-wearing and therefore ideal for roughing it, as he intended to do during this trip.

Following the custom at the time, the Farewell Committee, as Calica referred to their friends and family, had arrived with all sorts of delicacies as presents: trays of European-style pastries and of the national pastries known as *factura*, soft drinks and chocolates. The two mothers, Celia and Dolly, were distraught but disguised it well. However, Celia could not resist taking Calica aside and asking him to look after Ernesto, just as she had done when he left with Granado. Dolly, in the meantime, had taken Ernesto aside and reminded him that he had already travelled and had more experience than Calica, so it was up to him to behave reasonably. She especially recommended that they did not get drunk or get into brawls which might end with one of them getting hurt or, worse still, killed. Neither mother made recommendations about food because they both knew that Calica and Ernesto were capable of eating rocks, if necessary. That was how they had brought them up. In both their homes you ate what you were given and nobody ever got away with being picky or choosy.

The train was now ready to depart. According to Guevara Senior, Ernesto walked alongside the train, which left the station slowly as it was really long and had an engine at each end. When he finally jumped on board he turned towards the Farewell Committee and shouted, 'Here goes a soldier of the Americas.' Guevara Senior seems to have attached great importance to these words, as he was to call his memoir of his son *Aquí va un soldado de América*. Calica claims he either did not hear them or did not pay any attention to them, since Ernesto was wearing bits of uniform anyway and it could have been a joke. He had told Ernesto it was not a good idea to travel dressed as a conscript, as an officer might appear, ask him his name and rank, and shout '*Cuerpo a tierra*', and he would have to hit the deck.

Carlos Figueroa, Ernesto's other inseparable buddy, had offered his arm to Celia, who decided to walk along the platform until the train was right out of the station. Only then, at a considerable distance from the rest of the group, did she weep, Carlos confided to Calica years later, but she managed to compose herself as they walked back to the group on the platform.

The travellers inspected their little parcels of delicacies while the poor cholos (as the Indians were called by white people) indulged in a feast of stews, chicken, *empanadas* (a meat pasty which is a traditional Argentine staple) and other hearty dishes. It was customary for second-class passengers to bring their own food, since they could not afford the dining car. Soon Ernesto and Calica were invited to tuck in and they in turn contributed their own parcels, which amazed some of their new-found friends who had never seen or tasted *bonbons au chocolat*.

The train belonged to the General Belgrano line and it went as far as La Quiaca in northern Argentina, on the frontier with Bolivia. It had been Ernesto's idea to travel to Bolivia. He had not been there on his previous trip with Alberto Granado and he longed to see the Isla del Sol with its incredible Inca ruins. The island is in the middle of Lake Titicaca, which is not only the highest lake in the world but also a place of great natural beauty. And Bolivia was breaking the rules in Latin America. Its Movimiento Nacionalista Revolucionario had won the elections in 1952, defeating a dictatorial government, and it was in the process of launching much-needed and profound social changes. The new government had already nationalised the tin mines, initiated agrarian reform and dissolved the army.

The rest of Latin America was governed by men whose positions depended not on the ballot box but the support of the USA. In Peru, General Manuel Odría ruled with an iron fist, while Colonel Gustavo Rojas Pinilla in Colombia, Marcos Pérez-Jiménez in Venezuela and Alfredo Stroessner in Paraguay were all equally authoritarian and right wing. Central America fared no better: Fulgencio Batista had seized power in Cuba by means of a coup d'état, Anastasio 'Tacho' Somoza ruled Nicaragua as if it were his private fiefdom, and Héctor Trujillo in the Dominican Republic and Papa Doc Duvalier in Haiti were founding their own dynasties. All depended on American capital, and that depended on their willingness to bow to US imperialism. In Argentina, Juan Domingo Perón had now been democratically elected but he, too, would eventually become a strongman who only differed from the dictators in his confrontational attitude towards the USA.

The itinerary drawn up by Ernesto and Calica was Bolivia, Peru, Ecuador, Colombia and Venezuela. With the exception of Bolivia, obtaining a visa for any of these countries was an uphill job. Venezuela, in particular, could afford to be choosy as to whom it let in because it was oil-rich and everyone wanted to go and try their luck there. The Venezuelan consulate in Buenos Aires required to see a return ticket before issuing a visa. Ernesto and Calica made an appointment with the Venezuelan consul to request their visas. It did not go well. The Consul, an overweight mulatto with little patience, promptly informed them that unless they possessed return tickets there was no sense in even discussing a visa. Calica recited the lines he had carefully rehearsed the previous evening chez Guevara, to the effect that they would be travelling to research the fight against leprosy. Ernesto chimed in, informing the Consul that he was a doctor and was expected at the La Guaira leprosarium, where Granado was employed. The Consul was not interested. All he wanted was to see their return tickets. Ernesto insisted that he would contribute his knowledge and skills for the advancement of science in Venezuela. The Consul was unimpressed.

By now, all civility had gone by the wayside and Ernesto and the Consul were shouting at each other. The Consul decided to put an end to the meeting by stating that they would not be able to travel to Venezuela. Ernesto insisted they would. The Consul said it would be over his dead body and Ernesto replied that he would walk over the Consul's huge belly to enter Venezuela. Calica and Ernesto were unceremoniously told to leave the premises. Calica was crestfallen but Ernesto assured him they would find a way into Venezuela once they were en route. That was always his attitude towards any obstacles. And, of course, he was right because Calica ended up spending several years in Venezuela at the end of this trip. Ernesto, on the other hand, never set foot in the country again, but not for want of a visa.

Ernesto and Calica had managed to put together the modest sum of 14,000 Argentine pesos, the equivalent of about $700, by scrounging from friends and relatives. Calica carried their fortune in a cloth belt his mother had made, which he wore under his clothes. They referred to it as the chastity belt. Ernesto was not interested in their funds (or scarcity of them). On his previous trip with Granado, they had had no money almost from the outset and this had not stopped them reaching Venezuela. And in Calica's mind, the lack of funds was amply compensated for by the many letters of introduction from friends and relatives to their own friends and relatives in different parts of the continent. Sometimes having someone to look up was better than having money, as he or she might offer hospitality in the shape of lodgings or a lavish meal, or both.

The train roared north through the night and the crowd in the second-class compartment settled down to sleep. Even the babies and the parrots stopped making a noise. The first stop was Córdoba city next morning at seven and, as the train pulled in to the station, Calica and Ernesto caught sight of their close friends, Mario Salduna and Raúl Tisera, surrounded by snow and clutching their gifts: one roast chicken and two litres of table wine.

When the train finally reached the frontier at La Quiaca the following morning, at an altitude of 3,442 metres, they marvelled at the strange beauty of the vast arid desert landscape, unlike anything they had ever seen. Bolivia and Argentina are separated by a river which is but a trickle of water. They are joined by a railway bridge, in the middle of which both countries' flags are placed next to each other to mark the border. At the precise moment the journey came to an end and they were to disembark and cross the bridge on foot, Ernesto suffered a massive asthma attack. Calica had witnessed these attacks over the years but he had never been confronted with one so monumental. He was desperate to gather all their belongings before leaving the train. Dozens of Indians appeared and offered to carry their luggage in exchange for a few coins. Calica distributed their suitcases and parcels among them and put Ernesto over his shoulder to drag him to the nearest lodgings.

They arrived at a shabby pension, followed by a team of Indian porters with their many possessions. Some hours later, the attack subsided and Ernesto was breathing normally again. Calica was both livid and relieved. He angrily reproached Ernesto for not warning him that such a dangerous situation could arise. Ernesto simply admitted that Calica was right and said that he could give him an adrenalin shot next time, adding that it had to be into the muscle because, if it was injected into the vein, it would kill him.

Ernesto needed a whole day to recover completely and was unable to eat anything other than boiled rice and could only drink a few matés. He reached the conclusion that the cause of the asthma attack had been the gastronomic excesses of the previous days, when they had gone from one farewell party to the next, as well as gorging themselves on the train.

The tedium of the place and the never-changing arid landscape brought on a serious bout of nostalgia, which was remedied when they ran into Tiki Bildoza. He had been one of Ernesto's less privileged friends in Alta Gracia, had then joined the gendarmerie and now guarded the frontier. They chatted and laughed and were soon in the highest spirits again. In order to put the nasty shock of the asthma attack behind them and start the Bolivian journey with their best foot forward (and because the rate of exchange favoured them), Calica talked Ernesto into travelling to La Paz first class.

The altitude seemed to agree with Ernesto's health. He forsook his rice and maté and went back to a normal diet, taking advantage of the first-class dining car as well as of the concoctions and rare fruits offered by the locals every time the train stopped at a station. The landscape was similar to that of northern Argentina: the high plateau had scarce vegetation and the predominant colour was grey. 'The colour green has been banned,' Ernesto wrote in his diary. The monotony of the landscape was broken only by the multicoloured garments of the Indians. The women wore skirts in bright shades and the men ponchos of various hues. Both men and women wore tiny bowler hats perched on top of their heads, a legacy from the 1920s when British railway workers came to Bolivia wearing them. In spite of the extreme cold, the Indians went barefoot or wore sandals made from old tyres. It was impossible to start a conversation with them. Either they were extremely reserved and fearful or they did not speak Spanish. Among themselves, they spoke Aymara or Quechua. There was no sign of the exciting social revolution that was the talk of Buenos Aires.

However, Calica and Ernesto did make their first useful acquaintance on the train. José María Nougués, a young Argentine man of about their age, was travelling to La Paz to visit his father who lived in exile there. They discovered that they shared friends in Argentina – young men Ernesto had played rugby with and members of the medical profession who had known Calica's father. The train travelled through the night. It was so cold that, in the toilets, the water froze in the basins. And yet the Indians they saw en route were almost always barefoot and expressionless. They all chewed coca, which acts as an anaesthetic and can quench thirst, hunger, cold and fatigue. In the afternoon they reached their destination.

La Paz is the highest capital in the world, standing at an altitude of more than 4,000 metres and built in the crater of an extinct volcano. Calica and Ernesto bid farewell to their new friend and went in search of affordable lodgings. They found a guest house which was filthy but very cheap. Then they went in search of a meal, ending up in a canteen where the stew of the day was served at a long table which people joined as they arrived. They were famished and this was no time to think of Argentine fillet steak and chips, the traditional meal served in the restaurants of Buenos Aires. In the distance someone was playing the guitar. When they heard the familiar notes of a tango they were unable to look at each other for fear of betraying their emotions.

The next morning, washed and shaved and wearing fresh clothes, they went off to try their luck with the letters they had been given. Their first port of call was a Bolivian family who had relatives in Argentina. The introduction came from their buddy Carlos Figueroa. The Peñarambas had a good social and financial position in La Paz and were extremely helpful and friendly, not only feeding them but also taking them on a tour of the city and introducing them to their friends.

Both Calica and Ernesto admired the city: its colonial architecture, the tiny, steep side streets, the lively Camacho market with its exotic fruits and the cheerful little watering holes in Calle 16 de Julio. There were churches everywhere and their artistic treasures seemed ill matched with the aboriginal population of Aymara Indians, poorly dressed and inscrutable, who seemed to regard life with total apathy. When the women needed to answer a call of nature they would simply squat. They did not wear knickers but layers of skirts and petticoats of various colours. Hygiene was not a priority. The government had tried to change this habit by painting huge signs on the walls of the city stating that anyone caught urinating would be fined. The letters of the signs were blurred because men urinated against them.

La Paz was a far cry from Buenos Aires, but what made it so exciting was the revolution. There were armed men everywhere, belonging to the Movimiento Nacionalista Revolucionario which had put Víctor Paz Estenssoro in power. The government had nationalised the tin mines which were the property of the Aramayo, Patiño and Hochschild families. As the tin mines were the main source of foreign currency for Bolivia, these families had effectively controlled the country's economy, wielding absolute power over the indigenous population, which continued to live in subhuman conditions. The government had also dissolved the army and was preparing to implement a serious agrarian reform. The country was totally polarised, with staunch defenders of the government and those who were violently opposed to it. The fight had been without quarter, with many dead.

The *campesinos* (peasant farmers) were now attacking the privately owned *latifundios* (large estates), thus taking the law into their own hands rather than awaiting the promised agrarian reform, while the miners had joined the Central Obrera Boliviana (General Workers' Union of Bolivia) and organised demonstrations so the government, which they supported, could not go back on its promises. Ernesto tells us in his diary that a demonstration which took place by torchlight on 15th July was long and boring, but it was interesting to witness how the men expressed their support by firing their *piripipi* (the nickname they gave a repeater rifle). There was talk of counter-revolution as the ex-soldiers of the dissolved army were not happy either, and there were also internal divisions within the MNR, with two factions to the right and one to the left.

Much still needed to be changed. Calica tells us in his diary that, when they had been in La Paz a few days, they witnessed a scene which shocked them to the core. They were having a cup of coffee at the La Paz teahouse in the centre of town. At a table near theirs was a lady enjoying tea and sandwiches with her children. The Indian woman who would normally be looking after the children was sitting on the floor under the table. The children were throwing crusts and leftover bits of their sandwiches for her to catch and eat, as if she were a dog.

Calica and Ernesto were commenting on the scene when the young man they had met on the train appeared. José María was accompanied by his father, Don Isaías Nougués. He was the most prominent Argentine exile in La Paz, and it turned out he knew their parents. His home was the meeting place for both civilian and military exiles from Perón's Argentina, as well as the local high society and, at his frequent barbecues and dinner parties, Ernesto and Calica met everybody who was anybody in La Paz.

NINE

(1953)

Ernesto and Calica stayed in Bolivia for a month and a half instead of the week they had originally planned. Don Isaías Nougués was the main reason for their lingering in La Paz. He was quite a character, with the aura and authority of a medieval lord: 'an hidalgo from Tucumán' was how Ernesto described him.

Don Isaías found them modest but clean lodgings for the same price as their derelict and filthy guest house. Each morning they had something light to eat before setting out for the Sucre Palace Hotel, the most elegant in La Paz, where Nougués went for lunch almost every day. The patriarch and his guests never finished all the food on the table and, having once asked if they could help themselves to the leftovers, Ernesto and Calica were treated to all that had not been consumed, saved for them by the friendly waiters. And they could stand on the terrace to watch the workers parading in the streets of downtown La Paz, out to show their strength. The members of the oligarchy had never seen anything like it, but Ernesto remarked that many of the demonstrators seemed tired. There was no feeling of power emanating from them.

Another perk of their friendship with Nougués were the frequent visits to El Gallo de Oro, the most notorious nightclub in La Paz, which was owned by an Argentine exile. According to Calica, it was jokingly known as the second seat of government. Politicians, landowners, mine-owners and the heads of the revolution met there every night, in a convivial atmosphere in which everybody had far too much to drink, to discuss politics in the company of Argentine exiles and local beauties.

El Gallo de Oro was located on the outskirts of La Paz and was not easy to find unless you were escorted by one of its regular customers. Ernesto and Calica used to be driven there by Don Isaías and his brother Gogo. The road leading to the nightclub was controlled by a series of checkpoints manned by guards who stopped cars at gunpoint. Late one night, when they were leaving the club to go back to the city, they were stopped at one of these. Gogo Nougués had had too much to drink and told the guard to 'put down that gun for shooting partridges'. Surprisingly, the man let them through. Ernesto and Calica breathed a sigh of relief, for they had heard stories which ended with people being shot dead after similar confrontations.

During their nightly visits to the club, both Ernesto and Calica often had to bite their tongues when the people with whom they shared the main table (who came from utter privilege in Bolivia or Argentina) expressed their views on the current political situation and the upheaval to the social order caused by the new revolutionary government. But Ernesto claimed, 'Nobody denies the need for the state to put an end to things which symbolised the power of the three bosses of the tin mines, and the young believe that this has been a step forward in the struggle to have greater equality between peoples and fortunes.'

There was one area in which Calica was more worldly than Ernesto. One evening at El Gallo de Oro, Ernesto came back from the gents to tell Calica that he was mystified by the behaviour of some of the men. While in the lavatory they had brought out a little box and inhaled its contents. 'It's cocaine, you fool. This is Bolivia,' Calica told him. Ernesto had never come across it in all his travels, but Calica had an uncle who had shown him the nightlife of Buenos Aires as part of his adult education and taken him to some seedy tango joints, where cocaine was common.

Ernesto and Calica had been celibate since they left home and it was beginning to make them impatient. Once they were back in the city, Calica decided to put an end to their period of celibacy when, from his vantage point on the terrace of the Sucre Palace Hotel, he spotted two lovely-looking young women. He sallied forth and, once on the street, approached them. In those days when people travelled less, a well-mannered young Argentine male in La Paz would have been considered interesting and somewhat special. He was chatting up the girls when another man approached them and joined in the conversation. He was small, dark and in his mid-thirties.

When he suggested they all went for a drink together, Calica panicked. He had not a cent on him. But the girls had already accepted. He gestured to Ernesto, who was watching from the hotel terrace, but to no avail.

The group went into a bar and ordered cakes and sandwiches. The man ordered imported Scotch while Calica asked for a humble cup of coffee, the cheapest item on the menu. Not much later, the man ordered another Scotch. Calica gestured frantically to him, hoping the girls would not notice and be alerted to his dire predicament. The man laughed out loud, and said, 'Don't worry, I'm paying.' When the girls left, his new friend explained to Calica that he was a Venezuelan colonel who had been sent as military attaché to his country's embassy in Bolivia, as retribution for conspiring to overthrow the dictator Pérez-Jiménez. His salary was paid in a strong currency and, far from being punished, he was living a charmed existence.

Calica and Ramírez (for that was his name) continued to date the two girls they had met in the street. Meanwhile Ernesto was going out with a girl he had met at a party. She was Martha Pinilla and she came from a family of oligarchs whose lands started not far from La Paz and stretched for many kilometres. The long period of drought was over for both young men. Their rather schizophrenic existence (as Calica described it) continued, between high-society parties and the discovery of Bolivia's new social order in the streets. Their financial situation was deteriorating rapidly and something had to be done about it. Their new-found friends were all extremely generous but their purse, the famous chastity belt, was almost empty.

Visas for Ecuador were quickly obtained through old Nougués's contacts, then Calica's new camaraderie with the Venezuelan Colonel Ramírez proved providential. Informed of their lack of visas for his country over lunch, Ramírez said he would sort it out for them. And when Calica told him about their violent exchanges with the Venezuelan Consul in Buenos Aires, he discovered that Ramírez had a particular dislike for the man. The next day, Ernesto and Calica had their visas for Venezuela. Ernesto smiled triumphantly and said, 'I did walk over his belly in the end.'

In order to remedy their dreadful financial situation, Ernesto produced his trump card: a letter from Dr Ferreira in Buenos Aires for the Bolivian School of Medicine. Both men put on their best suits. In Ernesto's case this was one he had inherited from his uncle Jorge de la Serna, which they referred to as El Jorge. They saw a Dr Molina, who was politeness personified. He told Ernesto he could offer him a job as a doctor in a mine for three months, while Calica could work with him as a male nurse. They decided to accept the jobs for a month because their meagre funds would have disappeared totally if they stayed any longer, and they would be stuck in Bolivia (a salary in Bolivian currency would not be any use anywhere else). But when they returned the next day to report to Dr Molina, a secretary told them that he would be out of town for a few days. They went to the medical school in their best outfits every few days, only to return home empty-handed. In the end, Dr Molina did return but by now it was too late. And they had decided to move on.

Dr Molina was, however, instrumental in getting them an invitation to visit a tungsten mine in a mountainous area not far from La Paz. The doctor saw to it that they were offered lodgings at the mine but they did not have any money for transport. Ernesto remembered a useful tip from his previous trip: he went to the market, found out who was travelling in the required direction the next morning and arranged to hitch a ride. Not only did a lorry driver agree to take them but he offered them places next to him inside the cab. So off they went.

Ernesto suddenly remembered that his inamorata Martha Pinilla had told him her family's lands began just outside La Paz, and he asked the driver to tell him when they drove past them. The driver said they had been driving through the Pinillas' land for quite a while. Each time Ernesto asked the driver if they had now reached the other end of their land, he would reply that there was still some way to go. After hours on the road, the driver said they had now come to the end of the Pinillas' lands.

The men decided to make a brief halt to stretch their legs and have a look. Ernesto and Calica stopped to chat with some Indians whose huts were visible from the road. These indigenous workers told them their masters did not allow them to keep even one single animal, so that they could not have eggs from a hen or milk from a cow to supplement their diet.

It was almost dark when they arrived at the Bolsa Negra mine. The engineers greeted them cordially and they all had dinner together, after which they went off to bed. The next day was Sunday and they were taken to visit a glacier at Mururata and then shown the site where the tungsten was obtained by using a mill to crush the ore extracted by the miners. Ernesto wrote all the information down as if it were a school lesson. The following morning they were taken to see the mountain from which the ore was mined. Kitted out with rubber boots, raincoats and carbide lamps, they entered the mine.

It was quite an experience, but it was what they saw when they came out the other end of the tunnel that shocked them beyond belief. Not far from the exit of the mine was a village where the miners and their families lived. Pointing in the direction of the village there were machine guns. The mine had now been nationalised but the feudal lords who owned it until a few weeks earlier had seen fit to have these aimed at the miners' homes, to show them who was boss if they dared to ask for a pay rise or an improvement in working conditions. Now the miners had acquired social and labour rights and had also been given arms by the government, turning them into popular militias.

Miners carrying piripipi return to the mine from La Paz. Calica is the first on the left. Photo taken by Ernesto

On the day Calica and Ernesto visited the mine, the workers had gone to La Paz. It was 2nd August, marked in the new revolutionary calendar as the Day of Agrarian Reform as well as of the Indigenous Population. As rumours of a counter-revolution were rife, the miners went to the capital to show their solidarity with the government. When they returned in the late afternoon, they were an eerie sight. Their lorries could be seen in the distance, advancing in single file, and they could be heard as well: they were firing their rifles into the air and the sound reverberated in the valleys. They were a formidable lot, and even more so if you knew that until recently they had been at the mercy of the machine guns still pointing towards their village.

Ernesto noted in his diary, 'the miners have arrived with their stone-like faces and their multicoloured plastic helmets, which make them look like warriors from a foreign land'. They got out of their vehicles and handed in their weapons at the depot. They looked fifty or sixty years old but were only in their thirties. They had worked all their lives without any protection, without medical attention, without a limit to the hours they spent down the mine and without proper payment. Ernesto found out about sanitation from the only male nurse who lived in the village. He wanted to know about childbirth but was told the natives did not allow anyone to interfere in this very private event and had their own midwives.

Ernesto admired the Bolivian revolution as the much-needed reform that it was, but this did not prevent him from observing its flaws and commenting on them with irony and humour. One day Ernesto and Calica got themselves an invitation to visit the Minister for Indigenous Affairs. Ñuflo Chávez was Indian, had managed to obtain a degree in Law and spoke Quechua and Aymara as well as Spanish. He was about the same age as his guests. During the previous regime he had been persecuted for taking up the defence of trade unionists and political prisoners. He sat in his elegant office, with its curtains, carpets and upholstered leather armchairs, and listened to the delegations of indigenous peoples who came to see him and tell him their plight. As the government had passed an agrarian reform law, many came to see the minister in the hope of being given the lands they had been promised. There were lengthy queues of Indians wearing rustic clothes, coarse ponchos and multicoloured woollen hats. They advanced slowly along the corridors, silently waiting their turn.

At the end of the corridor, a *cholo* stood on a wooden box with a long rubber hose. He fed the hose into the waiting men's clothing, pushing it down their collars and fumigating them with insecticide. He did this methodically, leaving each of his victims covered in a whitish powder. Nobody batted an eyelid. Ernesto was angered by what he saw. 'The MNR makes the revolution with DDT,' he said bitterly. It was not unusual to see Indians walking down the streets in a cloud of DDT, identifying them as recent visitors to the minister.

Ñuflo Chávez was courteous and gave them a few books about the Bolivian revolutionary movement. But Ernesto could not control himself and had to ask why the Indians were subjected to such a humiliating ritual before entering his office. The minister said it was rather unfortunate but something had to be done: most Indians did not use soap and water and could not be expected to learn to do so overnight, and so they arrived covered in lice and other insects. For the moment, the revolution had to deal with the consequences; the time would come when they would be able to tackle the causes.

When they left the ministry Ernesto, standing in front of the statue of the liberator Simón Bolívar, after whom the country had been named, said, 'The thing would be to combat the causes and not to be content with suppressing the effects. This revolution will fail if it does not succeed in shaking the spiritual isolation of the Indians, if it does not touch them to the core and move them deeply, to give them back their status as human beings. Otherwise, what is it for?' And yet, Ernesto was still not interested in politics; his concerns were of a humanitarian nature.

Along with José Martí, Simón Bolívar, the man who played a key role in Latin America's struggle for independence from Spain, was a constant inspiration to Che. Bolívar saw the continent as a federation of nations that would jointly be able to resist the onslaught of foreign powers and preserve their independence and it was this that led to his leading role in the creation of the first union of independent nations in Latin America. Also deeply appealing to Che was Bolívar's emphasis on the importance of social justice. In his times the fight was against slavery, against the *criollos* and aboriginal populations being second class citizens in the continent of their birth. Bolívar may have picked his elite officers from Wellington's recently demobilised armies but the men who rode with him against the might of the Spanish were mulattos, half-breeds and freed black slaves as well as criollos. For Bolívar, in a post-colonial society man would not only be entitled to education, but also have access to medicine, the right to work without being exploited, and aboriginal peoples should have the right to be treated as equals. It's easy to see these themes running through Che's own concerns, though by Che's time the USA had replaced Spain as the main purveyor of oppression in Latin America.

He had always known that the real enemy was US imperialism but he had a very poor opinion of politicians as a whole. However, he recognised that Perón was due some credit, even though he did not care for him. For instance, his willingness to accept old Nougués's lavish hospitality did not deter him from speaking his mind one evening, when Nougués embarked on his usual anti-Perón diatribe. He went on and on about his personal sacrifices in the name of freedom and his prolonged self-imposed exile due to his many disagreements with the policies of those in power at home. Ernesto, who was thoroughly enjoying a *locro* (a sumptuous traditional Argentine stew), interrupted his host. 'Alright, alright, that is enough. Now, why don't you tell us a little bit about your sugar-processing industry?' The Nougués family at the time owned one of the country's largest sugar-cane factories in Tucumán, in northern Argentina.

Ernesto would also argue with his girlfriend Martha Pinilla about her family's *latifundios* and their political stance. The Pinillas were about to have some of their lands expropriated by the government. He would tell her he was not surprised the Pinillas were against the revolution when it was expropriating their land and cancelling the privileges of their social class.

As their date of departure arrived, old Nougués gave Ernesto and Calica a farewell party. They were both leaving behind their girlfriends, but it was a jolly affair with much joking and speech-making and far too much to drink. When Ernesto left the party at dawn, he did not realise he had forgotten to take his camera with him. In his account of the trip, Calica tells us that the two overslept the next morning and had to make a dash for the

Ernesto (left) and Calica (right) in Bolivia

bus station, where they had booked places in a lorry that would take them to the Bay of Copacabana on Lake Titicaca, on the border between Bolivia and Peru. They travelled part of the way in the cab but also rode in the back with the Indians, their hens, calves, boxes and whatever else they were carrying, to get a better view of the landscape. They were the only white people around, and stood out like sore thumbs. Halfway to Copacabana, Ernesto noticed the absence of his camera and decided to go back for it. He told Calica to carry on with all the luggage and wait for him, and then crossed the road and started hitchhiking in the opposite direction.

While in La Paz, Ernesto and Calica had met Ricardo Rojo, then a twenty-nine-year-old Argentine lawyer at one time imprisoned by Perón. In his book *My Friend Che*, Rojo tell us that he was of the party as well. From their respective published accounts, it seems that Rojo and Calica did not care for one another, as each makes snide remarks about the other.

According to Rojo, Calica later split from Ernesto in Ecuador because he was fed up with the way he was expected to travel: walking everywhere without ever tiring, totally disregarding hygiene and clothing and putting up uncomplainingly with the lack of money. According to Calica, who wrote his book in 2005, when Rojo had been dead many years, Rojo not only fantasised about some aspects of the trip – saying that he had travelled with Ernesto and Calica when in fact he had far more money than them and by comparison travelled in style – but also took liberties when describing Ernesto's political attitudes much later in Cuba. It is true that there are some inaccuracies in Rojo's book, which he wrote quite quickly, soon after Che's death, but there may have been rivalry between the two young men at the time, which could also account for some of the discrepancies between their accounts.

It is a fact, however, that Rojo stayed close to Ernesto's mother all her life. Once Ernesto became a public figure in Cuba, Rojo carried out some tasks abroad at his request. And in 1967, when Ernesto was heading a guerrilla force in Bolivia, Rojo rushed there to defend Ciro Bustos, an Argentine liaison operative who had been detained while attempting to leave the area. He was up before a military court, from which no one expected a fair trial.

Ernesto Guevara may have had many faults but he cared passionately for the truth, did not have an inflated ego and was not remotely interested in fame or posterity. He would have been uncomfortable with the attitude of those who wanted their moment of fame by osmosis, simply because they once knew him. He in fact once famously said to a French journalist, 'La gloire, ça m'enmerde.'

Calica tells us that he arrived at Copacabana alone and parked all their belongings at a modest guest house. He then went for a walk. The landscape was impressive, the place sad and silent. He noticed a five-star hotel by the lake and went to have a look. A woman approached him and he soon discovered that she too came from Argentina. She was the manager of the hotel and invited him to stay, since it was off season and the hotel was empty. She would throw in their meals as well. The woman was lonely and delighted to have some company for a while. She lived in this isolated and quiet resort because she had a seriously handicapped child to bring up, and no husband.

Ernesto rejoined him twenty-four hours later, after retrieving the camera and having a good night's sleep, and they planned their trip to the Isla del Sol, the purpose of their stay at Copacabana. They left at dawn, escorted by a local man who would be their boatman and guide, with a picnic basket courtesy of their landlady. There was no wind so they had to row. On arrival at the island, they were greeted by a couple of Indians who showed them the ruins close to the shore and claimed they had once been the Temple of the Sun. Ernesto had done his research and could not be duped. They all began to argue at the top of their voices until their boatman and guide admitted that the Temple of the Sun was situated in the middle of the island. He warned them it was a two-hour walk to get there and it would be too late to get back afterwards. They set off regardless.

When they reached the Temple of the Sun, they found a total ruin from which all artefacts had been stolen. But Ernesto gave Calica a guided tour anyway. He could tell where the great Inca sat and where the ritual sacrifices took place. In his memoir, Calica tells us it was a magical moment. From the elevation at the centre of the island they could see the beautiful lake, and they were surrounded by history and nature. Ernesto rummaged in the dust and finally found a little statue which he said was 'an idol representing a woman which complies with all my aspirations'.

Their guide put an end to this idyll by telling them how late it was. They started on their way back but reached the shore after dark. The boatman did not want to leave because it was too dangerous, but his charges persuaded him it would be worse to spend the night on the island, where there were no amenities. They were sailing along happily when a storm broke and the boat started to shake violently. The guide was so scared that he dropped the oars, flung himself to the bottom of the boat and prayed to Pacha Mama as well as to Our Father and the Virgin Mary, for good measure.

Ernesto and Calica took turns to row until their hands bled. Calica started to take off his elegant knee-high boots and Ernesto asked him why he was doing that. Calica said they might easily have to swim. 'Don't be such a fool! If you fall into the water you will die within five minutes, frozen,' Ernesto said logically. That was typical of him, Calica thought. There they were, in the pitch dark in the middle of a huge, freezing lake which seemed like an ocean because of the waves the storm was causing, and Ernesto still maintained his sangfroid.

They finally managed to land in a small bay. They could hear dogs barking and realised that men with lamps were out looking for them. Everybody was furious: they had endangered the boatman's life and now they had landed at a private establishment where they had no right to be.

Calica (right) rowing on Lake Titicaca in this photo taken by Ernesto

Nevertheless, they were allowed to stay for the night in a large shed and they decided to sleep against the large doors so that nobody could enter during the night and rob them. They fell asleep on the hay immediately, exhausted by their ordeal. The next morning they were woken by the sun on their faces, hens walking over them and Indians coming in and out to find their tools so they could get on with their work. The doors, it turned out, could be opened in both directions.

They set off for Copacabana with their boatman, to be greeted with much relief by their friend at the hotel, who had given them up for dead. They rested and then in the afternoon went out to visit the church of the Virgin of Copacabana, famous for its relics. They arrived to encounter lepers, beggars and a blind man who played a one-string violin, producing the saddest music from the altiplano. Entering the church, they came across an incredible scene: a fat priest, holding several Bolivian bank notes between his fingers as gamblers do, was attending to a lengthy file of Indians, whom he blessed one by one in Aymara or Quechua while they discreetly put their financial contribution between his fingers. It was a surreal scene, funny as well as infuriating.

Ernesto immediately started a conversation with some of the Indians to find out what was going on. He discovered that the priest was selling them places in heaven, which were allocated according to the amount of money the Indians paid. The best places were more costly, of course, but there was bargaining to be done. In order to establish the price, the priest and the Indian would hold a conversation; the Indian might decide that the price was too high and attempt to leave, at which point the priest would call him back and they would agree on a lower figure. The priest took advantage of the Indians, who came to him with all sorts of problems – illnesses, family dramas, unemployment. The scene surprised even Ernesto, who had never had any time for the Church and who had formed the worst possible opinion of the clergy ever since childhood.

TEN

(1953)

Peru was governed by the dictator Manuel Odría, a general who viewed the developments in Bolivia with a jaundiced eye. He was not about to let his country be ideologically contaminated, and he saw to it that no left-wing propaganda was tolerated in Peru. When Calica and Ernesto crossed the frontier from Bolivia into Peru, the guards confiscated *Man in the Soviet Union* which Ernesto had been carrying with him ever since they left Buenos Aires, as well as a publication by the Ministry of Indigenous Affairs which Ñuflo Chávez had given him in La Paz. A great argument ensued between Ernesto and the guards but it was to no avail. The guards told him he could retrieve his books once he arrived in Lima.

Ernesto proposed that they continue from Puno to Cuzco by train. He did not think there was anything of particular interest to visit between the two places and they would make up for lost time. Since their funds had continued to dwindle, they decided to travel second class. After a night in Puno, they went to the train station with all their gear to buy their tickets. The place was deserted and there was an eerie calm.

When they approached the window and asked for two second-class tickets, the man refused them, simply saying, 'No, no, I cannot sell second-class tickets to you.' They asked for clarification. The man could not be more explicit but Calica and Ernesto suspected they knew the reason: second-class carriages in Peru were really cattle-wagons. Indians, old and young, male and female and their children, as well as animals, all travelled piled inside them with no ventilation and no seats. The doors were padlocked from the outside and the train operators would decide on a whim whether to unlock them when they reached a station, leaving the Indians inside begging to be let out. When they were not, they had to get off at the next station and walk back to their homes or places of work. The station manager was refusing them second-class tickets because they were white and could not be subjected to such outrageous treatment without consequences.

Ernesto lost his cool. 'Who the hell do you think you are? You are going to sell us those tickets and that is that. We decide how we want to travel.'

'Well, I will sell you second-class tickets, but at your own risk. The train will be here in four hours, if it arrives on schedule,' the man said.

Ernesto and Calica paid for their tickets and went for a short walk to calm down. Soon Ernesto was sitting on the ground writing his diary. Calica was pacing up and down the platform when two men approached him. 'Do you have second-class tickets?' they enquired.

'Ah, no, not again! Stop breaking our balls with that second-class tickets saga. We've already enough trouble over them. Stop messing around. Hell, that's how we're going to travel and that's the end of it,' Calica said, as the whole episode had by now got on his nerves.

'Watch your language! We're Peruvian detectives,' the men said, producing their police IDs.

'Well, if that's the case . . .' Calica said, quickly backtracking. 'Look, all our papers are in order – passports, visas, proof of entry . . .'

'No, no, don't get upset, boys. We'd like to make a business proposal.'

Ernesto, trying to look like a businessman and stay calm, said, 'A business proposal? How interesting. What sort of business?'

'This is what I am proposing: we're supposed to be taking two prisoners from Puno to Cuzco in the first-class carriage, but unfortunately they've escaped. That means there are two free seats in first class, so we could resell your second-class tickets and you could keep the money from one of them and we the other. And we'll all be happy – you get to travel in first class and we all gain something.'

'Yes, of course,' Calica and Ernesto said simultaneously, after looking at each other.

'Don't get too excited because there's a catch,' the detectives said. 'As you have to impersonate the prisoners, you'll have to travel in handcuffs.'

Again Calica and Ernesto looked at each other and agreed. They were handcuffed and boarded the train with all their luggage, both embarrassed and amused. The two detectives sat in front of them while the entire compartment stared with great curiosity. What made the situation really funny was that people travelling in the carriage showed their solidarity with the prisoners by offering them something to eat or drink, while totally ignoring the policemen. Peru may have had a right-wing demagogue for a president, but ordinary people did not hesitate to show their sympathy with the downtrodden.

As the journey progressed, Ernesto chatted with the policemen and told them that he was a doctor, that he had already visited Peru, and that he and his travelling companion were particularly interested in observing the campaign against leprosy throughout South America. Through constant retelling during the trip, they had perfected the tale they had rehearsed before visiting the Venezuelan consul. The policemen relented and decided that the young men could be trusted. They removed the handcuffs and even lent them their police IDs, which they did not need themselves; nobody would question their identity because the railway workers had all seen them before. So Calica and Ernesto went from being prisoners to being Peruvian policemen in the space of a few seconds.

Once the ticket-collector had been round, the two policemen moved to another compartment where there was some gambling going on. Ernesto joined them briefly and lost all he had on him: 20 soles. He thought the gamblers had cheated him but was philosophical. He had learnt a lesson: gambling was not the answer to their dire financial straits. The train arrived in Cuzco at night and Calica and Ernesto managed to return the ID of one of the policemen but the other one was so drunk that he was being dragged away. 'I remember that his shoes were falling off,' Calica said when he told the story almost fifty years later.

They went in search of lodgings and found a guest house which was even filthier than usual but, as a consolation, cheaper than usual as well. The rate of exchange in Peru was not favourable to them and consequently all extras and little luxuries were now abolished. The next morning they went to the police station to show their passports and register as aliens – something that was compulsory at the time in countries with authoritarian regimes. Suddenly someone appeared and shouted, 'They are the ones who stole the ID.'

'We did not steal anything,' Ernesto said emphatically. Calica was dispatched to fetch the missing ID which they had left at the guest house, while the policemen held Ernesto as guarantee. By the time Calica got back, the drunk policeman, now sober, had arrived and apologised for the misunderstanding, saying, 'You understand, don't you?' Of course, they understood that they had to keep their mouths shut, since their friend could not explain to his colleagues that he had lent his ID to a foreigner and then gone on to lose sight of him because he was drunk.

'Have you ever eaten in a *picantería*?' he asked. They had not. So, that night, the policeman took them to a typical Peruvian restaurant, where food is prepared with every chilli (or *picante*) under the sun. Diners often compete in a machismo contest to see who can eat the hottest dish. The first course was soup. It was terribly hot and yet their host still added some chillies. Ernesto and Calica were very hungry, as usual, but they could hardly eat. Their friend explained to them that, in the days before refrigerators, chillies were used to dull the taste buds so that one could eat food that was well past its sell-by date. As they ate through their tears, Ernesto made a sign to Calica, pointing in the direction of the kitchen door, which was ajar. They could see the waiters pouring the leftovers from the soup plates back into the pot. Ernesto adopted the air of a scientist and said, sotto voce, 'Don't worry, just carry on eating – all the chillies will have killed any bacteria. It's like sterilising the food.'

They spent two days in Cuzco, looking at the multitude of churches with their art treasures. The attendant at a museum they visited told Ernesto, to his delight, that the little statue he had taken from the ruins at the Isla del Sol was genuine and was made from *tunyana*, the alloy for which the Incas were famous. He decided to call her Martha after his Bolivian sweetheart.

Nobody wanted to change their Argentine pesos, so Calica and Ernesto were stuck in Cuzco, unable to proceed to Machu Picchu, until they met an Argentine woman who sold antiques to tourists from the USA. She claimed to have collected the antiques herself from old Inca excavations in remote areas. The tourists paid handsomely for them but, as soon as they turned their backs, the woman brought out identical pieces and replaced them in her shop window. She made friends with Calica and Ernesto and helped them with the logistics of their excursion to Machu Picchu, giving them two rucksacks full of camping gear, which she claimed had belonged to soldiers in the Second World War, as well as provisions for the journey. But when it came to taking their pesos, she did so at a very unfavourable rate of exchange. Ernesto was philosophical: 'For the moment we won't starve.' They used the money to buy two second-class train tickets to Machu Picchu.

Calica in Machu Picchu wearing his famous knee boots made by López-Taibo. Photo taken by Ernesto

The landscape is spectacular as the small narrow-gauge train climbs up, following the course of the Urubamba river, and the tropical vegetation grows wilder and greener. Calica and Ernesto had left their heavy luggage in the care of their new Argentine friend and they decided to walk the eight kilometres up to the site from the station at Machu Picchu. In his diary, Calica tells us Ernesto was elated to be back at a place which had so impressed him the first time round. He was in excellent spirits, cheerful and talkative and, in spite of the altitude and the brisk walk, he did not have an asthma attack. With great enthusiasm, Ernesto showed Calica the 150 buildings that communicate with one another by means of corridors and stairs.

Machu Picchu also brought out in Ernesto his latent hatred of imperialism of any kind, including the latter-day imperialism of the good citizens of the USA who had discovered the ruins. He wrote an article that would be published by the Panamanian magazine *Siete* in December of that same year. In it he expressed his utter contempt for the devastation he witnessed and his anger that artefacts and treasures that represented a 'pure expression of America's most powerful native civilisation', one 'untainted by contact with the conquering hordes', were lying in far-away US museums in the hands of a people who are 'unaware of the moral divide between themselves and these descendants of a once-proud race, because it involves subtleties that only the semi-native spirit of us Latin Americans can appreciate.' Ernesto felt a sense of brotherhood with these native people, about whom he had known so little until recently. He ended the article with a poetic description of what Machu Picchu meant to him: 'For the freedom fighter who is pursuing something that is today dismissed as a fantasy, Machu Picchu is a symbol of the past holding out its hand to the future and calling out across the continent, "People of Indo-America, reclaim your history".'

Ernesto explained to Calica that during their earlier stay, he and Alberto had made friends with the manager of a luxury hotel and had even played a football match with him in the ruins. 'He is called Soto. He is a Peruvian who greatly admires Argentina because he loves football and the tango. His singing is atrocious and his football isn't any better, but you only have to tell him he does both things really well and everything will be paid for.'

Soto remembered Ernesto and welcomed them with open arms. 'Don't worry, boys, you can have one of the hotel's service rooms for a few soles.' The service room was, of course, much better than any they had slept in so far. It had two beds with clean sheets and a bathroom near by. That evening, they met up with Soto, who murdered a few tangos, and Calica even sang along with him. Tone deaf Ernesto knew better than to join them. But to make up for it, Soto knew a lot about Inca civilisation and Ernesto really enjoyed a long chat with him about it.

Machu Picchu

The following day they all played a football match among the ruins with several local men who arrived with a ball. Ernesto always played goalkeeper because of his asthma. He had developed his own style and was fearless when intercepting players who came at him at full speed. He had warned Calica that the altitude might affect him and he should not run too much. Calica did not heed his advice and ended up flat on the ground while Ernesto was regarded as star player by the assorted company, in spite of the fact that he had tactfully let in a couple of Soto goals.

They returned to Cuzco, where for lack of transport to Lima, they were forced to spend a whole week but they finally left by bus (in fact a converted truck with a tarpaulin for a roof and wooden seats). Even Ernesto, who never seemed to notice any discomfort or inconvenience, was rather fed up: 'The trip became endless. The hens had shitted under our seats and the smell of dirty feet was unbearable; you could have cut the atmosphere with a knife.' To ease the boredom and take a break from the smell, they would occasionally climb on to the tarpaulin and travel up there.

The landscape was beautiful along the Apurimac river and through the valleys and mountains, but they were able to appreciate how precarious the roads were, carved out of the rock and only wide enough for single-file traffic most of the time. When two lorries met face to face, one of them had to reverse and give way to let the other one through. And, of course, there was always the risk of a landslide. These sometimes blocked the road and the bus would have to wait until a tractor arrived and moved the rocks. Another landslide might begin as this was going on. Calica and Ernesto could not help noticing the skill and aplomb with which the Indians drove the lorries, tractors and buses. Their vehicles were often ancient and in bad repair, their tyres totally worn and their brakes almost non-existent. And the drivers were often so exhausted that they might ask a passenger to take over while they slept until the next stop.

During the stops, the passengers could have a plate of rice and chillies for next to nothing if they waited their turn to use the only spoon and plate available. And Calica and Ernesto helped load animals or sacks, in return for a glass of chicha or a *tamal*, a local snack made of cornmeal with a meat filling. Pisco, a kind of aquavit, is the national drink of Peru and it was the best thing for the cold as well as a better alternative than the water, which could give you diarrhoea. As the bus went up and down the hills, the climate changed from freezing cold at night to extremely hot in the afternoon, so the travellers had to put on and take off layers of clothing. During one stop, Ernesto and Calica decided to go for a swim in the Apurimac river. They took off all their clothes and jumped in. The other passengers were staring at them, which made Calica cover his private parts while Ernesto began to jump up and down, trying to shock the onlookers even more. But he paid for his prank because he got an asthma attack, and had to resort to his inhaler.

When they stopped for the night they slept under their vehicle or in a hut where the owners might make room for them in a corner. Although the Indians were willing to offer them hospitality, they were rarely prepared to talk to them, either because they were very reserved or because they spoke no Spanish. There was an exception, however. As the bus travelled on,

Calica was woken up by Ernesto's unmistakable laughter. The Indian he was talking to was also laughing, a rare occurrence. He was explaining to Ernesto, half in Spanish, half in his own language and with many gestures as well, that he had four days' travel ahead of him and the only food he had with him was a little bag of cooked chickpeas which he ate in small portions. He offered some to Ernesto, who remembered that he was carrying some tins they had been given by their Argentine friend in Cuzco.

He found a tin of sardines and some crackers. When he opened the tin, a jet of oil squirted out. Calica immediately warned him that the contents of the tin could be toxic, and he might be taken ill. 'You intend to eat that?' he asked in horror. 'Didn't you see what squirted out of it? It's rotten! It could kill a horse.'

Ernesto replied, 'Of course I'm going to eat it. It is fine.'

Calica screamed at Ernesto, 'You son of a bitch, listen to me. Your mother asked me to look after you. And you're going to eat that tin from 1940, you're going to fall ill here in the middle of the jungle and we're not even going to find a witch doctor to cure you. You're going to die, you idiot. What am I going to do with you dead?'

Ernesto and his pal devoured their canapés and lived to tell the tale. They even ate some ancient chocolate bars from the Second World War rucksacks. They climbed on the tarpaulin to enjoy the view. Suddenly, Calica, who had remained inside, heard Ernesto screaming at the top of his voice, 'Stop, stop, a passenger has fallen off.' The driver continued to the prescribed stop and after a while, the chickpea Indian appeared, covered in bruises and scratches: his luggage and his chickpeas were still in the bus, and he was not about to lose them. Ernesto was cheered by his arrival. He checked that he had no broken bones and cleaned his wounds.

Anywhere else there would have been fisticuffs with a driver who did not stop for his passenger, but the Indian demonstrated yet again that his race lived a life with no hope, utterly resigned to its lot. It was no wonder that a demagogue like Odría managed to stay in power, unchallenged, for so long. Even so, the military were to be seen on all the roads, armed to the teeth, and foreigners were constantly stopped and asked to show their passports, even in the smallest and most remote villages.

They finally reached Lima and parked themselves in a filthy little hotel.

Ernesto was looking forward to meeting up with Dr Hugo Pesce, who had been such a crucial friend and protector during his previous trip with Alberto, while Calica dreamt of catching up with Gogo Nougués, their friend from Bolivia, who would surely contribute to their well-being, just as he and his family had done in La Paz. Neither was disappointed.

But before they had a chance to organise their life in Lima, they had an incident with the police which made them realise to what extent the dictatorship of Odría was in control. They returned to their hotel room to find two policemen searching through their luggage. When asked for their papers, Ernesto immediately said, 'I'm an Argentine doctor, and together with my friend who is an advanced student, I'm investigating the fight against leprosy . . .'

'We're not interested in that,' one policeman interjected. 'You'll have to come with us.'

Ernesto replied, 'No, you can't take me with you. I need to talk to my Consul first.'

The policeman said, 'You're not going anywhere. You are both coming with us.'

They were taken to the police station and interrogated. The police wanted to know who they knew in Lima, where they were going and why they were travelling. After the interrogation they were locked up without any explanation for a couple of hours.

They racked their brains. Did this have anything to do with the books confiscated at the frontier? Did Ernesto's friendship with Dr Pesce compromise him? When the policemen came to let them out, their tone had changed. They even apologised, and told them they had been looking for someone from Argentina who had abducted his daughter after he'd fallen out with her Peruvian mother. Ernesto and Calica decided the story did not hold water. If a man had abducted a child, the last thing he would do was stay in Peru, where the repressiveness of the regime and brutality of the police were well known. They decided they would not make any attempt to recover the books confiscated from them at the frontier.

Their first port of call was, of course, Dr Hugo Pesce, who greeted Ernesto with great affection, which he extended to Calica as well. He invited them to visit him at the Hospital de Guía's leprosy section as well as at his home, where they were asked to dinner several times. Ernesto loved to listen to Dr Pesce, who could talk about so many subjects very knowledgeably. The doctor's wife, Soraya Sheier, was an excellent cook and their children, Lucho and Tito, joined them for dinner, turning the event into a family affair.

Again, as in La Paz, life proved to be schizophrenic as they went from one extreme to the other. The difference was that the right was in power and their left-wing friends were ostracised, with the government not even tolerating the existence of an opposition. The only reason Dr Pesce could not be touched was that he was well known abroad for his contribution to medicine, although some said it was because he was a higher-ranking freemason than President Odría himself. The same has been said of Simón Bolívar, to whom General San Martín deferred more than a hundred years earlier when they met in Guayaquil.

The other extreme, as it were, was provided by Gogo Nougués, who duly arrived in Lima and took over their social life, with invitations to the Country Club and the Hotel Gran Bolívar in downtown Lima where the elite met. Alas, there was no Gallo de Oro in Lima. Gogo saw to it that they were fed adequately and regularly, passing them off as his nephews whenever he had a personal invitation and justifying their voraciousness by their youth. Ricardo Rojo, who had flown in, was often of the party as well. According to Ernesto, he had also had problems at the frontier because of the books he was carrying.

They had now been on the road for two months. Ernesto was annoyed to be without letters from home, especially as he got news indirectly from Dolly, Calica's mother, who wrote often. He wrote to his father rather angrily, asking him to tell his mother that 'every time she wants to sit down to a game of patience, she should write to me first.'

For Ernesto, one of the most moving experiences in Lima was their visit to the patients at Dr Pesce's leprosy ward. They remembered Ernesto as someone very special, a kind of hero, a young doctor who was investigating their illness and who was free from prejudices. Calica and Ernesto often spent the afternoon with the patients (after first having lunch at the university, where they could get a good meal cheaply), discussing football, tango and movies. They even brought them some Argentine sports magazines they had received from home. Although Dr Pesce's patients were not as seriously ill as those sent to leprosaria in remote areas, their lot was a sad one. They were, on the whole, young and poor, and would not be able to find work because of the prejudice and lack of knowledge about the bacillus. Even Calica had serious reservations about being in contact with them.

When they decided to leave Lima, they went to make their farewells. It was an extremely moving parting. The patients gave Ernesto and Calica all sorts of little presents, such as a piece of fruit, a drawing, handicrafts. Calica got carried away, forgot his reservations and shook their hands. Everyone was on the verge of tears, although they were all pretending they would meet again soon. Once they had left and the emotion of the parting had receded, Calica asked Ernesto, 'Are you sure leprosy is not contagious? Tell me the truth: should I not touch anything with this hand?' Ernesto replied, 'Of course not, you fool. Put your hand down, you look as if you were hailing a bus. Leprosy is not transmitted like this. I am not suicidal either.'

They left for Piura in a lorry-bus like the one in which they had arrived. It travelled along the coast but it was far too cold to bathe in the sea, so they dreamt of Ecuador, where it would be warmer. They were back to a life of wooden seats, stews with mysterious ingredients, and long roads. As they reached Tumbes, on the frontier between Peru and Ecuador, Ernesto had an asthma attack and was forced to stay in their room until the next day. The Peruvian police stamped their passports on 27th September 1953.

ELEVEN

(1953–1954)

Celia had managed to stop playing patience long enough to organise a useful contact for her son in Guayaquil. She wrote to Ernesto telling him the president of Ecuador would be aware of their arrival and would assist them: this had been arranged by a friend of hers who knew the president's wife well. Calica was overjoyed, as by now he was beginning to tire of dilapidated buses, ghastly food and the lack of sanitary facilities.

On their last day in Lima, Ricardo Rojo had given them the address of a guest house in Guayaquil where they could make contact with him when they arrived. But in the event they met Rojo on the pier at Guayaquil, where they docked after a day and a night on a cattle boat, sleeping in hammocks slung above the cows. They had sailed from the port of Santa Marta, which they had reached by hitchhiking from Huaquillas, the border post on the Ecuador side, so depleted was the chastity belt by now.

Rojo was in the company of three law students whom he knew from the University of La Plata in Argentina: Eduardo García (or Gualo), Andro Herrero and Oscar Valdovinos (or Valdo). They were all waiting for transport by sea to Panama. From there they hoped to walk to Guatemala, their final destination. The group led the way to the guest house where they were staying. It had once been a luxurious colonial mansion but was now a semi-derelict, cheap hotel on the bank of the Guayas river. The owner, a kind-hearted woman called María Luisa, let the six of them stay in one room, which was really part of a much larger room that had been sectioned off with wooden boxes and old newspapers. The people on the other side could not be seen, but they could certainly be heard. The six young men spent their first day together drinking maté, joking, telling anecdotes, and discovering that they shared some friends at home. Thereafter they had to spend part of the day searching for funds and transport, but they still had a lot of time on their hands with nowhere to go and nothing to do: lack of funds made it impossible to move on.

According to Calica, Ernesto had begun to feel frustrated and become restless. He was also starting to take an interest in politics and had lengthy conversations with Rojo and Valdovinos, who were the two more politically aware members of the group. Perhaps finding a couple of interlocutors with whom to discuss at length what he had witnessed so far during the trip, formulating ideas which elicited a reaction from them and having the time to argue with them for days on end, provided the right environment for this awakening.

Ernesto played chess with the other inhabitants of the guest house and read a lot as usual. Their room had only two beds and those who got home first in the evening occupied them; the others slept on mattresses on the floor and were sometimes woken by a couple of rats who also lived in the room. Calica observed that, unlike the rats they had met before, these were not scared of humans. They held their ground and seemed to be ready to fight for the space they were forced to share. This, of course, was no joke: Calica, who came from a medical family, had recognised the mark left by the bubonic plague on the forehead of many of the Ecuadoreans they had come across in the poorer areas of Guayaquil. Swarms of mosquitoes, which reproduced easily in the filthy waters of the Guayas river near by, were also part of the menagerie, but none of the men paid much attention to them as they arrived home, exhausted from a day of walking in the tropical heat and eating not much more than the fruit (mainly bananas) on which they were now living.

As luck would have it, the president of the country, Mr Velasco Ibarra, was travelling to Guayaquil on an official engagement. Ernesto and Calica thought this might signal the end of their penury. They hoped they would get transport for all of them on some military aircraft out of this swamp, where they were wasting their time and running up debts. They put on clean clothes, had a shave and marched to the hotel where the president was staying with his entourage. They managed to get as far as his military aide-de-camp, a short, pompous, impeccably clad young man who could not have been less interested in being of assistance. He asked enough questions to discover that their connection with the president's wife was tenuous and then decided not to waste any more of his time, fobbing them off unceremoniously.

After this huge disappointment, Calica, Ernesto and their new friends regrouped. They all sold most of their possessions. Rojo surrendered his expensive overcoat and a gold ring, and also paid part of their debts (he was receiving a little money from the socialist government of Guatemala as a political exile). At this point Calica, who had been playing football with a group of local young men, received an offer to go to Quito to train a football team. Ernesto was also invited. Their travel expenses and lodgings would be covered and they would also get a salary. Calica was tempted but Ernesto chose to continue north. He had decided he wanted to see the socialist experiment in Guatemala where the new president, Colonel Jacobo Arbenz, led a left-leaning government, and to try to arrive there via Panama, like the other members of the group. He told Calica to go to Quito and try his luck. He would join him there if he was unable to get to Panama.

Eventually, Rojo and Valdovinos managed to board one of the United Fruit Company's White Fleet cargo vessels and leave for Panama. Rojo had a contact, a socialist lawyer to whom he had a letter of introduction from none other than Chilean socialist senator Salvador Allende, who arranged these passages. They were promised passage for six but they had to leave two at a time because no ship could carry that many free passengers in one go. In the end, Ernesto and Gualo also managed to board a ship for Panama, leaving behind Andro, who agreed to stay as guarantor of their debt and await rescue by his comrades.

Neither Andro nor Calica ever saw Ernesto again. Andro managed to find a job and pay the group's debts, but eventually he went home to Argentina rather than on to Guatemala, having tired of adventure and constant deprivation. Calica finally reached Venezuela, where he sought out Granado, got himself a job selling pharmaceutical products and stayed for nearly ten years before also going home to Argentina.

In his book, Ricardo Rojo claimed to see the irony of the situation: Ernesto Guevara entering the political fray in Central America thanks to an invitation from the all-powerful and reactionary United Fruit Company to travel on board one of its ships. This may or may not be true, as none of the other protagonists tells us that the *Guayos*, on which Ernesto and Gualo left for Panama, belonged to the United Fruit fleet. Writing in his diary, Ernesto tells us that their passage was arranged by a friend who was a friend of the captain. The *Guayos* finally set sail on 31st October and the days spent at sea were fine for Ernesto, the experienced sailor, but dreadful for Gualo García, who did nothing but be seasick when he was not asleep.

They reached Panama, docked at the port of Balboa in the Canal Zone, which was then controlled by the USA, and made their way to Panama City. Rojo had given them the address of a guest house where they were allowed to sleep in a corridor for a dollar each. They went to the Argentine consulate in search of letters from home, which contained the names of some Panamanian university students, who duly befriended them. Through these students Ernesto met a couple of magazine editors, one of whom published an article he had written about his previous trip with Alberto Granado, while the other eventually published his article about Machu Picchu. Their new student friends were also instrumental in providing the contacts for Ernesto to give a talk about allergies at the Faculty of Medicine of the University of Panama.

Ernesto and Gualo crossed Panama by lorry, train and on foot and arrived at the Pacific coast of Costa Rica. They visited Golfito, a banana port controlled by the United Fruit Company, and Ernesto reported that 'The town is divided into clearly defined zones, with guards who can prevent anyone from passing, and of course the best zone is that of the gringos.'

The next day, in the afternoon, Gualo and Ernesto left on board the *Rio Grande*. The captain lent them the fare and a couple of men who worked on board offered them the floor of their cabin to sleep on. That was good enough for Ernesto. As the ship made its way to Quepos, an abandoned banana port, shaking violently in the rough sea, almost all the passengers, including Gualo, were seasick. Ernesto was left alone with Socorro, an attractive and sexually voracious black young woman. He commented in his diary that she was '*más puta que las gallinas*' (more horny than a hen) – a typical piece of Argentine slang. La Pachuca, as Ernesto had nicknamed the ship because it carried *pachucos* (vagabonds), arrived at Puntarenas at six in the evening.

They disembarked and started for San José, the capital of Costa Rica, which sits in the Central Valley surrounded by volcanic mountains. It is 1,161 metres above sea level and, because it is one of the youngest capitals of Latin America, it has no interesting colonial buildings. Its temperature is pleasant all year round, averaging 23 degrees centigrade. Once there, they visited the consulate, where Ernesto received a letter from Alberto Granado which made him realise how much he missed him. The diplomats also gave them a supply of *yerba mate.*

Costa Rica was a perfect example of how a tiny Central American republic could be prosperous and stable without being told how to conduct its own affairs by the 'colossus to the north', although President Figueres did outlaw the Communist party and on the whole sought to be on good terms with the USA. He had abolished the army and stipulated that its budget should now be used to foster education and culture. He had nationalised the banks and ran an economy which was controlled by the government, but had not interfered with foreign capital. He had given citizenship to the children of black immigrants, given women the vote, and had promoted the drafting of a new constitution.

In San José Ernesto met two people who impressed him and who may well have fostered his growing political commitment: Manuel Mora-Valverde and Juan Bosch. Mora-Valverde was a communist leader whom Ernesto found intelligent and articulate in his analysis of recent Costa Rican history. Juan Bosch, a writer who later became president of the Dominican Republic, discussed politics in general with him and Ernesto noticed the clarity of his ideas and his left-leaning tendencies. He met a third politician, Rómulo Betancourt, who would also become president of his country, Venezuela. Ernesto was not impressed by him and found him to be like a political weathervane.

Ernesto also met the novelists Carlos Luis Fallas and Jorge Icaza while in Costa Rica. Fallas had been born in Alajuela in Costa Rica. As a young man, he had worked on the United Fruit Company's banana plantations, eventually becoming the leader of a banana workers' strike in 1934. His novel *Mamita Yunai* (*Yunai* being the phonetic spelling for United and *mamita* meaning little mother), published in 1940, denounced the unbearable conditions endured by the workers and their ill-treatment at the hands of the American foremen.

Jorge Icaza's *Huasipungo*, published in 1934, is an Indigenist novel which deals with the problems faced by Native Americans in Ecuador. The Indigenist movement preceded magic realism and is important in Latin American literature since it paved the way for writers such as Gabriel García-Márquez and Mario Vargas-Llosa. The novel made its author popular all over the world as it was translated into forty languages. Both writers gave Ernesto autographed copies of their books, which he dutifully read and annotated.

Ernesto and Gualo hitched their way to Nicaragua, where Anastasio 'Tacho' Somoza was ruling the country as if it were his private estate or estancia. Ernesto referred to Nicaragua, El Salvador and Honduras as the estancias of the strongmen in power rather than as countries, a description he had heard in Buenos Aires. As they were walking in pouring rain along a highway in Nicaragua, a car going in the opposite direction stopped. It was a 1946 Ford with US licence plates and, to their total amazement, their friend Ricardo Rojo emerged from it. He was travelling with two Argentine brothers, Walter and Domingo Beveraggi, one of whom was a professor at the University of Boston, hence the licence plates.

Gualo and Ernesto told them the road had become impassable, and so they decided to turn back and return to Rivas, with Gualo and Ernesto now part of the group as well. They spent the evening drinking maté and Rojo and Ernesto told each other how they had fared since they parted in Guayaquil. They dined on fried chicken and rice and the Beveraggi brothers brought out a guitar and sang folk songs from home, making the evening one of nostalgia and camaraderie. Ernesto and Gualo had not had a proper meal for days.

The group split into two the next day: Rojo and Walter Beveraggi flew to San José and Ernesto, Gualo and Domingo Beveraggi drove to Guatemala so that Domingo could sell his car. They drove through Honduras and El Salvador, paying the entry tax at the borders with coffee in one instance and a torch in the other. When they finally entered Guatemala, it was Christmas Eve and they were penniless.

Guatemala City, the capital of the tiny country, is surrounded by luscious tropical vegetation as it sits in the middle of volcanoes, lakes, forests and coffee plantations. Ernesto met up with Valdovinos and his very new Panamanian bride Luzmilla and found a guest house to stay in. Ricardo Rojo had returned from Costa Rica and it was he who introduced Ernesto to Hilda Gadea. A Peruvian exile of mixed Chinese and indigenous blood, she was an economist with a job at the Instituto de Fomento a la Producción (Institute for the Promotion of Production). In Peru, she had been a student leader of the youth wing of the Alianza Popular Revolucionaria Americana, a left-wing social democratic party with continent-wide aspirations. It influenced many Latin American movements, including Bolivia's Movimiento Nacionalista Revolucionario.

Hilda introduced Ernesto to Harold White, an American professor who wrote about Marxism and who wanted his work translated into Spanish. Luzmilla and Ernesto did the job and Ernesto also gave the professor some Spanish lessons. This was a stopgap to cover his most immediate expenses, as he was trying to find a decently paid job in his own field, through the Ministry of Public Health. He had not forgotten that Andro Herrero was still stuck in Guayaquil with their debts and that they had promised to relieve him.

Guatemala was far more interesting than any other place they had seen so far in the region, as the government was implementing agrarian reform. This required guts, since most of the land belonged to the ubiquitous United Fruit Company. Guatemala City was awash with political exiles from Latin American countries under right-wing military dictatorships. They came from Peru, Venezuela, Nicaragua, Honduras and even as far away as Chile. Hilda Gadea's social circle included Nicaraguan professor Edelberto Torres, an indefatigable fighter against Central American dictatorships. Professor Torres had been to China, and Ernesto learnt much from him about the revolution in that country. The Torres family entertained often and welcomed their friends' friends, so Ernesto and Gualo became their guests as well. And that was how, during a New Year's Eve party organised by Myrna Torres at her home, Ernesto met some of the Cuban exiles who had survived the disastrous recent attack on the Moncada Barracks in July: Ñico López, Mario Dalmau, Armando Arancibia and Antonio Darío López.

Fidel Castro's police photo   Fulgencio Batista in power

In Santiago, Cuba, a young lawyer by the name of Fidel Castro, his brother Raúl and a group of like-minded young men and women had plotted to overthrow the government of Fulgencio Batista, who attained power in 1952, with the acquiescence of the USA, by means of a coup. They attempted an assault on the Moncada Barracks on 26th July 1953. It was an abysmal failure. The Castro brothers ended up in jail and most of their co-conspirators were either in custody or dead. However, three times more soldiers than insurgents died in the skirmish.

Batista exacted revenge for this humiliating and dishonourable fact by ordering that ten prisoners be killed for each dead soldier. Seventy insurgents were shot in captivity and it was only the intervention of the Catholic archbishop of Santiago that put an end to the bloodbath.

When Fidel Castro was put on trial and asked who was behind the attack, he said, 'The intellectual author of this revolution is José Martí, the apostle of our independence.' Martí was the great promoter of Cuban independence from Spain, a cause for which he died fighting in 1895. Fidel Castro got fifteen years and his brother Raúl thirteen. But the attack on the

Moncada Barracks marked the beginning of the 26th July Movement which would continue to fight to free Cuba from Fulgencio Batista.

At first Ernesto was very reluctant to believe their exploits and would laugh them off, using an expression which was current in Buenos Aires at the time to mock and show disbelief: 'Now tell me one about cowboys.' But eventually Ñico López and Ernesto became close friends (and it was Ñico López who nicknamed Ernesto Che). The Cubans were marking time in Guatemala because they knew that their revolution would start in earnest as soon as Fidel Castro was set free.

Ernesto had hoped to go to the region of El Petén, where the indigenous population could have benefited from his services (and there was also a most impressive Maya temple, at Tikal). He volunteered to work as a doctor but the authorities demanded revalidation of his medical degree, which would have taken a year. He was eventually offered a post at the Dirección Nacional de Estadística (Office of National Statistics), but he turned it down because it came with the demand that he join the Partido Guatemalteco del Trabajo (the Labour Party of Guatemala), which was communist in its politics. He refused to do so. He told Hilda Gadea, who had been the mediator, 'It isn't that I'm not in agreement with communist ideology, it's the methods I don't like. They shouldn't try to recruit followers like that, it's not right.'

Since Ernesto was unable to work as a doctor, he and Ñico López became street vendors. They sold a framed picture of Nuestro Señor de Esquipulas, a black Christ who was very popular in Guatemala. Ñico had wired it with a small bulb so that it lit up and Ernesto went round peddling the gadget, constantly adding to the list of amazing miracles which he said the icon worked.

Ernesto had hit it off with Hilda Gadea because she was as well read as he was. He had found someone with whom he could discuss Marx's *Das Kapital*, Engels' *Socialism: Utopian and Scientific* and *Anti-Dühring*, and Lenin's *Imperialism, the Highest Stage of Capitalism*, as well as Tolstoy, Gorky, Dostoyevsky and Kropotkin. José Carlos Mariátegui, the Peruvian thinker who was the first Latin American to blend nationalist and indigenous thought with international Marxism in the 1920s, came up often in their discussions. He had lived his years of exile in Paris, a city that

Ernesto always dreamt of visiting, and Hilda would tease him, saying he was interested only in the bohemian aspects of life in Paris, sitting around in cafés all day long.

It may have been during this period of studies and discussions that Ernesto developed his idea that Marxism is a developing science, just like biology. However, throughout his life, he was reluctant to accept the label of Marxist, although he was familiar with Marxist ideas from an early age. He had read Marx as a young man in his father's library; Alberto Granado was already a Marxist when they met and decided to travel together; Tita Infante, whom he befriended at the Faculty of Medicine in Buenos Aires, was a member of the Communist party; his mentor in Peru, Maestro Hugo Pesce, had been a disciple of Mariátegui and also had an influence on his political development. His life-long friend Pepe González-Aguilar used to say that Ernesto developed his own political thought, taking Marx as a starting point but incorporating ideas from other more recent thinkers as well.

In his youth in Argentina Ernesto had found the Communist party stratified, monolithic and out of touch with the people. He would never change his perception of the established communist parties, wherever they were from, and this coloured his behaviour towards them: he did not consider them true followers of Marx, even if they had appropriated his ideas and used them as they saw fit.

While in Guatemala, Ernesto devoted time to working on a study of the role of the doctor in various Latin American countries. It dealt with the fact that in most cases the state did not offer any sort of medical assistance or protection, as well as describing the pitiful conditions in which the medical profession was forced to work, and their lack of resources. It was really a compendium of statistics he had been collecting from the countries he had visited. Like others before him, Ernesto was coming to the conclusion that the attitude of those countries' governments allowed exploitation by local oligarchies in cahoots with US big business. His reading was helping him to see that such matters were dealt with differently in the Soviet Union.

By mid-February 1954, there were persistent rumours that the USA was going to invade Guatemala, having had enough of President Arbenz's socialist reforms. Colonel Castillo-Armas, a Guatemalan, would lead the rebel forces but he was merely doing the dirty work for the US government and for the Dulles brothers. John Foster Dulles was the Eisenhower administration's secretary of state as well as a lawyer whose firm had represented the United Fruit Company in its various disputes with Central American governments. His brother Allen Dulles was the director of the CIA. Both were avowed opponents of communism.

Ricardo Rojo and Gualo García decided to leave. Rojo was going to head north to the USA, while Gualo was ready to go home to Argentina and settle down. Valdovinos had already left for Buenos Aires with his wife, who had been given a diplomatic posting at the Panamanian embassy there. So, of the group of six in Ecuador, only Ernesto was still on the road. He was keen to witness the American-sponsored invasion and thought that, even though the Guatemalan government had the army on its side, it should also arm the population, who would help defend their recent social advances.

In his book, *My Friend Che*, Ricardo Rojo tells us that American pilots dropped thousands of leaflets a week before the rumoured invasion. These informed the population that the liberating army of Colonel Castillo-Armas was massed on the frontier. The colonel himself frequently went on the air, calling on the population to abandon the Arbenz government. The Roman Catholic church also took advantage of the situation to exaggerate the leftist leanings of the men in power.

By 18th June the ground invasion had started, with the rebel army arriving from Honduras. During the first few days, they advanced fifteen kilometres without meeting any resistance. Then there was a clash with government troops, which dispersed the invaders. But everyone knew the real battle would be fought in the capital. The government had 7,000 armed men, but Jacobo Arbenz was a professional soldier and was not prepared to hand over weapons to trade unionists, university students or the political parties that claimed loyalty to his revolution, or to the *campesinos*, so as to swell this number. Instead, he resigned as president, arguing that he wanted to avoid bloodshed. He had hardly stepped down when his right-wing political enemies started plotting the bloodbath that would follow. It turned Guatemala into an extremely violent and unstable country for years to come.

According to Ricardo Rojo, the acting head of the Argentine embassy turned up at Ernesto's guest house at the crack of dawn. He had enjoyed a cordial relationship with Rojo, Valdo, Gualo and Ernesto, who had received gifts of *yerba mate* and Argentine newspapers from him (even if he was President Perón's envoy). He now demanded that Ernesto join him at the embassy, for his own safety. Ernesto argued that nobody knew him and he was not in real danger. The diplomat soon disabused him of that notion, saying he had been warned there was an Argentine troublemaker on the list of those to be executed. The CIA had noticed him in Guatemala and opened a file on him, following his movements with keen interest. The diplomat argued that it was absurd for Ernesto to imagine that he could do what the government was not prepared to do for its own survival. And that was how Ernesto ended up spending about a month at the Argentine embassy as the guest of Perón's government.

It later emerged that President Perón had a special relationship with Arbenz's predecessor: in May 1947, Guatemalan President Juan José Arévalo sanctioned the new Labour Code, as a result of which US shipping companies announced they would no longer serve Guatemalan ports. Since the country did not possess its own fleet, the decision was tantamount to a blockade. As soon as Perón heard of this, he simply ordered the Argentine merchant navy to include Guatemalan ports on their itinerary. He also took the opportunity to send a cargo of weapons with the first vessels to leave for Guatemala. Perón was awarded the Order of the Quetzal, Guatemala's highest decoration for a foreigner.

This explains why Perón was against the coup. In due course he obtained permission to land several military aircraft, so that those Argentines who had taken refuge at their embassy could go home. Ernesto refused to return to Argentina but instead got safe conduct to Mexico. Once there, he met up with Ricardo Rojo and told him what had happened in Guatemala after the fall of the Arbenz government. The United Fruit Company once again reigned supreme, Arbenz's followers had been massacred, there had been a political purge and the programmes for agrarian reform had been reversed. The landowners were back and the *campesinos* were disenfranchised once again.

Guatemala was a turning point in Ernesto's life, not only because of the lesson learnt that Arbenz, by not arming the people, students and workmen, had been instrumental in his own downfall, but also because, as he confided in a letter to his mother, he had enjoyed the skirmishes, the bombardments, and the violent struggle. In the letter he said: 'I am a little ashamed to admit that I had the most marvellous time during these past days. That magic feeling of invulnerability that I was telling you about in a previous letter made me relish seeing people running around like mad as soon as they saw the planes, or at night, during the blackouts when the city was filled with bullets.' He'd been impressed with the power of the bombers he'd witnessed, experiencing an excitement beyond anything he'd felt in even his most daredevil moments thus far.

It was in Guatemala that Ernesto espoused violence once and for all, as a means of liberating our continent from foreign domination. He would never renege on violence, for he truly thought it was the only way the enemy could be beaten. Gandhi's teachings on non-violence were but a distant memory. In fact, whether consciously or not, from then on he was on a quest for a people ready to rise up in arms so that he could throw in his lot with them. A man who had been flirting with death all his life – because of his infirmity – now seemed to be playing a perilous game, taunting death. He seemed to be saying, 'Come and get me.'

TWELVE

(1954–1955)

At the border crossing into Mexico Ernesto met a young Guatemalan, 'an engineering student called Julio Roberto Cáceres-Valle who also seems to be obsessed by travelling. He intends to go to Veracruz after a while and attempt the big jump (to the US) from there. We travelled to Mexico City together and now I am here alone although he may be back,' Ernesto wrote in a letter to his parents.

Patojo, as Cáceres was nicknamed because that is what young or small people are called in Guatemala, was to become Ernesto's inseparable companion. They worked together and they shared views about the struggle against US domination in Latin America. When the invasion of Cuba was being prepared in Mexico, Patojo volunteered to join the rebels, but Castro turned him down because he did not want to turn his guerrilla force into 'a mosaic of foreigners', as Ernesto put it. Once the revolution triumphed, Patojo disposed of his few possessions in Guatemala and turned up at Ernesto's door. Ernesto gave him a job in the public administration and before long he became the first head of personnel of the industrialisation department of the National Institute of Agrarian Reform, which Ernesto presided over in 1959. He eventually returned to Guatemala to rejoin the struggle and die in combat there.

En route to Mexico City, Ernesto and Patojo visited the archaeological ruins at Mitla, near Oaxaca. They were not as impressive as Machu Picchu but Ernesto thought they were interesting as a foretaste of the marvels of the Aztec and Mayan civilisations throughout Mexico to which he was so looking forward.

Once in Mexico City, Ernesto decided to look for work. He visited Ulises Petit de Murat, an Argentine friend of his parents who had exiled himself in Mexico because of his intense dislike of Perón. Petit worked as a screenwriter and was very successful. In those days, Mexico boasted a thriving film industry, with actors who became international stars, such as Pedro Armendáriz, Cantinflas and María Félix. Accompanied by his teenage daughter, Petit took Ernesto on a tour of the city, fed him and even invited him to stay with his family. Ernesto declined as he found it too bourgeois and religious for his taste: he was also very keen to preserve his independence.

In a letter to his father dated 30th September 1954, Ernesto says, 'I have seen enough of Mexico to realise that matters will not be very easy, but I have arrived here with a bullet-proof spirit ... Eventually, I will apply for a visa for the USA and will accept whatever is offered over there, but that would be in a few months' time.' Now that he could analyse the Guatemalan experience from a distance and with a cool head, he had arrived at the conclusion that the USA would continue to intervene in its 'back yard' whenever a Latin American country threatened its hegemony by taking crucial decisions independently and without seeking its agreement in advance. He also believed that the Soviet Union and the USA were on a collision course. But, more importantly, the Guatemalan fiasco had radicalised him. He was now, aged twenty-six, taking a serious interest in politics, although he was not yet a Marxist, and he had become convinced that armed struggle was the only way forward. As he would famously say later, 'I was born in Argentina, I fought in Cuba and I began to be a revolutionary in Guatemala.'

He visited the national museum, which proved to be extremely rewarding, satisfying his archaeological curiosity and introducing him to the frescoes of the big four: Rivera, Tamayo, Siqueiros and Orozco. These he found impressive, although he did not think they were properly displayed. The Mexican Muralist Movement to which the four artists belonged was born with the Mexican Revolution, which brought about political and social renovation, and the artists were all communists. The muralists decorated public buildings with huge colourful figures, some in the Maya tradition, some in a contemporary style.

Ernesto and Patojo had rented a room together in downtown Mexico City, and now, in order to stay afloat financially, they went into business together. Ernesto took photographs of children in the parks of Mexico City and, once they were developed, Patojo delivered them to their parents. Ernesto was also trying to insert himself into the world of medicine, one way or another, in order to continue the studies into allergy he had begun under Dr Pisani, as well as to find a position which brought in some regular cash.

He did the rounds of the hospitals, managing to meet Professor Mario Salazar-Mallén, Mexico's leading researcher into allergies, who invited him to cooperate with him at the Hospital General. There, Ernesto was able to put into practice all he had learnt in Buenos Aires some years earlier. He also worked at the children's hospital a few mornings a week. Towards the end of October, Ñico López, his Cuban friend from Guatemala, turned up at the allergies ward of the Hospital General, looking for a doctor to help a fellow Cuban who had been taken ill, and ran into Ernesto. They renewed their friendship and as a result Ernesto met up again with the exiled Cuban veterans of the Moncada Barracks attack whom he had first come across in Costa Rica.

By the beginning of December, Ernesto had met the Director of the Agencia Latina de Noticias (Latin American News Agency). The agency was created by Perón, who thought news about Latin America should be reported by fellow Latin Americans as opposed to North Americans. He offered Ernesto a job as a non-permanent correspondent, which meant that he could stop chasing Mexican children through the city's squares, being nice to their parents in the hope that they would purchase their photos. It had been exhausting and not very lucrative. He kept on with his research at the Hospital General because he was enjoying it and he was obtaining interesting results.

Hilda Gadea had not managed to go home to Peru as she had experienced problems in Guatemala City with the Peruvian embassy officials, who refused to renew her passport. She was taken into custody and then sent to a prison at the frontier by the Guatemalan authorities, because she had cooperated with the previous government. There she managed to buy her way out of jail and over the Mexican border.

Hilda and Ernesto in Mexico during their honeymoon at the Mayan ruins
at Papaloapan and Palenque, 1955

She and Ernesto began seeing each other again frequently, though their relationship had its ups and downs. Hilda was annoyed, for example, because Ernesto refused to escort her to a New Year's Eve party. Instead he chose to see the new year in serving as a night watchman at the premises of the Organization of American States.

Pepe González-Aguilar once told me that Ernesto had had a sexual relationship with a much older Indian woman, Sabina, who was a maid at his parents' house in Buenos Aires and had looked after him during his frequent bouts of asthma. Pepe thought that Hilda, half-Indian herself, perhaps subconsciously reminded him of that clandestine liaison. In his view, Ernesto had never been in love or wanted to settle down with her: he valued her as a loyal *compañera*, a good friend in hard times and his intellectual equal.

Ernesto was now spending more time with his Cuban friends, who gathered at the home of Cuban exile María Antonia González and her Mexican husband Dick Medrano, a professional boxer. Ernesto was operating on the ovaries of female cats he picked up from the streets as part of a scientific experiment and was reading John Reed's *Insurgent Mexico* and the memoirs of Pancho Villa. He wanted to know why the Mexican Revolution had failed and why the heroic exploits of its charismatic leaders

Pancho Villa and Emiliano Zapata had been forgotten. The Partido Revolucionario Institucional created by the revolution was still in power, but it had betrayed its raison d'être.

In a letter to his father dated 10th February 1955 he tells him that 'Mexico is totally in the hands of the Americans, so much so that for Nixon's arrival (for the Pan American Games) they threw all the Puerto Rican nationalists as well as dissidents of any other flavour into jail.' He talks about the censorship of the press and expresses concern about the impunity with which the FBI were operating in Mexico. In contrast to the corrupt, financially crippled Mexico, prevented by the United States from having any independent industry of its own, he regarded Argentina as 'an oasis in our America, we should give Perón all the support possible to avoid going into a war that promises to be terrible.' It is hard to know just what war Ernesto was fearful of Latin America being dragged into – presumably it was to be with the Soviet Union.

The Pan-American Games were held in Mexico City between 12th and 16th March 1955 and Ernesto was appointed to cover them as the correspondent and photographer for Agencia Latina de Noticias. But he told his aunt Beatriz Guevara-Lynch that, after they ended, 'a laconic telegram arrived from the Agencia Latina, in which it informed us that it was bringing to a close all operations and that each correspondent could do what he thought best with the personnel in his charge (not a word about salaries).'

In April Ernesto was congratulated on a paper he had submitted to a conference on allergy. His mentor, Professor Salazar-Mallén, said he would publish it in a specialist journal. He also offered Ernesto lodgings at the Hospital General, as well as a grant and some financial assistance. His salary was only 150 Mexican pesos a month but, as the arrangement included lodgings, meals and laundry services, he thought it was quite enough for the time he intended to spend in Mexico City. His paper 'Research into the treatment of skin conditions using the antigens in semi-digested foods' was published in the *Revista Iberoamericana de Alergología* (Latin American Magazine on Allergology) in May. The Professor also invited him home where Ernesto met his wife, Olvido Tapia. Years later, she would remember him:

My daughter, who was very little at the time, was fascinated by Ernesto and he by her. He used to put her on his back and walk long distances with her on his shoulders, simply to please her: he was both courteous and respectful. When the professor spoke with people Ernesto did not know, Ernesto would walk away from the group and if Mario did not call him, he would not take part in the conversation even if he knew the subject being discussed really well. We even invited him to live with us because we had the space and facilities for it but he refused. He said it was not right for a student to live in his teacher's house, that the Maestro needed privacy and that there were distances that should be kept. There was no way we could persuade him to come and live with us, he preferred to sleep in his sleeping bag on a hospital bed in a small room used for consultations and instruments, until he had his own apartment.

For Ernesto his need to be on his own at times and to come and go as he pleased was more important than having a home with regular meals and other creature comforts.

At the end of April 1955, Ricardo Rojo returned from New York, where he had spent a year at Columbia University doing a postgraduate degree. To support himself there, he had worked in a metal factory. He contacted Ernesto and they arranged to meet to watch the workers' parade on 1st May at the Zócalo, Mexico City's main square. According to Rojo, Ernesto said the parade looked like a funeral and that the Mexican Revolution was in fact dead, and had been dead for a while even though nobody had realised it.

Hilda Gadea went to the square with Ernesto. She later wrote that they met José Manuel Fortuny there. He had been the Secretary-General of the Partido Guatemalteco del Trabajo but Ernesto had never managed to meet him while in Guatemala City, although Hilda knew him. When Ernesto asked him why the Guatemalan government had decided not to fight and repel the invasion, Fortuny replied that they saw the situation as an extremely difficult one. They believed it was better to give up power and then go on fighting, and they were in fact trying to continue their struggle.

Ernesto insisted that it would have been better to fight from a position of power. Fortuny asked what he meant, in a tone verging on hostility. Ernesto replied, 'Exactly that. If President Arbenz had left the capital and gone to the countryside with a group of real revolutionaries, the possibility of fighting would have been very different, and besides, his legal position as president would have turned him into a symbol and a great moral encouragement, and then the chances of rebuilding the Revolutionary Government would have been infinitely more favourable.' Fortuny did not argue but bid them farewell. Ernesto concluded, 'Those are just excuses. There are many advantages when you fight while in power, but in any case, whether they were in power or not, the only thing to do was to fight.'

After they had spent a weekend together in Cuernavaca, Ernesto accepted Hilda's invitation to move in with her. On 15th May 1955, after twenty-two months in detention, Fidel Castro and some twenty survivors of the Moncada Barracks attack were set free in Cuba, following an amnesty. Batista had realised that if the Moncadistas were killed while in jail, the finger of blame would be pointed at him, while if they were bumped off out in the streets of Havana, it would be easier to disguise who was responsible. But the Moncadistas made a point of not going home, never sleeping in the same house twice and generally taking precautions to avoid being easy targets. It was all rather cloak and dagger, but Fidel Castro had always been good at deception, at duping his enemies and never being where he was expected to be. Ñico López, Ernesto's first Cuban friend, had already returned to Havana when Castro announced that the struggle would continue. He started organising his own political movement, the 26th July Movement, which took its name from the date of the failed attack on the Moncada Barracks in 1953. Its black and red colours have come to symbolise the Cuban Revolution.

Cuba had been the jewel in the Spanish colonial crown since its discovery by Christopher Columbus in 1492, and it would remain so for four centuries. Having decimated the aboriginal population through the diseases they brought to the island, the brutal treatment they meted out to them and the subhuman working conditions on the sugar plantations they had established, the Spanish needed to import African slaves to continue the thriving sugar industry. Cuba's economic dependence on a single crop would prove to be disastrous for the country throughout its history. In 1741

Britain invaded Cuba and held on to it for eleven months. Once the British were ousted, the Spanish built the Fortress of San Carlos de La Cabaña in Havana, the largest in the Americas, to deter the British from returning and to protect the island from any other intruders.

José Martí, Cuba's national hero, was born in Havana in 1853. The 1868–78 civil war against Spain and the cruelty of the Spanish masters towards their black slaves were formative influences. By the age of sixteen he was writing about what he was seeing. After being imprisoned in Havana and sent into exile in Spain in 1871 he published his *El Presidio Político en Cuba*, (Cuba's Political Jails) in which he denounced the horrors of colonial prisons. Martí was twenty-five when he returned to Cuba, having studied in Madrid, but in 1879 he was again deported to Spain, managing to escape to the USA a few years later. In 1895, while still in America, he created the Partido Revolucionario Cubano, the first party created in the Americas with the purpose of carrying out a revolution. It paved the way for the war of emancipation which would break out in 1895, bringing together the émigré community as well as Cubans of all classes and ideologies who sought the island's independence.

By 1886 slavery had been abolished; the sugar industry was modernised and the emancipated slaves became salaried workers. In 1893 Martí met with Máximo Gómez in the Dominican Republic and with Antonio Maceo in Costa Rica to secure the participation of the two generals who had become legendary heroes of the struggles of 1868–78. In 1895 all three arrived in Cuba to lead the country's indigenous insurgents to war against the occupying Spanish forces. Martí died in combat at Dos Ríos on 19th May 1895 but by now his revolutionary ideas had taken root. In the context of Che's involvement later in life it's interesting to note Martí's belief that the independence of Cuba was crucial to the independence of the whole continent because it would prevent the USA from using the island as a bridgehead from which to launch its attempt to conquer Spanish America.

In 1898 the USA declared war on Spain so as to be able to intervene in Cuba. After a naval blockade of the island and heavy shelling of the cities of Matanzas, Cárdenas, Baracoa, Manzanillo and Santa Cruz del Sur, and a particularly vicious attack on Santiago de Cuba by the Americans, the Spanish were ready to negotiate their exit. The Treaty of Paris, signed in

1898 by the USA and Spain, marked the end of Spanish rule in Cuba, but the Cubans themselves were not even present, let alone signatories. The island was handed over to its new masters in the capital city of a European country.

The Platt Amendment was imposed on the first Cuban constitution of 1901, which gave the USA the right to intervene in Cuba if it felt the political situation there to be threatening, a naval base on the southern tip of the island at Guantánamo Bay (which is still in operation to this day) and permission for American corporations to invest in the Cuban economy. By the 1950s, US citizens were in control of 80 per cent of Cuba's utilities, 90 per cent of the cattle ranches, most of the oil-refining industry, 50 per cent of the railways, 40 per cent of the sugar industry and 25 per cent of all bank deposits.

Between 1902 and 1959 a succession of governments in Cuba toed the American line. Some were legitimately elected, some corrupt, some bloody, but none sought Cuba's emancipation from the American yoke. However, the Cuban workforce organised itself as the Confederación Nacional Obrera de Cuba (Cuban National Workers' Confederation) in the 1920s, the students created the Federación Estudiantil Universitaria (Federation of University Students) and in 1925 the Partido Comunista de Cuba (Communist Party of Cuba) was founded. In 1939 the Confederación de Trabajadores de Cuba (Confederation of Cuban Workers) came into being. Between 1934 and 1937 militarism was on the rise. Sergeant Fulgencio Batista came to power for the first time in 1940, through the ballot box, and served a four-year term. On 5th July 1940 the new constitution was approved. It was advanced for its time and the communists participated in its drafting. Ramón Grau was in power from 1944 to 1948 and Carlos Prío from 1948 to 1952. Both were demagogues who continued with the policies of economic dependence on the USA.

On 10th March 1952 Fulgencio Batista returned to power by means of a coup. The Platt Amendment was removed from the Cuban constitution but the island continued to be an American colony in all but name. It was also a period of much violence and repression. Although Cuba was wealthy, its workforce was poor. The sugar industry only employed workers during the four-month season. The rest of the year they were expected to survive as best they could. American tourism companies and Mafia bosses had turned the island into a paradise for the rich and famous. Havana was the hemisphere's capital of vice: a giant combination of nightclub, casino and whorehouse.

In May 1955, Ernesto wrote to his father about his scientific work with Professor Salazar-Mallén and various projects he had begun or had in mind, saying, 'These same prospects enable me to suggest the possibility of a change in my aspiration to roam aimlessly.' With hindsight, his father was to find that another paragraph gave a more accurate picture of his son's future: 'I am waiting for some recommendation to march on the fields where dawn is maturing, as they say. In any case, although everything is green and although my convictions grow firmer by the day, I will not let slip the opportunity of embarking on some extra little trip: Havana in particular attracts my attention as somewhere to fill my heart with landscapes well interspersed with quotes from Lenin.'

On 14th June Ernesto had his twenty-seventh birthday and about this time the Agencia Latina paid him half of what he was owed, so he used some of it to pay off his debts. On 24th June Raúl Castro left Havana for Mexico City, having sought asylum at the Mexican embassy. The regime had accused him, falsely, of planting a bomb in a cinema in Havana. Fidel Castro's liberties, meanwhile, were curtailed. He was not allowed to broadcast and the newspaper La Calle (The Street), which he had used to publish his opinions, was shut down. He asked his brother Raúl to prepare those of his followers who were already in Mexico City for his arrival there.

A few days after Raúl arrived he met Ernesto at the home of María Antonia González and they became friends very quickly, as they shared many political points of view and aspirations. Raúl visited Ernesto at home and they also spent time together at the Librería Zaplana, a bookshop which sold Soviet books and had a cinema screen in the back of the premises where Soviet films were shown. The Instituto de Intercambio Cultural Mexicano-Ruso (Institute for Russo-Mexican Cultural Exchange) operated from the same premises. Raúl Castro had met Nikolai Leonov, a member of the Institute, on board ship when they were both travelling back from the Festival Mundial de las Juventudes, a worldwide youth festival held in Sofia, Bulgaria in 1953, but they had not seen each other since they disembarked in Havana. They ran into each other in Mexico City, where Leonov was posted at the Soviet embassy and in due course Ernesto also met the Russian. Years later, Nikolai Leonov, by then a KGB general, would be Ernesto's interpreter in the Soviet Union and they would become friends.

Fidel Castro arrived in Mexico City by bus on 8th July, having spent the night at Veracruz after flying from Cuba via Venezuela. A few days later, the bulk of the Cuban exiles met at Calle Emparán 49-C, where María Antonia González lived. Although neither Ernesto nor Fidel Castro made a note of the exact date of their first encounter, both agreed that they talked for hours right through the night. It was a meeting of minds. As Castro described his plans for an invasion of Cuba, the guerrilla army he was about to create, the travel arrangements, the supply of weapons and his ideas for the struggle, Ernesto was completely won over.

By the end of that very long night, the expedition might still have no boat, troops or weapons, but it had a doctor. Ernesto had enthusiastically accepted Castro's invitation to join him. Since, until then, only his brother Raúl had been selected by Castro and pledged his unconditional participation, Ernesto was able to claim in his diary that he was the third member of the expedition. Fidel Castro would later say, 'One could see he was imbued with a profound spirit of hatred ... for imperialism, not only because his political education had reached considerable development but also because not long before he had had the opportunity of witnessing in Guatemala the criminal imperialist intervention by means of which the mercenary soldiers put an end to the revolution of that country.'

Castro reckoned that Ernesto, who had never joined any political party, already thought like a Marxist at the time of their meeting. Ernesto admired Castro for attemping a coup d'état (something which he would have been unable to do in his own country), even if it was an abysmal failure. He, in turn, would eventually earn the respect of his Cuban comrades-in-arms for his willingness to risk his life for the liberation of a country in which he had never set foot. What better credentials could a man have than to follow the example of the great liberator Simón Bolívar himself?

There could not have been two more different men, coming from totally opposite backgrounds. While Ernesto could trace his ancestry to the last Spanish Viceroy of Peru, José de la Serna e Hinojosa, Count of Los Andes,

Fidel Castro was the illegitimate son of an illiterate Spanish peasant. Ángel Castro had originally gone to Cuba as a Spanish soldier in a regiment sent to quash a rebellion and had then returned there from Galicia and settled near Birán, on the north coast of Cuba's Oriente province, where he had acquired a sugar plantation. His son Fidel was born there. His mother was Lina Ruz, who was Cuban but also of Galician stock.

Ángel Castro had been married before and had two children from this first marriage: Lidia and Pedro. Lina Ruz had been a servant in his household while his wife was alive. Ángel and Lina had seven children: Ángela, Agustina, Ramón, Fidel, Raúl, Emma and Juana. Fidel was born on 13th August 1926, before his father married his mother. There was no love lost between Fidel and his father, whom he called a *latifundista* who exploited the *campesinos* working for him on his large sugar-cane plantation. With his mother he had an affectionate relationship, in spite of the fact that she disapproved of his and Raúl's revolutionary activities.

As a boy of six, Fidel Castro had asked to be sent to school. Neither parent had received an education. He was sent to the Jesuit school, Colegio Dolores, and then to the Colegio Belén, also run by Jesuits. He became interested in sports and was voted best athlete in 1944. He was a very good student and in 1945 he went to law school, where he was also a diligent student. His training as a lawyer stood him in good stead when he was tried in 1953 for leading the attack on the Moncada Barracks and he chose to defend himself. His impassioned speech, 'History will absolve me,' became an effective propaganda pamphlet after the triumph of the revolution (the phrase was originally coined by Adolf Hitler).

Fidel and Che complemented each other. Che was probably the only person capable of stimulating Castro's intellect until Gabriel García-Márquez came along many years later, and it is a shame that there is no record of their conversations.

When their paths crossed, both men had met their match. Che may have been shy and reserved but he was no less passionate. Fidel was a total extrovert and loved to talk. Che was both a thinker and a man of action. Fidel was a pragmatist while Che was a man of principles whatever the consequences. However, both men shared a devotion to José Martí – the Cuban scholar and patriot who was killed in battle in 1895, fighting for the island's independence from Spain. The twenty-eight volumes of his works are a staple in every Cuban's education. Che had discovered him, admired him and been inspired by his writings long before his arrival on the Cuban political scene.

On 26th July Castro and his fellow Cubans went to the Monument for the Child Heroes of Chapultepec in Mexico City to lay a floral offering on the second anniversary of the assault on the Moncada Barracks. Hilda and Ernesto attended as well. At the beginning of August Hilda told Ernesto she was pregnant. They decided they should get married, and a colleague of Ernesto's at the Hospital General, Dr Alberto Martínez-Lozano, made the necessary arrangements at his native village of Tepotzotlan, to the north of Mexico City, where they would be asked to provide only their passports and a prenuptial certificate.

Ernesto Guevara, Hilda Gadea, Raúl Castro, Jesús Montané (another Cuban who had just arrived in Mexico City), Lucila Velázquez and two colleagues of Ernesto's travelled to Tepotzotlan for the wedding on 18th August. It was a simple private ceremony, which Fidel Castro did not attend for security reasons. They all then went back to Mexico City and Ernesto prepared an *asado*, a typical Argentine barbecue. Fidel Castro and other Cuban friends were there.

A military coup in Argentina ousted President Perón in September, to the delight of the Roman Catholic church, the landed gentry and the cattle oligarchy, as well as the USA. Perón took refuge on a Paraguayan gunboat docked at the port of Buenos Aires and then sought asylum in Paraguay, a country governed by another strongman, General Alfredo Stroessner.

In his early youth in Argentina, Ernesto had been heavily influenced by his family's staunch opposition to the Perón government. Once he began travelling and saw how the rest of Latin America was being governed, how the people lived and died and were humiliatingly subjugated to US interests by the de facto military presidents that ruled most countries, he began to understand why Perón had captured the imagination of the disenfranchised and exploited working classes of Argentina. And Perón was ousted by a military junta of right-wing devout Roman Catholic men who would bend to the will of the USA. It could not possibly be an improvement on Perón who, even if he had many flaws, could be credited with standing up to American imperialism, Ernesto's chief bête noire. In a letter to his mother dated 24th September 1955, Ernesto confided his feelings:

> I confess, in all sincerity, that the fall of Perón made me very bitter – not for him, but for what it means to the whole of America, because whether you like it or not and in spite of the forced backing down of recent times, Argentina was the champion of those of us who believe that the enemy is in the north.

In the same letter, he also mentioned his marriage, quite casually. If it was really such an important event for him, would it not have merited a separate letter to his mother? According to Pepe González-Aguilar, contrary to the bride's protestations that Ernesto made constant requests for her hand in marriage, he married her because he had got her pregnant. Certainly in none of his writings of the time (granted that they were published posthumously and edited by his second wife Aleida March) does he make any mention of his desire to tie the knot, settle down, have a home or anything else along those lines. Hilda Gadea's book about her years with Ernesto was published in Mexico in 1972, when he had been dead five years and was therefore in no position to counter her version of events. Aleida March published *Otra Vez*, his diary of that period, in 2000. By then, Hilda Gadea was also dead and, like Ernesto, could not comment on any of it.

Ernesto and Hilda moved to a new home, and in October Ernesto was part of a group of some twenty amateur climbers who got together in an attempt to reach the top of Popocatepetl, Mexico's highest volcano, which is some sixty-five kilometres from the capital. Ernesto had met the others through a colleague at the Hospital General. The climb can be arduous and dangerous but on that day there was no wind and the group made it to the top. Ernesto left behind a small Argentine flag he had taken with him expressly for that purpose. The leader of the group, León Bessudo, who had been escorting similar groups for many years, took Ernesto's photograph with his flag. This story proves that for the moment he still thought of himself as Argentine, so much so that he had willingly accepted the nickname by which his Cuban friends addressed him (given to him because he had the very Argentine habit of interjecting the word when he spoke). He had become Che.

Ernesto in Mexico climbing Popocatepetl

The nickname suited him. It had an immediacy and brevity that went well with his personality, for he was a young man on the move. To be called by a word that was an adjective or an interjection rather than a noun or a proper name amused him. It appealed to the total iconoclast and debunker of myths he had always been. So Che it was from then on. Even Hilda now called him Che.

That month he and Hilda invited various Cuban friends to dinner to bid Castro farewell, as he was travelling to the United States in search of support for his forthcoming revolution. He planned to tour several US cities in search of Cuban exiles, just as José Martí had created clubs in support of the revolution he had led in 1895.

In November Che and Hilda took a few days off to go on their much postponed honeymoon. They visited Veracruz and the port and beach at

Mocambo. They went south and spent one night on the Coatzacoalcos river and then went by train to the Mayan ruins at Papaloapan and Palenque. They went to Campeche and then by bus to Mérida, in Yucatán. From there they travelled on to the ruins at Chichen Itza and Uxmal, returning to Veracruz by sea. There was an Argentine cargo ship at the port and Che went on board to ask his compatriots for some *yerba mate* before they returned to Mexico City by train and bus. Because she was pregnant, Hilda had not really enjoyed the two-week trek, but Che was elated by the Mayan ruins, which he had always wanted to see.

In December Fidel Castro returned from his seven-week tour of the USA, during which he had famously said, at a rally at the Palm Garden Hotel in New York at the end of October, 'In 1956 we will be free or we will be martyrs.' On 24th December 1955, the Cuban exiles met for the traditional Cuban Christmas dinner in the home of Haida Pi. It consisted of roast pork, *moros y cristianos* (black beans with rice) and yucca with *mojo* (a garlic, onion and lemon juice sauce). Che and Hilda heard Castro speak on agrarian reform, the nationalisation of Cuba's resources and the many other measures they would introduce once the revolution had triumphed.

THIRTEEN
(1956)

While Fidel Castro and his team of incipient revolutionaries started to make preparations for their invasion of the island of Cuba and Hilda's pregnancy progressed without incident, Che continued to carry out his scientific research at the Hospital General under Professor Salazar-Mallén and to read avidly. He was preparing another paper on his research for submission to a conference on allergies which would take place in Veracruz in March 1956. Hilda was expected to give birth at the end of February but she went into labour on 15th February 1956. Che took her to a clinic and their daughter was born that evening. They called her Hilda Beatriz (Beatriz Guevara-Lynch was Che's favourite aunt).

A few days later, Castro visited them with Faustino Pérez, a Cuban comrade newly arrived in Mexico City. Other followers were also arriving from different locations to start their training. They were lodged in various houses which had been rented for the purpose with the funds donated by Cubans living in the USA. Castro started acquiring the weapons needed for the expedition. Antonio del Conde, a Mexican arms dealer and sympathiser, was in charge of procurement. His Cuban friends nicknamed him El Cuate (a Mexican expression which means comrade or buddy).

The future guerrillas went into training, doing their best not to attract unwanted attention. They took long walks down Avenida de los Insurgentes, one of Mexico City's avenues, and rowed on the lake in Chapultepec Park. Che would join them when he was not required at the Hospital General. He would also go to the apartment at Calle Insurgentes 5, where some of the Cubans lived, whenever one of his comrades was in need of medical attention. Soon, the group began to climb nearby hills and practise gymnastics and personal defence as well as continuing with the long walks and rowing.

Towards the end of March, Castro arranged access to a shooting range called Los Gamitos in Santa Fé on the outskirts of the city. There they practised shooting at targets at various distances, as well as at live ones, using weapons with telescopic sights. They shot rabbits and turkeys, and those who killed them were allowed to eat them. Che now gave up his scientific research and trained with the rest of the future combatants during the day. In the early evenings they studied politics and discussed the Cuban situation or listened while Colonel Alberto Bayo, a veteran of the Spanish Civil War, gave them lessons on guerrilla warfare.

Ernesto, nbow having adopted his nickname, "Che,"
at target practice at Los Gamitos

As time passed and more future combatants arrived, it became necessary to find a location outside Mexico City in which training could take place in real campaign conditions. Colonel Bayo and Ciro Redondo finally located a house which met their requirements in Chalco, some forty kilometres from the capital. Surrounded by hills, it was hidden behind a high wall with watchtowers at the four corners, like a fortress. Che had been appointed the group's head of personnel and it fell to him to sign the contract for renting the property.

The men began to arrive in small groups to avoid arousing suspicion. Training continued under the tutelage of Colonel Bayo, with classes in the morning as well as practical exercises. They were taught how to launch grenades and clean and dismantle their weapons. At night they went on long marches in the neighbouring hills, carrying their weapons and ammunition. They initially marched for five hours in the dark and then gradually increased the number of hours. As the colonel was no longer very physically fit, it was Che who led the marches. His experience climbing Popocatepetl came in handy, as the weather conditions were often hard and the men had to climb tied to each other with only the Pole Star for orientation.

Che had been a good shot since his teenage years, when his father had taught him in Córdoba, and he participated in all the exercises – climbing, target practice, long walks and sentry duties – as well as looking after the sick and drafting daily reports for Castro. He managed, however, to find time to play chess with Colonel Bayo, who claimed to be the better player of the two (something that Che denied vehemently). By now, Castro had organised the arrival of more weapons from the USA which El Cuate had gone to collect. Castro would visit Chalco often.

As the weeks went by and new men arrived for training, the group reached almost thirty. On the night of 19th June some of the combatants left Chalco for a break in Mexico City. Among them was Antonio Darío López, who had contracted typhoid. Ciro Redondo drove groups of four to one of the movement's houses at Calle Kepler 26. On the evening of 20th June, Castro went to see them there, accompanied by Ramiro Valdés and Universo Sánchez. They noticed unusual movements near the house and decided to leave the area, but were detained by agents from the Dirección Federal de Seguridad. Ciro Redondo and Reinaldo Benítez were also taken into custody. The Mexican Secret Service then apprehended Cándido González and Alfonso Guillén-Zelaya.

On 21st June María Antonia's apartment at Calle Emparán 49 was searched by the police, and Juan Almeida, José Raúl Vega and María Antonia herself were taken into custody. Only Antonio Darío López was left behind, as he was too sick to get up. That same evening Carlos Bermúdez and Héctor Aldama drove to Chalco with Colonel Bayo and his son to inform

Raúl Castro. Raúl ordered those who were in the mountain outposts to return to the compound and hide the weapons. He then left with that group of trainees.

The search of María Antonia's apartment yielded a wealth of information about the revolutionaries and their activities. The combatants' passports were seized, as were documents relating to all the men who had joined in Mexico, as well as details of the arrival of members from abroad. The Mexican newspaper *Excelsior* came out with the headline 'Seven communists apprehended for conspiring against Batista; weapons confiscated'.

When Hilda read the report in the newspapers, she immediately removed anything that might incriminate her from the apartment, including the correspondence she had received for Castro, and asked a close friend, Laura de Albizu-Campos, to keep it all for her. She returned home to warn Patojo, who was still running the photographic business from a shed on the roof, but he and an Argentine friend of Che's, Cornelio Moyano, were detained as they attempted to leave the building. Patojo was released but Moyano did not have his papers in order and remained in detention. When the same agents came that night for Hilda, Patojo was in the room on the roof and she was able to let him know, so he could in turn inform Che and their friends. Patojo managed to inform Hilda's friends, but he was taken into custody when he returned.

Hilda had concocted a story that Che was in Veracruz investigating allergies. She told the police that she had been granted political asylum as well as being the mother of a very small child, but that did not prevent them taking her into custody with her baby. When she was brought back home that evening, the policemen settled down on the settee in her sitting room for the night, in the hope that Che or one of his Cuban friends would arrive.

When Castro realised the premises at Chalco had been discovered, he decided to go there himself with the police in order to avoid an armed confrontation, which might result in bloodshed and loss of life. On 24th June he led the police to the house and asked those of his followers who were still there to surrender. All thirteen men were taken to the jail at Calle Miguel Schultz 136, Che amongst them. A total of twenty-three men were now being held, and they were photographed and cross-examined.

The officials wanted to know their political affiliation, how they had entered the country, the nature of their relationship with the leader of the revolutionary movement, the activities they had been carrying out, the training they had received, their addresses in Mexico City and the origin and purpose of the weapons that had been confiscated. The men had been well schooled in this sort of interrogation and did not yield any new information to the Mexican authorities, so their friends still at large were not compromised. They stated that the weapons were used for training and were the only ones they had ever had.

Che's predicament was of a different order altogether, since he had signed the rental agreement. He admitted that he had rented the establishment at Chalco, that he had arrived in Mexico about a year and a half earlier from Guatemala, that he had wanted to defend the government of Jacobo Arbenz. He did not remember who had taken him to María Antonia's house, but he had met Fidel Castro there and had joined the 26th July Movement, while his wife had agreed to receive mail addressed to Castro. None of this was compromising, as the Mexican authorities were already aware of it, but a membership card of the Instituto de Intercambio Cultural Mexicano-Ruso had been discovered on him. He said he had joined to learn Russian and, as a doctor, to be able to study conditioned reflexes in the Soviet Union.

When asked about his political beliefs he did not hesitate to inform his interrogators that he was a student of Marxist philosophy and was in total agreement with it, although he believed the Soviet Union had committed many mistakes in its interpretation and implementation. He stated that there should be a one-party system, that the dictatorship of the proletariat would follow and that imperialist regimes would disappear in a violent upheaval, since imperialism carried within it the seed of its own destruction: quite a mouthful for the Mexican authorities. An ideological debate ensued between Che and one of the agents, Antonio Villeda, who claimed to be an expert in communism. His superior, Fernando Gutiérrez-Barrios, had to cut short the debate because Che's knowledge and articulacy made Villeda look foolish and lose his air of authority.

In spite of the enormity of the setback, those still free managed to conceal the remaining weapons and equipment and organise a campaign to get Castro and their comrades out of jail. Raúl Castro and Héctor Aldama set about finding a lawyer to represent all the detainees. Alejandro Guzmán-Gutiérrez accepted the task. The Mexican newspapers were full of sensationalist headlines about the detainees and their thwarted plans. In the meantime, Hilda informed the Argentine embassy of Che's plight and went to the jail with food and clean clothes, but she was not allowed to see him for two weeks. She then went there with Ulises Petit de Murat, Che's parents' Argentine friend, and Alfonso Bauer-Paiz, whom they knew from Guatemala. Petit asked if he could use a relative of Che's, who was posted at the Argentine embassy in Mexico, to obtain his freedom. Che flatly refused: he would share the fate of the Cubans. Petit wrote to Guevara Senior about this:

Batista has used the golden key of his corruption here and consequently there has been quite a fuss. But Mexico will not send the Cuban conspirators to Cuba. This is more than a certainty. As for Ernesto, the thing that causes him more concern is the fact that his Mexican papers were not in order. His original tourist visa had expired a long time ago. Consequently, it's almost certain that the strongest punishment for him will be deportation . . . He is in fine health, his wife and child are very charming and his wife is very courageous. Ernesto greeted me with laughter; he reads a lot and sunbathes a lot in the courtyard of the jail. He does not want anything special for himself. His moral attitude – whether one is in agreement with his ideals or not – is great. He rejects any attempts for anyone to do anything on his behalf before the Cubans are cleared. As you can imagine, I didn't pay any attention to this. I have made enquiries about him at the Argentine Embassy. This, of course, prevents the police from committing any atrocities . . . Batista has given a lot of money to lowly police elements who are not very different from thugs. That's why the police put on a show of heavy-handedness. And besides, Batista has used the influence of the United States, associating the young men – falsely, of course – with Russia. These reports must by now be in the hands of the Police in Buenos Aires, and this is why I believe Ernesto would be better off if he were able to stay in any country of this area. But you and Celia and the rest of your family can be perfectly reassured. Ernesto has been treated well, and he will be treated even better in future.

In jail the group studied, read, played ball games or chess. Che read mathematics and economics and the hours flew by for him. According to Ramiro Valdés, 'he would play chess with several comrades at the same time and with his back to the boards. He would tell them his moves and then listen to their moves. He could memorise several boards and the moves of all his opponents at once. It was quite a spectacle.'

Che wrote to his parents on 6th July 'from his new and luxurious residence at Calle Miguel Schultz', which was the prison address. Petit had told him of his parents' fears for him and he felt he owed them an explanation. Presumably the letter left the prison in the hands of a visitor as otherwise it would not have made it past the censor. 'I spent the last few months keeping up the lie to you that I had a job as a teacher, when I was in fact devoted to the task of giving physical instruction to the boys who must one day set foot again in Cuba.'

If it was designed to allay his parents' fears, his announcement that he would soon be embarking on a hunger strike in protest at his compañeros' treatment in prison can have done little to help, nor would his declaration that 'If for any reason, although I do not believe it will happen, I cannot write any more and it is my turn to lose out, consider these lines a farewell, not very grand, but sincere. I've gone through life in fits and starts looking for my truth and, now that I am on the right path and I have a daughter to perpetuate me, I have closed the cycle.' He then quoted some favourite words of Hikmet, 'I will take with me to the grave the sorrow of an unfinished song.'

Unexpectedly, on the evening of 9th July, most of the detainees were set free on condition they reported to the authorities every Monday until they left the country, something they had to do before their tourist visas expired. Four of the detainees, however, remained in jail. They were Fidel Castro, Ernesto Guevara, Calixto García and Jimmy Hirzel. The reason for this, the authorities alleged, was that their visas had expired. Jimmy Hirzel was then set free, but the other three spent several more weeks in jail. Castro and Che had ample time to discuss their political views and their ideas for the future, and to turn their relationship into a very solid friendship that would stand the test of time and adversity.

Fidel Castro and Che in custody in Mexico in the jail at Calle Miguel Schultz.
This is the first known picture of them together

On 15th July Che wrote to his mother, presumably replying to a letter from her telling him off for his intention to go on a hunger strike:

'I am neither Christ nor a philanthropist, I am exactly the opposite of a Christ . . . for the things I believe in I fight with all the weapons within my reach and I try to leave my opponent flat on the floor, instead of letting me be nailed to a cross or to any other place. What really horrifies me is your lack of understanding of all this and your advice on moderation, selfishness, etc. that are the most execrable qualities that a man can have . . . It's true that after dealing with the injustices in Cuba, I shall go to any other place and it's also true that, cooped up in a bureaucratic office or in a clinic for allergenic illnesses, I'd be so fed up.'

Significantly he signed the letter: Che. It's an extraordinary document in which he violently rejects any possibility that he may lead the kind of life his parents hoped, or (despite their unconventionality) expected he would follow. The days of training, then jail, had hardened him for the revolutionary life that lay ahead of him.

In this letter, Che offers an analysis of himself and his purpose in life in some detail for the first time, almost as if he were stating them to himself. Perhaps that is why it is so stark and unsympathetic, almost aggressive. He and his mother could be brutally honest with each other and both could take it, it was part of their special relationship.

But the recipients of the letter – his whole family shared his letters in Buenos Aires – were probably not aware of the importance to him of what he wrote. The letter seems to be evidence that Fidel Castro's promise to Che dates from this period. The promise to let him go after the triumph of the revolution was easy enough to make, since they had not yet even arrived in Cuba to begin the struggle, let alone won it. At this stage Castro did not know how brave Che was, or how he would distinguish himself as a leader of men and a guerrilla fighter.

Che and his new revolutionary colleagues in the courtyard of
the Miguel Schultz prison

As Fidel Castro, Calixto García and Ernesto Guevara were still being detained and their situation was far from clear, their comrades were fearful they might be killed while in custody or moved somewhere else. In order to prevent this, Ramiro Valdés and those members of the group recently freed took turns to be at the gates of the jail so that there was a constant watch on the only entrance to the building. Their defence lawyers also took the additional precaution of contacting General Lázaro

Cárdenas, the ex-president of Mexico who had granted political asylum to Leon Trotsky, asking him to contact the current president, Adolfo Ruíz-Cortines, and intercede on behalf of the detainees. On 24th July Fidel Castro was granted conditional freedom. He had been in custody for thirty-four days.

As soon as he was out of jail, Castro resumed preparations for the expedition. He rented several houses in Mexico City to accommodate those who had been set free, as well as disposing of those they had used before, which were now known to the authorities. He also met with General Cárdenas to thank him for his intervention. On 14th August Che and Calixto García were set free. Che had been in jail for fifty-seven days. He had told Castro he would fully understand if he was left behind, as the revolution should not wait, but Castro categorically refused, saying that he would not abandon him. Che had earned himself the right to be a Cuban revolutionary.

Both detainees were told to leave Mexico within five days or apply for a visa, which would probably have been refused. Che went home to Hilda and their child for three days and then left Mexico City for a seaside resort at Ixtapan, to dodge the police. There, nobody knew him or Calixto García, with whom he was travelling, and they both pretended to be students, registering under false names. They lived clandestinely for the next three and a half months.

By the end of August it had already become clear to Che that the humidity was causing him frequent asthma attacks. He sent for Hilda and Hildita, who paid a brief visit, and then he and Calixto moved to Toluca, where they continued to pretend they were students. They spent most of their time in their room or on the roof terrace. In a letter to his mother, he wrote, 'St Charles had acquired a devoted convert' and signed it 'your clandestine son'. At home they all knew that St Charles was Karl Marx.

On 1st September Fidel Castro and José Antonio Echeverría of the Directorio Revolucionario (who had flown in from Havana to meet with Castro) signed a document they called the Carta de México, in which they agreed to join forces against Batista's tyranny. The Directorio Revolucionario was a student organisation previously called the Directorio Estudiantil, founded by members of the Federation of University Students. Their methods against the Batista government differed from those of

Castro's 26th July Movement because they advocated urban violence. As a result of this, they were almost totally wiped out during a raid on the Palace of Government in Havana on 13th March 1957, though eventually a group from the Directorio led by Faure Chomón did fight alongside Che's troops in the Sierra del Escambray. During the meeting, both men agreed to inform each other beforehand of their actions and to act in unison once Castro and the expeditionary force had landed in Cuba, although the Directorio did not assist with the preparations or take part in the landing itself.

In mid-September Castro instructed Che and Calixto García to return to Mexico City and Che managed to spend a few days with Hilda and Hildita. He was then ordered to proceed to Veracruz, where the bulk of the expeditionary force was already staying. Che met the new comrades and gave them a lecture on what a revolution is. By now it was a Marxist one he had in mind: to totally change the social and economic apparatus. A few days later they returned to Mexico City and the group continued training in the nearby hills.

At the end of the month, Fidel Castro and El Cuate were in Tuxpán, a village on the coast, trying out some of the weapons which had just arrived, when they saw a small yacht being repaired. It was the *Granma*, a 1943 11.5-metre motor yacht which had seen better days, and had even sunk once, but it looked suitable for taking the invaders to Cuba. It belonged to a US citizen called Robert Bruce Erickson. The owner did not want to sell the yacht without selling his Mexican house as well, at an all-in price of $40,000. Castro was in funds, although their source is not clear. Some biographers claim that he had accepted $50,000 from his political rival, ex-president Prío Socarrás, whom he had met secretly during his recent trip (Socarrás was living in exile in the US, having been deposed by Batista). Others suggest that his funds came from groups of exiled Cubans in the USA who had organised themselves into clubs to help the revolution. In any case, Castro, who never clarified the matter, paid the $40,000 to the *Granma*'s owner and left El Cuate in charge of the repairs required to make the vessel seaworthy. The nearby property that came with the yacht turned out to be useful for their clandestine activities and as somewhere to conceal the weapons they were acquiring.

Frank País, a student in his twenties who was the coordinator of the underground activities of the 26th July Movement in the city of Santiago, in Oriente province, arrived in Mexico from Cuba in mid-October, hoping to convince Castro to postpone the departure of the *Granma*, as he believed his men in Cuba were not yet in a position to support the invasion. Castro told him they must do all in their power to be ready, because he and his men could not remain in Mexico much longer. In the meantime, Che spent some weekends at home with his family and asked Hilda to type up the instructions he had compiled for the expeditionary force on how to care for the wounded and administer first aid.

In Havana on 28th October, a commando belonging to the Directorio Revolucionario executed the Head of the Cuban Intelligence Service, Colonel Antonio Blanco-Rico, as he left the Cabaret Montmartre. The future combatants were overjoyed but Che explained to them that a revolution was far more than the liquidation of one enemy. 'We must make a more profound revolution,' were his words.

While the bulk of the revolutionary force travelled to a property in the state of Tamaulipas to receive training, Che decided to accept the offer of the Guatemalan politician, Alfonso Bauer-Paiz, to stay in a small servant's room on the roof terrace of the building in which he lived with his family in Mexico City. The preparations for the departure were now in full swing. Fidel Castro selected those who would travel on the *Granma* with him for the invasion on the basis of the discipline and skills they had demonstrated during the training period. Their size and weight were also taken into account because of the vessel's restricted capacity. Che would be travelling as the expedition's doctor.

On the morning of 23rd November the invaders began to leave their lodgings and make they way towards Tuxpán, where the *Granma* was moored. One group travelled from Abasolo, and another from Veracruz. The group from Mexico City received their last instructions from Castro just before they left, and he went personally to get Che from Bauer-Paiz's home. In order not to attract attention, Che left without saying goodbye to his hosts, who were holding a meeting of fellow Guatemalans. The various groups travelled by car, bus and taxi. Castro had asked Che, Calixto García and Roberto Roque to travel under their own steam as there was not enough transport for all of them. The three of them took a taxi to Poza Rica and then a second one on to Tuxpán.

They all gathered at a meeting point in a small wood nearby to await instructions to proceed. There was great activity all night as weapons, uniforms, equipment and food were loaded. Castro stood in the persistent drizzle in a dark cape, carrying a Thompson sub-machine gun and supervising the operation he had masterminded. It was no mean feat to have put it together in a country with a repressive police force, where many of the participants were living illegally. No doubt he was savouring the occasion.

The men finally boarded the vessel using a wooden plank and they all wrote down their full names, as well as that of their next of kin. Che realised he had reached a turning point in his life. He gave his name as Ernesto Guevara Serna, rather than de la Serna, with its aristocratic connotation. When Castro decided it was time to leave, he called the men who were guarding the mooring posts and told them to board, hugged those who had come to bid them farewell and climbed on board himself. Those who had not arrived by then were left behind.

The *Granma* once it had been restored. It is now at the Plaza de la Revolución in Havana

At two in the morning of 25th November 1956, the *Granma* left its moorings and started its engines. It made its way downriver in the wide channel without turning on its lights. The men on board travelled in total silence. Once the Tuxpán river had been left behind and the vessel entered the waters of the Gulf of Mexico, El Norte, a northern wind, blew ferociously. It was still raining, the yacht rocked from side to side and the waves were huge, reaching the roof of the vessel. Once they had cleared the coast, the lights came on. The men, some of whom had not met in a long time, embraced each other. They were all truly moved and they stood to sing the national anthem as well as the 26th July March and then shouted 'Long live the Revolution', 'Down with the dictatorship'.

A while before they left, Che had written to his mother:

This letter will only leave when the time has come and then you will know that your son, in a sunny country of Latin America, will be cursing himself for not having studied a little surgery to be able to help the injured, and will curse the Mexican government for not letting him practise his already respectable aim so as to topple targets with greater ease.

FOURTEEN

(1956–1957)

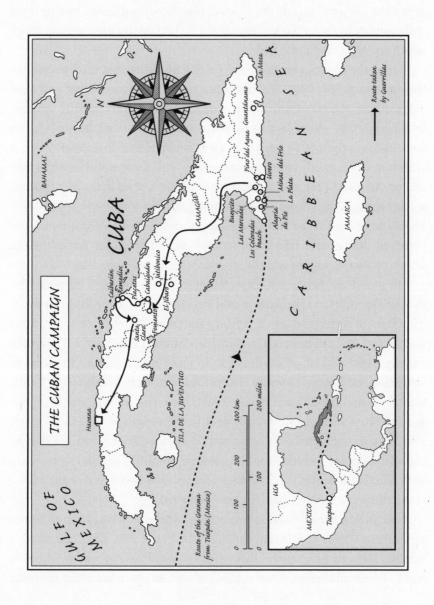

The *Granma* had capacity for twenty-four people and it was carrying eighty-two men, an arsenal of weapons, several crates full of boots and uniforms and some food. El Norte did not abate and the weather was foul throughout the crossing. The men were piled up on deck as well as below, and many were sick. The toilet, blocked by vomit, no longer flushed and instead let the water in, and the food supplies were insufficient, leaving them with nothing to eat for the last two days. Che had an almighty asthma attack which lasted a couple of days.

It took the *Granma* seven days to reach Cuba instead of the five planned (being so heavily loaded, she could not make the 10 knots that had been expected), so they were still at sea when Frank País launched the uprising in Santiago that was meant to coincide with their arrival. Batista's forces converged on the city to quell the revolt, while the air force and the navy were sent to the south-eastern coast to deal with the insurgents when they landed. All sorts of repressive measures were put in place in the area. Homes, workplaces and buildings where people gathered socially were searched. People were denied the right to assemble and vehicles were stopped and searched. Radio and television stations were put under armed guard, telephones were bugged and the troops were put on high alert.

On board the *Granma*, Castro distributed weapons and informed his men of the military organisation and structure of the expeditionary force. The chain of command was as follows: the commander-in-chief was Fidel Castro and his chiefs were Captain Juan Manuel Márquez and Captain Faustino Pérez; chief of administration was Pablo Díaz and the head of sanitation was Ernesto Guevara. The troops were led by Captain José Smith, Captain Juan Almeida and Captain Raúl Castro. The automatic rifles, which were the best weapons on board, went to the vanguard. Che deliberately asked for an old rifle because he was so afflicted by his asthma that he thought a decent weapon would be wasted on him. The men were issued with two sets of uniform, a backpack and a pair of boots, and changed into these, throwing their civilian clothes overboard.

Instead of reaching land at Cabo Cruz, where they had been meant to rendezvous with a contingent organised by Frank País, the *Granma* hit a sandbar some two kilometres from the beaches of Las Coloradas. The boat had to be abandoned as it had run out of fuel. At about six in the morning of 2nd December 1956, the men began to disembark. It was broad daylight. The auxiliary boat lowered to carry the weapons ashore soon sank. The men had to carry the weapons themselves and were unable to bring the heavier equipment ashore. Raúl Castro and Che were the last two to disembark.

They were forced to wade through the waters of a particularly inhospitable area: the mangrove roots formed a tangled web which, together with the thorny bushes and the sharp leaves of the *cortaderas*, drew blood. They were plagued by mosquitoes and gnats, and it took them two hours to reach land. Their clothes were in tatters and their weapons wet. Most had injured their feet and the lacerations were becoming infected. A group of seven men led by Juan Manuel Márquez was nowhere to be seen. They had accidentally separated from the main force and ended up reaching the shore further north. Che would later write, 'It was a shipwreck rather than a landing.'

While he waited for the rest of his men to reach land, Fidel Castro sent Luis Crespo to investigate a house that could be seen not far away. Crespo came back with the *campesino* who owned it, who took them home and cooked for them. Then shots were heard. The air force and the coastguard were attacking the mangroves at Las Coloradas. With the *campesino* as their guide, Castro and his men set off for a nearby hill where they could take cover and await the arrival of the missing men, before starting their long march towards the Sierra Maestra. Meanwhile, the local government forces at the Municipio de Niquero had received reinforcements in the shape of an artillery battalion with five officers and eighty-nine men.

Castro and his men reached the sugar-cane fields of the New Niquero Sugar Company. There they met another *campesino* who knew the area well and escorted them through the cane fields up to a place called Alegría del Pío. It was the morning of 5th December. The men camped next to the cane field and spent the night there. It was not a safe place because, that morning, government forces blocked the only exit from Alegría del Pío towards the Sierra Maestra. The guide had betrayed them, bringing the army close to the place where he had previously led the insurgents.

When the army fired its first shots, the men were taken by surprise but fired back. They were surrounded and invited to surrender. Che tells us in his *Reminiscences of the Cuban Revolutionary War* that it was Camilo Cienfuegos who shouted back, '*Aquí no se rinde nadie, carajo!*' (Nobody surrenders here, goddamit!) The army set the cane field on fire, and the air force joined the attack. Che recollected:

> A comrade dropped an ammunition box at my feet. I pointed questioningly to it and the man answered me with a face I remember perfectly, for the anguish it reflected seemed to say, 'It's no time for bullets,' and he immediately left along the path through the cane field (he was later murdered by the Batista forces). This was perhaps the first time I was faced with the dilemma of choosing between my dedication to medicine and my duty as a revolutionary soldier. At my feet were a pack full of medicines and a cartridge box: together, they were too heavy to carry. I chose the cartridge box, leaving behind the medicine pack, and crossed the clearing which separated me from the cane field.

As he ran, carrying the ammunition box, Che was hit by a bullet in the neck and began to lose a lot of blood. He thought the wound was lethal and prepared to die. (To this day the precise nature of the wound is unclear.) Coolly he considered the best way to do so, remembering the story 'To Build a Fire' by Jack London, in which the hero, knowing he will freeze to death in Alaska, leans against a tree and decides to end his life with dignity. But then Juan Almeida came over and it became apparent that his wound was not as serious as he had feared. They formed a small group with Ramiro Valdés, Rafael Chao and Reinaldo Benítez, crossing the cane field just as it burst into flames. They walked until nightfall and then decided to sleep huddled together. 'We were attacked by mosquitoes, tortured by thirst and hunger. Such was our baptism of fire on 5th December 1956, in the district of Niquero. Such was the beginning of what would become the Rebel Army,' Che tells us.

Castro withdrew to a nearby forest with Universo Sánchez; Faustino Pérez soon managed to join them. Raúl Castro, Efigenio Ameijeiras, René Rodríguez, Ciro Redondo, Armando Rodríguez and César Gómez also managed to abandon the flaming cane field and reach another part of the forest, amidst shots from all directions and the roar of aircraft. Another group, consisting of Calixto García, Calixto Morales and Carlos Bermúdez, reached a cane field and hid. In the confusion many men were unable to rejoin their comrades. Backpacks, weapons and equipment were lost. Three men were dead: Israel Cabrera-Rodríguez, Humberto Lamothe-Coronado and Oscar Rodríguez-Delgado.

Che in the Sierra with rebels and *guajiros*

Those combatants who survived tried to regroup and find their way to the Sierra Maestra without knowing the fate of their leader. Those who were caught were tortured and then murdered. Those who surrendered were also murdered. Of the eighty-two men on board the *Granma*, only about twenty survived, regrouped and fought on. Ñico López, Che's first Cuban friend, was captured, tortured and killed. The corpses of three captured men, their hands tied behind their backs, were thrown in front of the gates of the Niquero Cemetery.

Che and his group walked at night, following what he thought was the Pole Star (it was not, as he discovered later, but it still led them in the right direction), and hid during the day. They came across a sympathiser of the 26th July Movement who fed them and lodged them. After days of near starvation, they all ate too much. They were very sick with diarrhoea and had to spend time recovering before continuing.

They took the precaution of changing into civilian clothes, dressing like the *campesinos* (or *guajiros*, as the peasants of the region are known) and hid their weapons in someone's home. But the army was hot on their heels, their weapons were discovered and a comrade who had stayed behind because he was too sick to move was taken prisoner. The 26th July Movement soon dispatched a member to assist them. That was when they learnt that Castro was alive and was regrouping the survivors at a coffee plantation in the mountains. Che was delighted to discover a Cuban newspaper had reported his presence in the Rebel Army, describing him as an Argentine communist who had been expelled from his country.

Like the others who survived, Castro had hidden in cane fields and walked at night. He sent a messenger to Manzanillo and to Santiago to tell Frank País and Celia Sánchez his whereabouts, and it was Celia Sánchez who was now in charge of organising the network of *guajiros* who were operating so efficiently, combing the area for any of Castro's men who might have survived the fiasco of Alegría del Pío and capture and death by the army. They led Che's group to Castro's hideout, which they reached on 21st December. On arrival they discovered Raúl Castro had also survived and was there with four more comrades. Juan Manuel Márquez had been killed and Jesús Montané captured. Then Calixto García arrived with four more men. It was becoming clear how few had been spared.

Batista magnified the army's victory over the rebels at Alegría del Pío, stating that Fidel and Raúl Castro as well as Che were dead and that the revolt had been totally quashed. Che's family home in Buenos Aires, which had always been boisterous and cheerful, settled into an atmosphere of total gloom and silence. To make matters worse, the farewell letter Che had left with Hilda to be posted after his departure now arrived.

Guevara Senior decided he would find out his son's fate and got in touch with all possible contacts. He went to the offices of *La Prensa*, a right-wing broadsheet that was one of the largest-circulation newspapers in Buenos Aires. He was told there was no official confirmation yet, a small consolation. His wife Celia telephoned Associated Press but there was still no confirmation. Guevara Senior then went to see the president's private secretary. The president, General Pedro Eugenio Aramburu, ordered his Ministry of Foreign Affairs to make enquiries in Cuba.

A few days later, a cable arrived from Rear Admiral Raúl Lynch, the Argentine ambassador in Havana and Guevara Senior's cousin. It read: 'Dr Ernesto Guevara de la Serna, according to enquiries made by this embassy, is not among the dead, nor among the wounded, nor among the prisoners of Batista's army.' The social network of Argentina's privileged elite was going out of its way to discover the whereabouts and well-being of one of its own, regardless of the fact he had turned his back on them and taken up arms against what they stood for.

A muted New Year's Eve celebration took place at the Guevara home. Guevara Senior tells us, in his memoir *Young Che*:

> It must have been around ten o' clock that night when an envelope was slid under the front door by an anonymous benefactor acting as postman. It was a small airmail envelope addressed to Celia de la Serna postmarked Manzanillo in Cuba. Inside there was a little piece of paper. It was a page torn from a small notebook and was in handwriting we all knew well. It read, 'Dear Viejos: I am fine, I only used up 2 and have 5 still left. I am still doing the same job, news will reach you sporadically and will continue to do so, but trust that God is an Argentine. A big hug to you all. Teté'.

Teté was a nickname Ernesto had been given when he was a few days old, which had later been dropped in favour of Ernestito. In Spanish, cats have seven lives, which explains the reference to having used two and still having five. 'God is an Argentine' was a popular phrase at the time: whenever an Argentine was favoured by luck, he or she would say it was because '*Dios es argentino*'.

As the celebrations were in full swing chez Guevara, another envelope mysteriously appeared under the front door. It contained a card which said, 'Happy New Year. Teté is perfectly well.' The mood was buoyant and the new year was seen in with much champagne and toasting.

Meanwhile, weapons had reached Castro from Manzanillo and by 24th December he was on the move again. Che, in the Sierra Maestra, spent New Year's Eve sleeping out under the stars. He wrote in his diary that the day had been spent instructing the new recruits, reading, and doing minor things to do with war. Castro was reorganising his Rebel Army of about twenty-two men. He created a new five-man-strong leadership, or *Estado mayor*. It was composed of himself, Universo Sánchez, Crescencio Pérez, his son Sergio Pérez and Ernesto Guevara. Raúl Castro and Juan Almeida became platoon leaders and Ramiro Valdés, Calixto Morales and Armando Rodríguez were advance scouts.

This may have seemed an indulgence, considering he had lost most of his troops and his arms but, as far as he was concerned, it was much-needed planning for the future when he would have troops and weapons again. His faith in himself and the revolution was unshakable. After all, in spite of a disastrous beginning, he was in Cuba on the Sierra Maestra, the 26th July Movement's network had worked, the people in the cities were responding and most of the *guajiros* in the mountains were on his side.

Castro's faith in his ability to inspire a revolution was unwavering. Even when the odds seemed stacked against him, his confidence remained irrepressible. An anecdote from the Sierra campaign illustrates this. Not long after the *Granma* landing, Fidel Castro, Faustino Pérez and Universo Sánchez were trapped in a cane field, separated from the rest of their comrades and with just two weapons between them. They made the mistake of cutting sugar cane to feed themselves, dropping the discarded stalks as they walked deeper into the field. The army surrounded the area, and they lay between the rows of sugar cane in the field for three days, hoping they would not be discovered.

Fidel never stopped talking in a whisper about regrouping, finding the rest of the *Granma* survivors, meeting up with the 26th July Movement, reaching the Sierra Maestra, fighting and defeating Batista's army and winning the war. He went on to talk about creating a socialist revolution, organising the country and ending imperialism on the island. It was up to them to show the way, to take the initiative, to lead their people to victory. He quoted Martí frequently during his tirades.

They were eventually able to break free from the encirclement and Faustino Pérez and Universo Sánchez, who had thought Fidel was deluded at first, now realised here was a man with total self-confidence and faith in his struggle. For Che here was a man after his own heart, surely.

Now it was time to be on the march again and to take the fight to the enemy. The small barracks on the mouth of the La Plata river in the Sierra Maestra was the chosen spot. On the afternoon of 14th January, they climbed the last hillock before La Plata. The rebels had twenty-two weapons but little ammunition, so they would be defenceless if they did not take the barracks before it ran out. The plan was for some of the men to surround the overseer's palm-thatched house on the extreme right, while another group would attack from the centre and a third group from the left.

The rebels approached the enemy positions, stopping when they were forty metres from them. There was a full moon. At twenty to three in the morning, Castro started the shooting with his sub-machine gun. The soldiers were invited to surrender several times but invariably fired back as a reply. The rebels decided to set fire to the houses, in spite of the risk involved. Universo Sánchez and Camilo Cienfuegos attempted and failed, but Luis Crespo and Che managed to set fire to one of the buildings. Camilo Cienfuegos rushed into the burning house and was greeted by men surrendering. Their officers had fled.

The rebels were able to take eight Springfield rifles with 1,000 rounds of ammunition, a Thompson sub-machine gun with 150 rounds, clothes, backpacks and cartridge belts. Che observed that it was one of the few occasions when they had more weapons than men. They tended to the wounded (in sharp contrast with the way in which the army had treated their own wounded so far) and left them in the care of the men they had taken prisoner. The list of army casualties was two dead and five wounded. The rebels had not suffered any losses.

It was the Rebel Army's first attack and it did wonders for their morale. They needed to prove they were a force to be reckoned with and they needed the publicity that would result. Castro ordered their medicines to be left for the wounded soldiers, much to Che's chagrin, and the remaining buildings were set on fire. By dawn, they were safely on their way back to the Sierra Maestra.

The defeat at La Plata forced the government to admit the existence of the insurgents, and to send troops to encircle the Sierra Maestra. But the insurgents now convinced themselves their guerrilla-warfare tactics could defeat the regular army, in spite of its superior equipment and numbers: the army was ousting the *guajiros* from their homes and land in an attempt to intimidate them into turning in the guerrillas, and this meant that many of them were either joining the insurgents or assisting them as guides, giving them food and hiding them.

However, this was not true of all the men they encountered on the Sierra. Some spied on them for the army and some betrayed them. Such was the case of Eutimio Guerra, who had volunteered to be their guide in early January and had told the army their whereabouts on more than one occasion. When this was discovered, an ad hoc tribunal presided over by Fidel Castro decided he should be executed. It was Che who put a gun to his temple and shot him, thus putting an end to a situation that had become tense and uncomfortable for all those present as well as sparing his leader from having to do it himself.

Che's unflinching and decisive action has been criticised by many from the comfort of their armchairs, without taking into account that a lengthy debate might have led to the situation getting out of hand and been detrimental to the morale of the fighting men, many of whom were unsophisticated *guajiros* and the culprit's fellow Cubans, as well as extremely young and inexperienced in warfare. We must also remember that Che was someone who was prepared to die at the hands of his enemies (something he eventually did with great dignity) as much as he was ready to kill them.

In the early afternoon of 22nd January, the rebels again clashed with a small section of the army, at Arroyo del Infierno. Castro and his men had been waiting since dawn. When the soldiers were spotted coming towards them, he opened fire, followed by his men, and several soldiers fell. Those remaining retreated. The army lost five men. After this successful attack, the rebels continued on their way to Palma Mocha.

On 28th January Che discovered he had contracted malaria, and wrote a letter to Hilda: 'Here I am in the Cuban jungle, alive and thirsting for blood, writing these fiery lines inspired by Martí as if I were a real soldier (I am dirty and in rags, at least). I write on a field mess-plate with my weapon by my side and a new addition between my lips: a Havana cigar.

Havana cigars were the ideal complement to a guerrilla's kit. Like the maté Che had been in the habit of drinking since childhood in his native Argentina, they kept him awake and killed hunger pangs as well. He picked up the habit in the Sierra, when they rarely had enough to eat and the *guajiros* could provide them with home-made cigars. He did not abandon the habit once the revolution was in power and there was an enormous amount of work to do, as Dr Antonio Núñez-Jiménez tells us. He was put in charge of agrarian reform, and Che worked as director of one of his departments. Both men worked very long hours and never had time to stop for a bite. A Havana cigar did the trick. They were never hungry.

Che, who had never smoked cigarettes, found that cigars did not trigger his asthma; on the contrary, he thought they helped him avoid an attack. His doctor did not agree with this theory and at one point demanded that he smoke only one a day. Che promised he would comply but found a way round it by having the longest possible cigar made for him, so that it lasted him several hours. Havana cigars became his trademark, because he was so often photographed smoking them, but if he had not come to Cuba, a country in which tobacco has been cultivated since long before the Spaniards arrived and in which the manufacture

Che smoking a cigar during the campaign in the Sierra

of cigars is a central part of their economy and culture, it is unlikely he would ever have picked one up. In the Congo and Bolivia, where the tobacco leaves needed to roll them were not available, he smoked a pipe.

On 29th January Castro gave a speech to the men and warned them that from then on there were three offences punishable by death: insubordination, desertion and despotism. After many days of hunger, they ate abundantly that night as two pigs had been killed. On 30th January the air force bombed the area: Batista had acquired sixteen B-26 bombers from the USA.

February brought further bouts of malaria for Che so he was scarcely able to walk. When he also got diarrhoea he was forced to halt, Luis Crespo and Julio Zenón, a 47-year-old *guajiro*, staying behind with him. When they rejoined their comrades, at Cañón del Arroyo, they were attacked by the army and scattered. In the confusion, Che lost his rucksack, which was full of medicine, reserve food, his blanket (previously the property of Batista's army, it was taken as a trophy from La Plata) and his beloved books. Another blow was the loss of Zenón, a 'tireless worker' who had become almost invaluable around the camp and whom Che was beginning to teach to read.

On 17th February, Herbert Matthews, a correspondent with *The New York Times*, was brought to the Sierra Maestra by a group of Castro's men, to conduct an interview with him. It would turn out to be a huge scoop and became legendary. Herbert Matthews was a veteran reporter who had covered the Spanish Civil War, the Italian War in Abyssinia and the Second World War. The story goes that the guerrillas made a point of coming and going in the background, so he would think Castro had many more troops than he actually did; they were very pleased with themselves, as they were convinced they had duped him. Castro even had someone arrive with a message from the non-existent Second Column while he was talking to the reporter. Matthews later wrote that it was a ruse as old as warfare and he had not been deceived for a moment.

The Matthews interview gave the rebels a much-needed boost. It was reprinted in many newspapers and in translation as well. Everybody was talking about it. Batista could no longer get away with saying Castro and his guerrilla force had been wiped out. Matthews painted a very attractive picture of Castro and called him 'a man of ideals, of courage and of remarkable qualities of leadership'. Years later, when Castro and his revolution turned seriously to the left, Matthews was treated like a pariah in the USA for appearing to endorse such an anti-American movement.

On 23rd April Celia Sánchez and Haydée Santamaría, another veteran of the assault on the Moncada Barracks, arrived with a journalist and his cameraman: Bob Taber and Wendell Hoffman were covering the war for the Columbia Broadcasting Corporation. Their film was aired all over the USA on 18th May and there was a radio interview with Castro as well. The Cuban Revolution could no longer be dismissed or ignored.

In March Che received a consignment of weapons sent from Santiago de Cuba by Frank País and took part in the skirmishes at Palma Mocha. In April he made contact with various *campesinos* and created support centres for the troops within their area of operations, locating various houses which would be used to store supplies. During the first fortnight of May, the rebel forces marched every day and Che continued to fulfil his duties as a doctor. Without supplies of medicine there was little he could do to alleviate the suffering of the people who came to see him. Moreover, the symptoms he treated – prematurely aged and toothless women, children with distended bellies, parasitism, rickets, general avitaminosis – were a depressingly monotonous reminder of the grinding poverty in which many of his patients lived. His diary records one watchful girl who, having observed him carry out several examinations of local women in the *bohío* (hut) he used as an ad hoc clinic said, 'Mamá, this doctor says the same thing to all of them'. Ruefully he agreed that his knowledge was good for little else.

On 18th May a shipment of weapons arrived from Havana and filled the guerrillas with euphoria. Che was particularly happy as he was given a repeater rifle. He wrote in his diary, 'This way, I began to be a direct combatant since so far I had been an occasional one . . . With this a new stage began for me at the Sierra.'

On 28th May the attack on El Uvero, a well-fortified garrison in the Sierra Maestra, was a major victory for the rebels. Later, Che would say it had marked the coming of age of the rebel troops. He might now see himself as a combatant, but after the battle he had to revert to his old role of doctor and tend to the wounded of both sides, since the army's doctor, now a prisoner, totally forgot what should be done. This was due partly to inexperience and partly to fear. Che noted, 'I had to exchange my weapon for my doctor's uniform, which in actual fact consisted in washing my hands.'

During June Che tended to the wounded as well as to the *campesinos* of the area, recruited new combatants from among them and organised support bases. He prepared men who would become their means of communication with the city. He also found himself in the unenviable situation of being asked to extract a couple of teeth and was nicknamed El Sacamuelas (the tooth-puller) by his comrades. His first extraction met with success, although he referred to Israel Pardo as his victim. Of the second, Joel Iglesias, he said he would have needed dynamite to remove the tooth.

By the end of June Che had rejoined the main force, bringing new recruits with him, as well as men who had recovered from their wounds in his care. Castro made him a Captain. Che was teaching Israel Pardo and Joel Iglesias to read and write, and for those who had a higher level of education he organised courses on the history of Cuba as well as on guerrilla warfare. So he could play chess, he taught some of his men the game. He was also managing to read a lot. He was never without reading material as he always carried several books in his backpack.

Che reads Emil Ludwig's biography of Goethe while recovering from an asthma attack in the Sierra

On 21st July Che was made comandante by Castro, almost by stealth. The Rebel Army was sending a letter of condolence to Frank País because Josué, one of his brothers, had just been killed. The men queued to sign it, and their rank was included next to their signature. When Che signed, Castro ordered the word Comandante be placed next to his name. Celia Sánchez, who had become Castro's right-hand woman, gave Che a little star, which he pinned on his beret, while Castro gave him a wristwatch.

With his new rank came the command of Columna No. 4. It was actually the second column, the first being the one led by Castro, but it was called the fourth column to dupe the enemy. Che had seventy-five men under his command and had orders to march towards a new area to harass the troops led by Ángel Sánchez-Mosquera and Merob Sosa, two of the most brutal army generals. In his diary Che wrote about his promotion, 'The vanity which we all have in us made me the proudest man in the world that day.'

On 30th July Frank País was assassinated in the street in Santiago during one of the frequent security checks. On 31st July, after dark, Che's column encountered the army at Bueyecito. Nothing went according to plan. Some units did not arrive and when Che tried to start the action himself, his machine gun jammed and so did his pistol. A rebel fighter then tried to shoot the same sentry, but his weapon did not fire either. The soldier raked them with a hail of bullets from his Garand rifle. With his characteristic honesty, Che later wrote, 'I ran with a speed I have never matched since and in full flight turned the corner and ended up in the cross street where I fixed my machine gun.' By the time Che had sorted out his weapon and was ready for action, there was no more to be done: the garrison had surrendered to Ramiro Valdés, who arrived from the rear with his men. The rebels looted the garrison and left on board several trucks. Che abandoned his old Thompson sub-machine gun and awarded himself a Browning, the best weapon they had captured.

During August Che set up camp at El Hombrito and created a system of logistics with the population to keep his troops supplied. He won over the local *guajiros*, teaching many how to read and write alongside his troops. He involved them in the construction of an armoury, which was soon working at full capacity; he ordered the construction of two experimental models of grenade-launchers, and had some very powerful landmines made.

He installed a shoe-making facility which could make all kinds of shoes and other leather goods, although they did not yet have the materials to start operating. They also set up a poultry and pig farm and built a bread oven which would produce the first *keke* (literally, cake in the Cuban spelling, but meaning a bread loaf or bun) the next day. Many of the *guajiros* of the Sierra had never eaten bread. Two students newly arrived from Havana were put in charge of building a small dam on the nearby river, which would bring them hydroelectric power. Construction of a permanent hospital had also begun and a further one would be started soon.

From this stable base, his men could operate over a large area. They were also organising anti-aircraft shelters: he intended to stay put and not give it up for anything. His dogged determination and his capacity to plan, to create a working structure even under the most inhospitable conditions, came to the fore. From childhood he had had to manage with next to nothing, to make the best of what was available and what he had learnt was of immense use to him now. He had turned himself into the innovative leader of a small army who had inspired a variety of people to believe in his project and make the necessary effort to bring it to fruition.

On 29th August Che met up with Castro and they marched together towards Pino del Agua. The next day, Che's column put an end to General Sosa's offensive, in spite of his numerical superiority (140 men to Che's 75) and modern weaponry. It became known as the battle of El Hombrito. Che and Castro met up again at Dos Brazos del Guayabo and went through Pico Verde, Nuevo Mundo, La Bayamesa and María Tomasa together. On 10th September Columna No. 4 reached Pino del Agua, and there awaited the arrival of the army, against which Che subsequently fought a successful skirmish. Towards the end of September Castro sent Camilo Cienfuegos to join Che's column and lead the vanguard. Their friendship developed from that point on, until Camilo's untimely death a few years later, on 28th October 1959. Che would name his eldest son after him.

At the end of October Che returned to his base at El Hombrito and ordered a huge flag in black and red – the colours of the 26th July Movement – to be made, bearing the words, Feliz Año 1958. It was placed at the highest point of the plateau and Che hoped it would be visible from Las

Minas del Bueyecito, so Sánchez-Mosquera's troops would see it. On 4th November, at Altos de Conrado, Che launched a newssheet called *El Cubano Libre* (after the newspaper produced by the men who fought for independence from Spain in 1868–78 and in 1895), using a 1903 mimeograph machine to print it.

He wrote an article for the first issue, commenting ironically on the fate of a dog which the Soviets had sent into space on board a Sputnik, an action the Western press hastened to condemn as cruel. He signed it with the pseudonym El Francotirador (the Franc-tireur or Freelancer), the nickname Ricardo Rojo had given him during a political discussion in Ecuador when Che would not commit to any of the political options available to them at the time in Latin America. He sent a copy to Castro, telling him he hoped its poor quality would prompt him to draft a better piece to be published. Che also told him of his newly created base, which included what he referred to as 'our heavy industry'.

On 29th November Che led his men against Sánchez-Mosquera's troops in the battle of Mar Verde. It was a messy affair which ended in retreat. Joel Iglesias was shot several times and was unable to move. Che jumped down from his position behind a rock, picked Joel up, threw him over his shoulder and ran for cover. Fire rained from two sides but it was too late: Che and Joel were gone. After the battle, some of Sánchez-Mosquera's men, who had been taken prisoner, were asked why they had not shot at Che, giving him the time he needed to escape. They said it was such an unexpected thing for him to do, to jump into a spot where he would be under crossfire, that it had taken them those extra seconds to react. By the time they realised what he was doing and shot at him, he was gone. The most serious fatality of the battle was Ciro Redondo, who fell heroically leading his men. He had come on the *Granma* and had proved himself as a soldier and as a leader.

When Che and his men returned to their camp at El Hombrito they found devastation. Sánchez-Mosquera's troops had helped themselves to everything they were able to carry, from sacks of coffee to furniture, and totally destroyed the camp. Che remarked that the thoroughness of the looting gave him the impression Sánchez-Mosquera's men were not planning to return to the Sierra any time soon. Che moved his camp to the more inaccessible La Pata de La Mesa and organised it in the same way.

This was war and there was no point in dwelling on events, no matter how frustrating finding El Hombrito razed to the ground might have been.

On 8th December Che fought the battle of Altos de Conrado against Sánchez-Mosquera's troops and was wounded in his left foot. Unable to walk, he had to mount a horse to get to their makeshift hospital. A couple of days later, he had an M-1 carbine bullet removed from his foot with a razor blade. It was Machadito who performed the operation and Che mentions in his *Reminiscences of the Cuban Revolutionary War* that it was he, José Ramón Machado-Ventura, who went on to be the Minister for Public Health after their triumph. While Che was incapacitated, Ramiro Valdés took over the command of his column. Between 9th and 15th December Che was forced to stay in the home of Polo Torres to recover and there attempt his first steps after the operation.

Fidel Castro in the Sierra Maestra

FIFTEEN

(1958)

The New Year brought a new mimeograph machine on which to print *El Cubano Libre*; the third issue contained an article by El Francotirador called '*La ultima palabra la tiene el pueblo*' (The people have the last word). Tests were started for broadcasting news from the rebels' new base at La Mesa, using a small radio transmitter they had installed, and in mid-February Radio Rebelde went on air. It was a moving occasion as Che communicated with Camilo Cienfuegos across the airwaves: '*Camilo: soy el Che. Camilo, aquí habla el Che.*' The tremendous depth of affection that existed between the two men, as well as the sense of expectation and excitement over the first successful transmission, comes across clearly in the recording.

The new radio station boosted the morale of the troops on every front, but it also contributed to breaking the information blockade on the Sierra, as the government was using all means at its disposal to disseminate disinformation about the insurgency. It periodically announced the demise of the Castro brothers and Che Guevara, the failure of their campaign, the lack of cooperation from the *guajiros*, the army's success in routing the insurrection and the air force's carpet-bombing of the guerrilla bases in the Sierra Maestra.

Che and his radio transmitter

Radio Rebelde became the tool the guerrillas used to control and direct military operations and to disseminate war communiqués by means of coded messages. It also kept the people informed about developments in the political arena through occasional addresses to the population. It gave the troops of the 26th July Movement in the Sierra the means to be constantly in touch with their counterparts on other fronts and with their people in the cities, the section of the Movement referred to as El Llano. The station was originally located at the general command post in the Sierra and became the centre of a system that included thirty transmitters in both the First and Second War Fronts, as well as in Havana and even abroad. It was complementary to the telephone network organised in the liberated zones controlled by the rebels.

A radio technician from Bayamo had selected the necessary equipment in Havana and it had been transported to the Sierra by volunteers from the Movement. It was first installed in an abandoned house in Altos de Conrado and then moved to the region of La Plata for its safety, because it was known the army was preparing an offensive in the Sierra Maestra.

During the battle of Santo Domingo, loudspeakers were used for the first time to address enemy troops. They were used again during the battles of El Jigüe, Las Mercedes and Maffo, with great effect. The radio station was also used to communicate with the Red Cross and organise the handover of wounded combatants and prisoners. In Venezuela, long-wave transmitters recorded Radio Rebelde's programmes and retransmitted them to Colombia, Chile, Mexico and Peru, informing the continent of the events taking place in Cuba. Fidel Castro made the last broadcast towards the end of the two year struggle from Palma Soriano, just after the city's liberation.

The new base camp at La Mesa mirrored the one at El Hombrito as much as possible. It had a butcher's shop, an armoury and a shoe factory, as well as a cigar factory which manufactured the *habanos* which Castro – and by now Che as well – could not be without. Che would say in his *Reminiscences of the Cuban Revolutionary War*, 'the cigars we made were terrible, but, lacking better, we found them heavenly.'

On 6th January Che wrote to Castro, 'I told you that you will always have the merit of having demonstrated the possibility of armed struggle with the support of the people in America.' For him, this was the total vindication of what he had begun to believe in Guatemala. On 16th February Che participated in the second battle of Pino del Agua led by Castro. A company of the national army had established a permanent base there and it was necessary to eradicate them. Several rebel officers felt Castro had put himself at risk during the battle and wrote him a memo asking him to avoid exposing himself to danger unnecessarily, for the sake of the revolution. According to Che, who was one of the signatories, Castro did not even bother to acknowledge receipt.

Carlos María Gutiérrez, who wrote for the Uruguayan newspaper *Mañana*, arrived from Montevideo after travelling in the Sierra for several weeks. He interviewed Che at his base in La Mesa just after the battle of Pino del Agua. Che was always delighted to greet someone from his part of the world and receive first-hand news of what was going on in his own country. Prior to independence, Argentina and Uruguay had been governed jointly as part of the Provincias Unidas del Sur, so people on both sides of the Rio de la Plata have much in common. In fact, the people of Buenos Aires have more in common with those from Montevideo, the Uruguayan capital just across the river (albeit the widest river in the world), than with some of their fellow nationals from more remote areas of their own country. The two men chatted for hours over their maté, and not only about politics and revolution: Gutiérrez was carrying state-of-the-art professional photographic equipment and Che, always a keen amateur photographer, wanted to learn all about it. He then accompanied Gutiérrez to meet Castro.

When the journalist returned to his native Montevideo, he crossed over to Buenos Aires to share his news from the Sierra with the Guevara household. He was immediately adopted by them and treated as a member of the family whenever he visited Argentina. For the first time, Che's parents caught a glimpse of what their son really looked like from the photographs he brought (Che had been away from home almost six years and they had seen only a few published photos) and were told of his exploits as a guerrilla leader.

They heard he was idolised by his men, with whom he shared a camaraderie that had turned his unit into a brotherhood of fighters, prepared to lay down their lives for the common cause as well as for each other. The guerrillas would sing a ditty which went, '*Quítate de la acera/*

mira que te tumbo/ que aquí viene el Che Guevara/ acabando con el mundo'
(Stop hanging around on the sidelines/ and be careful not to fall/ because
here comes Che Guevara/ on his way to change the world). His parents were
told he had distinguished himself not only as a soldier in combat but also
as a strategist, that he always led from the front and set an example. They
learnt of his activities as a doctor among the *campesinos* and as a planner
who had devised ways to keep his army supplied and the morale of his men
high. And he had also become a primary-school teacher, as many of the
guajiros who fought alongside him were illiterate. The Guevaras were, of
course, immensely proud of him, but their feelings would always be tinged
by the anxiety they felt for his safety.

But the journalist whose visit to the Sierra would be of the greatest
importance, and who was eventually to become a key member of Che's
inner circle, was the Argentine Jorge Ricardo Masetti, from Radio El Mundo
of Buenos Aires. Masetti carried a letter for Che from Ricardo Rojo which
would no doubt yield him the scoop he sought, but first he had to find Che.
He had gone from Havana to Santiago, a distance of some 900 kilometres,
looking for a contact to make his existence known to the rebels. At last he
met a group of guerrillas who led him to the foot of the Sierra Maestra
where Juan Almeida, one of the *Granma* veterans, commanded the liberated
area and represented the 26th July Movement.

Masetti had been through much hardship by the time he arrived at Che's
base in the Sierra, wearing a torn and discoloured guerrilla uniform and
carrying a heavy backpack with cumbersome equipment to record his
interviews. The weather could go from extreme heat to intense cold and
there was frequent torrential rain. Food was not always available nor was it
possible to sleep much during the steep climb through the woodlands. His
guide, provided by the rebels at the foot of the Sierra, took short cuts to
avoid dangerous encounters, sometimes crawling through the mud on all
fours. By now the government was aware of the damage that foreign
correspondents' reports were causing, and Batista's men would not hesitate
to get rid of a member of the foreign press and then create circumstances
that made it look as though it had been the work of the guerrillas.

Che and his column had taken over an old uninhabited farmhouse
called La Otilia, near Las Minas, where the infamous Colonel Sánchez-

Mosquera continued to terrorise the population. Masetti arrived at Che's encampment after dark, to be told the Comandante was out on a sortie against the army. He was greeted with curiosity and asked many questions about Argentina, about President Frondizi and about Carlos Gardel, the tango singer and composer who had conquered Paris and Hollywood in the 1920s and 1930s with his good looks, inimitable style and voice. The men wanted to know if Masetti was Che's brother as he spoke like Che (an Argentine accent is very different from a Cuban one).

Che returns to camp on horseback after a skirmish in the
Escambray mountains, 1958

At about six in the morning, Che's men began to arrive. Che followed them, mounted on a mule, with rifle and ammunition as well as his camera, which hung from his neck. He dismounted and walked towards Masetti, whose first impression was that, in spite of his attire, Che still looked like a middle-class Argentine youth. The journalist was invited to have breakfast and the two men sat down together. They started a tentative formal conversation, but the ice soon broke after they discovered the many things they had in common. They began talking to each other using the familiar *vos*, which is how people of the same age (Masetti was a year younger than Che) and social background addressed each other in Argentina in those days. (Today everybody uses the familiar form, whether they have met before or not.) Masetti's political ideas, however, had thus far been the exact opposite of Che's Marxism, as he had been a militant in a right-wing nationalist organisation in Buenos Aires. They were both, nonetheless, against American imperialism and the new type of colonialism it represented throughout Latin America.

During the recorded interview, Masetti asked Che why he was fighting for Cuba. Che calmly replied that he knew of no other way to topple dictatorships and liberate the Americas. Masetti asked him whether he feared that his participation in the internal affairs of a country which was not his might be labelled as interference. Che took advantage of the opportunity to launch a tirade leaving no room for doubt as to his motives, principles and ideals:

> In the first place I consider my country not only Argentina, but the whole of America. I have predecessors as glorious as Martí and it is precisely in his homeland that I am complying with his doctrine. Also, I cannot conceive that it can be called interference that I give myself personally, that I give myself completely, when I offer my blood to a cause which I consider just and popular, to help a people free themselves from a tyranny that does admit the interference of a foreign power that assists it with weapons, aircraft, money and military instructors. No country up to now has denounced North American interference in Cuban affairs nor has any newspaper accused the Yankees of helping Batista to massacre his people. But many are concerned about me. I am the interfering foreigner who helps the rebels with his own flesh and blood. Those who provide the weapons for a civil war are not interfering. I am.

Che treated the interview as if it were a private conversation, although in the photographs of the event he is seen holding a small tape recorder next to his face. He spoke in a confidential, non-declamatory tone and he used language which anyone would understand. There was an intimacy about it that was in sharp contrast to the way politicians normally spoke in radio broadcasts at the time. He even used the recording to send greetings to his family, saying this was the first opportunity he had had in a couple of years to give them his news. He came across as a sincere young man who did not seek personal glory or benefits, was not aligned to any foreign cause, and was not an adventurer or a mercenary. When asked whether Castro was a communist, he replied, 'Fidel is not a communist. Politically one could call him a revolutionary nationalist.'

Masetti left for Jibacoa after their meeting, having agreed to meet up with Che again at his headquarters. When Masetti returned he was able to participate in a broadcast to the Cuban people from Radio Rebelde. To the guerrillas' surprise and delight, their improvised radio station could be heard in the USA as well as in the Caribbean. But not in Buenos Aires. Masetti had to return to the Sierra and record a further interview with Che. This time Che described the agrarian reform in progress. Masetti interviewed Fidel Castro as well, when he arrived at La Mesa. Castro spoke like an orator and a leader.

Masetti's return journey to Argentina was not easy, as by now he was a wanted man with a price on his head, but he had several hours of recordings which he turned into four radio programmes. They were an enormous success. His scoop had surpassed his wildest expectations. Because of their immediacy – the sound of enemy aircraft and machine guns could be heard in the background – the interviews were living evidence of what the guerrillas were experiencing.

The reports by Gutiérrez and Masetti marked the beginning of the Che Guevara legend in Latin America. The exploits of the young Argentine doctor, turned comandante, were the talk of the town in Buenos Aires and beyond. The capital's broadsheets were soon publishing accounts and photographs of the guerrilla leader, even if their line was to criticise him and what he fought for. It turned us all into his admirers, whatever our political convictions. The man had chutzpah and guts, and such good looks that he could compete in the glamour stakes with any of the foreign screen heroes of the period, imposed on us in the name of modern culture. Here was Errol Flynn or Clark Gable, except he was for real and he was one of us. Those of us too privileged or too young to understand his politics could still relate to the fact that he was putting his life on the line for what he believed in. There was something heroic about the man, and we were seduced. He was the rebel par excellence and the young could identify with that.

Masetti brought back a personal recording from Che for his family, which cheered them up but also marked their own serious involvement with the cause Che had embraced. Guevara Senior had ample experience in organising committees to assist worthy causes: he had been instrumental in the creation of one to assist the Spanish Republic in the 1930s. After the Republic fell, he turned his skills to aiding the refugees fleeing Franco's Spain. There was also his experience as an active member of Acción Argentina, the group formed to denounce Nazi infiltration in his country, so he had the know-how and the motivation. He did not hesitate in offering his home and office to members of the 26th July Movement operating in Buenos Aires. Soon he would rent more office space to house their activities. He organised fund-raising events and became an enthusiastic hands-on participant.

On 23rd February a group from the 26th July Movement in Havana, led by Faustino Pérez (a veteran of the *Granma* landing), kidnapped the Argentine racing driver and five-times world champion Juan Manuel Fangio, who was in Cuba for a Grand Prix race. Batista's government had organised a huge public-relations exercise around this international sporting event, to prove to the world the guerrillas were not really a threat and all was well in the country. Fangio had landed a couple of days earlier and was staying at the Lincoln Hotel in downtown Havana. The evening before the race, he was chatting in the lobby of the hotel with his friends and fellow drivers, Stirling Moss and Alejandro di Tomasso, when he was picked up by a rebel commando. He was driven to a safe house and kept there undetected for several days. The rebels thus turned the Batista publicity machine to their own advantage and created a furore which focused the eyes of the world on Cuba.

The race was an unmitigated disaster: it had to be abandoned because of an accident during the fifth lap when two cars drove off the track, killing six people and injuring forty. Once his captors decided it was safe to release Fangio, he asked to be put in touch with the Argentine ambassador, who was none other than Che's uncle, Rear Admiral Raúl Guevara-Lynch. Fangio's stay in Cuba had lasted only a week, but it had been a rather eventful one, even for him.

Reminiscing years later in Buenos Aires, Fangio told me that he had been happy to miss the race because he had not been altogether satisfied with his car's performance during practice. It was a Maserati, loaned to him by its American owner. He also told me he had been treated well by his captors and never blindfolded, although he had made a point of telling them from the outset that, even if he sympathised with their cause, he did not approve of their methods as he did not believe in violence. And what's more, Batista had given him the prize money as if he had won the race, as compensation. Fangio also told me that he returned to Cuba in 1981 as president of Mercedes-Benz Argentina (a firm with whom he had a long professional association and whose cars he had driven to victory over the years) and received an apology from Castro himself. 'He sent for me and greeted me with a huge hug,' Fangio said.

There was a lull in the fighting during April, which Che put to good use: he set up a school for future guerrillas at Minas del Frío, calling it the Escuela de Reclutas Ciro Redondo, in memory of their fallen comrade. He had trenches dug and ordered that fortifications be built while he inspected the surrounding areas. He was engrossed in Mao Tse-tung's book on guerrilla warfare but also took time to familiarise himself with the history of Cuba, something he would need at his fingertips after the triumph of the revolution, when he was frequently invited to speak in public. Castro put him in charge of the school, but this meant staying away from the front for the time being, which he was not particularly happy about. He continued to carry out his duties as a doctor and a dentist, as well as attending to local women during childbirth.

Che wrote to Camilo from his encampment at La Otilia, telling him to prepare some cigars as he would soon be joining him. In a jovial mood, he added kisses for everybody. Camilo replied, addressing Che as his soul brother, and said he was thrilled Castro had put him in charge of the Military School: not only because the result would be some first-class soldiers but also because he felt that he should be preserved for the future of the revolution, when he would be needed even more than during this early stage. He reminded Che that he had been his (Camilo's) commanding officer and would always be; thanks to Che, he was now able to be more useful to the revolution, and he would always strive to make him proud. He signed himself 'your eternal fan'.

Pablo Ribalta, a young black communist who had studied in Prague, arrived in the Sierra to join Che and participate in the political education of the recruits, although his left-wing credentials were kept under wraps. He even used a pseudonym. Ribalta would eventually be instrumental in the organisation of Che's Congo campaign, as he was by then the Cuban ambassador to Tanzania. Another young black man who would become inseparable from Che until his final days was Harry Villegas-Tamayo. He was sixteen years old and arrived at Minas del Frío to be trained. Today he is a revered figure of Cuba's *generación histórica* (historic generation), a general and a Hero of the Revolution.

On 9th April the 26th July Movement called a general strike, to take place all over the island, but it was a failure. Che tells us in his recollections of the event that 'An organisation was formed, the Frente Nacional Obrero [National Workers' Movement], led by remote control by the 26th July Movement. From inception it was a victim of the malady of sectarianism.' On 3rd May Castro called a meeting at Altos de Mompié to discuss this failure. He also announced that he had decided to create a new column, named Columna No. 8 Ciro Redondo. He put Che in charge of it. Many of the men under his command were graduates from his school at Minas del Frío.

On 25th May Batista launched the Great Summer Offensive, an all-out military campaign against the Rebel Army in the Sierra Maestra. It would last until the beginning of August. Ten thousand of Batista's troops, heavily armed, set out for Las Mercedes to the north of the Sierra Maestra. They were to attack Bueyecito and Las Mercedes simultaneously. Che was back in action, and not a moment too soon. The ground held by the rebels was to be defended at any cost.

Heavy fighting took place in June and July at Santo Domingo, Las Mercedes and Providencia. In mid-July the battle of El Jigüe lasted ten days and marked the beginning of the rebel counter-offensive. It was a decisive victory. Che and his men were defending Minas del Frío and later Las Mercedes, and did not take part in the battle of El Jigüe, which was fought by Castro and his men. The government troops were led by Major José Quevedo, who had been a classmate of Castro's at the University of Havana. Castro sent him a letter with one of his soldiers who had been taken prisoner, asking him to surrender: it would be an honourable action since he, Castro, was not an enemy of the fatherland but a sincere revolutionary, a man who fought for the welfare of all Cubans, and both he and Major Quevedo wanted the same things for Cuba. At first Quevedo rejected the offer, but eventually he met up with Castro and was swayed by his rhetoric. He decided to join the rebels and convinced several other military units to surrender or change sides, thus avoiding heavier losses on both sides.

In the course of the Great Summer Offensive the army lost more than a thousand combatants. Along with those killed, wounded or taken prisoner were a significant number of deserters. The rebels lost Comandante René Ramos-Latour, Andrés Cueva and Ramón Paz, who were both promoted to comandante posthumously, as well as many men. But they also availed themselves 'of six hundred abandoned weapons, including one tank, twelve mortars, twelve tripod machine guns, and an impressive quantity of automatic arms, not counting an incredible amount of ammunition of all sorts', in Che's words. The net result was that Batista's army had been broken and its men came out of the experience having lost the will to fight. But the rebels did not delude themselves. They knew they were still far from the end of the war.

Castro decided that the time had come to extend the war beyond the Sierra. On 21st August he signed a military order stating, 'The strategic objective of Column Number 8 will be to harass the enemy constantly throughout central Cuba and intercept enemy troop movements overland from west to east until they are completely paralysed, as well as other objectives which may be ordered as appropriate.'

So, Comandante Ernesto Che Guevara had his marching orders. He notified his men, in his usual blunt and direct manner, of the hardships ahead: a terrain they did not know, probable harassment from the enemy, hunger, thirst, cold and lack of resources. Perhaps 50 per cent of them would still be alive on arrival. Nobody budged. By now they were seasoned warriors. This fratricidal war had not been a picnic so far, and there was no reason for it to get any easier – plus, they knew who was leading them. Che may have been a hard taskmaster but the man he drove the hardest was himself, and he had always been fair. Comrades who had been with him so far were coming along too: Ramiro Valdés, Joel Iglesias and Oscarito Fernández-Mell. He was in good company.

They set off from the Sierra Maestra on 31st August, heading towards Las Villas province in central Cuba. Several days earlier Camilo Cienfuegos, who was by now leading his own column, No. 4, had been ordered to march towards Pinar del Río province on the western side of Cuba.

Che and Fidel Castro interrogate Evelio Lafaerte, one of the first
officers of Batista's army to join the guerrillas

Che and his men had planned to set off by lorry on 30th August but
their plans were thwarted after a succession of reverses. The plane carrying
weapons for them landed near the road and was spotted by the army, so
they had to set it alight. This prevented them reaching the lorry which had
brought them uniforms and petrol. They had expected to retrieve their
lorries after crossing the Manzanillo–Bayamo road but a cyclone prevented
them from driving, and they had no alternative but to continue on foot or
horseback, 'heavily loaded with ammunition, with forty rocket bazookas,
and everything necessary for a long march and a quick setting-up of camp',
as Che put it. Ahead of them were impassable roads plagued by mosquitoes,
with only water from puddles to drink. It was near impossible to keep their
weapons dry as they crossed rivers in flood. Finding fresh horses also
became a problem as they had to avoid densely populated areas.

Camilo Cienfuegos, who was not far off with his column, came to see
them on 2nd and 5th September. On 7th September Che wrote a report for
Castro about his column's progress so far, describing how tough it had been
on his men, some of whom were by now marching barefoot. On 8th
September the cyclone had turned into a hurricane. On 9th September Che
and Camilo Cienfuegos met up again and the same day, at La Federal, Che's
advance guard fell into an ambush and two men died. Then they lost four

more men when they were taken prisoner after a minor skirmish. They had, however, reduced the enemy garrison. Two days later they reached Laguna Grande and met up with Camilo Cienfuegos' forces, who had arrived before them and were in far better shape.

Che's vanguard next clashed with the enemy at Cuatro Compañeros, and an intense battle ensued. The air force spotted the rebels and bombarded them. They were flying B-26s, C-47s and C-3s and they cost the rebels one life and several wounded. By now Che's men were eating infrequently and were racked by fatigue and thirst. The vegetation which grew in the swamps had rotted their boots and was now lacerating their feet, so each step was a torment. Che wrote that they had become 'an army of shadows', encircled by enemy forces. They finally broke the encirclement and reached the road from Júcaro to Morón, but they were in really bad shape. And then the weather broke and it rained torrentially. They were compelled to march on, disheartened, sick and exhausted. Che resorted to a variety of verbal entreaties, from words of encouragement to violent insults, to keep them going until, at long last, they spotted the cordillera of Las Villas.

Most of them had never seen these mountains before but their appearance on the horizon seemed to have an incredible effect. A new spirit took hold. They marched on and managed to escape a second encirclement by swimming across the Júcaro river, which marks the boundary between the provinces of Camagüey and Las Villas. Two days later, they were at the Trinidad–Sancti Spiritus mountains and felt as if they had left the worst behind. They rested briefly and then moved on again, as time was of the essence. It was their intention to interfere with the elections due to take place on 3rd November. Batista had called national elections with the intention of providing legal cover for his dictatorship. The 26th July Movement had called for a boycott and organised ways in which to obstruct voter participation. In the event there was massive voter abstention and Batista's candidate (Andrés Rivero Agüero) was declared the winner.

On 16th October Che's column finally arrived in the Escambray mountains, where he established contact with other guerrilla forces. On 21st October he met the heads of the Directorio guerrillas in El Algarrobo. One of them, Faure Chomón, tells us, 'Che stopped at a place where we had a school for rural children . . . Everyone was resting on the ground, forming a circle round the school. It was a sight for sore eyes . . . we saw them with their clothes in rags and their shoes wrecked but still preserving intact all the spirited fighting presence of the revolutionary. Che rose to salute us, and we knew it was him from the gesture. We shook hands and spoke. We asked him why he had not made himself comfortable with his men inside the school, and he answered that the school was very nice and could not be messed up.' On 26th October, Che's column, fighting together with Faure Chomón's men, attacked and took the garrison at Güinía de Miranda. Che tells us that 'The days before the date set for the election were a time of extraordinary activity, our columns were moving in every direction and almost totally prevented voters from getting to the polls in these zones.'

By early December the rebel columns led by Che and Camilo Cienfuegos had captured a number of towns in Las Villas province and effectively cut the island in half, as they had been ordered by Castro. Che thought that 'there were increasing signs that the enemy was falling apart'. Between 15th and 18th December, the town of Fomento was attacked and taken. This was the last obstacle between the rebels and the main highway. On 23rd December the rebels attacked and took the town of Cabaiguán on the Central Highway. On the 24th, they attacked and took the town of Placetas, where Che installed his headquarters in the Hotel Tullerías. On the 25th, the towns of Remedios and Caibairén, on the northern coast of Las Villas, were liberated. Che's column began preparing for the battle for Santa Clara, the capital of Las Villas. Other troops were simultaneously taking Sancti Spiritus, Yaguajay, Santo Domingo and the neighbouring towns. Castro, in the meantime, wrote to Che to inform him they were winning in Oriente, too, as he had surrounded 10,000 men who had no way out.

As life got organised in the liberated territories, Che had resources at his disposal which he had never had before. Oscarito Fernández-Mell reports, 'We covered part of the distance to Las Vegas by jeep, and as it was raining the road was very bad and Che took short cuts through the narrow passes with plenty of determination but not a lot of skill, and all he said to me was: "as soon as we get there I am going to tell you something". And sure enough, as soon as we got out he told me it was the first time he had ever driven.'

Che and Ramiro Valdés stopped at their headquarters in Placetas to decide on their tactics for the assault on Santa Clara. At this point, Dr Antonio Núñez-Jiménez, who taught at the Central University of Las Villas in Santa Clara, arrived. He was carrying the master plan to the city, showing the access routes which Che had asked for. He had brought them himself because it was his intention to join the column. The information he provided was invaluable and soon Column No. 8 was on its way. News arrived from Oriente province telling them the rebels there had taken the city of Palma Soriano. At six in the morning of 28th December, Che and his column arrived at the university, where he established his headquarters. By half past eight the air force was bombing them, destroying the hospital's maternity ward as well as several neighbouring houses.

The government had 3,000 troops as well as an armoured train in Santa Clara. Che's forces comprised Captain Rogelio Acevedo's platoon of 30 men, Lieutenant Alberto Fernández-Montes de Oca's platoon of 10 men (Montes de Oca was to lose his life in Bolivia), Lieutenant Emerido Reyes' platoon of 30 men, Captain Alfonso Zayas's platoon of 50 men, Captain Ramón Pardo-Guerra's platoon of 40 men, Captain Miguel Álvarez's Command platoon of 30 men, plus 100 men from the Directorio Revolucionario led by Comandante Rolando Cubela and a reserve platoon of 50 men under Lieutenant Pablo Ribalta. Obviously, they were no match for Batista's army. Bombing by the air force continued intermittently during the day. That night Che took a walk along the railway track to try and find a weak point so he could get at the armoured train which lay in wait in the station at Santa Clara.

On 29th December he moved his headquarters less than a kilometre from the city. He had made a radio appeal to the population, asking them to cooperate with his rebel forces. At daybreak he ordered that a section of the railway track be destroyed. He then entered the city with his troops. After one in the afternoon the attack started. Roberto Rodríguez, the young guerrilla who led the squad of elite volunteers known as *el pelotón suicida* (the suicide squad) and had frequently distinguished himself in action since he joined Che's column, took the train station. At three in the afternoon, the armoured train started to move away while being attacked with Molotov cocktails and hand grenades. It turned into an inferno. Soon it reached the place where the tracks had been destroyed, where it derailed. The soldiers inside were now forced out and had to make a choice between fighting or surrendering to the guerrillas.

Batista was informed of the developments and chose to tell the international press that Comandante Guevara was dead. But Radio Rebelde was broadcasting very different news: not only was Guevara alive, but he had also captured the armoured train, and taken more than 300 enemy soldiers prisoner. His troops had taken innumerable weapons and two railway cars full of explosives. The rebel troops in Oriente were in the meantime taking the city of Maffo, Camilo Cienfuegos was taking the city of Yaguajay not far from Santa Clara, and Castro and his men were now poised to attack the city of Santiago de Cuba.

The two army commanders in Santa Clara retreated from their headquarters in disguise, leaving their men to their own devices. By midnight, as the year was coming to an end, there were only three places in the city which had not been taken: the Gran Hotel, the barracks of the 31st Squadron and the Leoncio Vidal Barracks. The Gran Hotel was the next to fall to the rebels when the sharpshooters on the tenth floor were isolated. They had to drop their weapons and leave the building with their hands above their heads. By the time the 31st Squadron surrendered, rumours that Batista had absconded were rife in Santa Clara.

In Havana, a military junta – aided and abetted by the US embassy – attempted to take office. Castro, who was in Palma Soriano, at the opposite end of the island, spoke on Radio Rebelde, calling a general strike as well as ordering that, as soon as Santa Clara was liberated, the Rebel Army columns led by Comandantes Camilo Cienfuegos and Che Guevara should advance on Havana. He also demanded the surrender of all remaining garrisons with his famous phrase, 'Yes to revolution, no to military coup.'

In Santa Clara, Che was busy trying to obtain the surrender of the Leoncio Vidal Barracks, the last piece of the puzzle which would give him overall victory in Las Villas. By midday, the exhausted government soldiers began to leave the building, having dropped their weapons. The rebels took the barracks and the fighting was over.

Che was heartbroken when he learnt of the death of Captain Roberto Rodríguez, nicknamed El Vaquerito (the cowboy). He was one of the most colourful members of his column because of his constant good humour and the tall stories he was in the habit of telling with great conviction, almost as if he believed them himself. 'They have killed a hundred of our men,' Che said, when confronted with the loss of a young man who would certainly have become a first-class soldier.

However, during the battle for Santa Clara something also took place which would bring Che great happiness. Aleida March de la Torre was an attractive twenty-four-year-old woman who had come to the Sierra with a large amount of money for Che's troops strapped to her body with bandages. She was originally from Santa Clara and had been ordered to stay there for her own protection, as the regime had discovered her activities as a courier for the 26th July Movement, but she had come to join Che's column. At first he considered her a hindrance – an attractive young woman surrounded by sex-starved young men, capable of being as brusque and blunt as he and who spoke her mind just as easily. But, after she had been with him for several days, he began to appreciate that she was serious about being a combatant and was eager to make herself useful. He even supplied her with a weapon.

Aleida on campaign with Che

Then, during the actual battle for Santa Clara, Che saw her expose herself to fire while crossing a street and realised that he cared for her. They stayed together from then on, and would eventually get married – once he had obtained a divorce from Hilda – and have four children in the eight years they spent together.

SIXTEEN
(1959)

On 1st January Fulgencio Batista was celebrating the arrival of the New Year with a ball at the Camp Columbia Barracks. At dawn he heard that Santa Clara had fallen to the rebels and decided it was time to make a move. He went straight to the airport with his family and closest associates (taking with him approximately $300 million), boarded his aircraft, which had been on standby for several days, and left for Santo Domingo and the sanctuary offered by fellow dictator and crony Rafael Trujillo of the Dominican Republic. The party was well and truly over. He would never return to his country and sat out his exile in the USA and Europe until his death at Estoril in Portugal in 1973.

The triumph of the *barbudos* also brought about the end of the good times in Cuba for Meyer Lansky, Frank Sinatra, George Raft, Lucky Luciano, Bugsy Seigel and their friends and associates in the gambling, narcotics and prostitution business. Lansky and company were on the next plane out of the country. Cuba had been a casino and brothel for its wealthy neighbours for a long time, while much of the native population were illiterate, toothless, underfed and had a life expectancy of about thirty years.

Others left in private yachts or took refuge in the embassies of friendly countries. But not everybody connected to Batista managed to abscond. Many military men discarded their uniforms, changed their names and tried to keep a low profile. It was not easy for them to hide because many had boasted of their crimes and photographs and souvenirs taken from their victims were found in their homes.

On 2nd January Che prepared to set off for Havana to comply with Castro's instructions and take the fortress of La Cabaña. Camilo Cienfuegos and his men had already left for the capital to take the barracks at Camp

Columbia. After a brief farewell speech in which he thanked Las Villas for its support, and with his ranks augmented by the local men who had joined the struggle there and fought alongside his veterans, Che's column was once more on the road. Che had his right arm in plaster as he had fallen climbing a parapet and broken a bone; Aleida had made him a sling with a big black gauze scarf.

The *Daily News* of New York announces the triumph
of the Revolution

Soon his caravan of cars, lorries and jeeps stopped at the town of Coliseo to refuel. Che and Aleida were briefly left alone in their jeep during the stop, so he took advantage of the opportunity to tell her he loved her. In her memoir of their time together, *Evocación* (published in Cuba in 2007), Aleida tells us she was daunted by what he said: partly because this man was a hero, the famous guerrilla leader and her commanding officer, but also because she was half-asleep and thought perhaps she had misheard him. So she said nothing, and wondered whether he was expecting a reply or a reaction which never came.

The fortress of San Carlos de la Cabaña occupies a commanding position over the bay of Havana

They reached Matanzas at sunset. He stopped at the telephone exchange to call Camilo, who had arrived at Camp Columbia, to ask how his troops had been received in the capital. The Fortress of San Carlos de La Cabaña is an overpowering structure. It was built on the east side of Havana harbour between 1763 and 1774 to defend the city from foreign invasions, mainly from Britain, and is the largest Spanish colonial fortress in the Americas, covering an area of 10 hectares. Batista used it as a military prison. It was dawn on 3rd January when Che and his men reached Havana and occupied La Cabaña, where there were still some government troops. He urged the soldiers and his own guerrillas to coexist in harmony.

Che took over the commandant's house in the grounds. (Aleida, and a couple of other women who were travelling with the column, took advantage of the fact that Lieutenant Colonel Fernández-Miranda and his wife, who was Batista's sister, had left in a hurry, to go through the clothes she left behind and help themselves to something clean to wear.) A few eyebrows were raised when Che lodged his black escort in the adjoining apartment. The Cubans were not ready for racial integration just yet, although many were of mixed race and many black and mulatto guerrillas had fought alongside their white comrades of Spanish descent, both in the Sierra and the cities. But until now black Cubans, descendants of slaves imported by the Spanish to work in the sugar mills, had not challenged their existing social status. They were not segregated, as in the USA, but they held no prominent positions in a Cuba ruled by a white elite.

Che settled in and then telephoned Castro, who was now in Bayamo. Manuel Urrutia, the choice of the 26th July Movement, assumed the presidency. Che gave several interviews to the local press as well as one over the telephone to an Argentine newspaper.

Camilo Cienfuegos and Fidel Castro enter Havana in triumph

On 8th January Castro arrived in Havana after a week's victory tour of the island. He travelled at the head of a caravan from Santiago to Havana in an open jeep or on top of a tank, stopping frequently in front of adoring crowds so that his fellow Cubans could discover what he looked like and get used to seeing him. His tour was covered by the television news every day. Che drove to Matanzas with Aleida to liaise with him before the final lap.

Castro spoke at Camp Columbia and the speech was broadcast live on television. The reception by the public was overwhelming. The newsreel of the event shows that two white doves alighted on his shoulder while he spoke. The crowds were ecstatic, but his detractors claimed it was stage-managed, as these docile birds can be trained to obey orders. This was the first example of something that was to become a life-long habit: haranguing the masses for several hours at a time. He called it 'direct democracy'. During these lengthy rallies he would ask the people for their opinions and seek their approval of his decisions. The term, coined by Castro on this occasion, would become a useful device for pretending the people were being consulted. In future there would be no need for the complicated and costly process of consultation via the ballot box, which might also come up with a result contradicting Castro.

The following day Che greeted his parents and his teenage brother Juan Martín, his sister Celia and her husband Luis Rodríguez-Argañaraz at the airport. His other two siblings, Roberto and Ana María, had stayed behind in Buenos Aires because of their work commitments. It was Camilo's idea to invite them and surprise Che, who might have preferred them to come later on, when the revolution had been consolidated. The Guevaras of Argentina travelled in an aircraft of the national carrier, Cubana de Aviación, sent to Buenos Aires to collect returning exiles. Che had not seen his family since 1953. On arrival Guevara Senior, never one to disguise his emotions, knelt and kissed the tarmac, long before Pope John Paul II turned the gesture into a much-repeated photo opportunity.

Che inaugurated the Military Cultural Academy at La Cabaña, founded the newssheet *La Cabaña Libre* and organised classes for all combatants wishing to learn to read and write. For those who were already able to read, there were courses on history, geography, and the social and economic features of the countries of Latin America, as well as the political and social situation throughout the world. Courses on military matters, mechanics and ballistics were set up for all combatants. Cultural and sports activities were organised and were open to all. In the evening, films were shown. He also created a riding school and set up chess courses.

He did away with cockfights; these entailed betting and Che believed they generated an atmosphere of rivalry, often ending in brawls and vendettas. He also created an internal supply system, called the Empresa Cabaña Libre, so his troops would never run out of provisions. He called upon a judge to conduct a mass wedding ceremony for all those guerrillas who were in a steady relationship. He even provided a priest for those who wanted their union to be blessed by the church. These were the days before the contraceptive pill and women's liberation, and Che was aware of the stigma on children without a father and the plight of single women struggling to bring up their children on their own. He gave his first speech since the triumph of the revolution at a ceremony in his honour organised by the Medical College in Havana, during which he was given an honorary doctorate.

On 21st January his wife Hilda Gadea and their daughter Hildita Guevara-Gadea arrived in Havana. It was only fair that Hilda, who had been so generous to Che when he was broke in Guatemala and Mexico and had then gone on to work for the 26th July Movement from her parents' home in Lima, should enjoy the fruits of the revolution. Besides, she was a Marxist economist and would be able to contribute to the general reorganisation that was now taking place. And Che wanted to see his little daughter, Hildita, now aged three, for whom he had always had a special affection.

Che and Hilda had been separated not by the revolution but by their own differences. Che had considered their marriage over for some time. While he was in Mexico, training for the invasion, he had even written to his parents announcing the termination of the relationship. If Hilda thought she was travelling to Cuba to retrieve her husband and resume married life she could not have been more misguided. With his characteristic bluntness, Che informed her he was now in a relationship with another woman and wanted a divorce. This time round Che was in love, in as much as a man who was married to the revolution could be in love with anyone.

In late January the Chilean socialist politician Dr Salvador Allende and his family visited Che at La Cabaña. Although there was great empathy between the two men, they agreed to disagree on the methods of attaining power. Allende was a staunch believer in the ballot box.

During February Che set up a tribunal at La Cabaña 'to judge the enemies of the Cuban people': those who had committed crimes, tortured and killed to keep Batista in power. (The number of people disposed of during the period 1952–8 was estimated at about 20,000.) Much has been written about Che's summary justice at La Cabaña, since he was in charge and had the final word after the appeals had been heard. The debate continues to this day, fifty years on. The enemies of the revolution claim that he sent thousands to their death. The exact figure cannot be ascertained but it is probably closer to two hundred, if that.

There are those who accuse Che of enjoying the executions, of being a sadist who went around cracking skulls and organising mock executions. I hesitate to trust these accounts because they originate with the enemies of the revolution, people who were forced to leave their country because they disagreed with Castro politically or because they were US employees and had lost their livelihood. They might well demonise those whose ideology differed from theirs.

Che was a sophisticated, well-read, worldly, refined man as well as a purist. He was in a loving relationship, had a home at last, and his parents and two of his siblings were in town. He had a fulfilling job, a revolutionary project to implement which included reorganising the armed forces, drafting laws and planning foreign policy. And he was learning to fly a twin-engine Cessna which Castro had put at his disposal, in view of his growing responsibilities throughout the island. Half the world was descending on Havana and wanted to see him, so where did he find the time to go around cracking skulls? He may have thought it was his duty to administer harsh justice but I do not believe he would have stooped to committing barbarous acts of revenge. There were identical tribunals in other Cuban cities and several hundred people were tried and executed across the island. Raúl Castro was in charge of a similar procedure at the opposite end of Cuba.

But Che has also been quoted as saying, 'It is not possible to tolerate even the suspicion of treason' and 'We do not need to use bourgeois legal methods – the proof is secondary.' It has been said that he sent teenagers to their death, but this was a war fought by very young men. Many who joined the guerrillas in the Sierra were as young as fifteen. Che seriously believed the revolution would not be consolidated if the enemy were given the opportunity to regroup and organise a resistance. (The lesson of Guatemala had been learnt.) There were still pockets of dissidents in the mountains who could cause trouble for the revolution. The general public in Cuba was in an unforgiving mood and ready to take the law into their own hands. They had done it before twenty years earlier, during a rebellion against the dictator Machado. There was a real fear the situation could deteriorate into a massacre and the city descend into chaos. So the revolutionary government proceeded to execute the enemy 'without due process', administering summary justice. Although witnesses and lawyers were present, there was no jury.

Che chose the judges carefully among those whose reputation was above reproach. He wanted revolutionary morality to triumph over vengeance and retribution. The prisoners were entitled to prepare their defence with their lawyers. The cases were heard in public. We are told by historians he preferred not to attend, but instead went through the cases in the evening with the judges and reviewed them on the basis of the existing evidence. But he thought that the only way to uphold their fragile revolution was to send its enemies before the firing squad and not allow any political or humanitarian plea to affect his decision. The two years in the Sierra and the revolutionary struggle had hardened him. He was a changed man. He had found his destiny and his life would not get any easier.

At this time, Che also held a series of secret meetings with Raúl Castro, Ramiro Valdés, Camilo Cienfuegos and Víctor Piña of the Popular Socialist Party, to plan the creation of a secret military body to ensure the security of the revolutionary government. Ramiro Valdés, who had been the second-in-command of Che's column, was put in charge of the newly created body, which went by the name of G-2.

Che was now granted Cuban citizenship in recognition of his contribution to Cuba's liberation. This privilege had previously only ever been awarded to the Dominican general, Máximo Gómez, during the war of independence from Spain, more than a hundred years earlier. Castro had to lower the age mentioned in the decree to thirty so it could apply to Guevara.

Che did not, however, renounce his Argentine citizenship. It is practically impossible to do this since Argentina, being a land of immigrants, vast and underpopulated, does not object to its citizens having more than one nationality. On the same day, there was a ceremony at Colón Cemetery, in the neighbourhood of Nuevo Vedado, to rebury the remains of those comrades who had fallen during the invasion.

On 16th February Fidel Castro became Prime Minister and the country embarked on an extensive programme of economic and social reforms. Two laws quickly followed, bringing down the price of electricity and reducing rents by between 30 and 50 per cent. Racial discrimination was outlawed, but it would be a very long time before the black population of the island saw themselves as equals, even though blacks and mulattos had helped in the fight against the Spanish in the 1890s. After all, their origins were totally different from the white population and their traditions and beliefs were unlike those of the white Cubans. Santería, a version of the Yoruba faith from Nigeria blended in with saints from the Roman Catholic pantheon to disguise its true origin, is with them to this day, and even doctors and professors would stop short of disputing the validity of its witchcraft and sorcery elements or calling it superstition. The Communist Party of Cuba was far more sensitive than Castro's middle-class revolutionaries in its attitude towards blacks, with the renowned communist poet Nicolás Guillén, probably the most famous black man in Cuba, leading the way. From his exile in Buenos Aires he had written a poem to Che comparing him to General San Martín, the legendary liberator of Argentina, Chile and Peru.

In March Che's whole body suffered a serious collapse and his doctors demanded he take a break. When told to move away from the city, he selected a large house which had been confiscated in the privileged neighbourhood of Tarará, famous for its turquoise sea and the immaculate sands of its exclusive beaches, with palm-lined streets and tropical gardens. He intended to continue working from home and it was large enough to accommodate him and Aleida and his bodyguards, as well as having space for meetings with members of his immediate entourage. It had previously belonged to a *batistiano* customs officer, who had obviously found a way to supplement his meagre state salary, since the house was quite luxurious.

When the magazine *Caretas* published something that could be read as an insinuation that he was abusing his privileges, Che wrote an irate letter to the editor, Carlos Franqui. He informed him that he was ill: he had not become ill in casinos or nightclubs but by working harder than his body could tolerate; the government had loaned him a house owned by a supporter of the previous regime because his salary as an officer of the Rebel Army was not large enough to pay for it; he had chosen the least luxurious of the requisitioned villas, and he would give it up as soon as his doctors allowed him to return to normal life. He asked that the letter be published, so the people to whom he was accountable would be aware of his situation. One can easily imagine the rage of this most austere of men, whose attitude verged on the puritanical and who thought it was his role to be an example.

Today, the area of Tarará is just as exclusive as the government uses it to house the foreigners who flock to the island's state-of-the-art medical clinics. Cuba continues to be in the vanguard of modern medicine and even exports doctors to third-world countries. The country likes its foreign currency to come from its clinics and eminent doctors as well as from tourism, which has given it a bad name because of the inequality and prostitution it has fostered.

The first Agrarian Reform law was proclaimed in May, fixing legal holdings at a maximum of 1,000 acres (400 hectares) and distributing land to the *campesinos*. By the end of May Che and Aleida had moved out of the house in Tarará to a rented house in the area of Los Cocos in Santiago de las Vegas, a suburb of Havana. Che and Hilda's divorce was finalised on 2nd June and Che married Aleida the same day. The ceremony took place at La Cabaña and very few people were invited. Castro arrived, complaining that he had not received an invitation, although he did not stay long. The shunned ex-wife had asked that no members of the press be present and a low-key affair was planned, but the event was in all the papers the following day, something that cannot have pleased Hilda.

Once Aleida and her new husband returned to their home, Hilda sent Hildita to stay with them as what Aleida believed was some sort of Greek gift. If that was the case, the ruse failed because Che was always thrilled to have his daughter with him. Hilda's office was in the same building as Che and Aleida's and she seemed to be constantly finding excuses to make an appearance on the floor where Che and Aleida worked. According to Pepe González-Aguilar, Aleida was irrationally jealous of anybody who had been part of Che's life prior to their acquaintance and she was always guarded with his Argentine friends. And Che was not particularly adept at handling the situation between his present and former wives, which generated tensions between all three.

I was having a chat with Aleida in her house in Miramar in January 2000 when we discussed some of the biographies which were being written or had appeared for the thirtieth anniversary of Che's death. She told me that Professor Salvador Vilaseca had called to tell her he was writing a book about the time he spent with Che (Vilaseca had travelled abroad with him and gave him lessons in higher mathematics for three years). Vilaseca asked Aleida to tell him about Che's defects. He felt he could not finish his book without mentioning them, as what he had written so far might make him seem unreal. Aleida replied that she was sure Che had flaws since nobody is perfect, but she had not had a chance to discover them because their time together had been so short. Eight years, she said, if you include the time when we were in the Sierra as guerrillas.

Aleida and Che leave the party just after their wedding. Their ever-present escorts Pombo, and Hernández-López, are in the back

Aleida dismissed much of what has been written as being by people who did not understand Che's political ideas. However, she was particularly incensed by an anecdote in which Che was said to have scolded her about a picture she had hung in their new home. The story was supposed to illustrate how dogmatic and rigorous he was in every sense. Aleida wondered how anyone could imagine that a man who had so many responsibilities and who slept only four hours most nights would concern himself with such trivia or try to undermine her authority in the home. 'He was too sensitive for that,' she said. 'In any case,' Aleida went on, 'we had a tacit agreement: he attended to his official duties and I gave him a functioning home as well as working with him in his office. I saw to the smooth running of our domestic life, the children, food, clothes, and so on.'

As phenomenally hard as he did work, there was still time for leisure in the household. On Sunday afternoons, when he returned from doing voluntary work cutting sugar cane or working in a factory, Che relaxed with the children. He would take off his shirt and sit on the floor to play with them. It was then that close friends such as Pepe González-Aguilar or the Granados dropped in.

Aleida and Che's house was full of people right from the start. As well as a loyal team of helpers, including a nanny once they started to have children, his escorts were always around. These were young men who would not leave his side and who were prepared to defend him with their lives. They slept on the sitting-room floor, and it was Aleida who saw to it that they did not go without a cup of coffee or a bite to eat, although there was rationing and she had to stretch her allowance to infinity. She never complained of the lack of privacy. On the contrary, she accepted their presence as her friends and allies. Che once said rather forlornly that his children saw more of his escorts than they did of him, and when they started to talk they called the men in his detachment Papa.

When Pepe González-Aguilar was interviewing Hildita as a grown woman for a Spanish magazine, she told him she had difficulty remembering her father. The myth had been created and was all around in Cuba, so she had trouble separating it from her own memories. When she was still very small, Hildita was often with Che at his office. He worked on his papers and she made drawings on hers. They could be seen arriving hand in hand, she immaculately dressed in white from head to foot, he in his usual crumpled and worn fatigues.

On 12th June Che set out on a long trip round Europe, Africa and Asia to negotiate commercial, technical and cultural agreements, returning on 8th September. Che gave a press conference at every stop on the trip, so the visits of the Cuban delegation were widely covered by the world press. Castro urged Che to take Aleida with him, and she had asked to be included as his secretary, but he would not hear of it. The other members of the delegation were not taking their wives along. Now, he pointed out, as well as being his secretary, she was married to him and so had to stay at home.

Some biographers have suggested that Castro wanted him out of the way as he had grown so popular, but in fact the trip was particularly important for the future of Cuba. Che had meetings with several Soviet diplomats at the USSR's embassies in the various countries he visited, as well as conversations with signatories to the Bandung Pact. These were the countries that would become the Non-Aligned Movement, which Cuba would eventually join. I spoke to American historian and diplomat Henry Butterfield Ryan, when he was in England writing about Che's achievements for his book *The Fall of Che Guevara*. He told me that he believed Che's efforts as a diplomat and economic envoy were amongst his main contributions to Cuba: they have probably not been sufficiently recognised as they have been overshadowed by his exploits as a guerrilla leader.

The delegation's first stop was Madrid. Che was followed around by a photographer who took his picture at the Palacio de la Moncloa, the Faculty of Medicine, the Palacio de Oriente and the Galerías Preciados department store. He expressed his wish to visit a bullring and was invited to the one at Vistalegre by its owner, Domingo Dominguín (whose family was known throughout Spain for their communist views). That evening Che was taken to the Corral de la Morería, just like Ernest Hemingway, Pablo Picasso and John Kennedy before him, to watch a flamenco show for tourists.

In Cairo President Nasser housed him in the summer palace of the deposed King Farouk. Che visited Gaza (then part of the United Arab Republic formed by Syria, Egypt and Yemen) and was proclaimed Great Liberator of the Oppressed. He also went to Damascus, the Suez Canal, Alexandria and Port Said, where he paid tribute to those who had fallen during the British-French-

Israeli invasion of 1956. He then spent a day on board an Egyptian destroyer, observing naval manoeuvres in the Mediterranean.

At first, according to Mohamed Heikal, a close friend and advisor to the president and the editor of *Al-Ahram*, the Arab world's largest circulation newspaper at the time, Nasser had not taken the *barbudos* very seriously. He did not think their revolution could succeed under the nose of the CIA and he found Castro's Latin exuberance too theatrical. But Che's visit changed all that. Although their revolutions were very different – Nasser was a devout Muslim and had only briefly flirted with communism, to then become the father of pan-Arabism and pan-Africanism – the two men struck up a good relationship. Cairo would be Che's point of departure during his secret visit to the area, when he was involved in preparations for his Congo campaign. Many years later, Mohamed Heikal told me in Cairo that he himself had been in charge of looking after Che on that occasion, on behalf of Nasser. The president was being closely watched by the American embassy and the CIA and did not want them to know of Che's presence.

From Cairo, Che and his delegation flew directly to New Delhi, where they were greeted by Prime Minister Nehru. Che had been a keen admirer of Nehru and his seminal autobiographical book, *The Discovery of India*, had been one of his favourites in his youth, when he had first read about Gandhi's adherence to non-violent protest during British colonial rule. In the flesh, however, Nehru was a great disappointment. He was only interested in polite conversation and chitchat. Che's various attempts to involve him in serious discussion failed abysmally. But India did not disappoint and he visited the sights of New Delhi, the Taj Mahal in Agra and Calcutta.

When the party arrived in New Delhi they were joined by José Pardo-Llada, a popular radio commentator with a sharp tongue. It had been Castro's idea to dispatch him to join the mission, and it may have been that he wanted him out of the way, since he suggested the radio commentator stay on as Cuban ambassador to India. Pardo-Llada and Che detested each other from day one and both found it difficult to disguise their feelings, making barbed and ironic remarks to each other every time they were together. Pardo-Llada would eventually defect and write a vindictive, venomous book about Castro and Che, with the accusation that Castro had sent Che to his certain death in Bolivia.

During their Asian trip together, Che and Pardo-Llada had to share a hotel room, as the Cubans were extremely penny-pinching with the revolution's funds. Pardo-Llada told American journalist Georgie Ann Geyer that Che had left a letter he was writing to Aleida on his desk when he was called out in a hurry. Pardo-Llada read it and found its sexually explicit contents pornographic. This story serves to illustrate their differences. For a sophisticated Argentine, the description of what a couple of consenting adults do together in private during their honeymoon might rate as erotic or daring, but never as pornographic.

From India, the delegation flew to Burma, Thailand, Hong Kong and Japan, being received by ministers and captains of industry wherever they went. In Japan, Che made a point of skipping the visit to the war memorial commemorating the unknown soldier and went to Hiroshima instead, where he used up four rolls of film capturing the devastation. The members of the Cuban delegation were each given pearl necklaces for their wives. Che went to the Mikimoto store in Tokyo and bought Hilda a necklace identical to the one he had been given for Aleida. Perhaps this gives an indication of the lengths to which he was willing to go in order to maintain the uneasy peace he had achieved between his current and former wives.

On 31st July the delegation reached Djakarta. The Argentine ambassador to Indonesia, whose English was far more fluent than Che's, kindly acted as his interpreter. He told Che that President Ahmed Sukarno had several young women at his disposal, whom he exhibited quite shamelessly at diplomatic receptions. The latest addition was very pretty and came from Russia. At the formal meeting with President Sukarno Che told the Ambassador to ask Sukarno about his Russian girlfriend. The Ambassador had to quickly dream up a question to translate as the President was keen to know what his guest had said.

In his retelling of the story, Pardo-Llada made a big song and dance about Che's improper behaviour, which had humiliated the ambassador. What was totally lost on Pardo-Llada was that the ambassador, Ricardo Mosquera-Eastman, and Ernesto Guevara de la Serna came from the same social background in Argentina, where that sort of practical joke would have been commonplace between equals. Moreover, the visit to Indonesia was a success and the following year Sukarno reciprocated by visiting Cuba.

Top: Che meets Marshal Tito of Yugoslavia, one of the driving forces behind the non-aligned movement. *Middle*: Che gives Prime Minister of India Jawaharlal Nehru a huge box of cigars. *Bottom*: Che with Prime Minister of Egypt Gamal Abdel Nasser in Cairo

In Ceylon (now Sri Lanka) they met the president and the minister for commerce, with whom an agreement was signed for the sale of 20,000 tons of sugar. In Pakistan, he was greeted by General Ayub Khan and his country's secretary for commerce. Their next destination was Belgrade in Yugoslavia, the only communist country on their itinerary. The Yugoslavs had won their independence through guerrilla warfare and their leader, Marshal Tito, had fought with the republicans in the Spanish Civil War and was a fluent Spanish speaker. He felt a great empathy for Cuba and also wanted to hear about the latest political developments in Latin America. The last stops were at Rome, Madrid, Seville and Casablanca, before going back to Madrid for the flight to Havana. On his return, Che was appointed head of the department for industrialisation of the National Institute of Agrarian Reform.

Castro had resigned as Prime Minister on 17th July because of a government crisis stemming from President Urrutia's opposition to revolutionary measures. In response, a massive popular outcry forced Urrutia to resign and he was replaced by Osvaldo Dorticós. By 26th July Castro had been returned to his post as Prime Minister. On 21st October Huber Matos, Rebel Army comandante of Camagüey province, was arrested for counter-revolutionary activities by the Army Chief of Staff Camilo Cienfuegos. In his biography he says that he never plotted against the revolution but had resigned his post because he disagreed with the pro-Soviet orientation the government was taking. However, he served twenty years in jail for counter-revolutionary activities and then went into exile. On 26th October the National Revolutionary Militias, incorporating thousands of workers and *campesinos*, were created to fight against the threat of counter-revolution. Che would be a key player in their development.

On 28th October Camilo Cienfuegos' plane disappeared over the sea on his return flight from Camagüey to Havana. In spite of days of intensive searching, no trace of the plane was found. In desperation, Che took to the air in his Cessna and spent many hours flying over the area. He had lost his dearest friend in Cuba.

The journalist Carlos Franqui, who would eventually fall out with the revolutionary leadership and go into an embittered exile, never ceased to accuse Castro of being behind Camilo's disappearance, a view Che did not share. According to Franqui, Camilo was the only one who could have become more popular than Fidel Castro. Raúl Castro's dry personality, unattractive looks and total lack of charm did not inspire. Although Che Guevara was a man of great charisma who was universally adored, he was also a reserved, almost shy man and not Cuban by birth. Camilo was the most charismatic of them all, a man full of mirth, a joker as well as a seasoned soldier, someone who could really communicate with the people, and the one who truly represented them. In a speech remembering him, Che said that Camilo was the people, Camilo was the revolution.

In November the Council of Ministers decided to appoint Che president of the National Bank of Cuba, with total responsibility for the country's finances. An apocryphal story, which amused him no end, did the rounds of the corridors of power. The story went that, at a meeting of the governing council, Castro asked if there was an economist in the room. Che raised his hand. Castro, surprised, exclaimed he did not know Che was an economist, to which Che replied, 'Oh, I thought you said a communist!'

Che (right) with his comrade Comandante Camilo Cienfuegos

Che might not have had any experience of banking or financial management at this level, but he was astute, and he made at least one far-sighted decision that prevented the loss of invaluable Cuban assets. By converting Cuba's gold and dollar reserves held in Fort Knox into several other currencies and transferring them to banks in Switzerland and Canada, Che saved significant sums from the later expropriation of all Cuban assets in the USA. In December, no doubt in response to his new duties, Che decided he should begin studying higher mathematics and asked Professor Salvador Vilaseca to teach him from seven to eight every morning, in his office, before his official day began. He continued these studies methodically for more than three years.

At the end of the year the Central University of Las Villas granted Che the title of Doctor Honoris Causa in pedagogy. He told the gathering that the university 'must paint itself black, mulatto, but not just the students but the tutors as well; they must paint themselves worker and peasant and the colour of the people, because the university is not the property of anyone and it belongs to the Cuban people . . . When we have achieved this nobody will have lost out, we will all be winners and Cuba will be able to continue its march into the future with a stronger step and will not need to include in its midst this doctor, comandante, president of the bank and today professor of pedagogy, who bids you all farewell.'

After the triumph of the revolution, the new government had been faced with improvising an apparatus for governing a nation, and the exodus of the disaffected created a brain drain which put a strain on their resources. Che's capacity for organisation and for working long hours, his sheer energy to learn what was necessary to create a socialist country, his lack of complacency, his charisma and qualities as a leader made him the ideal partner for Fidel Castro to take forward his huge undertaking. He was the perfect person to trust with so many key tasks: he had the intelligence, the education and the will and he did not seek power for himself. This was crucial in Castro's eyes. Consequently, he was entrusted with a remarkable amount of power considering he was a foreigner.

For Che, Fidel Castro was also the ideal partner since he was prepared to provide him with everything he needed to carry out his plans in other lands. Fidel Castro knew Che believed in world revolution and had no intention of staying in Cuba. In fact, he had promised to help him with his plans for the future once their revolution had been consolidated. And he kept his promise. Castro recognised Che's inspirational hard work and loyalty by supplying all his needs for his later campaigns in the Congo and Bolivia: men, weapons, equipment, logistics, false identities (travel documents and disguises) and money. (Had Che succeeded in either campaign it could only have benefited Castro's Cuba.)

Contrary to disinformation published by the Western press, Che was always loyal to Castro throughout his years in Cuba. Ciro Bustos, who was one of the last people close to Che to see him alive in Bolivia, told me Che always spoke of Fidel Castro with respect and affection during their conversations only days before he was captured and killed. Why would he not?

Time would prove that all Castro ever wanted was his island. Once he got it, he would do everything within his power to hang on to it – something he has done successfully for almost fifty years. At the time of the Revolution, he managed to persuade the Cuban people he truly was the embodiment of Cuban nationhood: unlike Batista, he was not an American stooge and under his tutelage their island would no longer be a casino and whorehouse. It would be for the Cuban people. In this he was different from Che, who wanted to end capitalism, exploitation, imperialism, foreign domination, racism, US supremacy, hunger, illiteracy and inequality wherever it was found. Che wanted the world and he was prepared to die for it. When they separated in March 1965 – Che left for his Congo campaign while Castro stayed at the helm of his island – their best days were over for both of them.

Fidel Castro, Che's daughter Aleida and Che

233

SEVENTEEN
(1960)

As Cuba reorganised its internal affairs, in both the political and economic spheres, its relationship with Washington was deteriorating. There was a massive exodus of disaffected people, who made their way to the USA, and Washington encouraged the emigration by providing special programmes to help Cubans settle in. The existence of these programmes also served to discredit the new Cuban government.

Between 1960 and 1962 about 200,000 people left the island, mainly members of the economic and social elite (white professionals, executives and managers) who had received technical and scientific training. This created an unprecedented brain drain. People who could take their places had to be found immediately but they also had to be ideologically trustworthy. Finding them was no mean feat. The rural population did not emigrate. Nor did the blacks, whether urban or rural.

The Cuban exiles in the USA were two distinct groups: those who had been in favour of Batista and had left with him, and those who had originally supported Castro and had fallen out with him or become disenchanted with the turn the revolution had taken. At first, those Cubans who left the island thought they were doing so temporarily, that they would soon be able to return home when the Castro regime was ousted. But with the passage of time came the realisation that it was not to be and so they organised themselves into a powerful anti-Castro lobby. It brought pressure on the US government to continue the embargo originally put in place in March 1958, when the Eisenhower administration banned the sale of arms to Cuba, having decided that Fulgencio Batista had gone too far with his attacks on his political enemies and had become an embarrassment to his American allies.

American companies had also left the island, taking their employees with them, including some who were Cuban. The net result of this exodus was that it was up to Che, first as president of the national bank and later as Minister of Industry, to keep the economy going. Once the Americans had left with the secret formula for Coca-Cola, he was faced with the absurd situation of having to taste the various concoctions, often revolting, prepared by the workforce in their attempts to keep the Coca-Cola plant in operation.

Fidel Castro Cuban President, Osvaldo Dorticós (second left), Che, Comandante Núñez-Jiménez (far right) and fellow revolutionaries present a common front to the world

In January 1960, delegates from news agencies from all over the world began arriving in Havana. They had been invited by the Prensa Latina news agency, newly created by Che, with his Argentine friend from the Sierra, Jorge Ricardo Masetti, as editor-in-chief. Che was on hand to greet the journalists. It was felt that the revolution, and its friends and allies, should receive fair news coverage throughout the world, to counter the barrage of hostile propaganda originating in the USA. This was a far more ambitious project than Argentina's Agencia Latina, for which Che had worked in Mexico and which had disappeared when Perón was toppled. Prensa Latina had some of the continent's best journalists as correspondents: Carlos María Gutiérrez in Uruguay (whom Che had met in the Sierra), Rogelio García-Lupo in Argentina, Gabriel García-Márquez and Plinio Apuleyo-Mendoza in Colombia, Carlos Fuentes and Ted Claure in Mexico. Many of them later became famous authors, during the golden period of the Latin American literary boom. Rodolfo Walsh, one of Argentina's most brilliant political analysts, moved to Cuba to work for Prensa Latina and lived in downtown Havana.

As part of this initiative to disseminate information and create a network of like-minded people, the Cuban government had also invited a group of representatives from the textile, metal, newspaper sellers' and journalists' trade unions of Argentina, who were accompanied by the writer Sara Gallardo, who had been invited at the last minute to cover the visit for her newspaper, La Nación, making a five-member delegation. In Germany recently I caught up with Osvaldo Bayer, the representative of the journalists' union on that occasion, who is an old friend. I asked him about their meeting with Che.

It was the sixth of January 1960. The day before, we had been in Santa Clara and received a telephone call from Che asking us to meet him the following day at the National Bank of Cuba where he had his office. We were to meet him at half past ten at night. That was Che for you. He often worked late into the night.

When we got to Havana, it suddenly struck me that I could spend the day that stretched out before me visiting Rodolfo Walsh. At Rodolfo's I met his Argentine partner Piri Lugones, and she was most insistent that I should take her with me to see Che. I told her I couldn't possibly do that, since only members of the delegation had been invited to the meeting. But she was determined. 'OK, if you don't want to take me, then I'll cling to you like a leech and come along anyway.' Which is precisely what happened.

When I left Rodolfo's, Piri came with me and we set off for my hotel, which was where the Argentine delegation was gathering before going to meet Che. On our way there we got caught up in a shoot-out between the green jackets, as the revolutionaries were called, and the *gusanos*, or counter-revolutionaries. We had to throw ourselves to the ground in the middle of the street and stay there until there was a pause in the shooting and we were able to take refuge in a baker's shop.

So, when the shooting finally stopped and we were able to leave, we were late and the cars taking the Argentine delegation to meet Che had already left the hotel. No problem. We were given a car with a driver and were taken to the Bank. Piri, clutching my arm, walked in with me without even being challenged by the guards (though I was in serious trouble with the Cuban authorities for it afterwards). But let's get to the important bit: the meeting with Che Guevara.

The meeting had already started when we arrived. After all the necessary introductions, Che had begun to describe his plan for starting a revolution in Argentina, following the model of guerrilla warfare that had been used in Cuba. The Argentines listened in complete silence, moving not a muscle as he spoke. Che was talking, in that amazing voice of his: Argentine Spanish with a hint of a Cuban accent. It was a voice that added to his already inimitable charm – a sort of tango or bolero with the music and rhythm provided simply by his accent. The meeting lasted about two hours.

'To launch a revolution in our beloved Argentina,' said Che, 'we need nothing more than a group of fifty young revolutionaries to start looking for a place to set up camp in the Córdoba mountains, without raising the suspicions of the local population. Once they have found the right place and set up camp there, they will have to learn how to live and feed themselves without being noticed by anybody in the area. They will stay there for about three months, getting fit and doing military exercises and building up their supplies.

'After ninety days, they will come down from the mountains for the first time. They will march on the nearest village, attack the police station and seize all its weapons. One member of the company will go to the village square, gather all the residents and talk to them about the

Latin American Revolution, which is on its way and cannot fail. Then they all return to camp. The next day, all the bourgeois newspapers' – that was the word Che used, 'bourgeois', I remember it well – 'will carry a front-page headline: Guerrillas in Córdoba. That's all the information Argentina's young revolutionaries will need to set off for Córdoba in search of the guerrilla camp. They will seek and they will find. And then there will be a hundred, maybe two hundred, young revolutionaries gathered together there.

'Now is the time for them to come down from the mountains for a second time to conquer a larger village. Once again, they will attack the police station and seize all its weapons. Once again, one of the revolutionaries will go to the village square to tell the people about the coming Revolution, which will begin in Córdoba. And so young people from all over Argentina will gather at the camp. Five hundred of them. Eight hundred.

'And when there are eight hundred of them, they will come down from the mountains again and march on the nearest town with a military barracks. They will attack the barracks and seize all their weapons, and a group of revolutionaries will gather in the main square and tell the people about the Latin American Revolution, which will be seizing power in the very near future. And all the young people of the town who had remained undecided about whether or not they were revolutionaries, will join the revolutionaries and follow them back up into the mountains. So, now there are twelve hundred of them, fifteen hundred of them.'

Che talked on in that bardic voice, reciting this revolutionary epic for us. He detailed every particular: how people would be taught to use weapons, the best food to stock at the camp, which exercises needed to be done every day, how to prepare the spirit for the imminent revolution.

Finally, he came to the ending: the final triumph, the Latin American socialist revolution. These were his closing words:

'When there are two thousand of them, that is when the revolutionaries come down from the mountains for the last time. In the towns and cities, the revolutionary workers' movement will declare a national strike and bring the country to a standstill. The guerrillas will go onto the streets, stopping lorries and buses to take them to Buenos Aires. The people will line the streets to cheer the revolutionaries as they pass and the streets will be filled with people celebrating. When they reach Buenos Aires, the revolutionaries will go to the Liniers area of the city and hold a great rally, inviting the people to go with them to the Plaza de Mayo. This is what will happen. The revolutionaries' vehicles will lead the way, followed by the crowd. They will reach the Plaza de Mayo and find it empty. The shameless and the ashamed have all fled. The young people take over Government House and declare a revolutionary socialist government.'

Che looked at us each in turn. None of us said a word. We were too moved and emotional, full of anxieties about what he was planning. The silence was broken once again by the voice of Che Guevara.

'Are there any questions?'

Silence. But then I suddenly felt ashamed. I have always thought that, when a speaker asks at the end of his talk if there are any questions and nobody responds, it must be a painful experience for the speaker. It always seems to me like a kind of insult, as though nobody has been interested in what's been said. So, I forced myself to ask a question – a question I shall be ashamed of asking until the end of my days. This is what I asked:

'We are most grateful for your words, *compañero* Che. We are all struck by the clarity and courage of your ideas, and what you say is quite extraordinary. But I'd like to ask you about a detail. You say that, when the guerrillas come down from the mountains for the first time and conquer a small village, the next day the bourgeois press will carry the headline: Guerrillas in Córdoba. I think that is the moment when the repression would begin.

'Supposing, to put it briefly, the government first sends in the provincial police, who are beaten by the guerrillas; then it sends in the gendarmerie, who are also beaten. After that, the government sends in the troops: two mountain infantry regiments, let's say, and an artillery regiment, and aerial bombing raids of the suspected area. And if the revolutionaries beat them, too, then they'll send in the *gorilas* (the special marine infantry set up to deal with possible guerrilla activities following the triumph of the Cuban Revolution). And if they too are beaten, they'll send in the real fanatics: the army, air force and marine cadets. Please, comrade Che, can you talk to us about the repressive forces that will be brought to bear.'

I shall never forget the enormous sadness in Ernesto Che Guevara's face as he looked at me. He looked at me as though I'd understood nothing at all, and said three words as his only response: 'They're all mercenaries.'

There was a tense and absolute silence. The other members of the Argentine delegation looked at me with utter contempt, as though they were silently saying to me, 'It's obvious, isn't it, idiot? Didn't you know they were all mercenaries?'

Taken aback, I repeated Che's three words to myself and looked at his calm face, with that deep sadness still in his eyes. And I asked myself how I could possibly have asked such a question of a genuine rebel and revolutionary. Who was I to voice doubts about his plans? I, who had never even taken part in a revolution, let alone led one. He had. I told myself that one should never ask such questions of a revolutionary, never raise doubts . . .

Years later, Che put his plan into action in Bolivia. And lost his life. I could say I told you so, that what happened there proved me right. But that's not how I see it. I shall always be ashamed of having asked that question of a revolutionary like Che.

'They're all mercenaries.' Yes, but they have all the weapons in the world, and the CIA behind them. Surely it wasn't a bad thing to call attention to the dangers? But yes, it was a bad thing, to do that to Che. You couldn't go around sowing seeds of doubt in the people's hero. He was the angel of revolution. You had no right to try to bring him down to earth. When I went to see the bronze statue of him in Rosario, where he was born, I touched the statue and asked for forgiveness. And I smiled up at the great man, who is now a hero in the history of popular struggle, in the ongoing quest for human dignity.

On 28th January Che gave a speech at the National Capitol during a ceremony to commemorate the anniversary of José Martí's birthday. He was in his element, as he had admired the Cuban patriot since his teens and had familiarised himself with his works and his career as a soldier. The Cuban audience was impressed by his knowledge, as well as flattered by the ease with which he quoted their hero. On the same day, an aircraft, suspected of coming from the USA, set fire to 15 million arrobas (one arroba is 11.5 kilograms) of sugar cane at the Adelaida central refinery in Camagüey. It would not be the last such act of sabotage, nor the last one whose origins could not be ascertained, as the aircraft involved often had no markings.

On 4th February the deputy premier of the USSR, Anastas Mikoyan, arrived in Havana from Mexico and Che was at the airport to greet him. Nikolai Leonov, Raúl Castro's friend from the cultural section of the USSR embassy in Mexico, came along to act as his interpreter. The official purpose of the visit was to bring to Havana an exhibition of USSR science, technology and culture which the Soviets had originally taken to Mexico, but the real motive was to hold discussions about a variety of subjects, such as the purchase of sugar and sale of weapons for the defence of the island, as well as about establishing diplomatic relations. The result was that the USSR agreed to buy nearly 500,000 tons of Cuban sugar during the first year and 1 million tons for each of the following four years. Payment would be made in Soviet goods, including oil. Cash payments would start in the fifth year of the agreement.

The Cuban leadership was extremely satisfied with the result of the negotiations. In its view, the agreement represented the beginning of financial independence, and the Soviet machinery they were importing would contribute to the industrialisation of the island. Other nations, members of the Soviet bloc, were soon sending their trade delegations to Havana and China was not far behind.

Che was allowed to fly solo for the first time in February. He had originally learnt the rudiments of flying in Buenos Aires with his uncle Jorge de la Serna, who owned a small aircraft. In the late 1920s a French entrepreneur had created the Courier Sud, the first airmail system in Latin America. Argentine men of Che's generation would have been exposed to all the media acclaim of the French pilots who defied the elements to fly over the cordillera between Santiago de Chile and Buenos Aires and as far south as Patagonia. The pilots who inaugurated the Aéropostale service, as it was officially called, were Jean Mermoz, Antoine de Saint-Exupéry and Henri

Guillaumet. Che was an avid reader of de Saint-Exupéry who wrote *Vol de nuit*, a vivid account of his experiences as a pilot in Argentina, as well as *Pilote de guerre*, about his life as a wartime pilot. His books were bestsellers at the time in Argentina and are aviation classics to this day. All three pilots enlisted when the Second World War broke out and were lost at sea.

When Pepe González-Aguilar, his childhood friend from Alta Gracia, discovered Che had not read de Saint-Exupéry's children's book, *Le Petit Prince*, he gave him his own copy. A few days later, Pepe telephoned Che, wanting to know what he thought of one of his favourite books. The phone lines in Cuba at the time were really bad as the original telephone operator, the American company ITT, had been nationalised and the service had fallen into disrepair. However, he heard Che clearly say the word 'crap'. He could not believe his ears. 'What?' he shouted down the line. 'I read it all in one crap. I could not put it down,' Che said. He was in the habit of locking himself up in the bathroom when he needed peace and quiet as it was the only place where his bodyguards and his children let him go on his own. He used to say it was his second office.

On 4th March, *La Coubre*, a French vessel which was carrying Belgian arms to Cuba, exploded in Havana harbour as a result of sabotage, allegedly instigated by the CIA. Eighty-one Cubans died. Che, who was on his way to work at the bank, went immediately to the waterfront, climbed on board the burning ship and assisted in the rescue of the injured. The following day there was a mass rally to honour the victims. Castro uttered for the first time the words which were to become the motto of the Cuban Revolution: '*Patria o Muerte*' (Homeland or death). It was during this mass rally that the Cuban photographer Alberto Korda took the snapshot of Che Guevara which Giacomo Feltrinelli, the Italian left-wing publisher, would turn into an iconic image of revolution's most handsome exponent and which to this day remains a symbol of defiance for the downtrodden of the world.

Castro now asked the Soviet Union for arms for the defence of Cuba and Nikita Khrushchev did not hesitate to oblige. French intellectuals Jean-Paul Sartre and Simone de Beauvoir had arrived in Cuba at the invitation of Alfredo Guevara, an old comrade of Castro's from their university days who was in charge of cultural events. They attended the funeral for the victims of the *La Coubre* explosion, and Che saw them in his office for a chat whenever the three of them could find the time. They were able to converse in French and enjoyed each other's company. For Che it was a particular pleasure to discuss seminal works which he had read in his youth with the authors themselves, while Sartre and de Beauvoir were seduced by Che's charisma and intellect. Sartre would famously say after Che's death that he considered him 'the most complete man of the century'.

Under orders from US President Eisenhower, the CIA now commenced training Cuban exiles who had volunteered for an invasion of the island. At the same time, Che published the first in a series of articles about military tactics '*Consejos al combatiente*' (Advice for combatants) in the magazine *Verde Olivo*, which would form the basis of his book *Guerrilla Warfare*. But he now felt, at least for the moment, that the people had first to be educated and taught to think like revolutionaries.

He embarked on writing a series of ironic political articles for *Verde Olivo*, while also making notes for his future books, and giving speeches whenever his commitments allowed. The literacy campaign which Cuba had undertaken was one of his favourite initiatives. He had always felt education was the birthright of free men and women and even as a child, when he was too sick to attend school, he would teach the women who helped his mother with the domestic chores to read and write. He used to read aloud to them to encourage them to learn, and the Spanish translation of *Robin Hood* was one of the books he chose. As a result of the attention he paid to the uneducated he became a well-known and much-loved figure throughout the island, although he was also feared by some who did not care for his revolutionary zeal and the tenacity with which he pursued his objectives. It was not unusual to hear *guajiros* exclaiming, '*Cuidado, que viene el Che*' (Careful, Che is coming), just as children in Europe might be told that the Big Bad Wolf would come and get them if they did not behave.

One of the great pleasures his newly acquired fame afforded Che was corresponding with many of the writers he had admired in his youth. Sometimes he was able to invite them to Cuba and meet them personally. This had been the case not only with Simone de Beauvoir and Jean-Paul Sartre, but also with María Rosa Oliver, an Argentine left-wing writer who, like him, came from a privileged background and was in Cuba as a member of the jury for the coveted annual literary prize awarded by The Casa de las Américas to an up-and-coming Latin American writer. 'Please let us not talk about Argentina any more,' he said to her once in his office over coffee. 'Why not, when it is obvious how much you love her?' she replied. 'That is why,' Che said.

The Casa de las Américas had been founded shortly after the revolution to help Cuba redefine its identity within the Latin American family. Cuba had spent most of its short life under either Spanish or US influence. It now needed to look to its fellow Latin American neighbours with whom it shared a language and a culture as well as a past history.

It was a non-governmental body devoted exclusively to socio-cultural relations. Its prestigious prize, created in 1960 and awarded every year by a rotating jury of renowned writers from all over the continent, helped to launch new writers in Latin America, where Cuba was now finding its rightful place through this initiative. Havana became a beacon for the region. It reflected the diversity of the continent at the same time as it unified it. Writers were no longer Peruvian or Colombian, Uruguayan or Argentine but Latin American, and they all read each other's literature and identified with it. Being Latin American went beyond politics or economics, and meant a wider community which encompassed the literature of the whole continent.

On 8th May Cuba and the USSR established diplomatic relations. The first Cuban ambassador was Faure Chomón. During the revolutionary struggle, he had led the Directorio troops in the Sierra del Escambray that had fought alongside Che's column. On 10th May President Osvaldo Dorticós gave a banquet at the presidential palace for President Ahmed Sukarno of Indonesia and Che attended, thus renewing his acquaintance. Sukarno was returning Che's visit to Indonesia as the head of a nation which was a member of the Non-Aligned Movement, originally founded by Presidents Tito of Yugoslavia, Nehru of India and Nasser of Egypt, with Sukarno of Indonesia and Nkrumah of Ghana, to counter the influence of the USA and USSR.

On 7th June Che and Castro attended a performance by the Peking Opera company, which was in Havana at the invitation of the Sino-Cuban Friendship Committee. Che and Aleida now moved to a house in Miramar, a suburb of Havana near the sea, which was to be their home for some time to come. During June Czechoslovakia's Minister for Foreign Trade arrived in Havana and a trade agreement was signed between the two countries. Trade with Czechoslovakia was not always without problems, and in Cuba people like to tell an anecdote about the Czechs selling the Cubans their obsolete machinery, including some ancient snowploughs!

Between 29th June and 1st July the revolutionary government nationalised all three US oil refineries (Texaco, Esso and Shell), which had refused to refine Soviet oil. The foreign companies were not compensated for their losses. On 6th July President Eisenhower retaliated by cancelling the sugar quota of about 700,000 tons which the USA was scheduled to purchase from Cuba that year. On 9th July the Soviet Union agreed to purchase all the Cuban sugar that the USA refused to buy. During this month, the vice-minister for commerce of the People's Republic of China visited Cuba at the head of a thirteen-strong delegation. Several scientific, technical and commercial agreements were signed. On 6th August several major US companies operating in Cuba were nationalised.

On 19th August Che inaugurated a training course at the Ministry for Public Health. The title of his brief lecture was 'The revolutionary doctor', but its focus was much wider. He seemed very aware of the fragility of the new Cuba's existence and correspondingly sure of what steps should be taken to ensure its survival: 'The isolated effort, the purity of ideals, the desire to sacrifice an entire lifetime to the noblest of ideas goes for naught if that effort is made alone, solitary, in some corner of Latin America … A revolution needs what we have in Cuba: an entire people mobilised, who have learned the use of arms and the practice of combative unity'. He finished by quoting from Martí: 'The best form of saying is doing' and his words were greeted with an ovation.

On 2nd September Castro issued the first Declaration of Havana, calling for the second independence of Latin America. He condemned the Declaration of San José in Costa Rica, in which, on 28th August, the Organization of American States had criticised Cuba for interfering in the affairs of other Latin American countries. Castro retaliated by condemning the exploitation of the workforce in the Third World, and rejecting the continuation of the Monroe Doctrine. Like Martí, he saw it as an instrument 'of the voracious imperialists to extend the domination of America'.

Che frequently addressed large audiences and developed a
distinctive rhetorical style

On 28th September Castro, with Che at his side, announced his decision
to create Committees for the Defence of the Revolution, which would be
popular organs of vigilance and mobilisation against counter-revolutionary
activities. Castro then left for New York to attend the twenty-fifth General
Assembly of the United Nations. Wherever he went, there were chants
of solidarity with the Cuban people. Castro and Nikita Khrushchev
indulged in a very public show of mutual affection although they had
never met before.

When the Hotel Shelburne, where the Cuban delegation was staying in
downtown New York, complained about their rowdy behaviour and talked to
the press about it, Castro decamped to a large but modest hotel in Harlem,
the Theresa, which was at the centre of black life in the neighbourhood. It had
been the home from home of Malcolm X, Duke Ellington, Louis Armstrong,
Muhammad Ali and Joe Louis, among others. He very loudly informed the
world that he was more at home amidst the poor and the humble people of
Harlem, which in those days was a strictly black area of New York.

The US airport authorities had impounded Castro's VC-10 as
compensation for American property expropriated in Cuba, so the Cuban
delegation went home in an Ilyushin-18, lent to them courtesy of the Soviet

premier. Castro was delighted to be able to make the point: what the USA took away from the Cubans, the Soviets gave back to them.

On 13th October the revolutionary government nationalised all Cuban and foreign-owned banks, as well as 382 large Cuban-owned industries. On 14th October the Urban Reform law was approved. It nationalised housing and Cubans were guaranteed the right to their own dwellings. On 19th October the USA imposed a partial trade embargo on Cuba and on the 24th all remaining US companies there were nationalised. There was no turning back now. The USA and Cuba would remain at loggerheads for the next fifty years and counting.

On 21st October Che left on a two-month-long trip that took him on his first visit to countries of the socialist bloc: the Soviet Union, the Democratic Republic of Germany, Czechoslovakia, China and North Korea. The decision to go had been prompted by the US trade embargo that had been imposed swiftly. Che and his delegation arrived in the People's Republic of China on 17th November, having travelled from Moscow, and he made a speech at the Palace

Che with Nikita Khrushchev

of the People's Congress on 21st November. He was accompanied by Chou En-lai, the Minister of Foreign Affairs.

During the visit, an economic cooperation agreement was signed between Cuba and China in the presence of Mao Tse-tung. Che used to tell an anecdote which illustrates his contempt for formalities as well as his ability to laugh at his asthma. The Cuban delegation had been taken to the Great Hall of the People and were respectfully lined up, waiting for Chairman Mao to make an entrance. At that precise moment, Che suffered such a strong bout of asthma that it gave him a cardiac arrest and he fell to the floor. His delegation knew just what to do: one of them leapt on him and started thumping his chest, while another gave him mouth-to-mouth resuscitation. Mao, who demanded that protocol and ceremony be strictly observed, now entered the Great Hall of the People, followed by his retinue.

Instead of a neat line of guests waiting to be introduced, there was a heap of agitated *barbudos* in olive-green fatigues lying on the floor, waving arms and legs in the air in utter desperation. He turned on his heel and left.

When Che had recovered, the delegation pulled themselves together and not much later Mao made his dignified and solemn entrance once more, as if nothing had happened. He had been briefed, and recommended that Che take a course of acupuncture. As we all know, this is the cure for everything, as it activates the nervous system and helps the body to fight any ailment. Che's conclusion was that his asthma was so macho that even Mao Tse-tung had not cowed it into submission.

On 24th November Aleida gave birth to their first child, a daughter, while Che was in Peking. Upon his return to Havana, Che chose the name Aleida for her, though he would call her Aliusha. From Peking he sent Aleida an affectionate postcard, telling her that she was always determined to make him look bad in front of others. Men always want their firstborn to be a boy, and he was no exception.

On 1st December the delegation travelled to Pyongyang in North Korea. Che met Kim Il-sung and agreements were signed for scientific, technical and commercial cooperation between Cuba and the Popular Democratic Republic of Korea. By 7th December they were back in Moscow. Che left Moscow for Berlin, in the then German Democratic Republic, on 13th December and held a meeting with Heinrich Rau, the Minister for Foreign Trade. Their interpreter was Tamara Bunke-Bider, a young German woman whose parents had moved to Argentina, and who had returned to Germany to study. She eventually moved to Cuba and was sent to Bolivia to prepare the ground for the arrival of the contingent led by Che in 1966.

In the meantime, in Washington DC, members of the US administration, the Pentagon and the CIA were discussing the possibility of liquidating Che.

EIGHTEEN
(1961)

The USA finally broke off diplomatic relations with Cuba on 3rd January, with inevitable consequences: no trade, no travel, no diplomacy. The government of Peru followed suit. Its president, Manuel Prado, a banker, was staunchly pro-USA. This signalled the beginning of Cuba's isolation by Latin American regimes, most of whom were keen to do Washington's bidding – some because they were bolstered by US support, others because they had not come to power via the ballot box and hoped US endorsement would legitimise them.

On 20th January John Fitzgerald Kennedy was inaugurated as the 35th president of the USA. During his election campaign he had talked about forming an Alliance for Progress to foster economic cooperation between the Americas, including programmes of assistance for countries willing to prevent the advance of communism in Latin America. On 13th March he entertained several Latin American leaders: Prado of Peru, Goulart of Brazil, Valencia of Colombia, Villeda of Honduras, Alessandri of Chile, Betancourt of Venezuela (whom Che had compared to a weathervane when they met in Costa Rica) and Paz Estenssoro of Bolivia, as well as the Governor of Puerto Rico. Some of them would reciprocate by asking Kennedy and his wife to visit their countries: Puerto Rico (by then an American colony in all but name), Mexico, Venezuela and Colombia. Mrs Kennedy even made a brief speech in Bogotá in what she thought was Spanish, which made us all cringe.

In 1960 the Pentagon had commissioned two academic investigations to further its interests on the island and the CIA had created a Centre for Cuban Studies. Its purpose was to generate disinformation, which would portray Cuba to the outside world in a negative light and deny the achievements of the revolution, as well as to plan future actions which would bring about the demise of the socialist government.

The government of Paraguay was the next to break off diplomatic relations with Cuba. The right-wing dictator General Alfredo Stroessner had been in power since 1954, holding periodic elections in which he was the sole candidate, and would stay on until 1989, when he was deposed by a coup d'état. In Latin America, only Fidel Castro would last longer in power.

On 6th January Che appeared on television to report on the outcome of his visit to the USSR. He stressed the fact that a whole bloc of countries had changed their economies to help Cuba: they were adjusting their levels of production for certain products and machinery in order to keep Cuba supplied, and were arranging to buy sugar and nickel from Cuba rather than any other country. He said the Soviets had been courteous enough to invite him to be in the Presidium for the march past on 7th November. And when the crowd spotted him there had been loud cheering for Cuba. (According to José Pardo-Llada, who was a member of the delegation, Che dreamt it all up: nobody noticed him or cared about his presence.) For his part, Che noticed Ho Chi Minh several rows behind him, ensconced between Romania's Ceauçescu and Poland's Gomulka, and made a point of approaching him at a reception after the parade.

Able to hold a conversation in French, the two men dispensed with the services of their interpreters, so we will never know what they said to each other. But Uncle Ho, as he is affectionately called in Vietnam, was the leader Che most admired. And of course, General Vo Nguyen Giap, the architect of Vietnam's victory over the French, Chinese, Japanese and eventually the Americans, was one of Che's military heroes. He expressed his admiration eloquently in the introduction he wrote to the Spanish language edition of the General's book on guerrilla warfare, *People's War, People's Army*, published in Cuba in 1964.

One wonders if Che ever marvelled at his meteoric transformation into the man he had become. Here he was, wearing the star of a comandante and dressed in the olive-green fatigues of the army of a nation newly freed from imperialism, talking as an equal with the premier of one of the two most powerful empires in the world, empowered to make crucial decisions on behalf of a country other than the one of his birth – and all this only seven years after he had left his native Argentina a penniless, aimless youth. Perhaps this tells us something about his continent: the need of the Latin American world to improvise, and the lack of people with knowledge and experience who are not corrupt which allowed a foreigner to rise to such heights in someone else's country.

I once said to Che's younger brother, 'Your brother was not very "tropical", for want of a better word,' and Juan Martín replied, 'No, he wasn't and he suffered for it in Cuba.' What I meant by this, which Juan Martín understood, was that Che was very unusual for the Caribbean: so driven, so hard-working, so willing to learn and to serve. Yet I don't think he was a goody-goody. He was enjoying himself thoroughly, because he thought it was his calling.

On 23rd February the Council of Ministers created a Ministry of Industry with Che as the new Minister. He accepted the position, stating that Cuba had now entered its industrialisation phase. On 26th February, even before he had been sworn in, Che organised a brigade of employees from his new ministry to join him in voluntary work at the Reparto Martí – a slum on the outskirts of the city which was particularly marginalised, with houses made from scrap metal, no electricity or running water and unpaved roads.

Che doing voluntary work at a building site, 1962

When he arrived at the Ministry of Industry Che found, unsurprisingly, that most Cuban industries depended heavily on raw materials, equipment and technological support from the USA. Those industries that were totally Cuban were mainly artisan manufacturing centres. The country did not produce spare parts and most equipment originated from the USA. There had not been many trained technical personnel to begin with and most of those who were qualified had now left. The remaining workforce had a very basic level of education, and little or no cultural and technical knowledge. No plans for economic or social development for either the medium or long term existed. None of the foreign groups that had been operational in the island was interested in its development. The revolution would have to face up to the fact that the country's main industries, those crucial to the economy, had been in the hands of the Americans: sugar, electric power, telephones, copper, oil refining. The tobacco industry (eight factories) had never been sufficiently mechanised and was backward and artisanal.

On 31st March President Kennedy abolished Cuba's sugar quota for good. The USA would no longer acquire any sugar from their southern neighbour. Since Cuba was a monoculture economy, Kennedy hoped the move would cause the country serious financial damage, but the Russians bought what the Americans no longer wanted. The effect of the decision was to push Cuba even further into the arms of the Russian bear.

The 9th April issue of *Verde Olivo* carried Che's article, '*Cuba, excepción histórica o vanguardia de la lucha anticolonialista?*' (Cuba, an historical exception or vanguard in the anti-colonial struggle?). In it, he described underdevelopment (a term he found particularly offensive), using a powerful image. It was

a dwarf with an enormous head and a swollen chest whose weak legs or short arms do not match the rest of his anatomy. He is the product of an abnormal formation distorting his development. In reality that is what we are – we, politely referred to as 'underdeveloped', in truth are colonial, semi-colonial or dependent countries. We are countries whose economies have been distorted by imperialism, which has abnormally developed those branches of industry or agriculture needed to complement its complex economy.

Che believed that underdevelopment was not what came before development but what some nations had to endure because others were developed at their expense.

On 15th April planes from the CIA's base in Nicaragua attacked the airports of Santiago de Cuba and San Antonio de los Baños, as well as the air force's Havana base, killing 7 and wounding 53 people. It was the prelude to the Bay of Pigs operation, masterminded by the CIA, to invade the island, depose the government and assassinate Fidel Castro. The following day, at a mass rally to honour the victims of the attacks, Castro proclaimed the socialist nature of the Cuban Revolution. The country was put on full alert in anticipation of the impending attack.

It had been Che's idea to arm the civilian population. He was keen not to repeat what he felt was the mistake made in Guatemala in 1954. Cuba had 25,000 regular soldiers and 200,000 in the militia. There was also a police force of 9,000 men and a navy of 5,000. Because many of the men who led them were graduates from his military schools in the Sierra and La Cabaña, historians have given some credit to Che for the success of the Cuban response at the Bay of Pigs, even though he was not there.

On 17th April approximately 1,500 Cuban exiles, trained and armed by the CIA, invaded Cuba at Playa Girón on the south coast of the island, west of the city of Cienfuegos. While the president of the USA sat in his office in Washington, anxiously awaiting news of a military operation that was not of his making, to which he had only reluctantly given the go-ahead, Castro rushed from Havana to Playa Girón at two thirty in the morning to coordinate and lead the defence himself. It was of paramount importance for Castro that the invading forces did not establish a beachhead and move deeper into Cuban territory. If they took a city and formed an alternative government, the USA and its Latin American allies might recognise it, which would be a key step in toppling his government.

The precise location of the attack had been detected by Cuban frogmen, and it had been expected for some time. Castro had concentrated his strength on Playa Girón, and most of his old comrades from the Sierra were there with him: Emilio Aragonés, Victor Dreke, Efigenio Ameijeiras, René Rodríguez, all with their men. A ferocious battle ensued, but the Sierra veterans had seen it all before.

The CIA had misled President Kennedy about the support the invading force would find once it was on the island. The men of Brigade 2506, as the invading force was called, believed they were a first wave of Cuban freedom fighters on their way to liberate their country from the tyranny of a communist dictator, but even Cubans who were not happy with Castro were ready to defend their country from what they saw as a foreign invasion. Resistance was seen more as a matter of national pride than as an endorsement of the regime. The invaders had been told that the second leg of the operation would consist of air support, provided by 16 B-26 light attack bombers. On 14th April Kennedy had reduced the number of bombers to 8, which meant that the invasion force had insufficient air cover on the day.

The 1,500 invaders, of whom only 135 were professional soldiers, soon discovered that the Cuban armed forces were stronger than expected; they did not have the substantial support they had counted on from within the island and found themselves in an untenable position. They were not able to advance inland, or to retreat, for behind them was the sea. The people who chose the Bay of Pigs as the site for the landing were ignorant of the terrain. It is thick with mangroves and infested with snakes, alligators, mosquitoes and flies. During the war of independence in the 1890s, General Máximo Gómez had called the area a geographic and military trap.

On 18th April Kennedy authorised six jet fighters from the aircraft carrier *Essex* to provide air cover to the B-26s that were allowed to attack Playa Girón, but they missed their rendezvous. When issuing its orders the Pentagon did not take into account the difference in time zones between Nicaragua, from where the B-26s took off, and Cuba.

On the afternoon of 19th April, the invaders surrendered. They had been in the country for a little over two days. Those who had managed to advance into Cuban territory were forced to retreat to the beaches where they had landed. When Kennedy discovered the invasion had failed he allowed two US destroyers patrolling the area to approach the Cuban coast to pick up any survivors at sea. The ships were not allowed closer to the coast than 5 miles (8 kilometres) during daylight and 2 miles (3 kilometres) after dark. Only those who managed to swim out to the bay's many cays could be retrieved. Many lay dead on the beach and 1,209 were captured by Castro's men. Nine of these died on the way to prison.

Castro's forces suffered 161 casualties. Within three days the battle of Playa Girón was over. President Kennedy's Cuban counter-revolutionaries had been routed and he had been humiliated. Cuba would eventually exchange its prisoners for baby food, powdered milk, medicines, pesticides and other goods in late 1962. The ransom was the equivalent of around $60 million.

Che had been put in charge of the troops at Pinar del Río province. Castro thought the coast of Cuba closest to the USA should be well defended, in case there was a second attack, in addition to the one expected at Playa Girón. While at his command post, Che accidentally dropped his revolver. Contrary to regulations, he always carried it without the safety catch on, an offence for which he would have severely punished his men. The gun went off and the bullet passed through his cheek and came out under his ear: a difference of a few centimetres and it would have blown out his brains.

He was taken to hospital and had his wound cleaned but, because he was on duty, he refused to have an anaesthetic. An anti-tetanus vaccine caused a violent allergic reaction, with much swelling. He jokingly told the doctors who treated him that they had almost succeeded in liquidating him, something the enemy had so far failed to do. Aleida rushed to his side and stayed with him until the conflict was over. He did not see action, as the skirmishes took place far from his base, so upon his return to Havana, everybody wondered why the Comandante was injured.

The new American president had inherited the invasion plan from his predecessor, General Eisenhower, and he had given the CIA operation his support half-heartedly. Kennedy did not really think the invasion was a good idea, but it was only three months into his presidency and he was poorly advised. The Cuban exiles had been training for more than a year and were ready to go, and the operation was sold to Kennedy as a golden opportunity to oust Castro before he had fully consolidated his power over the island. His motive for denying the operation proper air cover was that he did not want to be seen participating in the invasion of a neighbouring country. As a result the operation was a fiasco.

The small Cuban air force, on the other hand, gave a good account of itself, something the CIA had not anticipated. It consisted of only 15 B-26s,

3 or 4 lightly armed T-33s, fitted with .50-calibre machine guns for training, and a couple of Sea Fury fighters, but the Cuban pilots were defending their homeland and were ready to fly as many sorties as necessary to keep the enemy at bay. Castro also had newly acquired Soviet equipment in the shape of helicopters, armoured vehicles, personnel carriers, artillery, small arms and ammunition worth many millions of dollars. He had 54 Soviet tanks in place at Playa Girón within twenty-four hours and his helicopters flew overhead as the invading forces attempted to reach the beaches.

President Kennedy commissioned a report on the failed operation, to see what lessons could be learnt. The report attributed the failure to inadequate aircraft cover and weaponry, as well as to the loss of ships and ammunition. Historians tell us the invasion could only have succeeded if it had been launched with 10,000 men. In its own report, the CIA concluded that the agency had exceeded its capabilities, failed to assess risks realistically, failed at internal communications as well as communications with the government, had not involved the Cuban exiles sufficiently, had not organised internal resistance in Cuba sufficiently, had not collected or analysed intelligence on the Cuban military capability, did not have enough Spanish-speaking personnel and lacked contingency plans. The CIA had expected the Bay of Pigs to be a repeat of the invasion of Guatemala, which had been a walkover. But Cuba is an island. In a speech soon afterwards, Che called it the first defeat of American Imperialism in Latin America, he was convinced it would not be the last.

There were many interesting similarities between Kennedy and Castro. Both were lawyers, both had been brought up as Roman Catholics, both were sexually voracious, charismatic, ambitious, intelligent, considered good-looking, thirsty for power and used to getting what they wanted. But while Kennedy liked to surround himself with intelligent men who would argue with him and challenge his thinking, Castro only wanted yes-men around. Che Guevara was certainly not a yes-man but he was someone who shared his views.

Castro and Kennedy soon embarked on a battle of egos: Castro taunted Kennedy with attacks on the USA's behaviour towards her less fortunate neighbours, while Kennedy became obsessed with the elimination of Castro. This was unworthy of his intelligence and his status as well as not very rational, since the tiny island could not possibly pose a real threat to the country Castro referred to as 'the colossus of the north'. As Senator Fulbright said at the time, Castro was 'a thorn in the flesh, not a dagger at the heart'.

Cuba and the USA were not officially at war. The Bay of Pigs adventure would go down in history as the USA's first overt attempt at regime change. Perhaps Kennedy had been tempted into seeking a victory by proxy over the USSR early in his presidency, in view of the Cold War he had inherited from his predecessor. He may have hoped to impress the Soviet Union, which deemed him too young to hold office. There is speculation to this day on whether Kennedy's assassination in November 1963 was in any way connected to his stance on Castro and Cuba. Richard Goodwin, a trusted Kennedy aide, says in his memoir of the 1960s that by 1963 the president had begun secret discussions with members of the Cuban government, having understood the need for peaceful coexistence with his difficult neighbour. This gave the Cuban exiles a reason to want him removed.

Alina Fernández (Castro's daughter out of wedlock, who has always been an outspoken critic of her father's regime) has said that Castro and the CIA need each other and that the USA does not realise that its hostility towards Cuba's leader has helped him to perpetuate his hold on power. As demonstrated at the Bay of Pigs, Cubans do not take kindly to interventions from abroad, and they prefer to stick with a leader whom they know rather than risk being sold out to the USA. In its obsession with the liquidation of Castro, the CIA even joined forces with the leaders of organised crime at one point. These had their own motives for hating Castro, as they had lost their Batista-granted privileges on the island through his intervention, but this was not the most brilliant page of US history. In any event, the battle of egos across the Caribbean left a lasting legacy. The two countries have never yet found a way of living side by side.

The Bay of Pigs adventure led Soviet Premier Nikita Khrushchev to the erroneous belief that Kennedy was a weak president and this may have contributed to his idea that he could install missiles in Cuba with impunity not much later. But Kennedy had learnt much from the experience: in future he would act with a cool head, avoid taking decisions based on Group Think and manage to curb his 'passion for decisive action in foreign policy' as well as his competitive machismo instincts. His handling of the missile crisis in 1962 reflected this.

During May, June and July, Che continued to criss-cross the island, visiting numerous industries and factories and giving speeches. He would often appear unannounced, ask to see the attendance register and check for absenteeism. The Cuban population was not used to working long hours, to five-year plans and production targets, but Che's popularity meant that people welcomed him when he turned up at factories without warning and lectured them. Such was his charisma that what came across was not the disciplinarian in him but the leader who cared for their future.

Che believed that a revolutionary society needed to understand that there is a relationship between one's consciousness and production. He would impress upon the workforce the need to produce more for the revolution at this historic juncture for Cuba and for the rest of Latin America, and not to use patrol duty or political training as an excuse to stay away from work. He turned himself into living proof that you could do everything the revolution asked of you by working all hours of the day and most of the night during the week, and then joining the volunteer brigades cutting sugar cane on Sundays. And he still managed to look as if he was enjoying himself to the hilt. Whenever his friends from abroad were in Havana, he took them cane-cutting on Sundays. Even Aleida managed to go along in spite of working in his office all week, having a home and children to look after and often being pregnant.

Alberto Granado, Che, and Aleida, cutting sugar cane on a Sunday

Che realised that this couldn't be a one-way relationship. He always concerned himself with the safety of the workforce, the cleanliness of the premises and the relationship between the administration and the workers. Though extremely critical of anyone who was not doing his best, he also saw to it that the most able and willing received adequate training, and was quick to lavish praise when he saw a unit that achieved good results and had a happy workforce. He constantly made recommendations in relation to social aspects within the outfit, as well as designing measures for the adequate supply of the worker population, including sufficient housing and time off, as well as facilities to practise sports, and adequate clothing for those jobs that needed it.

Che with his family in Punta del Este. (From left to right): his sister Ana María, his brother Juan Martín, his father, Che, his brother Roberto, an unidentified friend and Che's childhood friend Carlos Figueroa

On 2nd August, Che left for Montevideo in Uruguay, at the head of a delegation representing Cuba at the Inter-American Economic and Social Council (CIES) of the Organization of American States, which was being held at the Uruguayan seaside resort of Punta del Este. The conference was scheduled to launch Kennedy's Alliance for Progress, but it was also an attempt to isolate Cuba from the rest of Latin America. It had almost been cancelled a couple of times due to teething problems, since it was a huge project which required the involvement of the whole American continent.

After an unplanned overnight stopover in Rio de Janeiro, which gave Che the chance to meet with the Finance Minister of Brazil, Clemente Mariani-Bittencourt, the Cuban delegation led by Che took over a floor at the Hotel Playa in Punta del Este, while the Americans led by Secretary of State Douglas Dillon stayed at the Vanguard. Journalists were split between the two camps.

Punta del Este was then, and still is, an enchanting seaside resort. It juts out into the sea (*punta* means point) and has beaches with golden sands and a charming port which accommodates yachts from all over the world during the regatta season. Its famous restaurants serve exquisite seafood and there are numerous nightclubs and a couple of casinos. It is a paradise for the rich and famous. But all this is in summer. In August it is the dead of winter in the southern hemisphere, and Punta del Este becomes a miserable, windswept, cold, damp, rainy, inhospitable place. Now, packed with delegates, politicians, journalists, spies, diplomats and weapons manufacturers, it was alive with rumours and conspiracy theories. Everyone wanted to see what would happen between the USA and Cuba. The rest of the conference was a sideshow.

Kennedy's brainchild, the Alliance for Progress, which he introduced at his gathering of Latin American leaders, had duped us all for one brief, shining moment. It took someone as articulate and thorough as El Comandante Guevara to analyse the proposed Alliance in detail, spelling it out for us and making us think again. What the continent needed was to develop its industries rather than receive aid with which to pay for imported materials. The policies of the USA towards 'the other America' had not changed at all; they had just been repackaged in a more glamorous outer layer.

Douglas Dillon, speaking for the USA, quoted Martí in his opening words to the conference, saying, 'We Americans are one people in origin, in hope and in danger.' It was a covert vindication of the Monroe Doctrine. Che, in his capacity as leader of the Cuban delegation, spoke on 8th August. It came as no surprise to anyone that he denounced Kennedy's Alliance for Progress and castigated the US president for proposing a project which would guarantee US hegemony in the Americas, thinly disguised as aid and cooperation.

He clearly stated that economics could not be separated from politics and he too quoted Martí, who had said, seventy years earlier, 'Whoever speaks of economic union speaks of political union. The nation that buys, commands; the nation that sells, serves. Commerce must be balanced to assure freedom. A nation that wants to die sells to one nation only, and a nation that would be saved sells to more than one. The excessive influence of one country over another's commerce becomes political influence . . . A nation that wants to be free must be free in matters of trade.'

Che went on to list all the US attacks Cuba had endured: the violation of its airspace by American planes; the burning of sugar-cane fields; the sabotage of the steamship *La Coubre* at Havana docks; the refusal of US oil companies based in Cuba to refine crude oil from the Soviet Union; the Declaration of San José at the Organization of American States conference the previous year, which denied Cuba the right to defend itself and led to the Declaration of Havana; and the cancellation of the sugar quota, followed by the invasion at Playa Girón.

Defending the humanist character of the Cuban Revolution, he quoted Martí again: 'Every true human must feel on their own cheek every blow dealt against the cheek of another.' He called for the independence of all occupied territories: the Panama Canal Zone; the Malvinas Islands off the coast of Argentina (called the Falkland Islands by the United Kingdom); and Swan Island off the coast of Honduras, from where the USA lambasted Cuba across the airwaves; the Guianas and the British Antilles. He went on to say that Cuba had given women and blacks equal rights, had eliminated illiteracy and had socialised medicine, and he mocked the colonial mentality of the USA, which offered to provide latrines – to improve the sanitary conditions of the poor Indians and blacks who lived in subhuman conditions – but not industrialisation, which would result in the poor of Latin America building their own latrines and ending financial dependency on a foreign power.

Che was, of course, aware that the eyes of the world were upon him. The Latin American press vied for his attention. Everybody wanted to interview him. Journalists had arrived from the most distant corners of the globe. He was followed around like a movie star, which left him mildly amused. On

9th August he gave a press conference which he began with the following words: '*Pregunten lo que quieran, pero después escriban lo que se conteste*' (You may ask what you like, but then write the reply as it was).

Che in Montevideo

Truth is the daughter of time, and while Kennedy may have proclaimed the Alliance's aims to be 'housing, work, land, health, education' for the peoples south of the Río Grande, the actual results of successive US governments' attempts to export their brand of democracy were the dictatorships of General Augusto Pinochet in Chile and General Jorge Rafael Videla in Argentina, the Contras in Nicaragua, the Death Squads in Guatemala, and many other US-fostered undemocratic initiatives throughout the Spanish-speaking Americas.

Che must have been elated to be in a country so like and so close to his own. Most of his family and friends had crossed over from Argentina to meet up with him. In those days, if you wanted to travel in style, you crossed on the Vapor de la Carrera service. Dinner was served on board, you sailed through the night and disembarked at Montevideo after breakfast. Or it was a 45-minute flight from Buenos Aires. Che spent time with his family, in particular his mother, whenever his official engagements permitted.

Meanwhile in Cuba, 17th August was the date new banknotes were issued, bearing Che's signature as president of the National Bank of Cuba. He had signed them simply Che, something that caused a furore in international finance circles. Many thought it was an indication of his contempt for money; others considered it a joke in poor taste. Now the red 3 peso note, issued after Che's death, still carries his image and many tourists take it home as a souvenir. It is an irony that the images of Karl Marx, who dreamt of a society that no longer used money, Vladimir Lenin, Mao Tse-tung and Che Guevara, each of whom enthusiastically attempted to put the concept into practice, have all appeared on their countries' currencies.

The CIES conference in Uruguay was perhaps the last opportunity for reconciliation between Cuba and the USA, to try and square Cuba's resentment at the invasion at Playa Girón with US fear of Cuba's socialism. A dialogue would be difficult, especially as Che's agenda was to expose Kennedy's Alliance for Progress. However, a meeting did take place. Che and Richard Goodwin, Kennedy's personal envoy, both attended the birthday party of a Brazilian diplomat in Montevideo and a room was set aside for them to talk privately.

Che asked Goodwin to thank the American president on his behalf for Playa Girón. He said that, prior to the failed invasion, the revolution had had its ups and downs, but the event had helped to consolidate it. According to Goodwin, Che said President Kennedy had handed the revolution over to 'us', by which he meant the Marxists in the higher echelons of power in Cuba. On a more conciliatory note, Che said he was aware of the impossibility of direct understanding between their two countries but Cuba would like to establish a modus vivendi, a sort of live and let live. They would not go back on the expropriation of US banks and factories, but were prepared to compensate the USA. Cuba could agree not to join any alliance with the socialist bloc countries, although this would not affect their natural empathy with them. They could even hold elections, but this would only be after a period required for the institutionalisation of the revolution. Che mentioned the US base at Guantánamo, on Cuban soil, something that violated Cuban sovereignty; and he said Washington would have to promise to decrease its covert operations in Latin America, formally renounce any further attempt to topple the Cuban government and lift the blockade. He said he would only discuss the meeting with Fidel Castro, to which

Goodwin replied he would also exercise discretion.

On 19th August, at the crack of dawn, Che boarded a Piper aircraft especially chartered to take him to Buenos Aires. The Argentine President Arturo Frondizi had arranged a secret visit because he saw himself as the only Latin American statesman who could mediate between Fidel Castro's Cuba and the new Kennedy administration. He wanted to avoid further confrontation, which would be detrimental to the rest of the hemisphere, as well as to the two main adversaries. He also hoped to strengthen his own position at home by gaining the support of the USA, who would perceive him as a statesman of stature. This was an accolade he needed, since he was constantly under threat of a military coup.

The aircraft landed at the small, private Don Torcuato airstrip some thirty kilometres from the capital. The two aides-de-camp sent by the president to collect a passenger could not believe their eyes when they saw who disembarked, and Che had to introduce himself and ask if the car next to the landing strip was their transport. He was then driven to the official presidential residence in Olivos, on the outskirts of Buenos Aires.

Che told the president that Cuba wanted to remain within the inter-American system. It was their intention to reach an accommodation with the USA, but it should take place in a dignified manner. Cuba also wanted to be independent from the Soviet Union: although Cuba received much aid from the USSR and sometimes even directives and instructions, Cuba wanted to build a totally autonomous socialist state. He believed the road of violence was the only one open to small and poor countries.

Frondizi told him he disagreed and that, even from a theoretical communist point of view, he was wrong. He asked Che if he had studied Marx, to which Che replied he had not (which may have been an act of humility on his part, for he did not consider he had totally mastered Marxist thought). In any case, he thought the only way forward was violence. He admitted that sending the enemies of the revolution before the firing squad had not yielded the expected results: it had created 'heroes'. The redistribution of land had also not been a success because there were undisciplined men who behaved like chieftains. But they were prepared to carry on. He hinted at the possibility of Argentina acting as mediator between Cuba and the USA. In response, Frondizi made a point of telling him Argentina had chosen a different path from Cuba and they would solve their problems by other means. Frondizi later said the meeting had been very cordial and Che Guevara sincere and measured.

The Argentine military were right wing and very powerful, but perhaps President Frondizi could have mediated between the USA and Cuba had the US emissary to Punta del Este not been Richard Goodwin who, as it turned out, totally misunderstood the Cuban position.

As the meeting drew to a close, Che told the president he had a favour to ask. His aunt, María Luisa Guevara-Lynch de Martínez-Castro, one of his father's sisters, was on her deathbed in Buenos Aires. He wanted to be driven to her home to say goodbye. The president, conscious of the danger this represented, checked the weather conditions for a later flight and reluctantly ordered a car to drive him to the Martínez-Castros' home. Che promised he would only stay with his aunt for five minutes and then he could be driven direct to the airport.

At this point, Mrs Frondizi, oblivious of protocol and secrecy, burst into the room, followed by her daughter Elenita, and asked Che if he cared for lunch. She could easily order a steak for him. 'On horseback?' Che asked. 'If that is how you like it,' she answered and left for the kitchen. (A steak on horseback, or *bife a caballo*, is an Argentine colloquialism which means a steak with two fried eggs on top.) Che had travelled on an empty stomach because of the early departure from Montevideo. Mrs Frondizi and Elenita enjoyed a quick lunch with him, and he was then sent to his aunt's home in a presidential car with tinted windows. He kept his promise and spent only a few minutes there, reaching the airport within the hour and returning to Montevideo. He flew on to Brasilia that same evening.

When it transpired that Che had been in Argentina, without their knowledge or authorisation, the military exacted their revenge. Before long, President Frondizi was deposed and sent to the island of Martín García, where there was a garrison and a military prison. The armed forces had been plotting his overthrow for some time: their relationship had always been fraught with problems and Guevara's visit was the last straw. Likewise, in Brazil, Janio Quadros was forced to resign the presidency after only eight months in office, because of his open support of the Cuban Revolution and the Soviet Union, something the Brazilian military would not tolerate.

In December, Cuba completed a year-long nationwide literacy campaign. Speaking at the UN in 1960, Castro had said that the revolution would eradicate illiteracy within a year. He had kept his word. Students were kitted out with uniforms and schoolbooks, and they travelled the length and breadth of the country, teaching those who needed to learn to read and write. The teenage students often taught men twice their age. It was quite a dangerous thing to do, as there were pockets of enemies of the revolution still lurking in the mountains. There were 40 fatalities among the teenage students-turned-educators, but even this did not diminish the success of the campaign. Cuba became an example to the rest of Latin America, where a project of this nature had never been undertaken. When Hugo Chávez came to power in Venezuela in 1998, he would ask Cuba's Ministry of Education to send its experts to Caracas to organise a literacy campaign which is still under way.

Che's book *Guerrilla Warfare* was now published in Cuba, and was translated into Russian, French and English soon after. It has since been criticised by military experts, who claim it does not add much to the subject compared, for instance, to the writings of Mao Tse-tung or General Vo Nguyen Giap of Vietnam. But the book served as a guide on how to overcome the prevailing defeatist attitude of the communist parties of Latin America during the 1960s. Those who claim it does not add much to the writings of Mao or Giap do not realise that their works were not available for free and in Spanish to guerrilla movements in Latin America.

In the book, Che set out to prove that armed struggle could result in victory even against established, entrenched regimes armed with modern weaponry, and that guerrilla movements based in the jungles and mountains of a country could lead the people to freedom, as had been the case in Cuba. It became known as the theory of the *foco guerrillero* (vanguard guerrilla group). *Guerrilla Warfare* would eventually become the bible of guerrilla movements in different parts of the world. For example, the Lion of Panjshir, Ahmed Shah Massoud, the charismatic Mujjaheddin leader, claimed he consulted it frequently. He died on 15th September 2001, after an attack by a bin Laden suicide squad, but previously had led the Northern Alliance of Afghanistan to victory, liberating their country from the Soviets. However, the American Green Berets, who would hound Che to death in Bolivia, read it as well, and so learnt about guerrilla warfare from an absolute expert on the subject.

It should be added that while Che may have inspired modern guerrilla groups, he was never an advocate of urban guerrilla warfare. He claimed it could not work because there was no possibility of having a vanguard and because it hurt civilians: women, children and other non-combatants.

The Italian journalist Roberto Savio was travelling in Latin America to write about the guerrilla movements at the time. An old friend, he told me an anecdote which illustrates Che's personality.

When Che was Minister of Industry, I made a long trip around Venezuela to see what the prospects were for a Cuban-style guerrilla movement there. The Venezuelan *campesinos* were not living in abject poverty and, most importantly, had faith in the future. Thanks to its oil receipts, the Venezuelan government was able to redistribute resources; this did not really change anything, but it gave the impression that the government cared about the people, including the *campesinos*.

The guerrilla movement was born in the cities, and in intellectual circles. North American imperialism and the liberation of Latin America were very abstract concepts for the average *campesino*. The more I travelled around the countryside, the more aware I became of the profound differences between people's lives and experiences in the countryside and in the cities. This was quite different from the situation in Cuba before the revolution. In the end, I came to the conclusion that the guerrilla movement had no future in Venezuela and that its chances of growth had been stemmed.

I decided to go back to Cuba and study the differences between the two countries before writing my articles on Venezuela. When I arrived in Cuba, I met up with friends who were also journalists, especially colleagues working for Prensa Latina, and told them of my doubts about the future of the guerrilla movement in Venezuela because of the different historical and socio-economic situation in the countryside. Of course, this led to huge arguments, because I seemed to be knocking the 'exportability' of the revolution. I told them that was not what I meant. What I meant was that specific models had to be developed to suit the situation in each country, and that that would require a lot more work.

Later that week, I was fast asleep in my room at the Hotel Riviera when someone came knocking at the door at three o'clock in the morning. I got up and opened the door to find myself face to face with a soldier, who promptly saluted me. 'I have orders to take you to Comandante Guevara,' he said. 'He wants to see you.' So, we got into a jeep and drove through the deserted streets of Havana to the Ministry of Industry. It must have been about seven storeys high and the whole building was in darkness apart from a light glowing on the very top floor. We took the lift and finally came to a room with a guard standing outside the door. The soldier who was accompanying me repeated what he had said to all the other guards we had met in the building – that the Comandante was expecting me – and the guard opened the door for me.

I found myself in a large office, whose walls were panelled with a dark, tropical wood of some kind. Che was sitting on the other side of a huge table covered with mountains of paper. 'My friend,' he said, 'I want to talk to you about the guerrilla movement in Venezuela. What's this you've been saying about it not having any future?' Suddenly realising that I was rather nervous because this felt like some kind of police interrogation, Che came over and shook my hand. 'Coffee?' he asked. I said I would love one, especially given what time of the night it was. He opened the door and asked the guard to bring us two cups of coffee. While we were waiting for the coffee to arrive, he asked me a few questions about my journey, whether I was keeping well, and when I had last been in Argentina.

The guard came in carrying a small tray with two cups on it and offered one to Che. 'Where are your manners?' said Che. 'You always serve the guest first.' And the guard, who was standing on my left, did an about-turn to hold the tray out to me instead. He had an AK47 over his shoulder and, as he turned towards me, he accidentally caught me just above my left eye with the barrel of the gun. It made me jump and the two cups of coffee went flying across the desk, soaking everything in sight with coffee. I was frozen to the spot and had no idea what to do. In that moment of panic, I heard Che saying, 'At last somebody has come along and got rid of some of this paper for me . . .' He was smiling. That was when I fell in love with the man.

Che kept me up until five o' clock in the morning, firing endless questions at me even though he was already very well informed about the situation in Venezuela. I answered each of his questions but he did not seem to be listening to me and ignored all my answers, constantly coming back at me with yet another question, sometimes on some minor detail. When we had finished, he gave me a copy of his book, *La Guerra de Guerrillas* (*Guerrilla Warfare*), with this personal dedication written in it: 'For Roberto Savio – a memento of a long summer's night, without any wish to indoctrinate – Che'. I left that meeting with huge admiration for the man, but believing that Che was very doctrinaire and had no time for other people's opinions if they failed to fit in with his scheme of things.

One day in the early 1990s, when I was in Rome in my office, my secretary said to me, 'There's a Venezuelan senator who'd like to see you.' As I was asking her who he was and why he wanted to see me, the door opened and a man walked in, saying, 'Oh, my friend, that was quite a night we spent with Che,' as though it were something that had happened only a few days before. Once I had invited him to take a seat and offered him a cup of coffee, he told me what had happened later that morning, after Che had let me go.

Apparently, the leaders of the Venezuelan guerrilla movement were on a secret visit to Cuba and Che went straight to the hotel in Havana where they were staying and woke them up. 'There's an Italian here who tells me the guerrilla movement in Venezuela is going to fail,' he said. 'I want you to listen to what he's told me and respond to his arguments one by one.' 'And, you know, my friend,' the Venezuelan senator went on, 'you were right about everything and we had quite a job calming Che down.' So, that was how I discovered, all those years later, that Che had not only been listening to me, he had been memorising every word I said so that he could repeat my arguments to the appropriate people.

NINETEEN
(1962)

Richard Goodwin returned home from Uruguay with a large box of Cuban cigars for his president, courtesy of El Comandante Guevara. The story goes that Kennedy invited Goodwin to light up first as he feared Castro might have learnt to make explosive cigars, a technique the CIA had perfected by then. Goodwin wrote President Kennedy a detailed memo of his conversation with Che, which was proof he had misread Cuba's desire to reach an accommodation with the USA. His conclusions perhaps tell us more about the Americans' innate inability to look at Cuba objectively than about Che's stance.

Goodwin advised Kennedy to escalate the blockade, exclude Cuba from international forums and ignore the peaceful coexistence sought by Castro. He recommended the intensification of anti-Castro propaganda in the hope of weakening the regime. He thought the USSR was not prepared to assist Cuba financially and believed Che had spoken from weakness. He was wrong on all counts.

President Kennedy set up a committee to discuss ways of bringing down Castro's regime and gave the green light to Operation Mongoose, named after the Asian snake killer. Known also as the Cuban Project, it was a secret CIA plan through which, as of November 1961, the president authorised aggressive covert operations against the government of Fidel Castro. These included plotting his death, as well as those of his closest allies. The CIA's director, Allen Dulles, had been replaced after the Bay of Pigs fiasco and the new man, John McCone, was given express powers to deal with the Cuban question. The agency was allotted a huge budget of around $50 million, four hundred officers and hundreds of motorboats.

The handsome, urbane, charismatic, wealthy, Harvard-educated, devout

Roman Catholic, war hero John Fitzgerald Kennedy seems to have considered it his birthright to order the removal (a euphemism for killing) of foreign leaders who did not see eye to eye with him. He may have been the president of the world's second-largest democracy, but he would not let that stand in his way. Ever since he entered politics as a senator for Massachusetts, he had had a relationship with the Mafia, something inherited from his father who had made his fortune as a bootlegger during Prohibition in the 1930s. As the Mafia had lost out to Castro in Cuba and would have relished a return to the island, it cannot have been averse to cooperating with any US initiative to dispose of the Cuban leader.

As a reply to Cuba's suspension from the Organization of American States on 31st January, Castro issued the Second Declaration of Havana on 4th February, underlining Cuba's support for revolutionary struggle throughout the Americas. In Havana, Che attended the ceremony at which it was proclaimed, together with Armando Hart, Osmany Cienfuegos, Augusto Martínez-Sánchez, Emilio Aragonés and Celia Sánchez. The declaration sought to unmask those countries in Europe, as well as the United States, which had attained a high level of industrial development by exploiting the rest of the world. Since the developed nations dominated mass communications and had infinite financial resources, the only way out of such a dire predicament was revolution. It was the duty of every revolutionary to make revolution. Guerrilla movements all over Latin America felt acknowledged and encouraged by Castro's words. He had reversed the role of continental pariah that Kennedy had so diligently sought for him and become instead the guerrillas' champion, inspiration and mentor.

Cuba now funded and trained guerrilla movements from all over Latin America, and Havana became their Mecca. They received financial assistance, weapons, training in guerrilla warfare and advice. Che Guevara's *Guerrilla Warfare* was both their manual and their source of inspiration: in it he claimed armed struggle was the only way forward for Latin Americans to lose their shackles. It would put guerrilla movements on a collision course with the established communist parties of the continent, which had not originated from revolutionary struggle and did not want to start insurgencies. Through the creation of a *foco* (or nucleus) in the mountains or wilderness, supplied and supported by the urban population, as had been the case in the Sierra, a guerrilla movement could successfully wage war against a dictatorial regime, even in the most unpromising circumstances.

For Che, the worker, the *campesino* and the student were at the centre of revolutionary struggle. This was anathema to the Soviets with their rigid centralised structures and echelons, and it differed from Lenin's model of insurrection, which had come from the cities during the October Revolution of 1917. Guevara's theory was different as well from Mao's doctrine of People's War. While Mao's theory counted on the support of the peasantry from the start to win the war, Che's theory stated that popular support would come during the struggle itself. This meant that a small group of insurgents could start a guerrilla war and develop the conditions to obtain popular support for their revolution at the same time. The theory of the *foco* rejects the orthodox Marxist emphasis on the working classes and the need to take objective conditions into account before launching an insurrection. He labelled this Vanguardism, pointing also to its moral value as an example.

In March 1962, Cuban Minister of Internal Affairs Ramiro Valdés tried to convince the Soviets to join the Cubans in their support of other Latin American revolutionary movements. He stated that, at a time when the Chinese were striving to exert their influence on every continent, the Russians were not doing so. The USSR and China had fallen out in 1960 and were becoming rivals in the sphere of influence over the rest of the world, but it may have been an exaggeration to state that China was active in every continent (though there had been serious skirmishes between the Chinese and the Indians in 1961–2 on their common border). Khrushchev's reaction to the criticism was to increase aid in the form of matériel and personnel, which indirectly benefited all those who came to Cuba for training in guerrilla warfare.

Cuba hosted an international chess tournament and Che took time off to indulge his passion for the game. He played the Argentine Grandmaster Miguel Najdorf and the match ended in stalemate. Che had once played Najdorf in the Argentine seaside resort of Mar del Plata when he was a medical student and the master was playing fifteen boards simultaneously. Che had lost, of course, but now he was better equipped, having amassed a library on the subject and practised regularly.

March also saw the creation of the Libreta de Consumo, or ration book. Castro explained the need for it on television. It was a system for the distribution of foodstuffs and industrial products to the population, and remains in operation to this day. When people complained that it was impossible to live on what the ration book prescribed, Che argued that his family managed well on their allowance. 'That is because you have two ration books,' came the reply. He went home and checked. Indeed he did. He had been issued one as minister and one

Che playing chess, a lifelong passion

as comandante. He told Aleida to return one ration book immediately. He went out of his way to explain that he had not known but had now put an end to the anomaly; they would manage on the same amounts as everyone else. Neither gastronomy nor abundance had ever been part of life in the Guevara household when Che was growing up in Argentina, so, unlike most middle-class Cubans, who have the reputation of being wasteful, he was comfortable with the rationing now required by the Cuban economy.

In April Che chaired the closing session of the National Council of the Central de Trabajadores de Cuba (Union of Cuban Workers), at which it was agreed that work should now begin on emulating socialist structures throughout the nation. He said, 'The Revolution has to be carried out at a violent pace; anyone who tires has the right to tire but not the right to call themselves part of the vanguard.' Che and Aleida's son Camilo was born on 20th May. Che was overjoyed at having a male heir. He was named after Camilo Cienfuegos, Che's comrade during the war in the Sierra.

On 26th August Che and Emilio Aragonés left for the Soviet Union, via Prague, for talks about cooperation on technical, agricultural, hydraulic, steel and military matters. Agreements were signed at Yalta on 31st August and 2nd September. A communiqué was issued to mark the satisfactory conclusion of the negotiations between the two countries, and Che gave an interview to the office of Prensa Latina in Moscow. They were back in Havana on 6th September.

It was not disclosed at the time that on 30th August Che and Aragonés had a meeting with Nikita Khrushchev at his summer house in the Crimea. Its purpose was to discuss the Soviet missiles being installed in Cuba as a result of negotiations between the Soviet leader and Fidel and Raúl Castro. When Che and Aragonés voiced their concern at the potential US reaction, Khrushchev simply said that if there was a problem he would send the Baltic fleet to the area. He was determined to have his missiles on Cuban soil.

On 16th October Ahmed Ben Bella, the Prime Minister of the Popular Democratic Republic of Algeria, arrived in Havana on an official visit, disregarding John F. Kennedy's advice. During his recent visit to New York, Kennedy had told him it would be wise to stay away from the island. He had cryptically suggested that something untoward was about to happen in Cuba.

In Washington DC, President Kennedy was informing his brother Bobby, the US attorney general, that a U2 spy plane had photographed a site in Cuba – a field near San Cristóbal in Pinar del Río – which was being prepared for the arrival of missiles and atomic weapons. In his memoir of the Cuban Missile Crisis, *Thirteen Days*, written in 1967 and published in 1969 when both he and the president were dead, Bobby Kennedy said that, to his untrained eye, the site looked like a football pitch. But the experts knew the photographic evidence could only mean one thing.

Arthur Lundahl, the man from the CIA who explained the photographs to the Kennedy brothers, had clearly marked the sites of erector launcher equipment, missile trailers and tent areas. The CIA had taken thousands of reconnaissance photographs of western Cuba and was able to assert that the missiles being installed were similar to those seen on military parades in Moscow's Red Square. They were probably but a week away from being operational. The Americans also suspected that the Soviet Union was building a large naval shipyard and a base for submarines in Havana's port.

The U2 spy planes continued their sorties. By 17th October the photographs were showing other installations, suitable for at least 16 and possibly as many as 32 missiles, with a range of more than 1,600 kilometres.

The missiles were all directed at American cities and, according to Bobby Kennedy, could kill as many as 80 million people within minutes if fired.

President Kennedy appeared on television on 22nd October to denounce Cuba's acquisition of Soviet nuclear missiles and to inform the world of his decision to impose a naval blockade or 'quarantine' on the island: the blockade was only the first step, and he had ordered the Pentagon to prepare for further military action. On 23rd October Khrushchev denounced the blockade. He had thought his missiles would prevent a war between the USA (still smarting from the Bay of Pigs) and Cuba, and he believed Kennedy was bluffing when he spoke on television the previous day. He knew Kennedy would have been as concerned as he was over the possibility of a nuclear war.

Kennedy had been in office for nearly two years, and he and Khrushchev had been playing a very dangerous game of nuclear tit for tat throughout that time. They had met at a summit conference in Vienna on 4th June 1961, not long after the failed Bay of Pigs invasion, and clashed over the future of West Berlin. Kennedy had come away from the meeting satisfied that he had held his ground with his policy of containment of communism in Europe. However, Khrushchev had then threatened to sign a peace agreement with East Germany that would block access to West Berlin because the roads and air routes would be under East German control. In August 1961, the East Germans suddenly closed their borders with their western neighbour and began construction of the Berlin Wall.

Since the Americans already had missiles stationed in Italy, Turkey and West Germany, aimed at Soviet cities such as Kiev, Odessa and Moscow, the Soviets thought they were only putting themselves on an equal footing with the USA when they offered their missiles to Castro. The American arsenal was also far greater than the Soviet one: they had 3,000 nuclear warheads and nearly 300 missile launchers, while the USSR had 250 warheads, including those now in Cuba.

Khrushchev originally wrote in his memoirs that, in addition to protecting Cuba, Soviet missiles would have equalised what the West calls 'the balance of power'. He deleted the section in further editions because he realised that admitting the missile deployment served any purpose beyond the defence of Cuba would cause him to lose face in the eyes of the world with their withdrawal.

While the Bay of Pigs invasion was the most outrageous act of war and imperialism in the hemisphere of the past fifty years, the Soviet placing of missiles in Cuba was a criminally insane act. The fact that the worst did not happen does not detract from that. At first, the Cuban leader had not been willing to contemplate the plan to install Soviet missiles in his country but eventually he gave in. He was quoted as saying, 'We did not like the missiles. If it was a matter of our defence alone, we would not have accepted the missiles here. But do not think it was because of the dangers that would come from having the missiles here, but rather because of the way this could damage the image of the Revolution in Latin America'.

Negotiations with Castro for the installation of the missiles on Cuban soil had started in May 1962, culminating in an agreement after much discussion between the parties over several weeks. Documents had been drafted, secret discussions had been held during trips to the Soviet Union by Raúl Castro and others, and by July, Soviet army personnel, technicians, engineers, materials and equipment were on their way to the island.

At one time the number of Soviet personnel in Cuba reached 42,000, twice the highest US estimate. During the next three months, as many as 85 cargo and passenger ships crossed the Atlantic, sailing towards Cuba. How could Khrushchev think the Americans would not notice? He was convinced he would be able to present them with a fait accompli and it is amazing that he almost did. By 4th October there had already been 114 shipments, and another 35 were on their way. Thirty-six R-12 medium-range missiles were already in situ. And it had all happened without the CIA detecting it. Khrushchev had not bothered to inform his embassy in Washington, so the Soviet ambassador there was not lying when he gave assertions to the Kennedy brothers that no offensive weapons were being sent to Cuba.

Cuba responded to the blockade by mobilising the population for its defence and putting its forces on wartime alert in preparation for the US invasion Castro thought imminent. Che was to command the forces stationed in Pinar del Río. He set up his headquarters in a cave in the mountains, not far from the San Cristóbal missiles site. His men built a structure inside the cave to provide him with some privacy and make it less damp, as excessive humidity could bring on an asthma attack.

On 24th October Castro replied to Kennedy's defiant declarations in an equally defiant tone. The whole affair was turning into a macho contest between the three men, as the whole world watched and held its breath. But the Soviet ships which were carrying incriminating cargo had been instructed to turn away from the quarantine zone. In any case, as Khrushchev would say later, the missiles were already in Cuba.

On 25th October a Soviet merchant ship bound for Cuba was intercepted by US warships, in compliance with the blockade Kennedy had ordered. She was boarded and inspected and allowed to continue without incident as her cargo did not pose any danger; but other ships had reached Cuba with cargo of a very different nature, and a number of IL-28 light bombers were already being assembled on the island.

On 26th October Khrushchev wrote to Kennedy saying that the missiles he had sent to Cuba were defensive and not offensive, but he did not expect him to believe it. In a conciliatory tone, he suggested that America should give him an undertaking not to attack Cuba and lift the naval blockade so that they could avoid a confrontation which would have no winners.

One of the most dangerous moments came on 27th October, when a U2 spy plane from the USA, which had violated Cuban airspace, was shot down north of Oriente province by a Soviet-supplied surface-to-air missile, launched from Banes. The pilot, Rudolf Anderson Junior, an American major, was killed. It was incontrovertible evidence that Kennedy was spying on Cuba.

Although negotiations between the two powers had already begun, the U2 had been shot down because Khrushchev had authorised the Soviet commander on the ground to fire missiles at his own discretion. It could have brought the whole negotiation process to an abrupt end. In addition, there was a grave risk of Kennedy now authorising retaliatory air strikes (although these had been vetoed earlier, for fear of them not disabling all the Soviet missiles and also prompting Soviet retaliation in Berlin).

President John F. Kennedy during the Cuban missile crisis

That same day, Khrushchev sent Kennedy another message, this time asking for the withdrawal of American missiles in Turkey. All Soviet vessels at sea turned round and returned to their home ports instead of proceeding to Cuba and confronting the blockade.

On 28th October Khrushchev brought the crisis to an end by announcing publicly that he would remove all missiles from Cuban soil and return them to the USSR in exchange for the United States pledging not to invade Cuba. Khrushchev had also accepted Kennedy's private assurances that he would remove US missiles from Turkey as part of the deal, but did not make this public. Kennedy agreed to this since the introduction of Polaris submarine-borne missiles would soon make them obsolete.

Castro was never consulted or informed of the exchanges between Kennedy and Khrushchev and only found out after the event. When the people of Cuba learnt of the Soviet premier's climbdown, they went out into the streets chanting, '*Nikita mariquita, lo que se da no se quita*' (You quitter, Nikita, you humble-pie eater). President Kennedy, on the other hand, regarded his handling of the Cuban Missile Crisis and the avoidance of conflict as his finest hour. The Western world applauded his cool attitude in averting a nuclear disaster and restoring stability to the balance of power. He was also credited with making Khrushchev blink first. However, he could be blamed for having contributed more than a little to the development of the crisis by his authorisation of Mongoose and for going on television rather than negotiating with Khrushchev offstage, so the Soviet leader could back down without losing face.

The Cuban Missile Crisis – or *la crisis del Caribe*, as the Spanish-speaking world called it – lasted thirteen days, from 16th to 28th October, while the world looked on in utter bewilderment and amazement, wondering how the two superpowers would resolve their differences. The alternative was the devastation of the entire planet.

Once the crisis was over, Kennedy would say that he thought it was folly that the behaviour of two men could have taken the world to the brink of destruction. The president would be judged severely by his contemporaries for having misread Khrushchev and not realising early enough that the man was a consummate liar. British Prime Minister Harold Macmillan thought Kennedy had been completely overwhelmed by the ruthlessness and barbarity of the Russian premier. Macmillan was quoted as saying that the young American president had never encountered someone who 'was impervious to his charm'. But Kennedy was aware that the Bay of Pigs fiasco had given the USSR the wrong impression. In Soviet eyes, he probably came across as inexperienced and gutless. He had disabused the Soviet premier of that notion.

Khrushchev's decision had a great impact on Castro. He needed to disappear from public view for a while. Taking refuge in his home in the Sierra, he brooded and sulked while he assessed the situation. He was truly disappointed in the Russian leadership. He felt their behaviour to be a personal betrayal, as a man with such a large ego was bound to do. He was frustrated and angry but, with his characteristic resilience, he licked his wounds, reviewed the events and decided on his next move with a cool head. Only he knew what was best for Cuba and best for Castro. After all, one of his most noteworthy qualities had always been his instinct for survival. He decided that he had to swallow his pride and remain best friends with the Soviets because he needed them. Perhaps he could even extract something from them as compensation for the missile climbdown.

Kennedy lifted the naval blockade around Cuba on 20th November but all other sanctions continued. Cuba had agreed to the removal of the IL-28 bombers along with all offensive weaponry, but Castro refused to allow on-site inspections. Forty-two IL-28s left Cuba on 5th, 6th and 7th December on board three Soviet vessels. Not all of them had been assembled and some were still crated. The planes were loaded on to the ships' decks and had to remain uncovered so that US surveillance planes could photograph them.

In early December Che granted an interview to British journalist Sam Russell, of the London-based communist newspaper, the *Daily Worker*. He told Russell that, if the Soviet missiles had been manned by Cubans, they would have launched them. And then went on to say, '*Frente al agresor solo cabe la lucha a muerte*' (If someone is out to get you, you have no choice but to fight to the death). It was proof of his continuing belief in the violent solution and of his disenchantment with the Soviet Union, which he made no effort to conceal, and which would eventually have dire consequences for him in Bolivia. But was it also posturing? Had he become obsessed with the missiles, as Russell suggested? Was he sending a message to the enemy by making such an extreme statement in an English-language publication? Was it a provocation? A man of his intelligence knew full well what the consequences of launching a missile would be, not just for the USA but for the whole world.

Che's mother Celia came to visit in October 1962, on her way to Europe. She had embarked on a career as a political activist and was in great demand as a public speaker. She and Ernesto Senior had separated amicably and Celia rented an apartment from her friend Susana Fiorito, who shared her political convictions. They were both members of the Movimiento de Liberación Nacional, a new left-wing movement. Celia earned a little money giving French lessons to private pupils and lived as frugally as she always had, but she was finally going to fulfil a cherished dream and visit Paris, Rome and Florence.

She flew to Havana from Montevideo, where she had gone to speak at a rally in solidarity with Cuba. She came to meet her newest grandchild, Camilo, who had been born earlier that year. She arrived just in time to live through the missile crisis and see her son's adopted country under threat and on a war footing. It was quite an experience, even for a woman who had grown accustomed to the dangers to which Che was constantly exposing himself. While she was away from home, the Federal Police in

Buenos Aires searched her apartment and that of her eldest daughter Celita, who worked as an architect and taught at university.

Celia was not in very good health as she was recovering from a recurrence of breast cancer, the illness that would eventually take her life. But she thoroughly enjoyed her stay at Che's home with Aleida and her grandchildren, and even managed to accompany Che on some of his engagements away from Havana. She also visited schools, hospitals and factories with the Cuban friends she had made on her previous visit.

She saw how the revolution had consolidated and was thrilled to witness the affection lavished on Che wherever they went. She was impressed by the way in which his ideas were accepted and implemented by people in every walk of life. Voluntary holiday work cutting sugar cane was one of his projects which workers undertook regularly. He told her that, for him, cutting cane was a sort of mental relaxation, a way of leaving all cares behind, as well as good physical exercise. Both Lenin and Mao had advocated the practice of manual labour before him, writing that it was good for the construction of socialism.

Celia was surprised that Harry Villegas-Tamayo, who had always been one of Che's four escorts, was nowhere to be seen. On her previous visit he had accompanied her everywhere and they had become friends. She was told that he had been sent to Cayo Largo as punishment for a misdemeanour. He had been driving a truck at an airport construction site for the past six months. She asked Che to take her to see him and, once they were there, she pleaded with Che to end his banishment. He deferred to his mother's wishes and gave his escort permission to return to Havana straightaway. Harry Villegas-Tamayo is today a five-star general and a national hero. He first served under Che in the Sierra when he was a teenage boy, then in the Congo, and finally in Bolivia, where he was one of five survivors. Years later he served in Angola with distinction. He has now retired and lives in Havana where he is better known as Pombo, his nom de guerre.

Operation Mongoose was eventually aborted towards the end of 1962. It had been a favourite project of Bobby Kennedy, who devoted much time to it and had his own full-time liaison officer inside the CIA, answerable to him rather than to the agency, but the White House was not in total control of it. Indeed, it blew up a Cuban factory on 8th November, after it was supposed to have ceased to exist. However, President Kennedy continued the covert sabotage of Cuba's government, Cuban cargo and shipping and Cuban installations, with the cooperation of willing and able Cuban exiles. There were also multiple attempts on Castro's life by the CIA during President Kennedy's tenure. These were both imaginative and original, as well as useless: exploding pens and cigars, lethal chemical agents doused on Castro's scuba-diving equipment and poisoned pills delivered by an ex-girlfriend.

The revolutionary government was now in its third year in power in Cuba, and was implementing a programme for the promotion of Cuban culture. The first book the revolution distributed for free was *Don Quijote de la Mancha*. New museums, art schools and theatres were created. Musicians were guaranteed a salary. All this was to a large extent due to the efforts of journalist Carlos Franqui, whose influence at the time was considerable. He took it upon himself to found the first publishing house in Cuba for native authors. At his invitation, many foreign intellectuals visited the island. There was state support for costly cultural activities for the masses, such as ballet, theatre and classical music. The intention was to counter the influence of US mass culture; Afro-Cuban cultural activities were encouraged, with the purpose of creating a cultural identity which reflected Cuban reality.

But soon the revolution would be controlling every initiative through its organisations, as the model of the Soviet Union and the eastern bloc was adopted. The state took over the different branches of culture, with the creation of institutions such as the Unión de Escritores y Artistas de Cuba or Union of Writers and Artists of Cuba (UNEAC), the Instituto Cubano de Artes e Industrias Cinematográficas or Cuban Institute for Film Arts and Industries (ICAIC), the Instituto del Libro or Book Institute and the Consejo Nacional de Cultura or National Council for Culture. Cultural activities had to be approved by the relevant bodies; official permission was required to publish a book or organise an exhibition of paintings.

According to the revolution's critics, strict adherence to Marxist-Leninist ideology was a grave mistake which cost Cuba dearly, as it resulted in a brain drain. Carlos Franqui got himself posted abroad as an unpaid representative of Cuban culture, but when Cuba endorsed the Soviet invasion of Czechoslovakia in 1968, he severed links with the island.

Author Guillermo Cabrera-Infante, whose parents had been founder members of the Communist Party of Cuba, was the editor of *Lunes de Revolución*, a literary supplement of the left-wing newspaper *Revolución*, which Castro banned in 1961. In 1962, Cabrera-Infante was appointed cultural attaché at the Cuban embassy in Brussels, where he served until 1965, when he too chose the road of exile. He was never to return to his homeland and his books about his lost paradise – *Tres Tristes Tigres* (*Three Trapped Tigers*), *Vista del amanecer en el trópico* (*A View of Dawn in the Tropics*) and *Havana para un Infante Difunto*, a play on Ravel's title *Pavane pour une Infante Défunte* (published in English as *Infante's Inferno*), to name but a few – became best-sellers in several languages. He died of septicaemia in a London hospital in 2005 aged seventy-five. Cuban newspapers did not carry an obituary or even a mention in the news.

Years later, Peruvian author Alfredo Bryce-Echenique, reminiscing about the period during a literary debate in Buenos Aires, said Che had been one of the guiding forces behind the initiative to promote culture in Cuba: by 1962 a golden age of the arts and literature had begun. And he mockingly added, 'In those days, spending fifteen minutes in the presence of Che Guevara gave you enormous kudos throughout the Spanish-speaking world.'

TWENTY

(1963–1964)

Khrushchev allowed some time for tempers to cool and anti-Soviet feeling to die down in Cuba after the missile crisis. Then he wrote to Castro in January 1963, inviting him to spend time in the Soviet Union. When Castro accepted, Khrushchev sent a TU-114, the most modern long-haul aircraft in the USSR, to collect him and his large entourage. Such was the political climate at the time, that they left Havana on 26th April without making their departure public, for fear of being shot down during the sixteen-hour journey.

Castro was given a hero's welcome in Moscow. He stayed forty days in the Soviet Union, visiting fourteen cities and touring military as well as civilian installations before returning to Havana on 3rd June. The media reported his every move. He was photographed next to the top leaders at the military parade in Red Square on 1st May, decorated with the Order of Lenin and made a Hero of the Soviet Union. It must have done wonders for his morale. In a joint statement issued on 24th May, the USSR endorsed Castro's demands at the UN, which had included dismantling the US naval base in Guantánamo and complete withdrawal from Cuban territory.

After his official tour was over, Castro was invited to Khrushchev's summer house at Pitzunda, on the Black Sea, where they were able to converse in private. Here Castro accidentally discovered that his friend Nikita had traded Cuba's missiles for the withdrawal of US missiles from Turkey. At the time, this had not been made public, allowing President Kennedy to save face. Castro was not amused at having been used as a bargaining chip. The discovery confirmed that his instincts were right when they told him to mistrust the Russians.

Khrushchev wanted to keep Cuba on the side of the Soviet Union in the new rift that was opening up between the USSR and China, and he thought Che might be growing pro-Chinese because he was constantly articulating his disagreements with the Soviets in no uncertain terms. In actual fact, Che had begun to be disillusioned with the Soviets even before the missile crisis. He found them too bureaucratic, did not care for their policy of monetary incentives for the workforce, thought they were indulging in a kind of state capitalism and disapproved of the privileges the upper echelons of the nomenklatura awarded themselves. He also despaired at the quality of some of the machinery and tools which had arrived from Russia, to replace the American ones which had been in Cuba when the revolution triumphed and had by now run out of spares, rusted and become useless. But this did not mean he was about to fall into the arms of Mao Tse-tung. He had developed his own version of Marxism, which he expressed in his speeches and his writing.

His vision of the New Man differed from the vision of Marx, Lenin and even Mao, all of whom had written about the concept. For him, the material incentives and the profitability the Soviets advocated for their enterprises, at the centre of the Soviet economy, were not advancing the cause of socialism. According to Che, it was a chimera to attempt to arrive at socialism using the tools of capitalism. He felt there was a better way, a more efficient one to arrive at communism, via the New Man. This man would understand that one should not work for the accumulation of material goods, something which was egotistical and individualistic. He would know that it was his selfless moral duty to work for society, and that society would in turn look after him and his family. To create this New Man, the revolution had provided for the eradication of illiteracy and a comprehensive healthcare system for all. Che so totally believed this to be the case that, when he left for his campaign in the Congo, he wrote a farewell letter to Castro stating he was not leaving his wife and children anything material because he knew the revolution would look after them.

Castro, for his part, had not been a communist to begin with and probably never would be, but saw the usefulness of the USSR. He realised that it could be instrumental in keeping him at the helm of his little Caribbean island if he was astute enough to play its game to his advantage.

He therefore allowed the Soviets to win him over to their ways. It was not too high a price to pay for what he got in return.

Meanwhile, in Havana, a strong and too dominant bureaucratic apparatus had been created, and the problem was compounded by a lack of qualified personnel. Even Che's own organisation, the Ministry of Industry, had undertaken a policy of centralisation which had discouraged initiative. It had gone from anarchy to total control, yet mistakes had not been spotted in time. The slogans of the day were: War on bureaucratism, Streamline the state apparatus, Production without restraints, and Responsibility for production.

As minister of industry, Che involved himself in every stage of production

Che spent five days at the Ciro Redondo sugar mill in February 1963, driving a cane-cutter. He worked for twelve consecutive hours a day as he checked out the machine. He then went on to close the National Sugar Industry plenary session in Camagüey, where he spoke about mechanisation and production as well as socialist emulation. This he considered to be an instrument for the development of the people's conscience which would motivate them to work productively, in turn creating greater riches and welfare for everyone. He had taken responsibility for overall production on the island and was determined to make a success of it, taking it upon himself to verify every aspect personally.

Celia Guevara eventually left Havana for Europe in March 1963. On her journey home, she was stopped by the Argentine customs under a fabricated charge of attempting to smuggle communist propaganda. She was taken into custody and transferred to a women's prison in Buenos Aires, about which her only complaints were the extreme cold and the lack of privacy. While she was still in jail, Che and Aleida's third child was born. They called her Celia, after her grandmother.

Celia could not be found guilty of anything but the military had suspended the constitution and were able to keep people who disagreed with them behind bars. The de la Sernas and the Guevaras were not without influential friends, and a judge intervened to reverse the injustice, setting up his court inside the jail in the middle of the night and decreeing that she should be set free immediately. By the time the military learnt what had happened, Celia, accompanied by a senior army officer whose name was never revealed, had slipped quietly across the border into Montevideo.

Che wrote to her, enclosing an air ticket to Havana but she declined his invitation. She was not about to give up her newly found calling as a political activist. As Che Guevara's mother, her opinions mattered, but it would not be until a new civilian president, Arturo Illia, had been inaugurated in Argentina that Celia could return home from Uruguay.

At the end of June 1963, Che flew to Algiers to represent Cuba at the ceremonies to commemorate the first anniversary of Algerian independence from France and to hold meetings with Prime Minister Ahmed Ben Bella. While Che was in Algiers, the USA declared a total embargo on Cuba. Then, while the Cubans celebrated the anniversary of the Moncada Barracks attack on 26th July, the American administration announced it was freezing all Cuban assets in the USA.

Che and Algerian Prime Minister Ahmed Ben Bella

Back in Havana, Che spoke at the closing ceremony of the first international meeting of architecture students since the revolution, at the end of September. He said, 'This generation has to pay the price of glory with sacrifice. It has to sacrifice itself day by day to build tomorrow with its efforts . . . Your obligations extend beyond the Cuban frontiers; the obligation to spread the ideological flame of the Revolution throughout every corner of the Americas, throughout every corner of the world where our voice is heard.'

On 22nd November 1963, President Kennedy was killed in Dallas. The man who allegedly shot him, Lee Harvey Oswald, had a Russian wife and had visited Cuba. He in turn was shot while in custody, in full view of the television networks' cameras. The president's assassination gave rise to a series of conspiracy theories: he had been liquidated by the Miami lobby of expatriate Cubans for going soft on Cuba; Oswald had shot him because he thought Castro wanted him dead; he had been killed by the Mafia; the Soviets had ordered his death. The speculation continues to this day. Guevara is alleged to have said that he did not want Kennedy dead because, although he was the enemy, he was an enemy they knew and whose behaviour they could predict.

Che had never given up on his idea of returning to Argentina to lead an insurrection against the right-wing military men. When Che joined the Cubans in Mexico to prepare for the liberation of their country, Castro had promised him that, when the time came, he would let him go to start an insurrection in Argentina, and would even help him. The time had come for Che's campaign in continental Latin America to enter its next phase.

Alberto Granado had already visited Argentina. He had made contact with the Communist party and interviewed men with technical skills who would like to work in Cuba. He had actually been recruiting men who would soon receive guerrilla training and join the insurgent group, initially led by Jorge Ricardo Masetti, and eventually by Che himself.

Cuba already had an espionage network in Prague, and Masetti had gone there on several secret missions for Che. He had also gone to Algeria to deliver weapons captured at Playa Girón. Cuba had contributed these to the Front Nationale de Libération (FLN), prior to its triumph, smuggling them in via Tunisia. Federico Méndez, one of Granado's Argentine recruits, travelled with Masetti and the arms. Both stayed on for several months at what had been the FLN headquarters and Méndez taught the Algerians to use their new US-made arsenal.

Masetti had moved to Cuba from Argentina after his scoop report of the revolution from the front for Radio El Mundo of Buenos Aires, and he had been editor-in-chief of Prensa Latina since it was founded, immediately after the triumph of the revolution. He left the paper in 1961, as a result of his and Che's constant clashes with the members of the Cuban government who were pro-Moscow communists, such as Aníbal Escalante and Carlos Rafael Rodríguez. These were among the first generation of guerrilla fighters from the Sierra (now known as the Historic Generation) who no longer needed to keep their affiliation under wraps. Masetti had then completed a guerrilla training course and obtained the rank of captain.

Ciro Bustos, an Argentine painter from Mendoza who was a sympathiser of the revolution, had arrived in Cuba in 1962 with his wife. He had accepted Granado's invitation to join Che's team preparing for the campaign in northern Argentina. He left his wife behind and moved to a safe house in Havana, where he underwent guerrilla training with Méndez and two other Argentine men, whose noms de guerre were Leonardo and Miguel. Hermes Peña, one of Che's bodyguards, joined them as Masetti's second in command.

The group received frequent visits from Che, Masetti and Comandante Manuel Piñeiro (also known as Barbarroja because of his long red beard), who was Head of Intelligence, and his deputy Juan Carretero, whose codename was Ariel. Havana's chief of police, Abelardo Colomé-Ibarra (everybody knew him as Furry) would be joining the Argentine group to command the rearguard base and be in charge of communications with Cuba. A Russian general on active service, who came from Catalonia and was a republican hero of the Spanish Civil War, was in charge of their training. His real name was Francisco Ciutat but he went under the pseudonym of Ángel Martínez. Everybody called him Angelito. Leonardo was a doctor, Miguel would be in charge of logistics and Bustos was to deal with security and intelligence.

The Argentine recruits were given a taste of what it might be like to be on a war footing when Che took them with him to Pinar del Río during the missile crisis, inserting them into a battalion of his Cuban troops, although they didn't see any action. When the missile crisis was over, Che knew that it was too dangerous to continue to have his trainees around, especially as there was bad blood between him and the Russians, who would now be going home with their missiles. So Piñeiro organised false travel papers for Che's men, with the idea that they would go to Algeria via Prague to complete their training.

According to Ciro Bustos, who wrote a detailed account of the experience in his 2005 book *El Che Quiere Verte* (*Che Wants to See You*), the papers were inadequate. He was balding, but what hair he still had was dark brown. Piñeiro gave him a passport for a much younger man with blond hair. He complained about it and was told there would be new passports for them in Prague, where they would be taken through passport control swiftly, as it was a city where they had good contacts. At this point each man got a nom de guerre. Bustos became Laureano. Masetti became Comandante Segundo, implying that there was a Comandante Primero. A lot has been written about these pseudonyms, but Bustos says there never was any doubt they were Che's men and that he would join them in due course as Comandante Primero. However, his work as part of the Cuban government remained unfinished. If it were discovered that a man in his position was actively involved in fomenting armed revolution in another country, there would probably have been diplomatic scandal on a grand scale, so the intention was for Che to bide his time in Cuba until conditions were right.

The men who came from Argentina had been selected by Alberto Granado, Che's trusted friend since their student days, and those Cubans who were invited to join came from Che's circle of intimates. These were men who were prepared to follow Che to the ends of the earth, who had proved their total loyalty to him as his comrades-in-arms and then as his escorts in civilian life, when he held office as a minister or travelled on behalf of the Cuban nation to various parts of the world. They were Alberto Castellanos, Hermes Peña, José María Martínez-Tamayo and Abelardo Colomé-Ibarra.

Once in Czechoslovakia, they were taken to an empty hotel by Lake Slapie, where they had to pretend they were students from Cuba on a scholarship. They were left to their own devices to await orders and for a couple of weeks it seemed they had been forgotten. Then Comandante Jorge Serguera, from the embassy there, took them to Prague, saying that the Czech authorities were upset because they had been too close to secret military installations during their country hikes. There had been nothing else for the bored men to do but go on marches to keep themselves fit. Once in Prague, Masetti thought they had waited long enough. He decided to fly to Algiers by himself. He was well received in Algiers and was back within two days. His request to Ben Bella and Boumedienne had met with success. He and his men were on the move immediately.

They flew to Paris, arriving on 1st January 1963, and stayed for a couple of days before flying on to Algiers. In Paris they passed themselves off as tourists and were never out together in more than twos or threes. They arrived in Algiers to witness the early stages of a revolutionary government in office. All non-Arabs were considered suspect, so Ben Bella arranged for Masetti and his men to be taken to a villa on the outskirts of the city, to protect them from any incident that might result from mistaken identity. The villa had a walled garden, and an armed detachment of Algerian security men escorted them on the rare occasions they went out. They spent a few months in the villa and continued their military training. There was great empathy between Masetti's men and their hosts, who took them to see the caves and tunnels in which they used to hide weapons during their civil war against the French. They were also taken to what had been the front lines during the conflict.

In Havana, Che continued to make his plans for Argentina. He invited the Argentine lawyer Ricardo Rojo to visit him. They had been friends since their days on the road, and Rojo had also been close to President Frondizi. He did not share Che's political views but he was well connected in Argentina, he would speak candidly and could be trusted to give an accurate analysis of the political situation in his country. Rojo stayed for two months briefing Che. In his book *Mi amigo el Che* (*My Friend Che*), Rojo says Che took copious notes, as if he were preparing for an exam. Perón's party was still outlawed. The old general had made it known that he admired the Cuban revolution and Che wondered if there was something to be made of that. Perón had already been invited to live in Cuba by the revolutionary government – an invitation he never acted upon.

Rojo went back to Argentina in April 1963, and in May Masetti and his men left Algiers for southern Bolivia, near the frontier with the province of Salta in northern Argentina, which was their intended destination. They were given Algerian diplomatic passports and left separately, accompanied by the Algerian security officers, whom they knew well by then. Their first stop was Rome, then São Paulo in Brazil and from there overland to Santa Cruz de la Sierra in eastern Bolivia. Algerian diplomats had carried their arms for them in the diplomatic pouch.

The men regrouped. Piñeiro's men, a network which had been in operation on the ground in Bolivia for some time, had bought them boots, uniforms and backpacks. They were of such poor quality that Bustos could not help thinking that they were being sabotaged. Fortunately, the Algerians had kitted them out properly. And the weapons which came from Cuba were also of good quality. On 21st June a five-man vanguard of the incipient Ejército Guerrillero del Pueblo (People's Guerilla Army) entered Argentina illegally and set up camp in a forest near the Pescado river, on the mountains south of the city of Orán in the province of Salta. They were Masetti, Bustos, Federico Méndez, Hermes Peña and Leonardo, who became ill and was released by Masetti. Furry escorted them to the crossing and then returned to their base inside Bolivia.

The political situation in Argentina was volatile. Perón's party continued to be banned although he wielded power from his exile in Madrid, where trade unionists and members of political parties, both of the left and the right, came calling. The military government was forced to call an election, and on 7th July the candidate for the Unión Cívica Radical del Pueblo, a decent, ageing provincial doctor, Arturo Illia, surprisingly won by a narrow margin. Voting is compulsory in Argentina and those who wanted Perón back voted with blank or spoilt ballot papers. The military had crafted an election which was fraudulent from the outset, seeking to install a 'tame civilian political leader' they could control. A large section of the electorate had been left without a voice.

Even before Perón's attempt at serious industrialisation in the 1950s, the country had always been divided into opposing groups. The agro-exporting oligarchy with their foreign connections, the new industrialists, the armed forces were on one side (both the oligarchy and the military were members of the Roman Catholic church, which was never far from the political scene). On the other side were the trade unions, which represented the exploited and the disenfranchised working classes. When Frondizi was ousted in 1962, the agro-exporting class was reinstated. The right wing of the trade union movement – the bureaucrats – were looking to throw in their lot with the highest bidder since they were opportunists in search of control. The real struggle was not for power but for the control of power. The military sought 'American style' hegemony, the poor demanded the return of Perón, and the country was in turmoil.

For a brief moment there was a new atmosphere in Argentina: the people were euphoric to be rid of the military. Masetti realised nobody would now join a guerrilla force to fight against a democratically elected government. He decided to call the whole thing off and sent emissaries to inform their urban network throughout the country. He then changed his mind, because he realised that things were not as they seemed. Perón's party was still outlawed and his working-class followers had voted for no one. For them nothing had changed and they still wanted Perón's return. Some recruits had joined, but after such an inauspicious beginning the enterprise was doomed.

Masetti began to show new aspects of his personality. He had always been impatient but now his behaviour became extreme. The reason is something of a mystery. He had behaved admirably in the Sierra, had been a top journalist both in Buenos Aires and at Prensa Latina, which he and Che had founded. His book *Los que luchan y los que lloran* (*Those Who Fight and Those Who Weep*) about his Cuban experience had been a best-seller, and an eye-opener for Latin Americans. It gave a vivid description of his conversion from someone who observes and chronicles the exploits of others to an active participant in a revolution. He had proved his worth when Che trusted him with carrying arms from Cuba to Ben Bella, with training the guerrillas in Algiers, with various secret missions. He and Che had shared much, there was enormous empathy between them and they saw eye to eye on all important aspects of the revolution. He was obviously the most suitable and fit young Argentine man Che knew, someone who could be trusted with such a vital mission. How could Che have guessed that he was not the man he thought he was? But the fact remains that the project's real leader was not present: Segundo was not Primero.

The jungle that surrounded Masetti and his men was unforgiving. Most of the new recruits were young men from the cities who were not accustomed to the rough terrain or to marching on an empty stomach. There were no *campesinos* to speak of in the region; neither were there any students or workers. It was impossible to recruit anyone locally. Without an urban network in the immediate vicinity to support them, the theory of the *foco* proved impossible to pursue.

Masetti started meting out extreme punishments, backed up by Hermes, his second in command, a veteran of the Sierra Maestra. Their networks in the main cities had begun sending recruits. One of these was a Jewish boy in his twenties, from Buenos Aires, whom they called Pupi. He suffered from asthma and became totally demoralised, could not keep up on the marches and cried like a child. He should have been released, but instead he was court-martialled and sentenced to death, on the grounds that he was having a negative effect on the rest. Masetti had sent Bustos away as a messenger, to get an open letter he had written to the president published, but he returned to camp at this point. Bustos tells us that Pirincho, another recent recruit, was put in charge of the execution to harden him up. He was a city boy from a wealthy upper-class background, something that jarred with Masetti. Pirincho botched the job and Bustos was sent to give Pupi the coup de grâce. It was a devastating experience.

Years later, Bustos wrote from his exile in Sweden, 'A fascist mentality had triumphed and dealt our libertarian utopia another mortal blow. For fascism is a mentality, a way of thinking, rather than an ideology . . . It is neither the preserve of the right nor alien to the left . . . a synthesis of pathological sadism and fundamentalist fanaticism. We thought we were imbued with revolutionary truth, when we were nothing but deluded dreamers, believing we could impose justice through the use of arms.'

In Salta, the local gendarmes had discovered the presence of Masetti's group and they began combing the area. Alberto Castellanos, a Cuban who had recently joined them after completing his liaison work in the cities, developed a serious throat infection and had to be sent to Córdoba to have an operation. New recruits arrived, only to be found wanting by Masetti. In March 1964 he held a court martial which condemned a recruit called Nardo to death. A bank clerk in Córdoba, his real name was Bernardo Groswald, and he was another Jewish boy. Because the two young men Masetti executed were Jewish, it was later said that he was an anti-Semite.

Ricardo Rojo told me in Buenos Aires, in the early 1990s, that in his youth Masetti had belonged to an extreme right-wing anti-Semitic political organisation called Tacuara, which was in existence from 1957 to 1964 and modelled itself on the Spanish Falange. However, when I discussed the matter with Ciro Bustos, in 2008, he claimed it was a coincidence that both men were Jews and that Masetti was just exhibiting a nasty character trait as he began to crack up, which nobody had spotted before.

While all this was taking place, Bustos had been sent on another errand, to find Grillo Frontini and escort him back to the camp. Grillo had been a coordinator for the guerrillas in the capital and had been injudicious with the group's money. Meanwhile Pirincho, who had been sent on a special mission to Buenos Aires, had absconded. He had probably left for Europe to escape the fiasco. By now Masetti, aware of the disaster their campaign had become, was looking for an escape route, but the group had been infiltrated by a couple of men from the DIPA (a political police force created during the military dictatorship), posing as recruits. At the same time, the gendarmes located their camp.

On 18th April 1964, the radio announced that the advance group had been scattered. Hermes Peña and Jorge Guille, a 24-year-old Argentine student, nearly qualified as a doctor, had been killed in an ambush set by the gendarmes. Others, led by Masetti, hid in the forests on a 300-metre-high hillside. They had not had any food for days, and several died of starvation in their sleep: they were the student César Augusto Carnevalli, 20, Marcos Szlachter, 25, born in Chile, and Diego Miguel Magliano, 21.

Antonio Paul, a worker in the oil industry, fell off a cliff on his way to assist Masetti, who could barely walk because of an old back injury suffered in Algiers. He and Atilio (Oscar Atilio Altamirano, 23, an office clerk) were at the top of the hill and probably died of hunger. Certainly neither was ever seen again and their bodies were never found. Ciro Bustos, who was making his way back to the camp when he heard on the radio that his comrades had been captured, made a quick about-turn. He would be spared to fight another day. His fate was now inextricably linked to that of Che.

Those who surrendered were taken into custody and tried. They were

Héctor Jouvé, Grillo Frontini and Alberto Castellanos. Grillo's father, Norberto Frontini, was one of their defence lawyers, and Gustavo Roca, who knew Che from his childhood in Córdoba, another, together with several colleagues. It was a formidable team and Argentina was no longer ruled by the military, but the sentences were still harsh. Federico Méndez, who had also been captured, was given 14 years, Héctor Jouvé 12 years, and Grillo Frontini, Alberto Castellanos and Henry Lerner, who surrendered, got 5 years each. Jouvé and Méndez were eventually released when an amnesty was declared in 1973. Furry, who was involved in the transport of weapons from Bolivia, was away from the camp and managed to make his way back to Cuba with the aid of false papers, after erasing all trace of the group's presence in Bolivia prior to their arrival in Salta.

Gabriel García-Márquez, the Colombian author and winner of the Nobel Prize in Literature in 1982, had worked at Prensa Latina under Masetti in the early 1960s but left Cuba quietly when the communists took over the news agency. He, like Che, considered Masetti had been responsible for the greatest achievement of Latin American journalism to date when he went up to the Sierra Maestra twice in a very short space of time to interview both Castro and Che. Many years later, having returned to Cuba and wishing to write about the episode, García-Márquez discovered the authorities had removed all reference to Masetti's campaign in Salta from the official archives, leaving no trace of the island's involvement in the fiasco.

In December there had been a Week of Solidarity with the people of South Vietnam, at which Che gave the closing speech in Havana. He ended by saying, 'We hail our brothers in South Vietnam as brothers in battle, as a fellow example in these difficult moments in world history, and even more, as our allies, as front-line soldiers, in the front trenches of the world proletariat against imperialism.' Che, in talking about the 'people of South Vietnam' and 'our brothers in South Vietnam' was implying that the vast majority of the South Vietnamese population were communists under foreign occupation.

1964 started with a reception at the Palace of the Revolution, followed by a mass rally at Revolution Square the next day. A delegation from the Communist National Front for the Liberation of South Vietnam, founded three years earlier, attended the celebrations, which marked the fifth anniversary of the triumph of the revolution.

Early January found Che signing a technical aid protocol with representatives from the USSR. At the end of the month he accompanied Castro to a farm at Oro de Guisa, near a sugar-cane plant at Aguacate, not far from Havana. They went to test some cane-cutting machines, manufactured in the USSR, which had recently arrived. Earlier that month, Castro had travelled to the Soviet Union and returned ten days later with an undertaking from the Russians to buy the bulk of the Cuban sugar crop at substantially above market prices. This demonstrated that the USSR was not interested in any of Che's ideas about industrialisation, the development of other industries or crop diversification.

On 3rd February, at the controls of his Cessna, Che went to Guanahacabibes, in Pinar del Río, where he had established an experimental correction centre. Officials of his ministry who had committed offences which undermined the progress of the revolution agreed to spend time there of their own free will. The inmates were allowed to carry weapons, since the camp was located in a remote area. Those who spent time there and proved they had learnt the error of their ways were able to return to their posts and no record was kept of their stint at Guanahacabibes. Those who did not volunteer could not continue to work for Che.

The camp was surrounded by a thick forest, with a great variety of timber, which was used to manufacture chairs. The establishment was self-sufficient and also produced honey and wax for sale, as well as fishmeal. Many species of wild animals and tropical birds lived in the forest. It was Che's intention to prove what man is capable of when he works collectively and for the good of the community.

He had met the Spanish writer León Felipe in Mexico, where he was exiled, and in 1964 he wrote to him to thank him for his book, *El Ciervo* (*The Deer*), which the poet had sent him with a dedication. In his letter Che apologised for his delay in acknowledging the gift, going on to explain that 'I have had little occasion to read it because, in Cuba, sleeping, having free time on one's hands, or resting, are simply sins of lese-leadership' but that in addressing a crowd of workers recently 'A drop of the failed poet that I carry within me came to the surface' and he quoted some lines of Felipe's – which he knew by heart – as a tribute to a man whom he admired so much. The letter finishes with a suggestion that Felipe come to Cuba. 'If the challenge tempts you, this invitation is sufficient.' There is, however, no record anywhere that he ever met the Turkish revolutionary poet Nazim Hikmet who was his favourite and whom he quoted frequently, although he visited the Soviet Union when Nazim lived there and Nazim visited Cuba in 1961 when Che was abroad.

Che had become a well-known figure on the international scene, and many people wrote to him from all over the world. He received a letter from María Rosario Guevara from Morocco, asking him if perhaps they were related. His reply, dated 20th February 1964, from Havana, said, '*Compañera*, Truthfully speaking, I don't know what part of Spain my family came from. Of course, my ancestors left there a long time ago with one hand in front and another behind, and if I don't keep mine in the same place, it is only because of the discomfort of the position. I don't think you and I are very closely related, but if you are capable of trembling with indignation each time an injustice is committed in the world, we are comrades, and that is more important. A revolutionary greeting,' and he signed. In Spanish '*una mano atrás y otra adelante*' (one hand in front and one behind) has the connotation of somebody being too poor even to possess something to cover their private parts. The phrase 'if you are capable of trembling with indignation each time an injustice is committed in the world' is from José Martí, whom he never missed an opportunity to quote.

Issue number five of the magazine *Nuestra Industria Económica* published an article also titled 'Nuestra Industria Económica' (On the Budgetary System of Financing) in which Che set out his economic thinking:

We maintain that in a relatively short time the development of conscience does more for the development of production than material incentives do. We base this on the general projection of the development of society necessary to achieve a communist society, which presupposes that work ceases to be a painful necessity and changes into a pleasant imperative. Because it is loaded with subjectivism, the statement requires confirmation by experience, and that is what we are witnessing. If in the course of that experience it were demonstrated that it is a dangerous deterrent to development of productive forces, we would have to decide to follow a healthy course and return to well-travelled roads. Until now this has not happened, and the method, with the improvement practice is providing, is acquiring more and more consistency and demonstrating its inner coherence.

In this he was at loggerheads with the Soviets, whose adherence to some parts of the law of value had strayed away from Marx and consequently from his own idea of the New Man. He was still more at loggerheads with much of the West's firm belief in the full-blown 'law of value', in wages for work, in the market as the best economic regulator, in capitalist institutions – what he calls here 'well-travelled roads'. For him, work was a social duty, a moral imperative, and solidarity would work in place of salaries.

Che left for Geneva in mid-March as head of the Cuban delegation to the UN Conference on Trade and Development. On 25th March he addressed the conference in plenary session. He said, 'It must be clearly understood, and we say it in all frankness, that the only way to solve the problems now besetting humanity is to eliminate completely the exploitation of dependent countries by developed capitalist countries, with all the consequences that implies . . . Just as it is the case that current prices are unjust, it is also the case that these prices are conditioned by the monopolistic limitation of markets and the establishment of political relations which give "competition" a purely one-sided meaning – freedom of competition for the monopolies, a free fox among the "free" chickens.'

Che at the United Nations in New York City, December 1964

He also castigated the assembly for the absence of North Korea, the Democratic Republic of (North) Vietnam and the Democratic Republic of (East) Germany from its midst, as well as for the presence of apartheid South Africa. He said all the participants had blood on their hands: the blood of Patrice Lumumba, the radical Prime Minister of the Congo, who had been assassinated in 1961 in the presence of UN troops, the very troops whose protection he had sought. Che did not mince words.

During a private chat in Geneva with Argentine Ambassador Mario Pico, he expressed his frustration at having to be at the conference giving speeches and surrounded by bureaucrats instead of returning to armed struggle, which by now he believed was the only way forward. Before leaving for Geneva, Che had met Tamara Bunke-Bider in Havana. She had just completed a course on counter-espionage, organised specifically for her by the head of Cuban intelligence, Barbarroja Piñeiro, and was about to be sent to Bolivia to attempt to infiltrate the higher echelons of government and report on the situation on the ground for the preparation of a guerrilla force there.

Back in Havana on 26th June, Che said in his closing speech at the Ministry of Industry's tribute to cane-cutters, 'Voluntary work on the land is deepening the awareness of all workers, and I think it is especially important for our white-collar workers, because it is the only way they can genuinely experience and understand the problems involved.' At a ceremony on 15th August, Che received a communist work certificate and badge from a worker called Félix Arnet-Silveira, for completing 240 hours of voluntary work during the half-year. Moments earlier he had given Arnet-Silveira a diploma recording his achievement as the most outstanding worker, with 1,600 hours of voluntary work. Che attached great importance to voluntary work, not only because of its contribution to the revolution but also because he felt it was necessary for the development of the social conscience that his New Man should have.

He thought that the young would fulfil his dream of the New Man because they were more open and willing to learn, and they did not have the cultural residues of a capitalist society. In 1961, Ricardo Rojo was spending time in Cuba. Che collected him from his hotel at five in the morning and drove him to the Plaza de la Revolución, where around 3,000 men and women sought a place on one of the buses and lorries leaving for a sugar-cane plantation some forty kilometres from Havana. Some carried Cuban flags, some were in military uniform, some wore *yarey* hats (made with the fibres of a local palm tree, the *yarey*). There were employees from the revolutionary government and the national bank, as well as from the other offices and industries that were grouped under the umbrella of the Ministry of Industry. Everybody was there, from the clerks right up to the higher echelons.

When they arrived at the plant they were all issued with *mochas*, the long knives used to cut cane. They worked from six thirty in the morning until half past eleven, when lunch was served under a tarpaulin. Everyone mucked in, regardless of status. The camaraderie was infectious and Guevara was exultant. Work resumed at three and lasted until seven thirty. Afterwards, Che gave an informal talk and answered questions from those present. He wanted to know what fears and anxieties the people might have, what their expectations and aspirations were, what they thought of the revolution and how prepared they would be to defend their country in the case of an American attack, which he had reason to suspect was imminent.

When the Swiss embassy celebrated its country's national day, 1st August, with the customary garden party, American journalist Lyle Stuart was present. He was a friend of Cuba and visited Havana often. In the introduction to *Memories of Che Guevara*, a collection of anecdotes by people who had known Che, issued in 1987 by Stuart's publishing house, he described the event: 'Dozens of people stood chatting, cocktails in hand. My back was to the entrance but I knew, without looking, that Che had arrived for you could literally feel the electricity. It's one of those things you had to experience to understand. He was charged with magnetism and charm and strength, and – yes, beauty. I.F. Stone (the American investigative journalist) once described him as "the most beautiful man I ever met".'

Following Brazil's recent lead, Bolivia broke off diplomatic relations with Cuba in August: US efforts to isolate Cuba were having the desired results. In October Castro decided to send Che to the USSR to represent Cuba officially at the festivities for the 47th anniversary of the 1917 revolution. It seems an odd choice in view of the way relations between Che and Moscow had soured. But off he went and spent two weeks in the Soviet Union, from 4th November to the 19th. He duly stood on the podium in Red Square to watch the march past, and acquainted himself with the new Soviet leader Leonid Brezhnev. He had recently replaced Khrushchev, who was ousted in part for his misunderstanding of the missile crisis. Che hosted the inauguration of Friendship House (a venue for people from the two countries, including the many Cubans who went to study in the USSR, to meet one another) with Yuri Gagarin, with whom he had become friends during the cosmonaut's visit to Cuba in 1961. He also met several officials to discuss the Sino-Soviet rift and see if he could act as a mediator, and to find out what was going on between the Soviet Union and the various communist parties of Latin America, some of which had voiced their disagreements with Cuba in Moscow.

Back in Cuba, in his tribute to the memory of those who fell in the Santiago uprising of 30th November 1956, Che made a premonitory speech: 'Cuba's name is the emblem of what can be achieved by the revolutionary struggle and the belief that the world can be a better place; it is the ideal for which it is worth risking one's life, even unto death, on the battlefields of every continent in the world.'

There has been much speculation about whether Che already knew he was leaving Cuba indefinitely, to spread the revolution, when he departed in early December for New York. Che had learnt that Masetti's Ejército Guerrillero del Pueblo had been entirely wiped out in Argentina, during February. He told Alberto Granado how badly he felt, saying that while men under his command went to fight and die, he was sitting behind a desk like a bureaucrat. He found the situation unbearable. He still wanted to go to Argentina, but for the time being it had become impossible.

Che looking thoroughly at ease on the CBS show *Face the Nation*

In New York, Che presided over the Cuban delegation to the United Nations and addressed the XIXth Annual General Assembly on 11th December. He quoted from the Second Declaration of Havana, 'Now this anonymous mass, this America of colour, sombre taciturn America, which all over the continent sings with the same sadness and disillusionment, now this mass is beginning to enter into its own history, is beginning to write it with its own blood, beginning to suffer and die for it.' And concluded with its final paragraph: 'For this great mass of humanity has said, Enough! and has begun to march. And their march of giants will not be halted until they conquer their true independence – for which they have vainly died more than once. Today, however, those who die will die like the Cubans at Playa Girón. They will die for their own true and never-to-be-surrendered independence.'

It was a rallying call for Latin Americans, for the Third World and the Non-Aligned. Here was somebody articulating their grievances as well as their aspirations on the world stage. His words may seem stilted and old fashioned today, because political discourse has moved on, but at the time they made us all sit up and listen. This was a man who was prepared to stand up for us, putting us on the world map. It was an awakening. We stood up to be counted. His speech made us aware of ourselves and our potential strength, if only we would unite under one banner, recognise what we had in common rather than what made us different from each other. Young men all over the continent were moved to take up arms for their cause.

His speech was attacked by representatives from five Latin American countries – Costa Rica, Nicaragua, Venezuela, Colombia and Panama – as well as by Adlai Stevenson of the USA. Che, exercising his right to reply but apologising for speaking for a second time, gave a detailed response and made his position clearer still: 'I am a patriot of Latin America and of all Latin American countries. Whenever necessary I would be ready to lay down my life for the liberation of any Latin American country, without asking anything from anyone, without demanding anything, without exploiting anyone. And this is not just the frame of mind of the individual addressing this assembly at present; it is the frame of mind of the entire Cuban people.'

Lisa Howard, a television journalist, was ABC's correspondent at the UN in New York. She had met Castro in Cuba and sought to mediate between him and the late President Kennedy. Now she invited Che to her apartment on Park Avenue to meet Democratic Senator Eugene McCarthy. According to McCarthy, Che expressed Cuba's interest in trading with the USA. When informed of the meeting, Lyndon Johnson did not show any interest, and that was the end of that initiative.

When his business in New York was done, Che did not go home. He left via Canada and Ireland for Africa, where he spent nearly three months, travelling to Algeria, Mali, Congo-Brazzaville, Guinea, Ghana, Dahomey, Tanzania and Egypt. He first called on President Ahmed Ben Bella in Algeria, where he was received with great warmth. He visited various organisations and delivered several speeches and addresses. He made it his base from which to come and go between the various African countries he visited. Che's friendship with Ben Bella had been strengthened by the assistance Cuba had given the Algerian government, in the shape of men and tanks, when the country was attacked by Morocco, duly armed by the CIA and France – the colonial power loath to give up its presence in the area.

TWENTY-ONE

(1965)

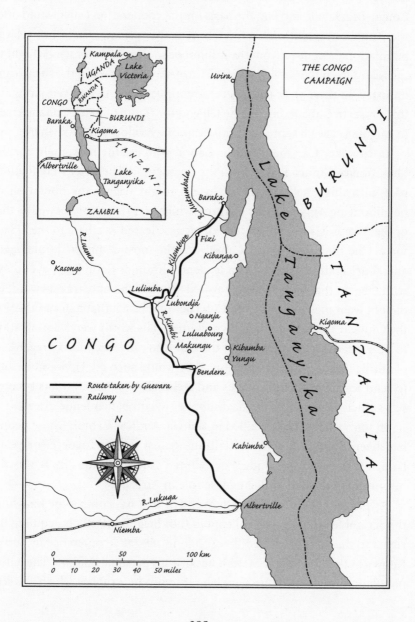

THE CONGO
CAMPAIGN

Uvira

Baraka

Fizi

Kibanga

Kasongo

Lulimba

Lubondja

Nganja

Luluabourg
Makungu

Kibamba
Yungu

Bendera

R. Mukumbata

R. Kilombwe

R. Luama

R. Kimbi

Lake Tanganyika

BURUNDI

TANZANIA

Kigoma

CONGO

Kabimba

——— Route taken by Guevara
- - - Railway

N

R. Lukuga

Albertville

Niemba

0   50   100 km

0   10   20   30   40   50 miles

Inset map

Kampala

UGANDA

Lake
Victoria

RWANDA

CONGO

Baraka

BURUNDI

Kigoma

Albertville

TANZANIA

Lake
Tanganyika

ZAMBIA

The purpose of Che's visits to African heads of state was to consolidate Cuba's relationship with the newly freed nations early in their post-colonial period, when they were at their most vulnerable. Some of them hosted meetings between Che and leaders of revolutionary movements not yet in power, such as Agostinho Neto of Angola. Che met him in Congo-Brazzaville and laid the basis for the cooperation Cuba would offer the Angolan revolutionary for the next thirty years. Cuba has a large population descended from the million or so men and women brought to the island from the west coast of Africa as slaves to work in the sugar-cane industry, so there were reasons for identification with and sympathy for this cause. In Cuba today, people tell you the figure of black Cubans killed in Angola is a well-kept secret but everyone has lost a relative there.

In Conakry Che met Amilcar Cabral who led the movement for the liberation of Guinea Bissau from the Portuguese. The latter were loath to part with this small colony because it might trigger the liberation of neighbouring Angola, a vast territory which was rich in oil, as well as that of the Azores islands, which the Portuguese leased as a base to the US air force. Che thought Amilcar Cabral was the most committed, intelligent and charismatic of the African leaders. Although Cabral saw eye to eye with Che, in that he considered armed struggle the only way forward, he did not want men or arms from Cuba because he felt that to forge a nation the Guineans should do their own fighting. His words were: 'For a nation to be born, the tribe must die'. If the Guineans all joined forces regardless of ethnic origins or tribal divisions they would succeed. He wanted Cuba to send teachers, doctors, nurses and technicians to help farmers become self-sufficient, as well as medical supplies to combat endemic diseases.

In 1967, when Che was killed in Bolivia, Amilcar Cabral, whose people had been fighting a war of attrition against the Portuguese for years, launched an offensive under the banner 'Che shall not die'. It was the beginning of the end of Portuguese rule in Africa.

As part of the Europe-wide movement that has come to be known as the Scramble for Africa, King Leopold II of Belgium formally acquired the rights to the territory called the Congo in 1885 at a conference in Berlin. Known as the Congo Free State, it became his personal fiefdom. The native population was turned into slave labour to produce rubber, which was sent abroad to be used in the budding automobile industry. A brutal army cut off the limbs of those who dared to rebel, failed to meet their allotted quotas of work or attempted to escape. It was only in 1908 that international pressure at the scandal forced the King to turn over his personal fiefdom to the government of his country, and the Congo became a Belgian colony.

By the 1950s the time for overt white domination and exploitation was coming to an end. To maintain their influence and dominance in Africa, Europeans saw that they would have to change tack, seek alliances with black leaders whom they could corrupt and so continue to benefit from the wealth of the continent by means of these special relations, which would never be to the advantage of the Africans.

The Belgians very reluctantly withdrew from the Congo in 1960, quite deliberately leaving a political vacuum. The left had thought they would be able to step in and govern, but it was not to be. Their leader, Patrice Lumumba, was an educated politician of unquestionable moral standing. Mercurial and charismatic, he was loved by his people. He was trouble. He could not be bought so he had to die.

Congolese troops had mutinied immediately after independence in July 1960, and then Moïse Tshombe staged a coup in Katanga, the area rich in cobalt, copper and uranium. (The province seceded until January 1963, when it returned to the fold with the assistance of UN forces.) In the capital, Leopoldville, the army under Colonel Mobutu staged a coup against Lumumba in September 1960. Backed by the USA and Belgium, the coup exacerbated the civil war. White mercenaries began arriving from nearby sanctuaries in apartheid South Africa, with 'Mad Mike' Hoare, a self-styled colonel, as their recruiting officer. Miami Cubans, of whom there was a surplus sloshing around aimlessly, salivating for revenge since their defeat at Playa Girón, were promptly regrouped and dispatched to the area by the CIA.

Lumumba, the champion of the newly independent Congo, was ignominiously murdered on 17th January 1961 as UN troops sent to his aid at his request simply looked the other way. After his assassination, Dag Hammarskjöld, the Swedish Secretary-General of the United Nations, was killed in a plane crash in September 1961. It appeared to be an accident, but many believed it was an act of sabotage. The suggested perpetrators ranged from the Soviet Union, Belgium, Tshombe and Britain to the USA.

There were rebellious factions everywhere, including Tutsi guerrillas from Rwanda who had escaped a massacre conducted by the country's other main tribe, their arch-enemies, the Hutus. The white mercenaries' excuse for their presence was that they were assisting the Congolese army to bolster the government and prevent the Congo from relapsing into communism. Lumumba's followers, on the other hand, were receiving assistance, men and arms, from both Nasser and Ben Bella. In a speech at the UN in December 1964, Che denounced the Belgian paratroopers who had descended on the Congo in 1961, with the endorsement of both Britain and the USA, to commit a crime – the assassination of Patrice Lumumba – which he claimed should be avenged.

By 24th January 1965, Che was back in Algiers, having flown in from Accra. On 29th January, in an interview with the newspaper *Argel Ce Soir*, he summed up his findings after visits to several African countries, saying, 'Africa was sick; now it is convalescent and it is getting better. Its sickness was colonialism, its risk of relapse is neo-colonialism.'

He flew to Paris for twenty-four hours. From the Louvre, he sent Aleida a postcard of Lucrezia Crivelli's portrait by Leonardo da Vinci, claiming Aleida looked like the lady in the picture. Then he travelled on to Tanzania on a five-day official visit, being received by President Julius Nyerere. Tanzania's capital, Dar es Salaam, was the headquarters of several of the African liberation movements, including the Congo's revolutionaries led by Gaston Soumialot and Laurent Kabila. They called themselves the People's Liberation Army (PLA) and saw themselves as Lumumba's heirs. Che would shortly throw in his lot with these men, but before leaving Dar es Salaam he, unsurprisingly, only made a generalised statement to the press: 'After completing my tour of seven African countries, I am convinced that it is possible to create a common front to fight against colonialism, imperialism and neo-colonialism.'

He made a brief stop in Cairo on the way back to Algeria, from where he, his escorts and Osmany Cienfuegos, Camilo's elder brother, went on a week-long visit to Peking. Che expressed his wish to learn more about planning, organisation and management of the Chinese economic project and the

Chinese leadership obliged by organising a meeting with two vice-Prime Ministers as well as a minister from the office of foreign trade. Che did not expect such a high-ranking delegation and was moved when Chou En-lai himself turned up as well.

Che believed China should be invited to join the United Nations and said so when he spoke at international forums, something that must have endeared him to both Chou En-lai and Deng Xiaoping, who was his host. Che and Chou En-lai had previously met in Moscow and were relaxed with each other, even sharing a joke about Che's unkempt beard. Both men came from a privileged background and were intellectuals as well as politicians. There was great empathy between them and their discussions were lengthy and fruitful. This empathy may have helped to ease the relationship between China and Cuba, which had become tense because of the rift between the Soviet Union and China. The Chinese were the main providers of arms to Soumialot and Kabila, and Chou En-lai had recently visited Africa twice.

The Organization of Afro-Asian Solidarity held a conference in Algiers in February 1965 for 63 African and Asian countries as well as 19 national liberation movements. When it was Che's turn to address the meeting, he spoke of his theory of moral rather than financial incentives, thus raising it to an international level. In the process, he was very critical of the Soviet Union and every socialist country which, in his view, continued to exploit people. He called for a new bond between all socialist peoples, to foster cooperation and coordination and lead to genuinely socialist relations among them, to the benefit of all. This was the famous speech that is supposed to have incensed Castro with its attack on the Soviets, but perhaps it would be nearer the truth to say that Che had made it to spare Castro from the need to say such things.

From Algiers, Che returned to the United Arab Republic, where he stayed from 3rd to 12th March. He visited the main industrial plants, speaking with Egyptian workers to learn from them about the reforms being implemented, as well as spending time with President Nasser. During their conversations, Mohamed Heikal, the editor-in-chief of *Al-Ahram* – the newspaper which boasted the greatest circulation in the Arab world – was often present. An adviser and close friend of Nasser, Heikal claims that Nasser was taken aback by Che's constant mention of death.

Che in Algiers at the Organization of Afro-Asian Solidarity

At one point Che said, 'The turning point in each man's life is the moment in which he decides to face death. If he faces death then he is a hero whether he becomes a success or not.' On the last day of his extended visit, Che said he hoped to find 'a place to fight for world revolution and to accept the challenge of death'. Nasser was intrigued by his words and asked, 'Why do you always talk about death? You are a young man. If necessary we should die for the Revolution but it would be much better if we could live for the Revolution.'

Nasser felt that Che was a man who knew his own destiny. Whether he was aware of it or not, he was inexorably walking towards it. As his countryman Jorge Luis Borges wrote, 'Any life, however long and complex it might be, is crystallised in a single moment: the moment when we discover who we really are.' Perhaps Che had, indeed, had an epiphany and discovered who he was.

He returned briefly to Cuba, arriving on 14th March. Che and Aleida's fourth child had been born on 24th February while he was in Algiers. Upon his return to Havana, he and Aleida agreed to call the boy Ernesto. He was always referred to by the Cuban diminutive, Ernestico, as there was already an Ernesto in the family, but the boy would grow up having barely known his father. After their fourth child was born, a letter written to Che by his mother tells us that Aleida had had a procedure. Celia says she is delighted to learn that 'the production line has closed' because she thought any more children would have been detrimental to Aleida's health, especially as they were born quite close to each other. I suspect Che closed the production line because he knew he would soon be leaving for a long time.

Che did not resume public duties. A lot has been written about the fact that Castro, Raúl and Che spent more than twenty-four hours locked up together talking from the moment he returned. Is that so surprising of Castro, a man whose shorter speeches lasted four hours? Che had been away for almost three months, so there was undoubtedly much to be discussed.

The last family portrait of Che and his children, 1965

A group of 150 men had begun training in guerrilla warfare before Che's departure three months earlier. They had no idea he would be amongst them or even that the Congo was to be their destination. Not even the Congolese were supposed to know. As Cuba did not want to be accused of foreign interference in an internal African matter, they were called military instructors, not fighters. They were all volunteers and all black, except for Che and José María Martínez-Tamayo, his head of intelligence.

The area of Luluabourg on the western shore of Lake Tanganyika had been liberated by Congolese rebels before Che's arrival (and it was where Che and his men first entered the Congo from Tanzania). Che believed that the creation of a *foco* led by the Cubans in this area would attract guerrillas from surrounding areas and neighbouring countries to contribute to the liberation of the Congo. After they had fought to liberate the rest of the Congo, those who came from other countries would leave, having acquired the necessary experience to liberate their homelands. Those who were Congolese would remain behind to govern their own country, and the Cubans would go home.

It was not a novel idea: the USA had been doing it rather successfully for some time from bases in Central America. But the method's success in Central America was no guarantee that it would work in the middle of Africa. Factors like tribal divisions and a fervent belief in black magic had a devastating effect on Che's hopes and expectations. It is not that he went into the Congo without any background knowledge or experience; it was simply that the background and experience had been gleaned on a different continent thousands of miles away. The region would not be ready for that sort of war of liberation for many years yet. The Congo was, after all, Conrad's *Heart of Darkness:* a far cry from a Hispanicised island in the Caribbean. And Laurent Kabila was no Fidel Castro.

The Congo is really a region rather than a country and as such it is a vast artificial construct, peopled by many tribes of different ethnic backgrounds who speak different languages and have different religions and belong to different political factions. Its enormous wealth is both its blessing and its curse, as it has made it overwhelmingly attractive to a variety of greedy foreigners throughout history.

At the height of the Cold War the Congo and the USSR were the only two regions that had the uranium needed to make atom bombs and the cobalt for advanced technology so the US had an interest in preventing the Congo falling into the USSR area of influence. Also, because of its size, had the Congo fallen into the USSR sphere of influence the US would have looked weak in the eyes of the world. President Eisenhower had understood this and during his tenure had given the green light to the assassination of Patrice Lumumba. In October 1963 a National Liberation Council had established itself in Brazzaville in the ex-French Congo and sponsored four specific rebellions. In 1964 Pierre Mulele led the one in the west, in the north-east the rebels were lead by Gaston Soumialot. A third rebel group led by Laurent Kabila had taken the western shore of Lake Tanganyika by June 1964. The fourth rebel group was led by Nicolas Olenga and took Kisangani (Stanleyville) in August 1964. Christophe Gbenye, who had been a minister in Lumumba's government, became the president of the People's Republic of Congo.

However, outside interference from Belgium, the USA, the UK and white mercenaries as well as the lack of unity among the different factions resulted in the loss of the liberated territories. But it was proof that if could be done. So Che was not deluded in thinking that he, an expert in guerrilla warfare, could succeed.

On 19th April Che left in disguise for Tanzania with Victor Dreke and José María Martínez-Tamayo. He had only been in Cuba for three weeks. Pablo Rivalta, one of his old comrades from the Sierra, had been appointed Cuban ambassador to Tanzania, and was on hand to greet them. Che's men began to arrive from Cuba in small groups.

Che (with hat) in disguise in Tanzania with some of his men

At the training camp in Cuba, before their departure, Che was seen concentrating intently on a text he was drafting with great care. It was a long farewell letter to Castro. He handed it to the leader on 1st April.

In a revolution one triumphs or dies (if it is a real one). Many comrades fall along the way to victory. Today everything has a less dramatic tone, because we are more mature, but the event repeats itself. I feel that I have fulfilled that part of my duty that tied me to the Cuban Revolution in its territory, and I say goodbye to you, to the comrades, to your people, who now are mine. I formally resign my positions in the leadership of the Party, my post as minister, my rank of comandante, and my Cuban citizenship. Nothing legal binds me to Cuba . . .

I have lived magnificent days, and at your side I felt the pride of belonging to our people in the brilliant yet sad days of the Caribbean crisis. Seldom has a statesman been more brilliant than you in those days. I am also proud of having followed you without hesitation, identified with your way of thinking and of seeing and appraising dangers and principles. Other nations of the world call for my modest efforts. I can do that which is denied you because of your responsibility at the head of Cuba, and the time has come for us to part . . . I free Cuba from any responsibility, except that which stems from its example. If my final hour finds me under other skies, my last thought will be of this people and especially of you . . . I am not ashamed that I leave nothing material to my children and my wife; I am happy it is that way. I ask nothing for them, as the state will provide them with enough to live and have an education. *Hasta la Victoria Siempre! Patria o Muerte!* I embrace you with all my revolutionary fervour.
Che

The words Hasta la Victoria Siempre! (Ever on to Victory) were adopted as the battle cry of liberation movements all over Latin America from then on.

It has been said that Che's letter was intended to exonerate Castro from any blame if his campaign failed and he was killed. But for Che, stripping himself of title, rank, nationality and all other responsibilities in order to go and fight imperialism, which was what he had always wanted, must have been a liberating experience.

He also wrote farewell letters to his parents and to his children. The letter to his parents said:

Viejos,

Once again I feel beneath my heels the ribs of Rocinante. Once more, I'm on the road with my shield on my arm. Many will call me an adventurer, and that I am – only one of a different sort: one who risks his skin to prove his truths . . .

I have loved you very much, only I have not known how to express my affection. I am extremely rigid in my actions, and I think that sometimes you did not understand me. It was not easy to understand me. Nevertheless, please believe me today. Now a willpower that I have polished with an artist's delight will sustain some shaky legs and some weary lungs . . .

big hug from your obstinate and prodigal son, Che

His mother never saw this letter. By the time it arrived in Buenos Aires, she had died. He wrote to his children to grow up as good revolutionaries, study hard and master technology. 'Remember that the revolution is what is important, and each one of us, alone, is worth nothing.'

He told the men who had trained with him to prepare for a campaign that could last up to twenty years. He left Aleida a tape recording of some poems by Neruda and promised he would send for her when the situation had become stable. His younger children saw him in disguise before he went, but he was already pretending to be somebody else so he could not make any show of affection. He left without seeing Hildita, his eldest, because she would have recognised him.

On 20th April Castro completed his last day of cane-cutting for the Noel Fernández mill in Camagüey before answering questions from the foreign press about Che's whereabouts. He said, cryptically, 'All I can tell you is that Comandante Guevara is always wherever he can be most useful to the revolution, and that relations between him and myself are excellent.'

In Buenos Aires, Che's mother's cancer had recurred. She wrote to Che, telling him that she wanted to come to Cuba to spend time with him. But she did not tell him she was dying. He did not guess what was going on because she was too tough to let it become apparent. But in any case, a man who was sufficiently driven to be leaving a happy home, a wife he loved and their tiny offspring, a country where he was a hero, and had friends and influence, in order to go back to soldiering, would probably not have altered his plans even if he had known how ill she was.

He wrote back saying that it was not possible for her to visit as he was about to take a break from his ministerial commitments and spend a month in Oriente cutting cane; he would then be spending five years running an industrial complex. She did not believe him and wrote back suggesting that if he had been ousted he could go and assist his friend Ben Bella in Algeria or Kwame Nkrumah in Ghana, both of whom would be happy to have his help. To her chagrin, she had to accept that she would not see him. The right-wing newspapers were awash with rumours which claimed Castro and Che had fallen out, Che had been shot, Che had gone mad and been locked up in a lunatic asylum, and these made her very unhappy.

The Argentine newspapers announced that Celia de la Serna de Guevara had died in a clinic in Buenos Aires at two thirty in the afternoon on 18th May. She was buried in the de la Serna family vault at the Recoleta cemetery in the centre of Buenos Aires. Many political figures of the left were present. Ricardo Rojo said a few words of farewell. Her husband and two of her sons carried her coffin on their shoulders to her final resting place. It was draped in both the Argentine and Cuban flags. Someone had sent a modest wreath on behalf of Che. Others sent orchids and roses. The federal police were on hand to prevent any demonstrations by right-wing militants.

Before she died, Castro had dispatched Osmany Cienfuegos to the Congo with a letter he had written to Che about his mother's condition. Osmany arrived at Che's camp on May 22nd. According to Osmany, Che was visibly upset and needed to be on his own. In his diary, Che wrote he suspected his mother was already dead by the time Osmany arrived in Africa, but confirmation would only come a month later. He wrote a moving short story about it, which was published with his African diaries many years later.

Che wrote to Aleida, describing his early days in the Congo as another Sierra Maestra which for the moment he could not have the satisfaction of feeling as his own. He also said that everything happened so slowly he felt as if the war was something which could be left till the day after tomorrow, so she should not fear he might get killed. He used his time to teach French, Spanish and mathematics from two to four in the afternoon and learnt Swahili as well. He did not think the lessons added much to the men's knowledge, but it kept them busy and gave the group some cohesion. Early in the morning he listened to the radio in French and occasionally in English, although he had never completely mastered that language. Physical training was yet to begin, but he walked two or three kilometres per day. He also practised medicine when someone needed attention, and was distressed to discover how many Congolese men suffered from venereal diseases.

In another letter to Aleida, in reply to one from her, he asked her not to blackmail him, saying she could not come now or in three months' time. He would reconsider when a year had gone by, but she should bear in mind she would not be coming as his wife but as a combatant, so she should prepare for that and at least learn French. He asked her to be strong and help him by not giving him problems he could not solve; he reminded her that she already knew who he was when she married him; if she fulfilled her duties, the road ahead, which was still long, would be easier to bear. He also said he had spent much of his time holding his feelings in check because of other considerations and, as a result, people thought he was a mechanical monster.

He asked her to love him passionately but also to understand him, since the only thing that could stop him from following his path would be death. 'Do not feel sorry for yourself,' he wrote, 'but face life and tame it, as we will yet be able to spend some of it together.' He wrote that what he felt was no carefree desire for adventure and she should know it. He asked her to educate their children and never consider leaving them behind because they were a part of both of them. He sent her a list of books he wanted her to send him: Pindar's *Triumphal Hymns*, the plays of Aeschylus, Sophocles, Euripides and Aristophanes, Herodotus, Xenophon's history of Greece, Demosthenes' speeches, Plato's *Dialogues* and *The Republic*, Aristotle's *Politics*, Plutarch's *Parallel Lives*, Cervantes' *Don Quixote*, Racine's plays, Dante's *Divine Comedy*, Ariosto's *Orlando Furioso*, Goethe's *Faust*, Shakespeare's Complete Works. And *Analytical Geometry Exercises*, which she would find in the sanctuary, as he referred to his office at home.

Che had moved from Tanzania to the Congo with thirteen Cubans on 24th April. They ran into difficulties almost immediately. Not everyone in the Congo spoke French, the colonial language, and some did not even speak Swahili, the African language spoken in Tanzania. He was accompanied by Godefroi Tchamaleso, the highest ranking Congolese rebel present in Dar es Salaam since Kabila was in Cairo and had announced that he would not be back for a fortnight. Che had to continue to hide his true

Che with a child in his arms and a Congolese soldier in the Congo

identity, something which suited him since the anonymity allowed him to observe what was going on in the camp. He noticed there were divisions among the men and between the officers as well. The lack of discipline was serious. He felt it necessary to inform Tchamaleso of his true identity. Tchamaleso was horrified. He begged Che to keep it a secret and departed for Cairo to inform Kabila.

Leonard Mitoudidi, Kabila's chief of staff, arrived on 8th May, bringing eighteen more Cubans with him. He brought news of Kabila, who asked that Che continue to conceal his identity. There was empathy between Che and Mitoudidi, and he approved of Che's plan to move the camp to an upper base on the mountains at Luluabourg. This was some five kilometres from their current base at Kibamba, an area normally enveloped in thick fog until mid-morning. On 7th June Mitoudidi drowned in mysterious circumstances while crossing Lake Tanganyika. Che and his men were on their own again.

Kabila was still absent, but on 17th June he sent instructions to attack Force Bendera, where there was a hydroelectric plant on the river Kimbi, further inland from Kibamba. It was a position held by Tshombe's forces. 'Mad Mike' Hoare, the infamous white mercenary, was defending the barracks at Force Bendera with a hundred Belgian paratroopers and a few hundred askaris sent by Tshombe from Katanga. Che thought it was madness to attack Bendera but was overruled by his Congolese hosts from the People's Liberation Army.

In the assault that followed, some men never fired a shot, the Tutsis ran away and four Cubans were killed. Their papers fell into enemy hands, so the presence of Cuban troops was no longer a secret. It went from bad to worse. Che's 'instructors' had not managed to teach the Congolese to shoot: they would simply close their eyes and fire their machine guns in the air. The Tutsis had hoped to benefit from a successful campaign in the Congo and sweep home to Rwanda on the momentum generated by their victory. Now they were disappointed, and abandoned the scene. The Cubans were disheartened, their morale at its lowest.

And then there was the *dawa*, a magic potion administered by the *muganga*, or witch doctor, which was supposed to make the Congolese invincible. When it didn't, they claimed it had not been properly administered and killed the *muganga*. Sometimes it took up to three hours to complete the ritual and the rest of the men were expected to wait until it had been performed. As if that were not enough, there was also the ill-treatment of prisoners, who were often tortured to death. Some Congolese seemed to have indulged in cannibalism, in the belief that to eat the heart of your enemy gave you his strength.

On 19th June Che's friend Ben Bella was overthrown in Algeria. This was a fatal blow to the Congolese PLA: he had supported them throughout, as one of their staunchest allies in the area. The deterioration of the situation accelerated. Che had claimed that his Congo campaign would probably last at least ten years, but it was to be over in seven months.

In early July, when the Cubans had already been in the Congo well over three months, Laurent Kabila put in a brief appearance at the camp. He soon returned to Dar es Salaam because he was having problems with Gaston Soumialot, the other leader of this Congolese group. It was early August when Che wrote that it would be impossible to win a war when the local leaders were always absent, the troops were undisciplined and totally lacking any spirit of sacrifice, there was no organisation to speak of, and the middle-ranking cadres did not inspire any confidence in their soldiers. As for himself, he had been plagued by frequent bouts of both asthma and malaria. In September Gaston Soumialot was invited to Cuba and given a hero's welcome. He asked for fifty doctors and gave a glowing picture of events at their camp which could not have been further from the truth.

In Cuba, the Communist Party of Cuba was officially formed on 1st October 1965. On 3rd October during a public meeting to announce the names of the members of its Central Committee, Castro publicly read out Che's farewell letter. He claimed that he had to do so: rumours and counter-rumours about Che's disappearance were rife, and he was under great pressure from the world press, as well as internally. Che heard it over the radio in the Congo and was very unhappy. It had the effect of alienating him from his men, because he said in the letter that he had given up his Cuban citizenship.

Che was at pains to explain to Castro that the Congolese led by Gaston Soumialot were duping him when they painted a positive picture of the developments in the Congo. Reality was rather different, but now they had found a way to obtain funds, trips abroad and various other benefits they were loath to give up their perks. On 5th October Che wrote to Castro. He was

> worried that, either because I have failed to write with sufficient seriousness or because you do not fully understand me, I may be thought to be suffering from the terrible disease of groundless pessimism . . . I will just say to you that, according to people close to me here, I have lost my reputation for objectivity by maintaining a groundless optimism in the face of the actual situation. I can assure you that were it not for me this fine dream would have collapsed with catastrophe all around. In my previous letters, I asked to be sent not many people but cadres; there is no real lack of arms here (except for special weapons) – indeed there are too many armed men; what is lacking are soldiers. I especially warned no more money should be given out . . .

By the end of September the white mercenaries led by Hoare had begun a two-pronged attack on Che's men and their Congolese allies. They encircled the rebels in Baraka, a town which they had held until then, and sent a third unit to Bendera and Lulimba. Baraka fell to the mercenaries and ten days later Fizi also fell. The mercenaries would now advance on Lubondja and Lulimba. Guevara and his men retreated back to their camp at Luluabourg to organise their resistance.

At this point the unexpected happened. On 23rd October the Congo's President Kasavubu attended a meeting of heads of state in Accra and informed the world that the white mercenaries would be leaving the Congo as he considered the rebellion in his country virtually over. It meant that other African states, including Tanzania, withdrew their support from Soumialot. By 20th November Guevara and his contingent had crossed back into Tanzania. Before the end of the month, Mobutu Sese Seko had deposed Kasavubu. He would stay in power for over thirty years and commit the greatest atrocities, aided and abetted by the US government who only saw in him a stalwart ally against communism.

'This is the story of a failure' were Che's opening words in his narrative of the Congo campaign. Right from the start, Che tells us about the disorganisation of the guerrilla force; the privileges the revolutionary leaders awarded themselves – the good life, alcohol and prostitutes – and their constant excuses to be away from the front. Kabila came and went from their camp at the wheel of a Mercedes-Benz and never stayed for very long. The Cubans were unable to blend in with their fellow combatants. Where was the internationalist spirit that had made them give up all the achievements of their own revolution and brought them to fight so far from home? The Cubans may by now have been internationalists, prepared to fight imperialism wherever it happened to be as part of a worldwide struggle, but the Congolese, with their different tribal ethnicities and political tendencies, were not even a nation yet.

Che's final words in the diaries were: 'I have learnt in the Congo, there are mistakes I will never make again, others might be repeated and new ones made. I leave with more faith than ever in guerrilla warfare, but we have failed. My responsibility is great; I will never forget the defeat nor its precious lessons.'

One of the lessons he had learnt was that leadership of a guerrilla force cannot be shared. If the group does not have a supreme commander to whom all parties are answerable, it will be doomed to fail. He should have led the campaign from the start, not only because he was the only member of the Cuban contingent who spoke French, a language some of his African colleagues also spoke, but because of his moral authority and knowledge of how to conduct a guerrilla war. By giving the noms de guerre Moja (number one in Swahili) to Victor Dreke and Mbili (number two) to José María Martínez-Tamayo, and putting himself in third place as Tatu, he confused the Congolese.

When Freddy Illunga, his interpreter between Swahili and French, first saw him using his asthma inhaler, he said, 'Who is this whitey Fidel has sent us who cannot stop putting perfume in his mouth?' Nobody could understand why Number Three was the man everybody consulted, when he was only the doctor and the Cuban interpreter between French and Spanish speakers. But that had not been the main reason for failure. Che wrote, 'you cannot liberate a country which does not want to fight'. Their situation had become untenable: they were not invaders, nor were they mercenaries. They had to leave. Besides, there was now a CIA-backed naval patrol on Lake Tanganyika, threatening their lines of communication back to Tanzania.

On 28th November 1965, Che wrote a letter to Aleida, describing the failure of his Congo campaign and telling her he was now in Tanzania. He also wrote about the final and definitive stage of his road, in which he would be accompanied by only a handful of chosen men 'with a star on their forehead'. The star would not be that of a comandante but the star that Martí referred to in his writings. Had he already turned his attention to Bolivia? He wrote that he had hoped to see her during what he thought would be a long war, but it would not be possible. He asked her to carry her cross with revolutionary fervour and told her he would always find a way of sending her his news. He said that now that he was hidden away, far from the front, with no enemies nor wrongs to right in sight, his need for her had become violent as well as physiological, and neither Karl Marx nor Vladimir Illich could always assuage it.

The Cubans were evacuated after the failure of the campaign, returning home via Europe and China. Between December 1965 and January 1966, Che stayed in Tanzania, hiding in a small apartment in the grounds of the Cuban embassy in Dar es Salaam. He needed to take stock of the disastrous events of the past months. Using his notes, scribbled as events were unfolding, he wrote his account of the experience. His prose is immediate and uncompromising. His criticism of the participants is scathing, and he does not spare even himself. Laurent Kabila cannot have been pleased with the picture Che painted of him.

Kabila would eventually oust the tyrannical Western-sponsored Mobutu Sese Seko from Zaire (as Congo-Kinshasa was then called), in 1997, thirty-two years after he attained power. Kabila, Soumialot and Christophe Gbenye had never been able to agree on anything, let alone assume the leadership of a united force – or even be present during the campaign. Che referred to the People's Liberation Army of the Congo as 'a parasitical army, it did not train, it did not fight and it demanded labour and provisions from the locals.'

Che's narrative of the unmitigated disaster that was the Congo campaign, told in unstinting detail, served for Castro as a lucid report on the conditions in Africa. When Che was in the former Belgian Congo,

Castro had sent 250 Cubans under Comandante Jorge Risquet to the neighbouring country that was once French Congo. The two groups were intended to meet in a pincer movement on Kinshasa. But Che's failure in the Congo meant this never happened. But that did not deter Castro from continuing to assist African liberation movements.

During a visit to Guinea-Bissau in 1972, Castro offered Amilcar Cabral to send men to teach the rebels how to use Soviet weapons as well as doctors and teachers. The Cubans stayed until 1974 when the independence of Guinea–Bissau was declared. When Portugal's dictatorship was finally overthrown in April 1974, Castro's interventions in Africa changed in nature. He had learnt from Che's experiences who should be helped and how. With Portugal now out of the scene the war in Angola became an international conflict between the super powers. The USSR and the US both sought to further their own interests by supporting rival factions, effectively conducting a war by proxy, and former colonial powers Great Britain and France also looked to exert an influence despite, or perhaps because of their diminishing stature on the world stage. Cuban troops would fight a lengthy war against South African forces in Angola which lasted until 1987–8. The Cubans were able to frustrate the ambitions of the South Africans in both Angola and Namibia and a stalemate ensued, which was resolved during a conference between the parties, mediated by the United States. The South Africans agreed to withdraw from both nations if the Cubans also left the area, but the last Cubans only returned home from Angola in 1991, leaving 4,000 dead and 10,000 wounded. This was no small-scale guerrilla warfare such as Che had attempted to wage in the Congo in 1965.

In Cuba in 1991, Nelson Mandela went so far as to claim that the defeat Castro's forces inflicted on the enemies of the Angolan movement led by Agostinho Neto had been a first step towards the triumph of the ANC and the dismantling of apartheid in South Africa, as well as being instrumental in helping Namibia gain its independence, after the 1988 stalemate. This had been negotiated in return for the final Cuban withdrawal from Angola. Che's Congo campaign would now be viewed under a different light.

While Che was still in Tanzania Castro sent Aleida to be with him. They had never had so much time alone together before, and the fact that they were not able to leave the small apartment did not matter at all. In Cuba, El Patojo and Oscarito Fernández-Mell had been their guests for lengthy periods, and Che's escorts were always around, some of them refusing to go home at night in case he staged one of his disappearing acts and went out alone, for he was always trying to dodge them. And then there were the children: Hildita had been around since day one and, when they began to have their own, they needed nannies and home helpers, as Aleida worked in Che's office as well as accompanying him to diplomatic receptions when her pregnancies allowed.

Aleida welcomed this Tanzanian interlude as a sort of honeymoon, the one they had never had. They established a routine in their restricted lodgings: after breakfast Aleida read or studied French which Che was teaching her, while he read, wrote or developed the photographs he took with a small camera. He also recorded some children's stories for her to take home for their family and wrote Castro a letter, in which he commented on some of the revolutionary movements which were active in Latin America at the time. He had kept himself well informed. He was clean-shaven except for a moustache. If it were not for the fact that he had gone back to wearing his olive-green fatigues, he could have been taken for someone else.

Che's personal appearance was striking, as the poster on the walls of a million student bedrooms testifies. This is borne out by the story that I heard from María Florez, one-time Cuban ambassador in London. In the early 1990s, when Pepe González-Aguilar and I were putting together a proposal for a documentary film about Che, I went to see the ambassador to conduct a preliminary interview. She started by saying Che's message would always be relevant. New generations would see in him an example, not for his political convictions or his feats as a guerrilla leader, but because he was a man who had been true to himself: he had never betrayed his beliefs, had paid the price and laid down his life uncomplainingly.

When her husband was appointed Cuban ambassador in Ghana, María, a career diplomat herself, had taken a sabbatical to accompany him on his posting. Che arrived in Accra on an official visit early in 1965, and the embassy organised a reception in his honour. They stood in line to receive their guests: the ambassador, his wife María, Che and the rest of the delegation. The visitors advanced down the line and were introduced to their hosts. Everybody in diplomatic, social and political circles in Accra had managed to get an invitation, such was the curiosity over Che. A worldly, mature and elegant lady, the wife of an Italian official, was introduced to Che and could not refrain from exclaiming to María: '*Ma é bellissimo, quanto é bello!*' (He is very beautiful, how beautiful he is!) María looked sideways at Che to see the reaction of this man who took himself and his role on the world stage very seriously. He was trying to look circumspect but could hardly contain a broad grin.

Pepe González-Aguilar used to say that Che was not aware of his magnetism and power of seduction as a young man. As he grew older and it became obvious, because of the response he elicited, he never made use of it to charm anyone or to gain an advantage: this quality was combined with a kind of reserve which in his early years had verged on shyness. Later on he got used to his new persona of Comandante Che Guevara, but he still had too much respect for the feelings of others to profit from his gift of seduction. According to Pepe, the words used to describe Ignacio Sánchez-Mejía, Federico García-Lorca's bullfighter friend, could easily be applied to Che: '*No era un seductor, era la seducción misma*' (He was not a seducer, he was seduction itself).

The morning after the reception, María accompanied Che and his men on a visit away from Accra. They drove a long distance in an open vehicle over the red soil, through beautiful green countryside. To pass the time they sang Cuban songs, such as José Martí's *Guantanamera*, of which they all knew the lyrics. Che did not join in. María wanted to know why the Comandante would not sing, since the atmosphere was so friendly and they were all having such a good time. 'I am tone deaf,' came the reply. 'You would all be very unhappy if I massacred a Cuban song.'

María told him he would not be let off the hook. He too had to contribute to the entertainment. He could sing a tango if he so wished. Che smiled at the prospect. He said he would recite some poetry instead and plunged into *La Canción Desesperada*, which he knew by heart: '*Ah mujer, no se como pudiste contenerme en la tierra de tu alma, y en la cruz de tus brazos!*' (Ah woman, I do not know how you could contain me in the earth of your soul, in the cross of your arms!) As he recited Pablo Neruda's moving words in his half-Argentine half-Cuban accent, with the backdrop of the rolling green hills and the soft breeze in their hair, María thought El Comandante was indeed a very beautiful man.

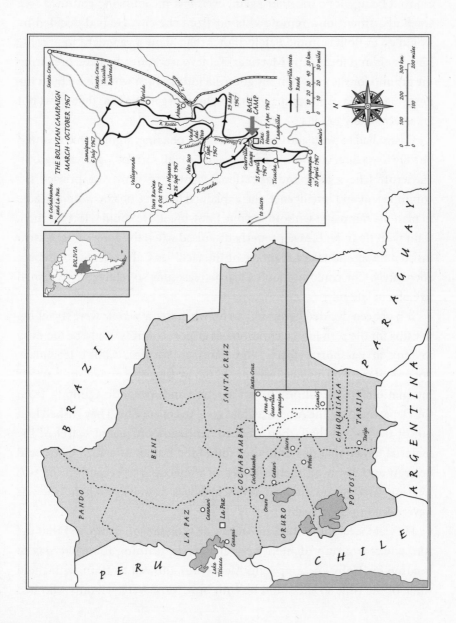

THE BOLIVIAN CAMPAIGN
MARCH – OCTOBER 1967

327

Che left Tanzania in early 1966 and went to Prague, where he spent several weeks. Aleida followed him there, in the disguise she wore while travelling to visit Che (a long black wig and thick glasses which made her look much older), and with a false passport in the name of Josefina González. They enjoyed being alone together again, even if it meant being confined to a small apartment or a remote villa far from the city. He had decided he would go to Bolivia immediately, rather than allow a vanguard to precede him. Tania and José María Martínez-Tamayo were already there, preparing the ground for the arrival of his guerrilla force, which would have been the next stage of Masetti's campaign in northern Argentina, had that effort not failed abysmally in 1964.

Castro had to persuade Che to return to Cuba first, arguing that it would be folly to go direct to Bolivia from Prague, for all sorts of logistical reasons. He wrote Che a long and affectionate letter, in which he praised his commitment and intelligence and explained that in Cuba he would be able to plan his campaign without anyone knowing it. He could select his men, train with them and leave properly disguised when the time came. Castro insisted he should take advantage of the facilities Cuba offered to prepare adequately. Che could not fault Castro's reasoning so reluctantly returned to Cuba in late July.

It had been decided he should arrive when many people were travelling to Cuba for the 26th July celebrations, as airport controls would be too busy to look at passports closely. But Santiago Álvarez, Cuba's legendary documentary film-maker, was on hand to film the arrival of various international personalities. Juan Carretero and Armando Campos, from the Department of the Americas, had gone to collect Che. They rushed him out of the arrivals hall, then went to Santiago's office and searched the material filmed that day until they found the frames on which Che could be seen and removed them. It was an unnecessary precaution: he was wearing thick glasses and had a hunched back as well as no hair. Che was never seen in public again.

He went straight to the San Andrés de Caiguanabo camp, in Pinar del Río, where a group of men were already in training for what was to become his Bolivian campaign. Aleida was allowed to train with them some of the time so she could be with him. Most were veterans who had already served under him and who had volunteered for the new assignment.

The men included (in alphabetical order of their Bolivian noms de guerre) Gustavo Machín Hoede de Beche (Alejandro in Bolivia), who had fought with Che's column in the decisive battle of Santa Clara; Orlando Pantoja-Tamayo (Antonio/Olo in Bolivia), a founder member of the 26th July Movement and a captain in Che's column in the Sierra; and René Martínez-Tamayo (Arturo in Bolivia), who was José María Martínez-Tamayo's brother and a radio operator with the Cuban air force.

Dariel Alarcón Ramírez (Benigno in Bolivia) had been an illiterate *campesino* when he joined the Rebel Army in the Sierra and fought alongside Camilo Cienfuegos (Che inherited him when Camilo was killed in 1959; he went with Che to China, Europe, the USSR and Algeria and then fought with him in the Congo; he was one of the survivors who made it back to Cuba and would eventually defect). Israel Reyes-Zayas (Braulio in Bolivia) was a labourer in the Sierra Maestra until he joined Raúl Castro's column as his escort and was then promoted to first lieutenant, afterwards joining Che's forces in the Congo.

Juan Vitalio Acuña-Núñez (Joaquín/Vilo in Bolivia), originally a *campesino* from the Sierra Maestra, had fought in Che's column until he was promoted to comandante and given his own column in the Rebel Army; he was a member of the Central Committee of the Communist Party. Antonio Sánchez-Díaz (Marcos/Pinares in Bolivia) was originally a bricklayer who also rose to the rank of comandante of the Rebel Army in Cuba and became a member of the Central Committee of the Communist Party.

Manuel Hernández-Osorio (Miguel/Manuel in Bolivia) was one of the founders of the 26th July Movement; he had fought in Che's column and been made a captain, and went on to hold various posts in the Cuban armed forces. Octavio de la Concepción de la Pedraja (Moro/Morogoro/Muganga in Bolivia) was a surgeon who had fought with the Rebel Army and then held various medical posts in Cuba, before becoming a member of Che's Congo guerrillas. Alberto Montes de Oca (Pacho/Pachungo in Bolivia) served in Che's column in the Sierra and was promoted to captain, before holding several administrative posts in Cuba and becoming head of the State Mining Enterprise.

Harry Villegas-Tamayo (Pombo in Bolivia) was a captain in the Rebel Army who became Che's personal escort in Cuba and then in the Congo; he survived the Bolivian campaign, reached Cuba in 1968, returned to Bolivia in 1968 and, having survived the failed Teoponte uprising, went on to serve three tours of duty in Angola. Today he is a retired five-star general in the Cuban army.

José María Martínez-Tamayo (Ricardo/Papi/Chinchu in Bolivia) had been living in La Paz for some time; he was a founder member of the 26th July Movement, had been involved in the preliminary stages of the insurrection in Salta, northern Argentina, had returned to Cuba, and then gone to the Congo with Che as his head of intelligence.

Eliseo Reyes-Rodríguez (Rolando/Capitán San Luis in Bolivia) served in Che's column in the Sierra, was appointed head of the military police at La Cabaña garrison when Che was stationed there, and participated in operations against counter-revolutionaries; he was another member of the Central Committee of the Communist Party. Jesús Suárez-Gayol (Rubio/Félix in Bolivia) was a member of the 26th July Movement who had joined Che's column at Las Villas and been promoted to lieutenant, then held various posts in the army and in government, such as vice-minister for the sugar industry.

Carlos Coello (Tuma/Tumaini in Bolivia) was an agricultural worker and a member of the 26th July Movement who joined the Rebel Army and fought with Che both in Cuba and in the Congo. Urbano Tamayo-Núñez (Urbano in Bolivia), originally a *campesino* in the Sierra Maestra, had joined the Rebel Army and served in Che's column, then became Che's adjutant and travelled abroad with him (he was one of the survivors who made it back to Cuba in 1968, to then go on internationalist missions to Angola and Nicaragua).

Pacho, Pombo and Tuma had been with Che in Prague when he and Aleida stayed there incognito for several weeks. They made a formidable guerrilla force of experienced, tough men, accustomed to all sorts of deprivations and used to fighting together in the roughest terrain and most unforgiving conditions.

Before leaving for Bolivia, Che was driven to a safe house in Havana, where he saw Aleida and the children for the last time. He was in his disguise and the children did not recognise him. In her memoir, Aleida describes how painful it was to see her husband prevented from behaving like their father. They were told he was a friend of Che and they decided to show off all they had learnt so he would tell their father. They even attempted to play the piano. As she raced around the room, Aliusha banged her head against the furniture and hurt herself. Che attended to her bruised forehead and tried to console her, and she turned to her mother and said she thought the old man was in love with her. Hildita, his eldest child, had not been brought for fear she would see through the disguise.

Che had to get to Bolivia via East Germany and Prague. He arrived in La Paz in November 1966, impersonating a Uruguayan bureaucrat. His passport, in the name of Adolfo Mena-González, had allegedly been issued in Montevideo. He was carrying a letter from none other than the Organization of American States, stating he had been commissioned to write a report on social and economic conditions in the Bolivian countryside.

He checked in to the Hotel Copacabana in La Paz, where he took some photos of himself in disguise. These eventually fell into the hands of the Bolivian military and only resurfaced in 1991, when the Swiss documentary film-maker, Richard Dindo, shot a film based on Che's *Bolivian Diary* on location. Dindo borrowed the roll of undeveloped photos from an officer of the Bolivian army who had helped himself to it, probably not knowing he was handing over a unique document.

La Paz was the city where, as a young man, Che had so much fun that he found it hard to leave. This was where he had a romance with a local millionaire's daughter and was wined and dined by his fellow Argentines, who preferred to lead a life of privilege abroad rather than live in constant fear under Perón at home. All this had been only thirteen years earlier, but it must have seemed like a lifetime. Bolivia, the country named after the Liberator Simón Bolívar, was (and still is) one of the poorest in Latin America, and its aboriginal inhabitants were the most needy members of the population, disenfranchised, marginalised and deprived, despite being the majority.

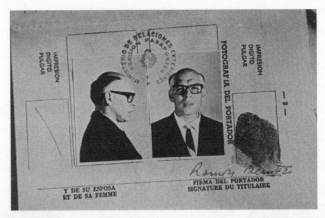

(Top): The false passport Che used to enter Bolivia as Adolfo Mena-González
(Bottom): Che in his room at the hotel Copacabana in La Paz.
Photos taken by Che

Some land reform had been initiated by the president, René Barrientos, an air force general of mixed blood who had seized power in 1964. The latest in a long line of military strong men who had governed the country, Barrientos had initially presented himself as being on the side of the people but had ended up ordering brutal repression and was on the payroll of the CIA.

During his previous stay in Bolivia Che had seen their attempt at revolution and predicted it would fail. According to his Bolivian lieutenant Inti Peredo (one of the five survivors of the campaign, who was killed later in La Paz), Che thought it was inhumane that a population of 4 million people were on a diet of less than 1,800 calories per capita (the doctor in him surfacing?) and 42 per cent of the population died of malnutrition, that 10 per cent of the population did not have a roof over their heads and 86 per cent of housing did not have proper sanitation.

More pertinently to Che's plans for continent-wide revolution, Bolivia shared a frontier with five countries: Argentina, Chile, Peru, Paraguay and Brazil. And these were countries whose politico-economic situation was growing more critical all the time. An insurrection initiated in Bolivia could be exported to any of the frontier countries by land. It is possible to walk from southern Bolivia into Argentina without being noticed, something that must have been a significant factor in Che's decision to begin the revolution in Bolivia.

He met up with Pacho, Tuma and Pombo on the evening of 5th November and they were driven to a farm in Ñacahuasú which was to be the site of their Bolivian camp. They drove for nearly two days, passing through Cochabamba, Santa Cruz, Camiri, Tatarenda, Caraguatarenda, Gutiérrez and Lagunillas, and crossing several rivers. Jorge Vázquez-Viaña, a member of the Communist Party of Bolivia who had joined the guerrilla force, drove one of the vehicles. When he was told the person sitting next to him, whom everyone addressed as Ramón, was Che Guevara in disguise, he was so startled he drove into a gully and they had to abandon the jeep. They continued on foot for the final twenty kilometres.

On arrival at the farm, they met three men from the Communist Party of Bolivia – Apolinar, Serapio and León – who had already moved in. Che asked them to wait until Mario Monje-Molina, their leader and Secretary-General of the Communist Party of Bolivia, returned from a trip to Bulgaria, to get his approval to join the force. The following day was spent in a recce of the area and Loro (Vázquez-Viaña's nom de guerre) went to retrieve his jeep with the help of a man called Argañaraz. He lived at a neighbouring farm and they bought some pigs and hens from him.

The first week at camp went by quietly enough. Tuma went with Che on an inspection tour of the river which bordered their land and verified that the area was deserted. Che then decided they would move out into the scrubland because he felt Argañaraz and his labourers had become too interested in their activities. Argañaraz thought his new neighbours were setting up a cocaine factory and dropped hints that he wanted a share of the business. Che wrote in his diary that he would only feel at ease when the rest of his men had joined them. He also mentioned that his hair and beard, both of which he had shaven off, were beginning to grow. 'In a couple of months I will be myself again,' he wrote.

Days went by. They dug a tunnel to hide anything that might compromise them if there was a sudden visit by neighbours, and then camouflaged it with branches and twigs. Ticks and mosquitoes continued to feast on their flesh, leaving them with painful sores and infected bites.

Marcos and Rolando arrived, having travelled via São Paulo in Brazil. They came with a group of Bolivians. Heavy rains continued to drench them but they settled in. Some weapons arrived, as well as Joaquín and Urbano, who were driven by Coco Peredo, a member of the Communist Party of Bolivia. He left, to return with Ricardo, Miguel and Braulio. Inti Peredo, Coco's elder brother, had also arrived to join the group. He told Che that he thought Estanislao (the name by which Mario Monje-Molina went) would not join the struggle but he, Inti, would stay anyway.

Coco left again to collect Chino from Santa Cruz. Juan Pablo Chang-Navarro (Chino) had been active in Peru against the military dictatorship and was exiled after spending time in jail. He had been a member of the Ejército de Liberación Nacional del Peru in 1963 and lived clandestinely in Bolivia for a couple of years after its defeat. He was arriving from Peru and had offered to bring twenty men. The group had a meeting and decided Chino should wait until they had seen some action before bringing in Peruvians, as they did not want to become an international force just yet.

The recce of the area and the nearby streams continued. At the end of November Che wrote in his diary that it had all gone rather well. His trip had been without incident and half the group had already arrived. He felt they

Che (third from left) and his men in Bolivia

would be able to spend a long time there. They should try to recruit some twenty more Bolivians, and wait for Mario Monje-Molina's reaction and Moisés Guevara's arrival as well as seeing how his men behaved. Moisés was a Bolivian leader of the Miners' Union and had been a member of the Communist party until there was a split. He was to join Che's guerrillas with twelve of his men.

Marcos and Rolando had arrived with Rodolfo Saldaña, a militant of the Communist Party of Bolivia who had provided logistical support to Masetti's failed campaign in northern Argentina in 1963–4. He was the leader of the clandestine urban support network in the cities and mining regions for the present campaign, and was fluent in Quechua, the language spoken by some of the native inhabitants of the region.

The rest of the Cubans arrived during December. Che and the men took turns to dig a cave in the rock, in which to install their radio equipment. Work started on a second cave near the stream, to hide weapons and food. They baked their first batch of bread in the house.

In his Analysis of the Month, Che wrote that the Bolivians were still too few, and he needed to talk to Moisés Guevara, the miners' leader, and to

Mauricio and Jozami. Mauricio was Ciro Bustos, the Argentine painter who had survived Comandante Segundo's disastrous campaign. Bustos had previously been summoned to Havana and had written an extensive report for Che about the political situation in Bolivia and its neighbouring countries while he was there. Jozami was an Argentine lawyer and journalist who had once been a militant with the Communist Party of Argentina and had pledged his support.

But the most important event that month was the arrival of Mario Monje-Molina (Estanislao) on 31st December. Tania had driven him with a new Bolivian recruit, whose nom de guerre was Pan Divino (Holy Bread), and Ricardo, who had been coming and going, bringing in recruits, but had now come to stay. Monje demanded the political and military leadership of the guerrilla force for himself, as long as the insurrection took place in Bolivia. It was an absurd demand, since he had no experience of guerrilla warfare.

Che could not tolerate any ambiguity in the matter. The African fiasco, brought about in part by an unclear chain of command, was not to be repeated. Che made it very clear he was in charge. The conversation went round in circles. Monje said he would think about it, but was further disconcerted when the men from the Communist Party of Bolivia, who were there at his behest, were given the choice of following the party line or remaining at the camp; they all chose to stay. This decided Monje to withdraw his backing.

The Communist party would have provided a much needed urban network, and Che could not have been happy about losing its support. Its absence meant delays in the development of his force, but he felt the decision had a positive effect on him as it liberated him from any compromise. There were muted celebrations to mark the end of the year and Che made a speech invoking Murillo, the Bolivian patriot who had made the first declaration of independence by a Spanish colony in the Americas in the 1810s. He wrote in his diary that Monje left the next morning, looking like a man going to the gallows.

In the early 1990s, I had an opportunity to see Mario Monje-Molina in Moscow. He had asked for asylum there in 1968, after resigning from his post as Secretary-General of the Communist Party of Bolivia when he saw Che's guerrillas were doomed to failure. He lived in Moscow with his family and taught at Patrice Lumumba University. My friend Boris Koval, who taught at the same university, invited him to lunch at his daughter Tatiana's apartment where I was staying, saying that I would like to meet him.

Monje had rarely spoken in public about his meeting with Che at the camp in Ñacahuasú on 31st December 1966, and I was unsure whether he would be willing to talk to me, but in the event he was delighted to be interviewed: he was fed up with being Castro's scapegoat, and was particularly offended by the introduction Castro had written to Che's *Bolivian Diary* when it was published in 1968. He claimed he had been duped by the Cubans about Che's guerrilla movement and was told Bolivia would merely be used as a base from which to launch a guerrilla campaign in Argentina or Peru.

I then asked him why he, who had no military experience, had challenged Che's leadership of the guerrilla force. We were sitting quite close to each other on a small sofa. Monje gently picked up my left hand from my lap and placed it next to his. 'This is why,' he said. 'Che was as white as you.' Next to mine, his hand was the colour of copper. His implication was that the Indians of Bolivia would not follow a white man. 'Bolivia was not ripe for a guerrilla war,' he went on to say. 'I always used to say to Che, "You have a machine gun up here in place of a brain," and we would both laugh together.' He must have thought he had coined a rather inspired phrase, because it appears in biographies written years later, published on the thirtieth anniversary of Che's death.

By the end of January, Che was describing Monje's behaviour as at first evasive and then outright treacherous. He wrote, 'The Communist party is up in arms against us, and I do not know how far they will go. But this will not stop us and maybe in the long run it will be to our advantage (I am most certain of this). The most honest and militant people will be with us, even if they have to go through a crisis of conscience that may be quite serious.'

Moisés Guevara, the Miners' Union leader, had finally arrived with Loyola Guzmán-Lara, who was in charge of finances for the guerrilla organisation in La Paz. Che was particularly impressed by Loyola. She was a member of the Bolivian Communist Youth, but would later be expelled for supporting the guerrillas. In 1967, after the guerrillas were routed and she was arrested and tortured, she tried to commit suicide for fear of betraying her comrades. She spent three years in jail, until released in 1970, and now heads the Latin American organisation of the relatives of the 'disappeared'.

Che wrote that he was happy with Moisés Guevara's attitude so far and would be observing how his men behaved in future. He had told Moisés there would be no ranks for anyone and all arguments to do with international or national differences were to be avoided. Moisés then left, returning with some of his men in February. Tania also left, to liaise with the Argentines (Ciro Bustos and Eduardo Jozami) who had not yet given signs of life. Che noted that the real guerrilla phase which was about to begin would test the men and give him some idea of the prospects for the Bolivian revolution. He saw the recruitment of Bolivian combatants as the hardest task of all.

Che with Loyola Guzmán at his guerrilla camp in Ñacahuasú

In February Che organised a march to explore the area and give his new recruits a taste of the life of a guerrilla force on the move. Leaving a few men in charge of the camp, his group marched through thick vegetation, opening paths with their machetes as they went up and down steep mountains. They had their first fatality on day twenty-five when Benjamín, a young Bolivian, fell into a river and drowned. He could not swim, and Rolando jumped in to try to save him but the current was too strong and he was swept away. Che remarked that Benjamín was a weak and inept young man but had enormous willpower. He thought that some of the Bolivians would not be able to withstand the rigours of their new life. Even some Cubans, veterans of previous campaigns, were not responding well.

March was eventful: Che wrote that his forces had successfully completed the stage of purification and consolidation but in mid-March they lost Carlos, who had been sucked down by a whirlpool when they were crossing a river. It was a serious loss, for he was the most disciplined, serious and enthusiastic of the Bolivians. They also lost a Brno, two M-1s and three Mausers, as well as some bullets and rucksacks. Some of Moisés Guevara's men had been a disappointment: two had deserted, one had talked to the army, three had been thrown out and two feeble ones remained.

On 20th March all his men returned to camp at dusk. Tania had arrived with Chino, Ciro Bustos and Régis Debray, a French intellectual in his early twenties who spoke Spanish fluently. He had lived in Cuba and written *Révolution dans la Révolution*, a book which explained the theory of the *foco*. His erudition had impressed Castro, whose idea it was that he visit the guerrillas in Bolivia, but as later entries in his diary show, Che was quite disparaging of the Frenchman, even suggesting that he had 'sung' when he was detained and taken into custody by the Bolivian army.

Che wrote there was a climate of defeat and confusion because the army had discovered one of their camps and had captured Salustio, one of Moisés Guevara's men, as well as taking a mule. The jeep had also been lost, and Loro had disappeared from his watch at their second camp. Che had a serious talk with the Peruvian Chino, who said he intended to take up arms in the area of Ayacucho, in Peru, where he would be creating a new *foco*, with fifteen men under his command. They agreed Che would take some of Chino's men immediately and some more later; after they had trained with him and been in combat, they would be sent back to Chino with their weapons. They would use medium-range transmitters to stay in touch, which Chino would procure. Loro then resurfaced and said he had killed a soldier.

The following day Che chatted with Bustos, Debray, Tania and Chino. Debray said he wanted to stay but Che told him it was best he return to France, via Cuba, and organise a support network there. He would be taking letters from Che to Bertrand Russell and Jean-Paul Sartre, asking them to organise an international fund to support the Bolivian Liberation

Movement and send assistance in the shape of medicines, money, electronics, equipment and an electrical engineer. Che invited Bustos to become the group's coordinator in Argentina and to start by getting in touch with Jozami, Hellman and Stamponi there. Bustos was also asked to give Che's news to the writer María Rosa Oliver, with whom he had made friends when she visited Cuba, and to his father in Buenos Aires. In the event, neither Debray nor Bustos would be able to do what he asked.

Life at the camps continued: the operators decoded messages sent from La Paz, while the men hunted for food, laid ambushes for the army and quarrelled with each other. There were some discipline problems and Che often had to intervene. There was rivalry between the Cubans and the Bolivians, with some of the Cubans perhaps displaying an air of superiority, as they had seen it all before in the Sierra. Che considered such behaviour intolerable.

On 23rd March the first guerrilla action took place. They successfully routed a Bolivian army column that fell into an ambush: 7 soldiers were killed, 14 taken prisoner and 4 wounded. Many weapons were captured and some of the prisoners gave away army plans. They were set free and given time to collect their dead before leaving, having been stripped of all articles of clothing the guerrillas could use. On 25th March Che held a meeting to evaluate the situation. There had been planes flying overhead and, on 26th March, they saw a helicopter landing. By the end of March, Che noted that Debray 'emphasised rather too vehemently how useful he could be outside'. Maybe Debray had realised the life of a guerrilla was not for him after all.

In his diary, Che noted they would have to start on their march away from the camp sooner than he had originally planned, taking with them four men who might otherwise turn into informers. The army now knew the location of their camp, yet he was optimistic. He split his men into three groups. The vanguard would be led by Miguel, the rearguard by Joaquín and he would lead the main force. The visitors Tania, Bustos, Debray and Chino were in his group as well as Serapio, whom he referred to as a refugee, as he would not be joining the guerrilla force but had to wait for an opportunity to leave the area undetected.

At the end of April Che, ever the optimist, wrote in his Analysis of the Month that things were developing normally although they had suffered the loss of two Cubans: Rubio and Rolando. Strategically, Rolando's death was a severe blow as Che had planned to put him in charge of a second front. It was also a serious personal loss, because he was very fond of Rolando. In his diary he wrote, 'We have lost the best man in the guerrilla force, one of its pillars. He was a comrade of mine from the time when he was still almost a child, and came as a messenger for Column No. 4, then throughout the invasion, and now in this new revolutionary venture. All I can say about his obscure and unheralded death, for a hypothetical future for all that may come out of this, is: "Thy little brave captain's corpse has stretched to immensity its metallic form."' These lines are from Pablo Neruda's tribute to Simón Bolívar in his 'Canto General'.

Che carried a green notebook with him in his rucksack, containing a collection of poems he had copied out. It had Arabic letters on its cover, so Che may have had it with him since his time in Dar es Salaam and taken it with him to Prague, then Bolivia. Although the notebook does not include the names of the writers whose work has been copied, most of the poems are immediately recognisable, as their authors were four well-known contemporary Spanish language poets: Pablo Neruda from Chile, León Felipe from Spain, Nicolás Guillén from Cuba and César Vallejo from Peru. Che had their books with him in Bolivia, so perhaps copying out the poems was the method he used to memorise them. The notebook was in any case a kind of personal anthology, and an interesting complement to the vast number of books he had taken with him. The list below is only a small, but representative, part of his library in Bolivia.

War Memoirs General Charles De Gaulle
Memoirs Sir Winston Churchill
Memoirs Field Marshal Bernard Montgomery of Alamein
Phenomenology of Spirit Georg Wilhelm Friedrich Hegel
The Permanent Revolution Leon Trotsky
The Bankers in Bolivia Margaret Alexander Marsh
The Rebellion of Tupac Amaru Boleslao Lewin
History of Colonialism J. Arnault
The Prince, Political works Niccoló Machiavelli
Stamboul Train Graham Greene

The Town William Faulkner
The Charterhouse of Parma Stendhal
Twentieth Century Physics Jordan
Life is Lovely, Brother Nazim Hikmet
Biological Foundations of Surgery Surgical Hospitals of North America
Revolution in the Revolution Régis Debray
Habits and Curiosities of the Aymara M. L. Valda de J. Freire
The Guide for Blind Walkers from Buenos Aires to Lima Concolorcorvo

As yet, Che's group had not recruited any local men and they had not been able to make contact with Joaquín's rearguard group. The groups were meant to stay in touch using their walkie-talkies (which Che referred to as radio transmitters), but they were now out of range and all possibility of communication was lost. They had also lost Loro, who disappeared after a skirmish at Taperillas. The Bolivian army was now using three German shepherd dogs to track them, but they had not detected the guerrillas, who shot at them and killed one.

Che wrote and dispatched a document entitled 'Message to the Tricontinental Conference of Solidarity with the Peoples of Asia, Africa and Latin America', which was published in Havana on 16th April. He called for the creation of 'two, three, many Vietnams', the purpose being to dilute US forces in Vietnam by forcing the Americans to fight on more than one front, and its publication in his absence lent credence to the rumour that he was in Bolivia. His closing words could have been his epitaph.

> Our very action is a battle cry against imperialism, and a battle hymn for
> the people's unity against the great enemy of mankind: the United States
> of America. Wherever death may surprise us, let it be welcome, provided
> that this, our battle cry, reaches a receptive ear, that another hand picks
> up our weapons, and that other men are ready to intone our funeral dirge
> with the staccato sound of machine guns and new battle cries of war and
> victory.

An Anglo-Chilean photographer suddenly appeared, led by some Indian children. He had managed to do what nobody else had: reaching the guerrillas without being detected by the army. Che proposed that George Roth, for that was his name, accompany Bustos and Debray on the road to the village of Muyupampa as cover for them: his papers were in order and he had been issued with a permit by the authorities to be in the area. Once in Muyupampa, they would be able to make their way to the Sucre–Cochabamba road. They left at night and walked by moonlight. It was extremely cold and Bustos was in his shirtsleeves, so Che had given him the topcoat he had worn when he flew into Bolivia, a large imitation-suede jacket with a quilted lining. He also gave him some Bolivian money and $2,000, which Bustos hid inside the lining of the jacket.

The three were captured by the army the following day and taken into custody. The detention of Régis Debray caused such a commotion in France, where his parents mobilised even the president of the republic, Charles de Gaulle, that when Che was captured as well, only weeks later, the army decided to execute him rather than try him, for fear of another international uproar. George Roth was allowed to go home, but Debray and Bustos were tried by a military court in Camiri and sentenced to thirty years in jail. They served only three, thanks to the intervention of the French president and the change of government in Bolivia when the president, René Barrientos, was killed in a helicopter crash.

Ciro Bustos in jail in Camiri, Bolivia

Che heard over his radio that the USA was mobilising the Green Berets and sending helicopters to Bolivia, and he recorded it in his diary as a matter of fact, without attaching much importance to it. He also mentioned that Chino would be joining the ranks of combatants until a second or third front could be developed. He observed that the capture of Debray and Bustos had been the result of their haste to leave, thus cutting off communication with Cuba, where Debray would have gone, and Argentina, where Bustos should have carried out a plan of action. And yet, Che insisted, 'everything has evolved normally . . . and the morale of the combatants is good because they have passed their first test as guerrilla fighters.'

May Day was celebrated by listening to their Cuban comrade Comandante Juan Almeida on the radio, making a speech in Havana lauding Che and his guerrilla fighters. They also heard over the radio that Loro had been wounded in the leg and captured. Che commented ironically in his diary that Ñato had killed a little bird with a slingshot for their dinner, so they were entering the era of the bird. By now, they barely had enough to eat and were not sure of their geographical position. They continued to be unable to make contact with Joaquín and his group. But the army had stopped using dogs to track them as it had proved a fruitless exercise.

Che noted calmly in his diary that they had been totally unable to get in touch with Cuba, that his group was reduced to twenty-five men, and that no *campesinos* had been recruited. The army, however, was in a state of disarray and were not improving their tactics. They were attempting to intimidate the population by arresting those who had collaborated with the guerrillas in the area of Masicuri. Che felt the *campesinos* would now be pressured by both sides, but the final triumph of the guerrillas would bring about a qualitative change in them.

Che continued to lament the lack of recruits in late June. It was a vicious circle: for more men to join they needed to attract attention to themselves by being permanently in action in populated areas, but this was impossible because they lacked men. The guerrillas' most urgent need was to re-establish contact with La Paz. They needed medicines and military supplies as well as another 50–100 men, even if only 10–25 of them became active combatants. On 21st June, Che's diary tells us that during the two previous days he had devoted time to the extraction of teeth from various members of his guerrilla force, earning him the nickname 'Fernando Tooth-puller'.

There was a massacre in the mines. The governing military junta of Barrientos and Ovando had reduced the salaries of Bolivian Mining Corporation workers by 45 per cent. The clandestine Mining Workers' Federation had called a meeting, during which the workers of the Catavi mine voted to give a day's salary to the guerrillas, as well as a consignment of medicines. At dawn on 24th June, when many men were still drunk after the celebrations for the feast of St John, the Bolivian army opened fire on their houses at the Siglo XX mine, the largest in Bolivia. It went down in history as the Massacre of St John.

At the end of July Che noted in his diary that the Bolivian army was continuing to reveal its incompetence, although some units seemed more combative. His forces, on the other hand, were gaining combat experience through participating in skirmishes, and their morale was high. Only Camba and Chapaco were still weak. However, there was still a total lack of contact with the population and the absence of recruits continued to be felt, although some *campesinos* now recognised them and were no longer afraid of them. The legend of the guerrillas was acquiring continental dimensions: the de facto president of Argentina, General Juan Carlos Onganía, had sealed the frontier between the two countries, and Peru, another frontier country, was taking precautions. The Bolivian government was in crisis but the USA was giving it some small loans, which were helping to raise the standard of living and mitigate general discontent.

The Organisation of Latin American Solidarity held a conference in Havana from 31st July to 10th August. Che was made its Honorary Chairman in absentia. But on 4th August, a deserter led the Bolivian army to the guerrillas' main arms cache at their camp. Che called August the worst month they had had so far. The loss of all documents and medicines as well was a terrible blow, they had lost two men, they had marched with horsemeat as their only food and Camba had become separated from the group, with Che thinking he might have deserted. There was still no contact with Joaquín and his group or with the outside world. The men were demoralised and some of them were sick. They had encountered the enemy only once and had not inflicted the losses they should have, and they had too little water.

All this was beginning to affect the men adversely. As Che put it, they were at a low point in their revolutionary legend. The remark makes one think he was divorced from reality: writing about legends when they were sick, had no water, no food, no contact with the outside world and no recruits. His only positive comment was that Inti and Coco Peredo were emerging as revolutionary and military leaders. But of course he had known equally dire circumstances in Cuba and had bounced back. He knew that was what guerrilla warfare could be like.

Towards the end of September the guerrillas lost León, and the radio said a guerrilla group had been wiped out. If true, it could only be Joaquín and his men, although some might have escaped and be wandering around on their own. Che noted that he and his men now needed to move to more suitable terrain. He also thought the army was becoming more efficient. Of his men, he only had doubts about Willy. These turned out to be unfounded, as Willy behaved heroically and even looked after him when he was wounded in their final encounter with the army. Che also mentioned that their structure in La Paz was shattered. On 15th September Loyola Guzmán-Lara had been detained; her house was raided and compromising photos of her in the guerrilla camp at Ñacahuasú were found. The house of the guerrillas' urban network's radio operator, Hugo Lozano, was also raided but fortunately he had gone underground and was not there.

By 26th September the guerrillas were encircled by government forces. Che started the day's entry in his diary with the word 'Defeat'. They had reached Picacho, at an altitude of 2,280 metres. They moved on to La Higuera, where the women had been left behind but there were no men around. Colonel Ovando of the ruling junta said over the radio that Che Guevara would be captured at any moment. Miguel, Coco and Julio fell in an ambush and Camba disappeared, leaving his rucksack behind. In his diary Che mourned the death of his three comrades, saying Coco's death was the worst to bear, while acknowledging Miguel and Julio as magnificent fighters. In his Analysis of the Month Che admitted they were in a dangerous position and that the news of the deaths of Joaquín's group might be true.

October began without incident, with Che noting in his diary on the 7th that it was the eleventh month of their becoming a guerrilla army and that the day was 'almost bucolic'. He thought their position was about one league from the village of La Higuera and around two from Pucara. A woman herding her goats entered the canyon where they were hiding and they had to detain her for fear she would give them away. In the afternoon Inti, Pablito and Aniceto went to the woman's house; she had a bedridden daughter and another one who was a dwarf. Chino had lost his glasses and could barely see; he had become a real burden when they were forced to march by night. Che believed the news he heard on the radio was deliberately misleading.

That was his last entry in his diary. On 8th October, the remaining seventeen guerrillas were trapped; many were killed and others captured, including Che who was wounded in the skirmish. Willy, who had fought alongside him, was also captured. Che's Bolivian diaries, one for 1966 and one for 1967, were taken from him and analysed in great detail by the Bolivian military and their CIA minders. The US rangers, the CIA agent and the Bolivian military involved in his capture took great interest in his twelve rolls of film, his twenty maps with corrections in crayons of different colours, and a portable radio which did not work.

On the evening of 9th October, La Voz de las Américas radio station broadcast detailed information about the event:

The Bolivian Army announced today that Ernesto Che Guevara was presumed dead yesterday in an encounter between government forces and the guerrillas in the south-east of Bolivia. A violent confrontation with a communist group took place yesterday, six kilometres north-east of Higueras, according to the statement issued by Army Command. The insurgents put up a desperate resistance and suffered five fatalities, believed to include Che Guevara. The military statement issued at midday reports that four soldiers died and there were four wounded. Press reports from Vallegrande, the nearest town to Higueras, said today the encounter took place at approximately 1.00 pm yesterday and lasted for some five or six hours. Later reports provided details of the area in which they were trapped: it is mountainous, consisting of a series of dry peaks devoid of cover, separated by a series of ravines filled with dense jungle vegetation. Towards midday on Sunday 8th October, Guevara's guerrilla group was cut off in one of these gullies between two openings controlled by the rangers.

347

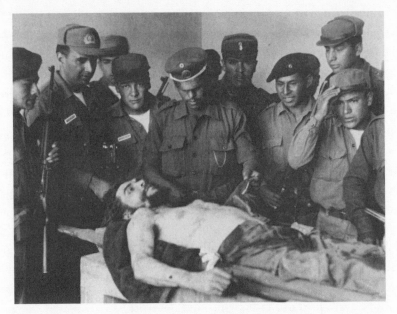

Che's body at the laundry of the Nuestro Señor de Malta Hospital in Valle Grande

On 9th October, Sergeant Mario Terán volunteered to shoot the wounded Guevara, who was lying on the floor of the school in the village of La Higuera. He was told not to shoot at his face because he was supposed to have died in battle. He was promised a reward. He had several stiff drinks and did the deed.

Epilogue

Confused and trembling voices will tell us that the death of Che
Guevara is a useless sacrifice, though a generous one. A desperate act.
An explosion, very beautiful but ineffectual, of the romantic revolution.
But no – this death is the culmination of a life, of a series of rational
decisions. Isn't it rational for a Marxist to plan to transform reality, to
change the apparent dark purpose of the world, such as it is and such as
is determined by the economic structures and dominant ideologies of
imperialism? This death is a political action and it is our duty to clarify
and preserve its political significance: its reasons, its causes, its
consequences. To learn from his death. To live from his death, fighting.

Jorge Semprún

On 9th October 1967, Che Guevara was young, extremely good-looking and
one of the most photographed men in the world. He had held a succession
of important posts in Cuba and befriended many artists and world leaders.
His iconoclastic views, his speeches on behalf of the downtrodden and
disenfranchised, had filled US presidents with trepidation and the poor of his
continent with expectation. He was also dead.

What happened next? His hands were cut off so the Argentine police
could ascertain whether he was really Ernesto Guevara de la Serna. The
Bolivian military who disposed of him cut locks of his hair as souvenirs;
the nuns in the hospital kept his filthy socks as a relic. He had said that a
guerrilla had no grave and should be left where he fell. Over thirty years
later, his corpse was found, taken to Cuba and given a mausoleum. It would
not have interested him in the least.

At the time of Che's execution there was no capital punishment in Bolivia,
but the government got away with it because it had the tacit agreement of the
United States. Since he had renounced his Cuban citizenship, it fell to the

Argentine government to demand justice, but the country was ruled by the de facto dictator General Juan Carlos Onganía, the first in a long line of right-wing, devoutly Roman Catholic military men.

The man who had turned himself into a myth in his lifetime was no more. His men were either dead or in hiding. (Rodolfo Saldaña, a member of the urban network in Bolivia, helped the five survivors escape to Chile and later published a book on the campaign called *Fertile Ground.*) So he left his mortal remains for his captors to squabble over. His assassins could make up whatever stories they wanted about his last twenty-four hours.

We are asked to believe that Che—who had an untreated wound in his leg, had lost twenty kilos since the start of the campaign, was suffering from malaria and had always had difficulty expressing his feelings— suddenly became as talkative as a chat show host, giving interviews to every Bolivian army and CIA officer who came to see him lying in the mud hut which passed for a schoolroom in the hamlet of La Higuera. It was even claimed by his captors that he sent his wife Aleida a message giving her permission to remarry, something she has never mentioned. History is written by the victors.

The American press was happy to perpetuate the Hollywood-style myths they had created. The establishment was overjoyed at its success. An exchange of telegrams between the US, Argentine and Bolivian governments gloated with obscenities, referring to their prey as the Red Beast.

On 12th October 1970, *Time* magazine fabricated a story about Che and Tania being lovers. According to Ciro Bustos, who was actually there, not only were they never alone together but they addressed each other with the formality of their military rank. He was their comandante, she a foot soldier.

As might be expected in a continent that had been Christianised by the sword five centuries earlier, from Che's ashes rose San Ernesto de la Higuera, who has performed a miracle or two and to whom Bolivian *campesinos* pray to this day.

For the black population of Cuba, who were forcibly transported to the island as slave labour and are still practising Santería, the religious rituals of their Yoruba faith, he joined the pantheon of Ologún and is worshipped alongside Yemanyá, Oshún and Oxalá.

For the rebellious youth of the 1960s, Che had already become the poster boy of campuses across the Americas, a symbol of revolt against the status quo and the Vietnam War.

For the consumer societies of the Western world, obsessed with celebrity, he became the face on the compulsory T-shirt churned out by merchants who know a good deal when they see one. It is ironic that the very system he tried to destroy is keeping his image alive today.

As with many icons, Che's image has been co-opted, disputed and distorted. Andy Warhol produced a series of prints of him, alongside film stars like Marilyn Monroe and James Dean. Smirnoff was sued by Alberto Korda for using a version of his celebrated photograph in their advertising campaigns. Madonna is only the most famous of the many performers who believe they can acquire radical chic simply by dressing up as Che.

For the family he left behind in Cuba, the heirs to his estate, he bridged the gap between communist Cuba and the capitalist world, with a little help from Walter Salles and Robert Redford, who made a moving film about Che's early wanderings across the continent of his birth, and later from Benicio del Toro and Steven Sodebergh, with whom they cooperated on a film and tie-in book launching a new edition of Che's works.

His widow, Aleida March, after years of being taken for a ride by so-called left-wing publishers, sold the rights to Che's works to Mondadori, owned by none other than the right-wing tycoon Silvio Berlusconi.

His two elder Cuban children (Hildita died of cancer in 1995, aged thirty-nine) went on the conference circuit, talking to enthusiastic left-wing audiences and enjoying new careers as public speakers.

Mario Terán, the sergeant who had volunteered to shoot the wounded Che at La Higuera, went into hiding, turned to alcohol and lost his eyesight. In 2007 a team of Cuban

Sergeant Mario Terán, the man who killed Che

eye surgeons working in Bolivia as part of a good will mission restored his eyesight. He was overjoyed at seeing his grandchildren for the first time.

In the 1990s several journalists came out with biographies. An American wrote a mammoth book which he called the definitive biography. The press was happy to endorse this claim, thereby confirming what Che had always said: the American media shape world opinion.

With the fall of the Soviet Union in the 1990s, an event Che had predicted many years earlier, the Cuban establishment was free to readopt him and turn him into an icon again. He could no longer embarrass them with his brutal honesty.

When Che's comrade-in-arms and fast friend Camilo Cienfuegos' aircraft disappeared into the ocean, never to be found again, he was declared missing. In a moving speech, Che said that he did not want Camilo to be turned into bronze, to be made into a statue that was venerated, because Camilo had been a man of flesh and blood and would remain so for him for ever.

Despite many attempts, it has proved impossible to turn Guevara himself simply into a bronze statue, an object of veneration. He was not black, he was not hungry, nobody had trampled him underfoot, he had access to education and yet he understood like no one else the plight of those who had nothing. He became the spirit of a continent in arms.

Most of the heroes of Latin America fought to take their countries back from invaders, colonisers and conquerors. Che saw himself as part of this history, as someone following in the footsteps of Martí and Bolívar. This was not arrogance, since he believed anyone who studied the lives and writings of the continent's patriots could choose to emulate them, to follow in their wake. He now undoubtedly ranks among their number.

In his teens, Guevara had been attracted to the ideas of Mahatma Gandhi, who advocated non-violence. But when he was captured in Bolivia at the age of thirty-nine he had a weapon in his hand. He had turned to violence early in life when he decided on the futility of any other way of resisting European and US dominance.

One does not have to accept all his ideals and political choices to see that Che's was a remarkable, inspiring and, in many ways, exemplary life. He died for the future and thus became what he always wanted to be – a man of the twenty-first century. His intention was to create a civilised society by changing himself first, thus proving that it is possible for anyone else to do the same thing. He started life as a carefree upper-class Argentine boy in search of fun and adventure, and became a revolutionary who fought on behalf of the downtrodden of two continents and laid down his life for his fellow man and for his beliefs.

In a public speech on this theme, he once said, 'At the risk of sounding ridiculous, let me say that the true revolutionary is inspired by a great feeling of love . . . it is not enough to interpret the world – the world must be transformed. Humans must stop being the slaves and tools of their environment and transform themselves into architects of their own destiny.'

Che was a man who followed his ideals, who was able to put his ideas to the test, to turn himself into a role model and to make many decisions of enormous significance, all before his fortieth birthday. Yet what most of his biographers seem to miss is that he also enjoyed every minute of it. Perhaps it takes a fellow Argentine to detect from his style that he was having the time of his life. He is doing what he regards as his duty, but there is nothing else that he would rather be doing.

Che in a relaxed mood

What makes Che so attractive – and why his photo remains empowering for the youth of today – is that he was always true to himself. He went to his death like a man, almost cheerfully. His turn had come and that was that. He meant it when he said, 'Wherever death may surprise us, it will be welcome, provided this, our cry of war, has reached a receptive ear and a hand extends to pick up our weapon.'

He had always risked and so far won. But now his luck had run out. Vast numbers of Latin Americans, by no means all of them his political supporters, felt that our luck had also run out. We were left orphaned and bereaved. Che Guevara was larger than life, so his enemies felt they had to kill him – only to discover that he was larger than death. He lives on as something that is still very real in Latin America, a part of our collective psyche.

He was an intellectual as well as a medical doctor and a soldier. Che could have been a scientist, a researcher, a writer, a teacher, a photographer, but he had to become a guerrilla leader because that was where he felt he was most needed. He believed he had no choice. As Francesco Rosi said, 'Some ideas are greater than men, but some men are as great as their ideas. I don't just say that because I believe it is true, but because Che Guevara proved that it is true.'

His dedication to his revolutionary beliefs was deeply religious. Che had a missionary's faith in the innate goodness of man, in the ability of workers to dedicate themselves to ideals and to overcome selfishness and prejudices. It was the other side of the coin of his passionate indignation against injustice and exploitation of the humble. He saw the solution in an exalted form of Marxism that would bring freedom and brotherhood. Such men are born to be martyrs.

Herbert L. Matthews, *Revolution in Cuba*

Biographical Notes

Juan Almeida-Bosque (1927–2009) Cuban writer and guerrilla, fought in the attack on the Moncada Barracks, was on board the Granma for the invasion of Cuba. Distinguished himself during the revolutionary struggle, held various government posts and was one of Castro's most loyal followers.

Fulgencio Batista (1901–1973) Cuban Major General, military leader and dictator. Was de facto President from 1940 to 1944 and then again from 1954 until 1959 when he was overthrown by Fidel Castro and fled the country.

Colonel Alberto Bayo (1892–1967) A military leader of the defeated left-wing Republicans in the Spanish Civil War, was a prominent figure in the Cuban Revolution and died a general of the Cuban armed forces.

Ahmed Ben Bella (1916–) Leader of the Algerian National Liberation Front, fought a long war of independence from France and his country's first Prime Minister in 1962 and President in 1963. Deposed in a military coup in 1965 by Houari Boumedienne.

Simón Bolívar (1783–1830) Venezuelan general, patriot and statesman who liberated six countries from Spanish rule and established the foundations of democratic ideology in much of Hispanic America.

Tamara Bunke-Bider (1937–1967) Better known as Tania, her nom de guerre, she was a communist revolutionary and spy. Born in Argentina of German parents, lived in East Germany and Cuba. Member of the Communist Party. Translator. Trained for clandestine work. Went to Bolivia in 1964 to prepare the ground for Che Guevara's campaign. When her cover was blown she remained with the guerrillas and fell during an ambush at Puerto Mauricio in

August 1967. Many believe she may have been a double agent spying on Che Guevara for the Soviets.

Ciro Roberto Bustos (1932–) Argentine painter and writer, close to Che Guevara, survived Masetti's failed insurrection in Northern Argentina, was taken prisoner in Bolivia and sentenced to thirty years, released in 1970. Lives in Sweden. Author of *Che Wants to See You*, a seminal book on Che Guevara's campaigns.

Julio Roberto Cáceres-Valle a.k.a Patojo Communist journalist, poet and member of the Guatemalan Labour Party. Went to Mexico to escape persecution and there met Che Guevara under whom he worked in Cuba after the victory of the Cuban revolution. He returned to the Guatemalan mountains, where he was killed by army forces.

Faure Chomón (1929–) Although he had previously been a member of anti-communist organisations, he became a key leader in the Revolutionary Directorate and ambassador to the USSR after the triumph of the revolution.

Camilo Cienfuegos-Gorriarán (1932–1959) An early participant in the struggle against Fulgencio Batista in Cuba, he attained the rank of comandante and with Che Guevara led the invasion of 1958 from east to west which accelerated the triumph of the Revolution, but died shortly afterwards when his aircraft was lost at sea.

Chou En-lai: (1898–1976) Chinese communist leader and first premier of the People's Republic of China from 1949 to 1976.

Abelardo Colomé-Ibarra a.k.a. Furry (1939–) Cuban guerrilla and survivor of Masetti's failed insurrection in Northern Argentina. Fought with Cuban forces in Angola. Vice President of the Council of State and Minister of the Interior and the recipient of many honours.

Régis Debray (1940–) French intellectual, journalist, captured leaving Che Guevara's camp in Bolivia and sentenced to thirty years in jail by a military tribunal, serving only three. Was later a foreign affairs adviser to President Mitterrand.

Carlos Ferrer a.k.a. Calica (1929–) Argentine author of *Becoming Che*, the story of his journey with his childhood friend Che Guevara across Latin America.

Carlos Franqui (1921–2010) Cuban revolutionary, literary critic and former ally of Fidel Castro. Editor of the Cuban magazine *Caretas*, he broke with the revolutionary government and went into exile in 1968.

Hilda Gadea-Acosta (1921–1974) Peruvian economist of mixed Chinese and Indian ancestry. Left wing student leader, member of the American Popular Revolutionary Alliance of Peru. Met Che Guevara in Guatemala and married him in Mexico. They were divorced in 1959. Mother of his first daughter Hildita.

Calixto García (1931–) Cuban Brigadier General, was in jail in Mexico for 55 days with Che Guevara, was a member of the force that sailed in the Granma, fought in the Sierra, became a Comandante and held various key posts in the Cuban administration.

Albino Gómez (1928–) Argentine journalist, writer, diplomat, radio and television advisor, foreign correspondent for Clarín (one of Argentina's leading newspapers) in the USA. Ambassador to Sweden, Kenya and Egypt. Advisor to President Frondizi's cabinet in 1961 when Che visited the president secretly. Currently works as a journalist for various Argentine publications.

Maria Antonia González Cuban revolutionary married to a Mexican professional boxer, helped organise the Cuban underground movement when Castro was in Mexico.

Richard Goodwin (1931–) Close friend of US president John F. Kennedy, a Harvard law graduate, Deputy Assistant Secretary of State for Inter-American Affairs, helped develop the Alliance for Progress and was Secretary-General of the International Peace Corps.

Alberto Granado (1922–) Argentine scientist and lifelong friend of Che Guevara, travelled with him from Argentina to Venezuela. Moved to Cuba in 1961 and became professor of medical biochemistry at the University of Havana, was director of the Department of Genetics until 1994 when he retired.

Moisés Guevara (1938–1967) Bolivian miner and communist leader who fought with Che Guevara and was killed at Vado del Yeso in 1967.

Loyola Guzmán-Lara Bolivian human rights and political activist who supported Che Guevara's Ñacahuasú guerrilla movement in 1966–1967. Arrested in 1967 and released in 1970. Currently member of the Socialist Movement led by President Evo Morales.

Berta Gilda (Tita) Infante Argentine medical student and active member of the Argentine Communist Youth. Was a close friend of Ernesto Guevara when they were medical students and they corresponded throughout their lives. She committed suicide in 1976.

Laurent Kabila (1939–2001) Born in the then Belgian Congo, studied political philosophy and was an activist since independence, was supported briefly by Che Guevara in the early 1960s, finally achieved his aim of toppling president Mobutu in 1997.

Joseph Kasavubu (c.1915–1969) African political leader and first president of the Republic of Congo (1960) who dismissed Lumumba as Prime Minister. He himself was ousted in 1965.

Patrice Lumumba (1925–1961) Congolese independence leader and first elected Primer Minister of the Republic. In 1961 he was deposed by a coup, imprisoned and assassinated.

José María Martínez-Tamayo (1936-1967) Cuban guerrilla. Founder member of the 26th July Movement, survived Masetti's failed insurrection in northern Argentina, went to the Congo with Che Guevara as his head of intelligence and then to Bolivia where he was wounded and died.

Juan Manuel Márquez (1928–1956) Cuban revolutionary, sailed in the Granma, a valued adviser to Fidel Castro, he was captured and executed by Batista's men not long after the landing.

Aleida March de la Torre (1936–) Cuban member of the 26th July Movement, married Che Guevara in 1959 and bore him four children.

José Martí (1853–1895) Writer, journalist, essayist, poet and freedom fighter, Cuba's national hero, managed to unite all factions during the war of independence from Spain and died fighting Spanish colonialism.

Jorge Ricardo Masetti (1929–1964) Argentine journalist, the first Latin American to interview Fidel Castro in the Sierra Maestra. Close friend of Che Guevara. Founder and first director of the news agency Prensa Latina in Cuba. Led an insurrection in Salta, Northern Argentina, disappearing in April 1964. His nom de guerre was Comandante Segundo.

Mario Monje-Molina General Secretary of the Communist Party of Bolivia until December 1967. Lives in exile in Moscow.

Isaías Nougués Argentine provincial politician who owned a sugar processing industry in the province of Tucumán and lived in self-imposed exile in La Paz, Bolivia.

Frank País (1934–1957) Formed a revolutionary group in Santiago, Cuba, which in 1955 merged with Fidel Castro's 26th July movement to support the revolutionary effort. He was captured and killed by Santiago police in 1957.

José Pardo-Llada (1923–2009) Journalist and political commentator, the most aggressive and influential radio commentator in pre-Castro Cuba in the 1940s and 1950s. Went into exile not long after the triumph of the revolution.

Hermes Peña (1938–1964) One Che Guevara's escorts in Cuba. Died in combat in northern Argentina in 1964 during the Salta campaign led by Masetti.

Faustino Pérez (1920–1992) Cuban doctor, politician and member of Fidel's Castro's original rebel contingent.

Hugo Pesce (1900–1969) Doctor who specialised in leprosy and tropical diseases. Was a member of the Peruvian Communist party and a positive influence on Che Guevara during the 1950s.

Ulises Petit de Murat (1907–1983) Argentine poet and screenwriter, friend of Che's father, lived in self-imposed exile in Mexico City during Perón's regime.

Manuel Piñeiro-Losada (1933–1998) Also known as Barbarroja (Red Beard). Cuban politician and soldier and head of the Americas Department for decades. An expert on espionage and counter-espionage, in charge of logistics for Che Guevara's clandestine operations.

Pablo Ribalta (1940–) Cuban black communist who joined the revolution in the Sierra as a youth, fought alongside Che Guevara in the campaign of Las Villas and was later appointed Cuban ambassador to Tanzania to assist Che Guevara's Congo campaign.

Ricardo Rojo (1923–1996) Argentine lawyer, author of My Friend Che (1968). Politician and member of the Unión Cívica Radical Party in Argentina. In 1953 made a spectacular escape from a police station in Buenos Aires and was granted political asylum in Guatemala. Defended political prisoners in Bolivia after the failure of Che Guevara's Bolivian campaign.

Mario Salazar-Mallén Mexican professor and immunology specialist who was Guevara's employer at Mexico City's General Hospital.

Celia Sánchez-Manduley (1920–1980) Member of the 26th July Movement in Cuba, aide, close friend and confidante of Fidel Castro.

José Francisco de San Martín (1778–1850) General. Argentine patriot who liberated Argentina, Chile and Peru from Spanish domination. He died in self-imposed exile in France.

Ángel Sánchez-Mosquera Colonel who commanded Batista's 11th battalion during the Cuban revolution, pursued the guerrillas in spite of repeated ambushes and being wounded in one of the battles in 1958.

Mobutu Sese-Seko (1930–1997) Congolese activist who overthrew the nationalist government of Patrice Lumumba in 1960 and later ruled Zaire (now the Democratic Republic of Congo) for over three decades maintaining an anti-communist stance.

Moïse Tshombe (1919–1969) Congolese politician who won control of Katanga Province in 1960 and declared its secession. Defeated and exiled in 1963, he returned as Prime Minister in 1964 but was later dismissed and when charged with treason by the new ruler Mobutu, fled the country.

Ramiro Valdés-Menéndez (1932–) Cuban Comandante, revolutionary and politician, fought along Fidel Castro in the attack on the Moncada Barracks in 1953. Has held several portfolios and is vice-president of the Cuban council of state and ministers.

Jorge Rafael Videla (1925–) Argentine general. De facto President of Argentina from 1976 to 1981 under whom state terrorism took hold, lasting until 1983 when democracy was restored.

Harry Villegas-Tamayo a.k.a Pombo (1940-) Cuban Brigadier-General who was Che's personal escort in Cuba, the Congo and Bolivia. Survivor of the battle of Quebrada del Yuro in Bolivia, escaped to Chile, returned to Cuba in 1968 and later served three tours of duty in Angola.

Acknowledgements

At Quercus, Mark Smith gave me his unwavering support and enthusiasm and, in Josh Ireland an editor who brought stamina and resilience to my project.

I had the good fortune of working with veteran editor Roger Hudson, who guided me through the minefield of conflicting versions of recent US-Cuba history, and made many valuable suggestions during the early stages which enabled me to create a coherent text.

My friend, editor and author Matthew Reisz, whom I had frequently consulted when editing and translating three books about Che Guevara, was always available with advice and was a sounding board with whom to discuss ideas and help me draft controversial paragraphs, thus making an invaluable contribution to the project.

Fellow Argentine and long-time friend Laszlo Papas, a frequent visitor to Cuba, was involved at every stage of the project, reading and commenting on the manuscript, finding out-of-print books for me both in Havana and Buenos Aires, and liaising on my behalf with my Cuban contacts to obtain relevant photographs and publications.

From Sweden via email Ciro Bustos, who was close to Che Guevara from when they met in 1962 to the date of his death, was a daily source of relevant detail, precise information and guidance on life in Cuba at the time as well as during the Salta and Bolivia campaigns. He also introduced me to Adriano Zecca, who kindly gave me the photograph of Ciro in 1967.

Richard Dindo kindly made available to me several photos from his collection of Che Guevara in Bolivia. Jorge Semprún generously allowed me to quote his moving words on Guevara's death in the Epilogue.

Suzy Adams in Machinlleth, mid-Wales provided a reassuring and calm influence when I was drafting the manuscript and ensured that my English was English enough as it is not my first language and much of my source material was in Spanish, French and Italian.

My neighbour Tony Waller was always at hand to cow the most unruly and opinionated computers into submission.

In Cuba, historians Heberto Norman-Acosta, Juan José Soto, Adys Cupull

362

and Froilán González kindly provided books, research and information and Olguita Méndez-Colina gave me a home from home in Havana. Aleida March, who chairs the Che Guevara Studies Centre in Havana, made time from her busy schedule to see me during my visits to the island.

In Argentina, life-long friends Golo Pico, Silvina Márquez, Federico Urioste and Duilio Marzio made enquiries on my behalf, found detailed information and supplied books on Argentine history and politics. Horacio López das Eiras, who wrote a book about Ernesto Guevara's early years, provided relevant details and filled information gaps.

Osvaldo Bayer and Roberto Savio wrote detailed accounts of their respective meetings with Che Guevara especially for my book. Tito Drago shared with me his recollections of Argentina in the early period of the story which I am too young to remember.

Roberto and Juan Martin Guevara de la Serna spoke candidly with me, pointed me in the right direction and cleared the many misconceptions that existed all those years ago when Che was a taboo subject in Argentina.

Calica Ferrer shared with me his memories of childhood and teenage years with Ernesto Guevara in Córdoba and Buenos Aires, where he continues to work to keep the memory of his friend alive. In Buenos Aires, Miguel Bersaiz welcomed me into his home and helped me to overcome my initial bewilderment at having become a stranger in the city where I was born. In Cairo, Albino Gómez, then Argentine Ambassador to Egypt, extended hospitality and arranged my meeting with Mohamed Heikal.

In the United Kingdom, Antonio Carvallo-Quintana organised my stay in Moscow with Boris and Tatiana Koval who looked after me and introduced me to Mario Monje-Molina. Covadonga de la Campa translated various texts for me when I was too pressed for time to do the work myself. Willie Makin was a constant source of specific political information on Perón's presidency. Simon Reid-Henry, who had just completed his book on Guevara and Castro, kindly let me have some of his books on the subject and shared insights and opinions.

Charles Carlino, Françoise Delas-Reisz, Alicia Gilardoni, Tomás González, Horacio Lacunza, Michele Cantoni, Martin Lovell-Pank, Alex Potts, Doris Plummer and Celia Waller (in the United Kingdom), Med Hondo, Pascal Aron, Ricardo Aronovich and Nathalie Civrais (in Paris), Blanca Alvear and Charo Álvarez de Toledo (in Madrid), Grant Munro (in Montreal), Marcos Celesia (in Monterey), Susan Pierres (in Miami) and Tarun J. Tejpal (in New Delhi) contributed press cuttings, research, books, always accompanied by large quantities of patience and affection.

Photo Credits

17 Photo taken by Ernesto Guevara-Lynch. Ernesto Guevara-Lynch's Personal Archives

27, 30, 34, 35, 40, 57, 58, 59, 60, 63, 75, 95, 102, 152, 163, 166, 172, 173, 177, 183, 189, 192, 196, 197, 201, 208, 229 (top and middle), 235, 246, 258, 259, 273, 286, 287, 299, 311, 313, 335 all © OFICINA DE HISTORIA DEL CONSEJO DE ESTADO DE CUBA

70, 143 (right), 224, 229, 247 © Bettmann/CORBIS

80 © Hulton-Deutsch Collection/CORBIS

115, 119, 122, 128 reproduced by kind permission of Calica Ferrer

130, 217, 231, 233, 251, 262, 302, 318, 353 © Getty

143 (left), © Mary Evans/Rue des Archives/Tallandier

213 © Alain Nogues/Sygma/Corbis

215 © NY Daily News via Getty Images

216 © Rolando Pujol/ South American Pictures

278 © CORBIS

343 Photo by Adriano Zecca, extracted from his documentary 'Bolivia 1970'.

348 © Freddy Alborta

Select Bibliography

Che's Works

Socialism and Man in Cuba, Pathfinder, 1992

The Motorcycle Diaries, Ocean Press, Melbourne and New York, 2006

Self portrait, Ocean Press, 2006

The Great Debate on Political Economy, Ocean Press, Melbourne and New York, 2006

Global Justice: Liberation and Socialism, Ocean Press, Melbourne and New York, 2006

Our America and Theirs. Kennedy's Alliance for Progress: The Debate at Punta del Este, Ocean Press, Melbourne and New York, 2006

Reminiscences of the Cuban Revolutionary War, Ocean Press, Melbourne and New York, 2006

Guerrilla Warfare, Ocean Press, Melbourne and New York, 2006

Latin America: Awakening of a Continent, Ocean Press, Melbourne and New York, 2006

Critical Notes on Political Economy: A Revolutionary Humanist Approach to Marxist Economics, Ocean Press, Melbourne and New York, 2007

The African Dream: The Diaries of the Revolutionary War in the Congo, The Harvill Press, London, 1999

The Bolivian Diary, Pimlico, London, 2004

Che Guevara and the Cuban Revolution, Deutschmann, David (ed), Pathfinder Pacific and Asia, 1987

Che Guevara Reader, Deutschmann David (ed), Ocean Press, Melbourne and New York, 2003

Ana, Marcos, *Decidme Cómo Es Un Árbol*, Umbriel Editores – Tabla Rasa, Barcelona, 2007

Ariet García, María del Carmen, *Che: Pensamiento Político*, Editora Política, La Habana, 1988

Benasayag, Miguel, *Il mio Ernesto Che Guevara*, Erickson, Roma, 2006

Besancenot Olivier, Löwy Michael *Che Guevara – Une braise qui brûle encore*, Mille Et Une Nuits, Fayard, 2007

Bethell, Leslie, *Cuba: A Short Story*, Cambridge University Press, 1993

Bornot, Thelma, (et al), *De Tuxpán a la Plata*, Editora Política, La Habana, 1985

Borrego, Orlando, *El Camino Del Fuego,* Imagen Contemporánea, La Habana, 2001

Bridgland, Fred, *Jonas Savimbi: A Key to Africa,* Mainstream Publishing Company, Edinburgh, 1986

Bustos, Ciro, *El Che quiere verte,* Javier Vergara Editor, Buenos Aires, 2007

Caistor, Nick, *Che Guevara: A Life,* Interlink Publishing Group, Inc, Northampton Massachusetts, 2010

Cortazar, Julio, *Todos los fuegos el fuego,* Sudamericana Planeta, Buenos Aires, 1996

Cupull Adys, González Froilán, *De Ñacahuasú a La Higuera,* Editora Política, La Habana, 1989

Cupull Adys, González Froilán, *Che: Recuerdos Profundos,* Editora Política, La Habana, 2007

Cupull Adys, González Froilán, *Un Hombre Bravo,* Editorial San Luis, La Habana, 1994

Das Eiras, Horacio *Ernestito antes de ser el Che,* Ediciones del Boulevar, Córdoba, 2006

De Palma, Anthony, *The Man Who Invented Fidel,* Public Affairs, New York, 2006

Dietrich, Heinz, *Diarios de Guerra. Raúl Castro y Che Guevara,* La Fábrica Editorial, Madrid 2006

Dobbs, Michael, *One Minute to Midnight,* Arrow Books, 2009

Drago, Tito, *Cara y Cruz: El Che y Fidel,* Sepha, Malaga, 2007

Dunkerley, James, *Barrientos and Debray: All Gone or More to Come? Occasional Papers No.2,* University of London, 1992

Engels, Frederick, *The Origin of the Family, Private Property and the State,* Lawrence & Wishart, London 1972

Fanon, Frantz, *The Wretched of the Earth,* Penguin Books, London, 1963

Farago, Ladislas, *Aftermath,* Pan Books, London, 1974

Fernández, Alina, *Memorias de la hija rebelde de Fidel Castro,* Plaza & Janes, Barcelona, 1997

Fernández Montes de Oca, Alberto *Ejército de Cuba: El Diario De Pacho,* Editorial Punto y Coma S.R.L., Santa Cruz, 1987

Fernández-Madrid, Félix, *Che Guevara and the Incurable Disease,* Dorrance Publishing Co. Inc, Pittsburgh, Pennsylvania, 1997

Ferrer Calica, Carlos, *De Ernesto al Che,* Txalaparta, Tafalla, 2007

Franqui, Carlos, *Camilo Cienfuegos,* Seix Barral S.A, Barcelona, 2001

Freud, Sigmund, *The Future of an Illusion,* W. W. Norton & Company Ltd, New York and London, 1961

Gadea, Hilda, *My Life with Che,* Palgrave Macmillan, London, 2009

Galeano, Eduardo, *Las Venas Abiertas de América Latina,* Siglo Veintiuno Editores, Madrid, 1981

Gálvez, William, *Che in Africa, Ocean Press,* Melbourne, 1999

Giap Vo, Nguyen, *Guerre du Peuple Armée du Peuple*, FM Petite Collection Maspero, Paris, 1968

Gilbert, Abel, *Cuba de Vuelta*, Planeta, Buenos Aires, 1993

Glasman, Gabriel, *Breve Historia del Che Guevara*, Nowtilus, Madrid, 2008

Goksu, Saime, and Timms, Edward, *Romantic Communist: The Life and Works of Nazim Hikmet*, Hurts & Company, London, 1999

Gómez, Albino, *Arturo Frondizi El Último Estadista: La vigencia de un proyecto de desarrollo*, Ediciones Lumiere S A, Argentina 2004

Goñi, Uki, *The Real Odessa*, Granta Books, London, 2002

González, Mike, *Che Guevara and the Cuban Revolution*, Bookmarks, London and Sydney, 2004

Goodwin, Richard, *Remembering America: A Voice From the Sixties*, Little, Brown & Company, Boston Toronto, 1988

Gott, Richard, *Cuba: A New History*, Yale University Press, New Haven, 2004

Gott, Richard, *Fabian Research Series 266*

Gott, Richard, *Guerrilla Movements in Latin America*, Seagull books, London and New York, 2008

Granado, Alberto, *Travelling with Che Guevara*, Pimlico, London, 2003

Green, John, *Engels: A Revolutionary Life*, Artery Publications, London, 2008

Guerra-Alemán, José, *Barro y Cenizas: Diálogos con Fidel Castro y el Che Guevara*, Fomento Editorial, Madrid, 1971

Guevara Lynch, Ernesto, *The Young Che: Memories of Che Guevara*, Vintage, London, 2007

Harris, Richard, *Death of a Revolutionary: Che Guevara's Last Mission*, W.W. Norton & Company, New York, 2007

Hart Dávalos, Armando (et al), *Pensar Al Che Tomos 1 y 2*, Editorial José Marti, La Habana, 1989

Heikal, Mohamed, *Nasser: The Cairo Documents*, New English Liberty, London, 1972

Herren, Ricardo *La conquista erótica de las Indias*, Planeta, Barcelona, 1991

Hoare, Mike, *Congo Mercenaries*, Robert Hale, London, 1967

Hobsbawm, Eric, *Revolutionaries*, Little, Brown and Company, London, 1973

Hochschild, Adam *King Leopold's Ghost*, MacMillan, 1999

Jones, Howard, *The Bay of Pigs*, Oxford University Press, 2008

Kamenka, Eugene, *The Portable Karl Marx*, Viking, 1983

Kennedy, F. Robert, *Thirteen Days*, W W Norton & Company, New York, 1969

Leante, César, *Fidel Castro: El fin de un mito*, Editorial Pliegos, Madrid, 1991

Lenin V. I., *Karl Marx*, Foreign Languages Press, Peking , 1967

López, Coco, *Mate y Ron: de Rosario a La Habana*, Ameghino, Rosario, 1997

Löwy, Michael, *La Pensée de Che Guevara: Un humanisme revolutionnaire*, François Maspero, Paris, 1970

Luna, Félix, *Breve Historia de los Argentinos*, Planeta Argentina, Buenos Aires,

1993

MacKenzie, M. John, *The Partition of Africa 1700-1900 and European Imperialism in the Nineteenth Century*, Methuen, London and New York, 1983

March, Aleida, *Evocación*, La Casa de las Américas, La Habana, 2007

Mark, Karl and Engels, Frederick, *The Communist Manifesto*, Pathfinder, New York, 1987

Martens, Ludo, *Pierre Mulele ou la seconde: vie de Patrice Lumumba*, Editions Epo, 1985

Martí, José, *José Martí Reader: Writings on the Americas*, Ocean Press, Melbourne, 2007

Masetti, Jorge, *El Furor Y El Delirio*, Fábula Tusquets, Barcelona, 1993

Masetti, Jorge Ricardo, *Los que luchan y los que lloran*, Nuestra América, Buenos Aires, 2006

Matos, Huber, *Cómo Llegó la Noche*, Tusquets Editores, Barcelona, 2002

Matthews, Herbert L., *Castro: Political Leaders of the Twentieth Century*, Pelican, Middlesex, 1969

May, Ernest and Zelikow, Philip, *The Kennedy Tapes: Inside the White House During the Cuban Missile Crisis*, W.W.Norton & Company, New York, 2002

Nehru, Jawaharlal, *The Discovery of India*, Oxford University Press, 1985

Neruda, Pablo, Felipe León, Guillén Nicolás, Vallejo. César *El Cuaderno Verde del Che*, Seix Barral, Mexico, 2007

Neruda, Pablo, *Twenty Love Poems and a Song of Despair*, Jonathan Cape, London, 2004

Niess, Frank, *Che Guevara*, Haus Publishing, London, 2005

Norman Acosta, Heberto, *Preludio de una Leyenda*, Editora Política, La Habana, 2009

Norman Acosta, Heberto, *La Palabra Empeñada*, Oficina de Publicaciones del Consejo de Estado, La Habana, 2005

O'Donnell, Pacho, *Che: La vida por un mundo major*, Plaza Janés, Barcelona, 2003

Ocampo, Emilio, *De la Doctrina Monroe al Destino Manifiesto*, Buenos Aires, Claridad, 2009

Oltuski, Enrique, *Vida Clandestina: My life in the Cuban Revolution*, John Wiley & Sons Inc, 2002

Patterson, James T., *Grand Expectations, The United States 1945–1974: The Oxford History of the United States*, Oxford University Press, 1996

Peredo-Leigue, Guido Alvaro Inti, *Mi Campaña junto al Che*, Editorial Diógenes S A, México, 1972

Pigna, Felipe, *Los Mitos de la Historia Argentina*, Planeta 2008

Pilard, Olivier Pierre et Masetti, Ricardo Jorge, *Un revolutionaire guevarien et guevariste de 1957 a 1964*, L'Harmattan, Paris, 2007

Barbarroja Piñeiro, Manuel, *Che Guevara and the Latin American Revolution*,

Ocean Press, Melbourne 2006

Reid-Henry, Simon, *Fidel & Che: A Revolutionary Friendship*, Hodder & Stoughton, London, 2007

Rojo, Ricardo, *Mi Amigo El Che*, Editorial Legasa, Buenos Aires, 1987

Ryan, Henry Butterfield, *The Fall of Che Guevara*, Oxford University Press, Oxford, 1998

Sábato, Ernesto, *Antes del fin: Memorias*, Seix Barral, Buenos Aires, 1998

Sáenz Tirso, W., *El Che Ministro*, Editorial de Ciencias Sociales, La Habana, 2005

Saer, José Juan, *El Río Sin Orillas*, Alianza Singular, Buenos Aires, 1991

Saldaña, Rodolfo, *Terreno Fértil: Che Guevara y Bolivia*, Editora Política, La Habana, 2001

Seminario Científico Internacional: El pensamiento revolucionario del Che, Buenos Aires, 1989

Serguera Riveri, Jorge, *Caminos Del Che*, Plaza y Valdés Editores, Mexico, 1997

Shetterley, Aran, *The Americano: Fighting for Freedom in Castro's Cuba*, Algonquin Books of Chapel Hill, 2007

Sinclair, Andrew, *Che Guevara*, The Viking Press, New York, 1970

Sinclair, Andrew, *Viva Che! The Strange Death and Life of Che Guevara*, Sutton Publishing, Stroud, 2006

Skierka, Volker, *Fidel Castro: A Biography*, Polity, 2006

Soria-Galvarro, Carlos, *El Che En Bolivia: Documentos y Testimonios 1-5*, Edición Segunda, La Paz, 1994

Suchlicki, Jaime, *Cuba: From Columbus to Castro and Beyond*, Brassey's, Washington and London, 1997

Sweig, Julia, *Inside the Cuban Revolution: Fidel Castro and the Urban Underground*, Harvard University Press, London, 2002

Szulc, Tad, *Fidel: A Critical Portrait*, Coronet Books, Australia, 1986

Tablada, Carlos, *Che Guevara: L'economie et la politique dans la transition au socialisme*, Pathfinder, New York, 1992

Trotsky, Leon, *The Essential Marx*, Dover Publications Inc, New York, 2006

Vanden, Harry E., *National Marxism in Latin America: José Carlos Mariátegui's Thought and Politics*, Lynne Rienner Publishers, Boulder Colorado, 1986

Villegas, Harry, *Un Hombre De La Guerrilla Del Che*, Editora Política, La Habana, 1996

Wheen, Francis, *Karl Marx*, Fourth Estate, London, 1999

Wright, Ronald, *Stolen Continents: The Indian Story*, Cambridge University Press, 1992

Wrong, Michaela, *In the Footsteps of Mr.Kurtz: Living on the Brink of Disaster in the Congo*, Fourth Estate, London, 2000

Yaffe Helen, *Che Guevara: The Economics of Revolution*, Palgrave MacMillan, London, 2009

Index

Massacre of St John (1967), 345
Massoud, Ahmed Shah, 266
Matos, Huber, 230
Matthews, Herbert, 190, 354
Medrano, Dick, 152
Méndez, Federico, 288–9, 292, 296
Mengele, Josef, 54
Las Mercedes, battle of (1958), 198, 206–7
Mermoz, Jean, 242
La Mesa, La Pata de, 196, 197
mestizos, 20–1
Mexico: boundary treaty with USA, 45; Che's travels round, 149–55, 158, 163–4; film industry, 150; politics and governments, 152–3; USA's influence, 153; Cuban revolutionary activity in, 165–76; US overtures, 249
Mexico City, 149–55, 158; Librería Zaplana, 158
Mexican Muralist Movement, 150
Miguel (Argentine guerrilla), 289
Miguel (Cuban guerrilla in Bolivia) *see* Hernández-Osorio, Manuel
Mikoyan, Anastas, 241
Minas del Frío guerrilla training school, 205–6
Miramar, Argentina, 74
Misiones province, Argentina, 22–3
Mitla, Mexico, 149
Mitoudidi, Leonard, 317–18
MNR *see* Movimiento Nacionalista Revolucionario
Mobutu Sese Seko, 307, 321, 322
Molina, Dr, 114
Molina-Luco, Mr, 80
Monje-Molina, Mario (Estanislao), 333–4, 335, 336–7
monkey hunts, 95
Monroe Doctrine, 46, 246, 261
Montané, Jesús, 161, 184
Montejo, Mr, 90–1
Montes de Oca, Alberto (Pacho/Pachungo), 330, 331, 333

Moore, Ernesto, 22, 23, 38–9
Mora-Valverde, Manuel, 140
Morales, Calixto, 183, 186
Moro *see* Concepción de la Pedraja, Octavio de la
Morocco, 304
Morogoro *see* Concepción de la Pedraja, Octavio de la
Mosquera-Eastman, Ricardo, 228
Moss, Stirling, 204
Mothers of Plaza de Mayo, 5
The Motorcycle Diaries (film), 95
Moulin, Tatave, 3
Moussy, Martin de, 23
Movimento de Liberación Nacional (Argentina), 280
Movimiento Nacionalista Revolucionario (MNR), Bolivia, 109, 110
Moyano, Cornelio, 168
Moyano, Daniel, 43
Muganga *see* Concepción de la Pedraja, Octavio de la
Murillo, Pedro Domingo, 336

Najdorf, Miguel, 272
Namibia, 324
Nardo *see* Groswald, Bernardo
Nasser, Gamal Abdel, 226–7, 245, 308, 310
National Revolutionary Militias, Cuba, 230
Ñato (Bolivian guerrilla), 344
Necochea, Argentina, 75
Nehru, Jawaharlal, 227, 244
Neruda, Pablo, 77, 101, 315, 326, 341
Neto, Agostinho, 306, 324
Nicaragua, 105, 141, 253, 262, 303
Nixon, Richard, 77, 153
Nkrumah, Kwame, 245
Non-Aligned Movement, 226, 244–5
North Korea, 247, 300
Nougués, Gogo, 112, 133, 134
Nougués, Don Isaías, 110, 111–12, 118–19
Nougués, José María, 108, 110

coup in Guatemala, 146–7; Che
meets in Mexico, 147; returns to
Mexico after postgraduate degree in
New York, 154; nickname given to
Che, 195; recommends Masetti to
Che, 200; briefs Che on affairs in
Argentina, 291; on Masetti's alleged
anti-Semitism, 295; Che takes him
cane-cutting, 300–1; speaks at Che's
mother's funeral, 316
Rolando *see* Reyes-Rodríguez, Eliseo
Roman Catholic church: in Bolivia,
122–3
Roque, Roberto, 176
Rosario, Argentina, 15–16, 73
Rosas, Juan Manuel de, 21, 35
Rosi, Francesco, 352
Roth, George, 341
Rubio *see* Suárez-Gayol, Jesús
Ruiz-Cortines, Adolfo, 173
Runciman, Sir Walter, 44
Russell, Bertrand, 339
Russell, Sam, 280
Ruz, Lina, 160
Rwanda, 308, 319
Ryan, Henry Butterfield, 226

Sabina (Guevara family maid), 152
Saint-Exupéry, Antoine de, 242
Salazar-Mallén, Professor Mario, 151,
153–4, 158
Saldaña, Rodolfo, 335, 350
Salduna, Mario, 107
Salles, Walter, 95, 351
Salta, Argentina, 4, 66–7, 292–6
Salustio (Bolivian guerrilla), 339
San Andrés de Caiguanabo camp, 328
San Antonio de los Baños, Cuba, 253
San Francisco del Chañar, Argentina, 73
San José, Costa Rica, 140
San José, Declaration of (1960), 245, 261
San Martín, José de, 19, 65, 134
San Pablo leprosarium, Peru, 93–5
Sánchez, Celia, 184, 190, 193, 271
Sánchez, Universo, 167, 182, 186, 187

Sánchez-Díaz, Antonio
(Marcos/Pinares), 327, 332, 333
Sánchez-Mosquera, General, 193, 195–
6, 201
Sancti Spiritus, Cuba, 210–11
Santa Clara, battle for (1958), 210–13
Santamaría, Haydée, 190
Santería religion, 6, 222, 350
Santiago, 79
Santiago de Cuba, 180, 191, 212, 253
Santo Domingo, battle of (1958), 198,
206, 211
Sartre, Jean-Paul, 242–3, 339
Savio, Roberto, 267–9
Second World War (1939–45), 44, 46,
48, 51
Siegel, Bugsy, 214
Semprún, Jorge, 349
Serapio (Bolivian communist), 333, 340
Serguera, Jorge, 290–1
Serna, Juan Martín de la, 21
Serna y de la Llosa, Carmen de la, 22,
41–2
Serna y de la Llosa, Celia de la (Che's
mother): background, 16, 18–19,
21–2; character, 24, 27–8, 34; and
politics, 22, 33; marriage and married life, 22–5; moves to Buenos
Aires, 26; relationship with Che, 27;
moves to Córdoba for Che's health,
28; hospitality to children's friends,
34–5, 37; and religion, 36; family
holidays, 39; nurses González-
Aguilar back to health, 42–3; moves
to Córdoba city for children's education, 49; rescued by police from
pro-Peronist demonstrators, 53;
moves back to Buenos Aires, 55;
breast cancer operation, 55; attitude
to Che's motorcycle journeys, 73;
and Che's education, 102; delight at
Che's qualification as doctor, 102;
sees Che off on second trip round
Latin America, 103–4; Che ticks off
for not writing to him more often,

PO

Mr
Dec/14